Troubleshooting & Repairing PC Drives & Memory Systems

Troubleshooting & Repairing PC Drives & Memory Systems

Stephen J. Bigelow

Windcrest®/McGraw-Hill

New York San Francisco Washington, D.C. Auckland Bogotá
Caracas Lisbon London Madrid Mexico City Milan
Montreal New Delhi San Juan Singapore
Sydney Tokyo Toronto

pbk   5 6 7 8 9 10 11 12 DOC/DOC 9 9 8 7 6 5
hc   2 3 4 5 6 7 8 9 10 11 DOC/DOC 9 9 8 7 6 5 4

Library of Congress Cataloging-in-Publication Data
Bigelov , Stephen J.
        Troubleshooting and repairing PC drives and memory systems /
    Stephen J. Bigelow.
            p.   cm
    Includes index.
    ISBN 0-8306-4550-0 (H)   ISBN 0-8306-4551-9 (P)
    1. Computer storage devices—Repairing. 2. Data disk drives-
  -Repairing.   I. Title
  TK7895.M4B5   1993
  621.39'7'0288—dc20   93-32537
                                                            CIP

Acquisitions editor: Roland S. Phelps
Editorial team: Joanne Slike, Executive Editor
                Susan Wahlman Kagey, Managing Editor
                Mark Vanderslice, Book Editor
                Jodi L. Tyler, Indexer
Production team: Katherine G. Brown, Director
                Cindi Bell, Proofreading
Design team: Jaclyn J. Boone, Designer
                Brian Allison, Associate Designer   EL1
Cover photograph: © W. Cody/Westlight   4491

IBM™ **PC/XT**™ **PC/AT**™ **PS/2**™	International Business Machines, Inc.
Iomega™	Iomega Corp.
Innoventions™ **RAMCHECK**™ **SIMCHECK**™	Innoventions, Inc.
QuadClip™	ITT Pomona
AlignIt™	Landmark Research International Corp.
Lotus 1-2-3™	Lotus Development Corp.
Maxtor™	Maxtor Corp.
Windows™ **MS**™ **MS-DOS**™ **Microsoft**™ **Windows for Pen Computing**™	Microsoft Corp.
FileSafe SideCar™ **FileSafe**™ **Mountain**™	Mountain Network Solutions, Inc.
Tri-State™	National Semiconductor Corp.
ST™ **SensaTemp**™ **Cir-Kit**™ **PACE**™	PACE Inc.
PCMCIA™	Personal Computer Memory Card Industry Association
ProDrive ELS™ **ProDrive LPS**™ **HardCard EZ**™ **GoDrive**™ **Quantum**™ **ProDrive**™	Quantum Corp.
CleanSphere™	Safetech Limited
Seagate™	Seagate Technology, Inc.
SunDisk™ **SDP**™	SunDisk Corp.
Tandy™ **Radio Shack**™	Tandy Corp.
TI™ **Texas Instruments**™ **Travelmate**™	Texas Instruments, Inc.
Satellite™	Toshiba America Information Systems, Inc.

This book is dedicated to
my wonderful wife, Kathleen.
Without her loving encouragement and support,
this book would still have been possible,
but not nearly worth the effort.

Contents

Acknowledgments

It is simply impossible to prepare a state-of-the-art troubleshooting and repair text such as this without the encouragement, cooperation, and support of a great many talented and generous individuals. I would like to thank the following individuals and organizations for their gracious contributions to this book.

- Ms. May Adachi, Teac Coordinator
- Ms. Karen J. Baker, PACE Inc.
- Ms. Lea Baker, Simon/McGarry Public Relations
- Ms. Debbie Beech, Hewlett-Packard Limited (U.K.)
- Ms. Randi Braunwalder, Hewlett-Packard Co. (Boise Division)
- Mr. Jim Ciraulo, Adtron Corporation
- Ms. Deirdre D'Amico, OK Industries, Inc.
- Ms. Elizabeth R. Dessuge, Accurite Technologies Inc.
- Mr. Gregg Elmore, B+K Precision (a division of Maxtec International)
- Mr. David Y. Feinstein, Innoventions, Inc.
- Mr. Mark Fisher, ITT Pomona
- Ms. Paula Fisher, NEC Technologies, Inc.
- Ms. Elizabeth Foley, Graseby Plastic Systems
- Ms. Sandy Garcia, Mountain Network Solutions, Inc.
- Mr. Howie Greenhalgh, Lynx Technology, Inc.
- Ms. Sharon Gregory, SunDisk Corp.
- Ms. Traci Hayes, Hill and Knowlton (for Toshiba America Information Systems, Inc.)
- Ms. Jennifer B. Hennigan, AMP Inc.
- Ms. Susan Johnson, National Labnet Co.
- Mr. Steve Hire, Cooper Hand Tools
- Ms. Andrea Mace, Maxtor Corp.

- Ms. Fran McGehee, Tandy Corp./Radio Shack
- Ms. Cara O'Sullivan, Iomega
- Ms. Karrin L. Pate, Quantum Corp.
- Ms. Rickie Rosenberg, Texas Instruments, Inc.
- Mr. Todd Schreibman, Link Computer Graphics, Inc.
- Mr. Mike Siewruk, Landmark Research International, Inc.
- Ms. Stephanie Smith, Sony Corp. of America
- Mr. Daniel Sternglass, Databook Inc.
- Mr. William B. White, Elan Systems, Inc.

Special thanks to my electronics acquisitions editor, Roland S. Phelps, executive editor, Joanne Slike, and the entire staff at TAB/McGraw-Hill for their outstanding advice and limitless patience. Finally, thanks to my friends and colleagues at the Millipore Corporation: Chet, George, Dave, and Brian. Your interest and encouragement has made a big difference—thanks a lot!

Preface

My father introduced me to electronics when I was in my early teens. Through the GI bill and a lot of hard work, he made his way through an array of home-study courses. It didn't take long before he could follow just about any circuit. The cellar was his shop. A small arsenal of home-built test equipment took up a better part of the workbench. Any sick or dying television, radio, or tape deck was considered fair game for his soldering iron. I can remember long evenings assisting Dad in "emergency surgery," trying to save ailing home electronics from certain destruction. Some were rescued, while others went on to "hardware heaven." Although I was too young to understand the math and science of electronics at the time, I caught the bug—troubleshooting and repair was fun.

In the years that followed, I've learned a lot about electronics and troubleshooting. Perhaps the most important thing of all is the need for information. With a clear understanding of how and why circuits and systems work, tracking down trouble becomes much less difficult. That is why I wrote this book. Since computers and peripherals have become so prevalent in our everyday lives, it seemed only natural to provide a thorough, comprehensive text on computer technology and repair for personal computers. It is written for electronics enthusiasts and technicians who want to tackle their own computer problems as quickly and painlessly as possible.

After all, troubleshooting and repair should be fun. Thanks Dad!

Introduction

Troubleshooting has always been a bizarre pursuit—an activity that falls somewhere between art and science, often requiring a healthy mix of both. I've had to do a lot of computer troubleshooting, and the advice I give to novice troubleshooters is always the same; troubleshooting is a three-legged stool. That is, three important elements are needed to achieve a successful repair:

- the right tools (and test equipment) for the job
- the right replacement parts
- the right technical information

If any of these three elements is weak or missing, your repair will probably be difficult, and maybe even impossible.

Unfortunately, it's not always easy to establish each of these three legs. After all, tools and test equipment can be expensive (especially when compared to the price of the unit you're going to fix), specialized parts can sometimes be difficult to obtain, and information may be scarce or nonexistent.

That's why I've written this book. With the startling advances in computer systems and the rapid acceptance of notebook, palmtop, and pen-computers, it seems only natural to provide a book for computer users and electronics enthusiasts that can help you make better repairs in less time. This book shows you what tools and equipment you need and how to use them, where to go for many replacement parts, and provides not only information about how and why your computer works, but explains a comprehensive set of troubleshooting techniques that you can put to work right away. This book is intended to maximize your troubleshooting success, and to help you make the most of your resources.

I am interested in your success! I've made every effort to ensure a thorough and thoughtful guide. Feel free to contact me with your questions or comments. Hope to hear from you!

Stephen J. Bigelow
Dynamic Learning Systems
P.O. Box 805
Marlboro, MA 01752
Fax: (508) 366-9487

1
Mass-storage devices

The ability to retain information is as important to a computer as its microprocessor. Computers must have immediate access to program instructions and data during processing. Programs and data must also be retained while the computer is turned off. Otherwise, a human operator would have to manually enter each instruction and data item by hand as the program executes. As you can imagine, the computer as we know it simply would not exist without some type of storage mechanism (Fig. 1-1).

Since the introduction of the earliest computers, the insatiable demand for more and faster storage has given rise to several families of powerful storage devices, each of which is capable of retaining substantial amounts of information. They have become known collectively as *mass-storage devices*. With today's storage-hungry

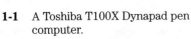

1-1 A Toshiba T100X Dynapad pen computer.

application programs and operating systems such as Windows or OS/2, the need for large, fast storage is more acute than ever. The need for even more storage will likely be a driving force behind computer development for many years to come. This book is devoted to the study and repair of PC drives and memory systems.

There are three major technologies at work in modern mass-storage systems: *electronic, magnetic,* and *optical.* Electronic mass-storage uses semiconductor devices (primarily integrated circuits). Magnetic mass-storage employs a delicate interaction of magnetic material, mechanics, and electronics to hold its data. Optical mass-storage employs electronics and mechanics in conjunction with optical materials and principles to access vast quantities of information. Each of these mass-storage technologies enjoys its own unique advantages, and suffers its own particular limitations. Each one has also secured an important place in computer applications. You will learn about these technologies in detail throughout the course of this book.

Before we jump right into the particulars of mass-storage devices, however, you should know a bit about computers in general. If you already have a good knowledge of computer basics, feel free to skip these sections. For those of you whose technical computer background is weak, the following material can give you an appreciation of today's IBM-compatible computers, and a better understanding of where mass-storage devices fit in the overall scheme of computer operations.

Computer primer

In order to understand a computer, there are two important concepts that you must grasp: *digital logic* and *number systems.* These concepts are absolutely fundamental to the operation of every computer system ever made, because they define the ways in which information is interpreted and represented by electronic circuitry. Let's start at the beginning.

Digital logic

The lineage of modern digital logic can be traced back to 1854. George Boole developed a new way of thinking by substituting symbols instead of words to reach logical conclusions. This symbolic logic became known as *Boolean logic* or *Boolean algebra.* The interesting feature of this Boolean logic is that input and output conditions can only be expressed as true or false (yes or no). While Boolean concepts had little practical application during the mid nineteenth century, they would form the basis for electronic logic devices less than 100 years later.

With the advent of electron tubes, it became possible to implement Boolean logic in the form of electronic circuits which could "automatically" solve the simple addition and multiplication relationships envisioned by Boole. Because logic circuits only dealt with two conditions (on/off or 1/0), they were dubbed *binary logic circuits.* As electron tubes gave way to semiconductor components such as diodes and transistors, additional logic functions appeared which took their roots in Boole's principles (i.e., NAND, NOR, INVERTER, BUFFER, XOR, XNOR). Each logic function was implemented using fairly standard electronic circuitry, so they became known as *logic gates*. Logic also became known as *digital logic* due to the use of logic circuits to perform mathematical computations. When discrete logic circuits were finally fabricated as integrated circuits, the gate concept stuck, and remains in use to this day. You can see a chart of the eight major logic gates in chapter 2. For the purposes of this book, the terms Boolean logic, binary logic, and digital logic are all identical.

For an electronic circuit to deal with binary logic, there must be a direct relationship between logic states and electrical signals . This relationship is critical because logic circuits perform operations based upon the voltage signals existing at each input. As you can imagine, an incorrect signal voltage might result in an erroneous logic output. A binary true (or on) condition usually indicates the presence of a voltage, while a binary false (or off) indicates the absence of a voltage. This is generally known as conventional or *active-high logic.* In some cases, however, the active-high convention is reversed where an on state is represented by an absence of voltage and an off state is shown by a presence of a voltage. This is called *active-low logic.* Active-low logic signals are represented with a solid bar over the signal label. Occasionally, active-low signals are also shown with a minus sign (–) or apostrophe (') after the label.

In the first example in Fig. 1-2, the label Error indicates an active-high signal. When a logic 1 signal voltage is present, the condition is true. When a logic 0 signal voltage is present, the condition is false. In the second example, the label is marked Error, so an active-low signal is indicated. Here, a logic 1 signal voltage is considered false, indicating that there is no error condition. A logic 0 signal voltage represents a true state, indicating that an error condition does exist. Active-low logic is used because it is often faster to make a signal logic 0 than logic 1, so active-low signals help to boost logic system performance at the hardware level.

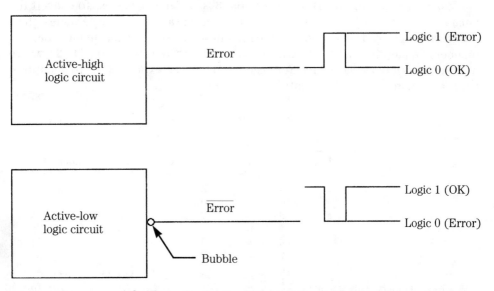

1-2   Example of active-high vs. active-low logic.

When troubleshooting, you need only realize the difference between active-high and active-low signals during your testing. Some schematics and block diagrams accent active-low signal lines using small circles (called *bubbles*) at the circuit's output.

Binary numbers

You are familiar with the decimal number system, which consists of ten digits, 0 through 9. Each digit represents a discrete quantity that we all can associate with. By combining digits using basic rules of place values, you can represent virtually any quantity. The same is true of *binary logic.*

Binary logic uses a number system of two characters instead of ten. A true condition is considered to be a logic 1, and a false condition is considered to be a logic 0. These binary digits (or *bits*) can also be combined to represent almost any quantity. Where a decimal digit can be 0 through 9, a binary digit can only be 0 or 1.

In the decimal number system, a single digit alone can express ten discrete levels or magnitudes (0 to 9). When the quantity to be expressed exceeds the capacity of a single digit, the number *carries over* into the next higher place value. Decimal place values are based on powers of 10, because there are ten digits in the decimal system. The decimal place values are 1s, 10s, 100s, 1000s, 10,000s, and so on. As an example, the number 35 has a 3 in the 10s place and a 5 in the 1s place. The number would be resolved as $(3 \times 10) + (5 \times 1)$. The number 256 has a 2 in the 100s place, a 5 in the 10s place, and a 6 in the 1s place, and would be resolved as $(2 \times 100) + (5 \times 10) + (6 \times 1)$. You have done this subconsciously since early grade school.

Because the binary number system uses only two digits instead of 10, each place value is based on powers of 2. This creates the place value system as shown in Fig. 1-3 using 1s, 2s, 4s, 8s, 16s, 32s, 64s, etc. The binary number 100110 (pronounced *one zero zero one one zero*) uses a 1 in the 32s, 4s, and 2s places. To convert the binary number to a decimal equivalent, you add up the associated place values wherever 1s are present. The number 100110 is equivalent to the decimal number 38. The number of quantities that can be expressed by a binary number is equal to 2^n, where n is the number of available bits. For instance, 4 bits can express 2^4 or 16 quantities, 8 bits can express 2^8 or 256 quantities, and so on.

2^7	2^6	2^5	2^4	2^3	2^2	2^1	2^0	
128s	64s	32s	16s	8s	4s	2s	1s	
		1	0	0	1	1	0	Binary number
		1	x	32	=	32		
		0	x	16	=	0		
		0	x	8	=	0		
		1	x	4	=	4		
		1	x	2	=	2		
		0	x	1	=	0		
						38		Decimal equivalent

100110 binary = 38 decimal

1-3   Example of binary number formation.

Binary-coded decimal

Binary-coded decimal (BCD) is a common technique of representing decimal dig-its with their binary equivalent numbers. For example, the decimal number 25 would be represented as 0010 0101 in BCD (in straight binary, decimal 25 would be repre-sented as binary 11001). Because each decimal number is directly replaced by its four-bit binary equivalent, BCD offers fast and easy conversion from BCD to decimal and vice versa. It has historically found use with variable-state input devices such as thumbwheel switches and as raw data to drive seven-segment LEDs. Today, BCD is typically used for data coding in certain optical disk systems, which are covered later in this book.

Hexadecimal numbers

While the decimal number system uses 10 digits and the binary number system uses two digits, the hexadecimal (or *hex*) number system uses sixteen digits. The char-acters 0 to 9 are used, along with the letters A, B, C, D, E, and F, which represent the values 10 to 15. The place value technique used to form hexadecimal numbers is the same used with decimal or binary numbers, but each place value is now a power of 16 rather than a power of 10 or 2. Figure 1-4 illustrates two hexadecimal examples. In the first example, the hexadecimal number 3C has a 3 in the 16s place and a C (12) in the 1s place. This results in a decimal equivalent of $(3 \times 16) + (12 \times 1)$, or 60. The second example has an F (15) in the 16ths place and an F (15) in the 1s place. A hex FF represents decimal 255.

16^4	16^3	16^2	16^1	16^0
65,536s	4096s	256s	16s	1s

3C hex   FF hex

3	x	16	=	48		15	x	16	=	240
12	x	1	=	12		15	x	1	=	15
				60 Decimal						255 Decimal

3C = 0011 1100 Binary   FF = 1111 1111 Binary

1-4   Example of hexadecimal number formation.

It is interesting to note that there are exactly four binary bits in every hexa-decimal character. For example, the hexadecimal number 5 can be represented with a binary number 0101, while the hexadecimal number F equals a binary 1111. This relationship makes it very easy to translate between hexadecimal and binary num-bers, and is the main reason why hexadecimal notation has been widely embraced in the computer field. A 16-digit binary address can be represented with only four hex characters.

Octal numbers

Octal numbers are yet another way of expressing quantities using a number system of eight digits. The characters 0 to 7 are used to represent the eight digits. Octal place values, however, utilize powers of eight instead of powers of 10, 2, or 16. Figure 1-5 shows how a typical octal number is formed. Once an actual number counts from 0 to 7, the next numbers are 10 to 17, 20 to 27, and 20 on. The octal number 170 has a 1 in the 64s place, a 7 in the 8s place, and a 0 in the 1s place, so the equivalent decimal number is 120.

8^4	8^3	8^2	8^1	8^0
4096s	512s	64s	8s	1s
		1	7	0

170 octal

1	x	64	=	64
7	x	8	=	56
0	x	1	=	0
				120 Decimal

170 octal = 001 111 000 Binary

1-5   Example of octal number formation.

You should note that with eight digits, only three binary digits are needed to represent each octal digit. Octal 1 equates to binary 001, octal 4 is the same as binary 100, and octal 7 equates to binary 111. This relationship also makes it very convenient to translate between octal and binary number systems. Like hexadecimal, the octal system was developed to facilitate fast back-and-forth conversion. However, octal is used less than hex, because hex can represent more bits with fewer characters. The relationship between decimal, hexadecimal, octal, and binary numbers is illustrated in Table 1-1.

Table 1-1. Relationship between decimal, binary, and hexadecimal, and octal numbers

Decimal	Binary	Hexadecimal	Octal
0	0	0	0
1	1	1	1
2	10	2	2
3	11	3	3
4	100	4	4
5	101	5	5
6	110	6	6
7	111	7	7
8	1000	8	10
9	1001	9	11
10	1010	A	12
11	1011	B	13
12	1100	C	14
13	1101	D	15
14	1110	E	16
15	1111	F	17

A basic computer

In the broadest sense, a *digital computer* is an electronic device utilizing the rules of Boolean logic to input, store, manipulate, and output binary information—nothing more. Every computer ever made finds its foundations in this fundamental concept. To fulfill such a broad definition, a computer must contain at least four major functional elements as illustrated in Fig. 1-6: a processing unit, memory, input devices, and output devices. While a modern, full-featured computer can contain many specialized functions, each function can generally be categorized as one of these four elements.

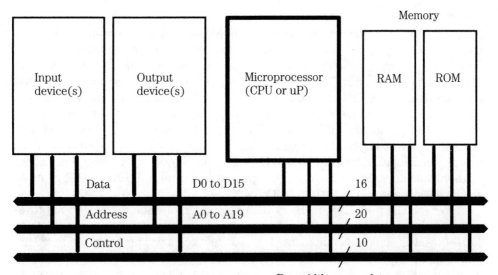

1-6 · Diagram of a simple computer system.

Central processing unit

The *central processing unit* (also called a CPU, uP, or microprocessor) is at the heart of every modern computer system. It is the CPU that provides a computer with much of its processing power. Strangely, a CPU is only capable of three types of operations: *arithmetic, logic,* and *control*—that's it. Arithmetic operations allow the CPU to add, subtract, multiply, and divide. Logical operations let the CPU make comparisons and conditional decisions about various pieces of data. Control operations allow a CPU to access ports and data anywhere within the computer, and move information from one place to another. Even the hundreds of unique and powerful instructions found in sophisticated CPUs can be grouped into these three categories.

The great advantage to a CPU is not in its internal design. In fact, CPUs make use of very generalized internal designs which actually tend to be much slower than streamlined integrated circuits (ICs) that are dedicated to performing one particular function. What CPUs might lack in speed performance, they make up for in flexibility—the ability to carry out operations in any order as instructed. The instructions which direct a microprocessor's operations are called a *program*. Programs are held in mass-storage areas outside of the CPU (typically in a bank of memory ICs). The CPU accesses its instructions and data from the program in storage, then executes each operation as the particular instruction specifies. Thus, by altering the pattern of instructions and data in storage, the same CPU can perform an entirely different set of operations. Even though today's computers utilize an assortment of powerful ICs to achieve high-level control over drives, displays, and keyboards, the actual program instructions which make those parts work together are still executed exclusively by the CPU.

Storage

A CPU functions through the use of instructions contained in a program. However, the CPU is merely a processing tool. Aside from a few internal registers used to store temporary information, microprocessors offer no way to retain the program that they are supposed to run. This limitation requires the program (and any associated program data) to be held outside of the CPU. The CPU can then simply access the stored program and execute it as directed. Computers use solid-state memory ICs to retain current program information. Temporary random-access memory (RAM) holds the current application program (e.g., a word processor or spreadsheet) as well as the computer's operating system (e.g., DOS, Windows, or OS/2). Permanent read-only memory (ROM) holds the computer's power-on self-test (POST) routines and its basic input/output system (BIOS).

Over the last few years, memory ICs have undergone some dramatic improvements in speed and capacity. Many commercial computers now come with 2Mb to 4Mb of RAM as standard equipment. The next few years will probably see those figures double. With so much inexpensive memory available, solid-state memory ICs have become an important branch on the mass-storage family tree. You will see more about memory ICs later in this chapter. Chapter 5 covers memory devices in detail, and chapter 6 discusses a powerful new application of memory ICs in self-contained solid-state memory cards.

Input and output devices

Although a CPU and memory together can technically constitute a working "computer," such a computer would have very little practical value, as the device would have no interaction with the outside world. In order to be useful, a computer must be able to carry information to or from the outside world. For our purposes, we can consider the "outside world" to be any component or mechanism outside of the CPU or its memory devices.

Input devices include a wide variety of circuits and electromechanical systems that can provide information to the CPU and its memory. The CPU can then make use of input information to adapt to any changes in the outside world. A *keyboard* is one of the most common and well-recognized input devices. When you press a key, a numerical code is generated by the keyboard circuitry. The CPU recognizes that a key has been pressed and interrupts its current activity to acquire the key's numerical code.

Even when a computer can read and process data from the outside world, no computer is complete until the results of a computer's processing are made available to the outside world in some coherent, meaningful form. We can consider an output device to be any circuit or electromechanical device to which a computer can provide data. A computer monitor or flat-panel display are two typical output devices. The CPU outputs numerical codes representing commands, text, or graphics to a video controller IC. The video controller IC stores and processes those codes, and generates the information needed to form the display image.

Many other circuits and electromechanical devices are capable of acting as both input and output devices. A serial communication port is a popular input/output (I/O) circuit which allows data to flow into and out of a computer under program control. Many I/O devices are the mass-storage systems that are covered in this book: floppy disk drives, hard disk drives, CD-ROM drives, tape drives, and solid-state memory cards. Each of these devices can receive data output from the CPU (except for the CD-ROM), and provide data input to the CPU as well.

Busses

As you look over the simple computer diagram of Fig. 1-6, you can see that each part of the classical computer is interconnected using three major sets of signals called *busses*. It is important for you to realize that even though the bus might appear as a single solid line, it represents a collection of individual signals all traveling together. The exact number of lines in a bus depends on the particular microprocessor and memory arrangement being used. The number of lines is usually marked on the bus line with a slash, or indicated discretely with labels (i.e., D0 to D7 would suggest an 8-bit bus).

There are three major busses in a computer: the *address bus,* the *data bus,* and the *control bus.* The address bus is controlled exclusively by the CPU. Binary information placed on the address bus defines the precise location in the computer where information can be read or written by the CPU. Microprocessors typically offer more than 20 address lines (A0 to A19), but advanced addressing techniques allow most newer CPUs to access more than 1 billion theoretical locations.

A data bus carries binary information to or from the unique locations specified by the address bus. Such binary information might be an instruction needed by the CPU, the result of a calculation or comparison, or the destination address of a program subroutine or jump. At any given time, the CPU can either input or output data using the data bus.

The control bus carries a selection of digital signals that are used to direct system operations. Control signals can vary quite a bit between computer models and manufacturers, so it is difficult to define one bus that is common to all computers. The number and purpose of control signals depends on the CPU being used, and the overall complexity of the system. One common control is the read/write (R/W) signal generated by the CPU. If the read/write signal indicates a read, the CPU inputs the contents of the databus at the location specified by the address bus. If a write is directed by the read/write line, the CPU outputs data to the address specified by the address bus. Busses are extremely important for this book because most mass-storage devices are interfaced to a computer through its major busses.

Motherboards and bus architecture

The circuitry required to implement a working computer is fabricated onto printed circuit boards that are mounted in a desktop case. It is a simple matter to provide a complete computer on a single PC board, which is how notebook and laptop computers are manufactured today. In fact, early computers such as Commodore's VIC-20 used a single-board design.

However, when IBM designed their personal computers in the early 1980s, they cut costs by providing only the essential (or *core*) components on the *motherboard*. Core components include the microprocessor, a socket for an optional math coprocessor, base memory (now exceeding 4Mb in many desktop systems), BIOS memory (ROM), and support circuitry supplying clocks, system controllers, and signal converters. Other computer functions such as video controllers, drive controllers, and communication circuits must be added to the computer as plug-in expansion boards.

Active backplanes

Classical desktop systems incorporate the core components on a main system PC board (also called a motherboard or *backplane*) as shown in Fig. 1-7. The major signal busses are provided to a series of large card-edge connectors. Each card-edge connector can accept a standard-size expansion board. When a new feature is plugged in to upgrade the computer, it interfaces directly to the main system busses. This approach is known as an *active backplane* system. The term *active* indicates that active semiconductor components are at work on the backplane PC board.

Expansion slot

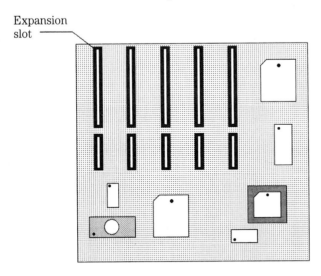

1-7 An "active backplane" motherboard.

Passive backplanes

The disadvantage of active backplane systems is their large size; a substantial amount of motherboard area (or *real estate*) is needed to hold the active components as well as the expansion board connectors. With so many computer systems struggling to reduce the overall case size (or *footprint*), an active backplane is often too large. Another problem with active backplane systems is that the core components are fixed—everything can be changed except for the core components. To overcome the limitations imposed by active backplane systems, computer designers have introduced the *passive backplane* architecture.

A passive backplane uses no active components. This results in a simple, much more petite PC board as shown in Fig. 1-8. The CPU, BIOS, core memory, math co-processor, and support circuitry are removed from the motherboard and placed on a plug-in board of their own. This CPU board occupies its own expansion slot. You can upgrade or repair the computer's core functions simply by removing the old CPU board and installing a new CPU board. All other expansion boards such as video controllers and drive controllers are exactly the same as for active backplane systems.

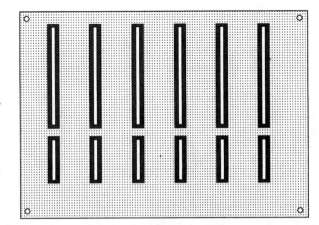

1-8   A "passive backplane" motherboard.

Because you will probably have to deal with expansion boards and computer backplanes during mass-storage troubleshooting, you should be familiar with PC busses as well. This book shows you three popular IBM PC busses, the PC/XT bus, the PC/AT bus, and the PC/MicroChannel bus.

PC/XT bus

The original backplane bus for the IBM PC/XT uses a card-edge connector with 62 pins marked A1 to A31 and B1 to B31 as illustrated in Fig. 1-9. There are three ground lines, five power lines, twenty address lines, eight data lines, ten interrupt lines, and sixteen control signals. The labels for each bus pin are described in Table 1-2.

A1   A31

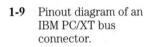

1-9   Pinout diagram of an IBM PC/XT bus connector.

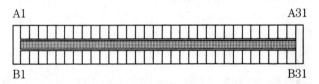

B1   B31

Table 1-2. Expansion board pinout for the PC/XT bus

B1	Ground	A1	I/O Channel Check
B2	Reset Driver	A2	Data 7
B3	+5 Vdc	A3	Data 6
B4	Interrupt Request 2	A4	Data 5
B5	–5 Vdc	A5	Data 4
B6	DMA Request 2	A6	Data 3
B7	–12 Vdc	A7	Data 2
B8	Card Selected (XT Only)	A8	Data 1
B9	+12 Vdc	A9	Data 0
B10	Ground	A10	I/O Channel Ready
B11	Memory Write	A11	Address Enable
B12	Memory Read	A12	Address 19
B13	I/O Write	A13	Address 18
B14	I/O Read	A14	Address 17
B15	DMA Acknowledge 3	A15	Address 16
B16	DMA Request 3	A16	Address 15
B17	DMA Acknowledge 1	A17	Address 14
B18	DMA Request 1	A18	Address 13
B19	DMA Acknowledge 0	A19	Address 12
B20	Clock	A20	Address 11
B21	Interrupt Request 7	A21	Address 10
B22	Interrupt Request 6	A22	Address 9
B23	Interrupt Request 5	A23	Address 8
B24	Interrupt Request 4	A24	Address 7
B25	Interrupt Request 3	A25	Address 6
B26	DMA Acknowledge 2	A26	Address 5
B27	Terminal Count	A27	Address 4
B28	Address Latch Enable	A28	Address 3
B29	+5 Vdc	A29	Address 2
B30	Oscillator	A30	Address 1
B31	Ground	A31	Address 0

The oscillator signal (pin B30) is a multipurpose clock generated directly by a crystal oscillator. The 14.31818-MHz clock is precisely three times the frequency needed by the CPU and four times the frequency at which TVs and monitors achieve a color signal lock. This way, the oscillator not only drives the CPU, but the display system as well. The oscillator signal can also be used by any expansion circuit requiring synchronization with the CPU. The clock signal (pin B20) is a 4.77-MHz square wave derived by dividing the oscillator signal by 3, and is used to drive the CPU directly. It can also be used to operate other expansion boards in the system.

An I/O Channel Check (pin A1) is a check of memory and devices attached to the system bus. When the signal is logic 1, parity check is correct, and the CPU knows that processing is continuing normally. When a parity check error occurs, the signal becomes logic 0. This effectively crashes the computer. When a pulse is applied to the Reset Driver line (pin B2), the entire system is reinitialized (also known as a *warm boot* or *warm start*).

When the CPU places an address on its address bus (pins A12 to A31), a brief pulse is placed on the Address Latch Enable (ALE, pin B 28) to indicate that the address is valid. External circuitry uses the ALE to address the address while the CPU goes on to other work. During a memory read, the CPU activates the Memory Read Command (pin B12) which inputs data on the data lines (pins A2 to A9) from the specified address. Conversely, the CPU activates its Memory Write Command (pin B11) during a write operation. This causes data to be output to the specified address. If the CPU is working with an I/O port instead of memory, the CPU can input data from an I/O port address by activating the I/O Read Command (pin B14), or output data to an I/O port address by activating the I/O Write Command (pin B13). Because a microprocessor can access I/O much faster than I/O devices can respond, the I/O Channel Ready line (pin A10) can cause the CPU to wait until the I/O circuit has caught up.

IBM bus architectures also allow for data transfers under Direct Memory Access (DMA) control. DMA transfers can be accomplished much faster than working through a microprocessor, but a DMA controller circuit must take control of the address and data bus lines. An Address Enable signal (pin A11) tells the DMA controller when to take charge of the system and begin its data transfer . The number of bytes to be moved is declared, and the controller counts each byte as it is transferred. When all bytes have been moved, the Terminal Count signal (pin B27) is asserted to indicate that the data transfer has been completed.

Devices requiring direct memory access make their requests by asserting one of three DMA Request lines (pins B18, B6, and B16) where DMA request level 1 is the highest system priority, and DMA request level 3 is the lowest system priority. When a DMA request is accepted, the DMA controller confirms the request by asserting the appropriate DMA Acknowledge line (pins B19, B17, B 26, and B15). Only DMA Acknowledge lines 1, 2, and 3 are available to the system for general use. DMA Acknowledge line 0 (pin B19) is the highest priority acknowledge signal used to handle memory refresh operations.

Another way to obtain the microprocessor's attention is to assert one of the CPU's Interrupt lines (pins B4, B25, B24, B23, B22, and B21). There are six interrupts available to the bus (labeled Interrupt 2 to Interrupt 7) where level 2 is the highest priority interrupt, and level 7 is the lowest priority. Interrupt 0 is a system timer interrupt, and Interrupt 1 is devoted to servicing the keyboard. After an interrupt routine is serviced, the CPU returns to its original program.

While the IBM PC/XT and all XT-compatible computers have been obsolete for several years, the many XTs that have been sold during the early 1980s will have a place in homes, offices, and schools for years to come. As a result, you need to be familiar with the XT bus architecture.

PC/AT bus

It did not take long before the limitations of XT computers became painfully apparent. The XT proved far too limited in its memory capacity, its Intel 8088 microprocessor could support only an 8 bit data bus, and its system services (i.e., interrupts and DMA) were inadequate for all but simple processing applications. Computer designers had to upgrade the XT without obsoleting the broad base of XT expansion products that had been created. The next generation of computer from IBM was dubbed the PC/AT. The AT computer is centered around the 16-bit Intel 80286 microprocessor, but retains compatibility with just about all 8-bit XT expansion products.

Instead of redesigning the XT bus, the AT bus simply added a second connector along with the original 62-pin card-edge connector. This supplemental connector is a 36-pin card-edge connector marked C1 to C18 and D1 to D18, as shown in Fig. 1-10. The AT extention adds five interrupts, eight data lines (D8 to D15), four DMA Request/Acknowledge pairs, four extra address lines (A20 to A23), and some additional control lines. Table 1-3 lists the labels for each AT pin. The AT bus has proved to be so versatile and resilient that the Institute of Electrical and Electronic Engineers (IEEE) adopted the bus as an industry standard called the Industry Standard Architecture (ISA) bus.

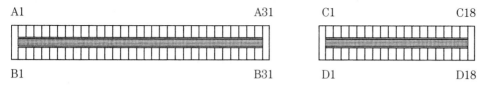

1-10   Pinout diagram of an IBM PC/AT bus connector.

Table 1-3. Expansion board pinout for the PC/AT bus

B1	Ground	A1	I/O Channel Check
B2	Reset Driver	A2	Data 7
B3	+5 Vdc	A3	Data 6
B4	Interrupt Request 9	A4	Data 5
B5	−5 Vdc	A5	Data 4
B6	DMA Request 2	A6	Data 3
B7	−12 Vdc	A7	Data 2
B8	Zero Wait State	A8	Data 1
B9	+12 Vdc	A9	Data 0
B10	Ground	A10	I/O Channel Ready
B11	Real Memory Write	A11	Address Enable
B12	Real Memory Read	A12	Address 19
B13	I/O Write	A13	Address 18
B14	I/O Read	A14	Address 17
B15	DMA Acknowledge 3	A15	Address 16
B16	DMA Request 3	A16	Address 15
B17	DMA Acknowledge 1	A17	Address 14
B18	DMA Request 1	A18	Address 13
B19	Refresh	A19	Address 12
B20	Clock	A20	Address 11
B21	Interrupt Request 7	A21	Address 10
B22	Interrupt Request 6	A22	Address 9
B23	Interrupt Request 5	A23	Address 8

Table 1-3. Continued.

B24	Interrupt Request 4	A24	Address 7
B25	Interrupt Request 3	A25	Address 6
B26	DMA Acknowledge 2	A26	Address 5
B27	Terminal Count	A27	Address 4
B28	Address Latch Enable	A28	Address 3
B29	+5 Vdc	A29	Address 2
B30	Oscillator	A30	Address 1
B31	Ground	A31	Address 0
D1	Memory 16 bit Chip Sel.	C1	System Bus High Enable
D2	I/O 16 bit Chip Select	C2	Unlatched Address 23
D3	Interrupt Request 10	C3	Unlatched Address 22
D4	Interrupt Request 11	C4	Unlatched Address 21
D5	Interrupt Request 12	C5	Unlatched Address 20
D6	Interrupt Request 15	C6	Unlatched Address 19
D7	Interrupt Request 14	C7	Unlatched Address 18
D8	DMA Acknowledge 0	C8	Unlatched Address 17
D9	DMA Request 0	C9	Memory Read
D10	DMA Acknowledge 5	C10	Memory Write
D11	DMA Request 5	C11	Data 8
D12	DMA Acknowledge 6	C12	Data 9
D13	DMA Request 6	C13	Data 10
D14	DMA Acknowledge 7	C14	Data 11
D15	DMA Request 7	C15	Data 12
D16	+5 Vdc	C16	Data 13
D17	Master	C17	Data 14
D18	Ground	C18	Data 15

Because the AT bus allows both 8-bit and 16-bit expansion boards to be used in the same computer, the System Bus High Enable (pin C1) must be asserted for a 16-bit data transfer to occur. An expansion board uses the Memory 16-bit Chip Select (pin D1) or the I/O 16 bit Chip Select (pin D2) to request data transfer to or from memory or an I/O port. The Zero Wait State signal (pin B8) allows an expansion board to essentially speed up bus operation by eliminating wait states between bus cycles.

Addressing in the 16-bit range is facilitated with supplemental Memory Read (pin C9) and Memory Write (pin C10) signals. Any addressing below the 1Mb real addressing range use the memory read and memory write lines on the original 62 pin connector, while any addressing performed above 1Mb uses the additional read and write signals.

The AT bus also allows a limited amount of bus sharing (similar to DMA) with other microprocessors. A new CPU can take control of the system for a few milliseconds by asserting the Master line (pin D17). When the original CPU must resume bus control, a Refresh signal (pin B19) is asserted which warns the "visiting" CPU to relinquish control so the original CPU can refresh its local memory.

PC MicroChannel bus

The IBM MicroChannel bus, created in 1987, is a rethinking of computer expansion slot capabilities which have been extended into the realm of 32-bit data processing. MicroChannel expansion boards are physically smaller than full-slot AT boards, and use smaller, denser connectors, but the differences are more than physical. The MicroChannel bus is designed to be faster and more powerful than the AT bus. With 32 bits of data, 32 address lines capable of addressing 4Gb of memory, a built-in audio channel carrying signals from 50 Hz to 10 kHz, and a built-in Video Graphics Array (VGA) capacity, the MicroChannel bus is intended for high-performance computing. The MicroChannel bus is also designed to handle bus arbitration—the ability of various CPUs to take control of the bus. Figure 1-11 illustrates the pinout for a typical MicroChannel card slot, and each pin is labeled in Table 1-4.

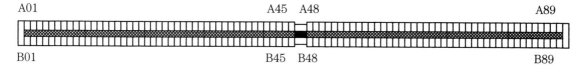

1-11 Pinout diagram of an IBM MicroChannel bus connector.

Table 1-4. Expansion board pinout for the PC MicroChannel Bus

A01	Card Setup	B01	Audio Ground
A02	Make 24	B02	Audio Signal
A03	Ground	B03	Ground
A04	Address 11	B04	14.3 MHz Oscillator
A05	Address 10	B05	Ground
A06	Address 09	B06	Address 23
A07	+5 Vdc	B07	Address 22
A08	Address 08	B08	Address 21
A09	Address 07	B09	Ground
A10	Address 06	B10	Address 20
A11	+5 Vdc	B11	Address 19
A12	Address 05	B12	Address 18
A13	Address 04	B13	Ground
A14	Address 03	B14	Address 17
A15	+5 Vdc	B15	Address 16
A16	Address 02	B16	Address 15
A17	Address 01	B17	Ground
A18	Address 00	B18	Address 14
A19	+12 Vdc	B19	Address 13
A20	Address Decode Latch	B20	Address 12
A21	Preempt	B21	Ground
A22	Burst	B22	Interrupt 09
A23	−12 Vdc	B23	Interrupt 03
A24	Arbitration 00	B24	Interrupt 04
A25	Arbitration 01	B25	Ground

Table 1-4. Continued.

A26	Arbitration 02	B26	Interrupt 05
A27	–12 Vdc	B27	Interrrput 06
A28	Arbitration 03	B28	Interrupt 07
A29	Arbitration Grant	B29	Ground
A30	Terminal Count	B30	reserved
A31	+5 Vdc	B31	reserved
A32	Status Bit 0	B32	Channel Check
A33	Status Bit 1	B33	Ground
A34	Memory I/O	B34	Command
A35	+12 Vdc	B35	Channel Ready Return
A36	Card Ready	B36	Card Selected Feedback
A37	Data Line 00	B37	Ground
A38	Data Line 02	B38	Data Line 01
A39	+5 Vdc	B39	Data Line 03
A40	Data Line 05	B40	Data Line 04
A41	Data Line 06	B41	Ground
A42	Data Line 07	B42	Channel Reset
A43	Ground	B43	reserved
A44	Data Size 16 Return	B44	reserved
A45	Refresh	B45	Ground
A46	KEY (empty position)	B46	KEY (empty position)
A47	KEY (empty position)	B47	KEY (empty position)
A48	+5 Vdc	B48	Data Line 08
A49	Data Line 10	B49	Data Line 09
A50	Data Line 11	B50	Ground
A51	Data Line 13	B51	Data Line 12
A52	+12 Vdc	B52	Data Line 14
A53	reserved	B53	Data Line 15
A54	Status Byte High Enable	B54	Ground
A55	Card Data Size 16	B55	Interrupt 10
A56	+5 Vdc	B56	Interrupt 11
A57	Interrupt 14	B57	Interrupt 12
A58	Interrupt 15	B58	Ground
A59	reserved	B59	reserved
A60	reserved	B60	reserved
A61	Ground	B61	reserved
A62	reserved	B62	reserved
A63	reserved	B63	Ground
A64	reserved	B64	Data Line 16
A65	+12 Vdc	B65	Data Line 17
A66	Data Line 19	B66	Data Line 18
A67	Data Line 20	B67	Ground
A68	Data Line 21	B68	Data Line 22
A69	+5 Vdc	B69	Data Line 23
A70	Data Line 24	B70	reserved
A71	Data Line 25	B71	Ground
A72	Data Line 26	B72	Data Line 27
A73	+5 Vdc	B73	Data Line 28

Table 1-4. Continued.

A74	Data Line 30	B74	Data Line 29
A75	Data Line 31	B75	Ground
A76	reserved	B76	Byte Enable 0
A77	+12 Vdc	B77	Byte Enable 1
A78	Byte Enable 3	B78	Byte Enable 2
A79	Data Size 32 Return	B79	Ground
A80	Card Data Size 32	B80	Translate 32
A81	+12 Vdc	B81	Address 24
A82	Address 26	B82	Address 25
A83	Address 27	B83	Ground
A84	Address 28	B84	Address 29
A85	+5 Vdc	B85	Address 30
A86	reserved	B86	Address 31
A87	reserved	B87	Ground
A88	reserved	B88	reserved
A89	Ground	B89	reserved

Although the MicroChannel architecture offers some performance advantages over the AT bus, it is not widely accepted. As a result, this edition of the book will not look at the MicroChannel bus any further.

Mass-storage overview

Now that you have an understanding of rudimentary computer concepts and expansion bus architectures, this section gives you an overview of the mass-storage devices that are covered in this book.

The ability to store large amounts of information is a critical aspect of all computer systems. Storage allows programs and data to become a working part of the computer. Without storage ability, program instructions and data would have to be entered manually as the computer runs—not a feasible option. In addition to existing programs and data, storage devices often serve as a repository for the results of program operations. For example, you can load and run a word processor, then save the created document back to a storage device as a unique computer file. Clearly, computers as we know them would be absolutely useless without mass-storage devices.

As you might expect, there are many ways to store digital information. Some of the earliest methods utilized punched paper cards or tape. While punched paper storage has long since disappeared into history, other technologies have evolved to serve the needs of today's computers. This book discusses the three major storage technologies currently in use: solid-state ICs, magnetic media, and optical media. You will also learn about some hybrid storage devices that incorporate features from more than one storage technology.

Memory ICs

Solid-state storage technology uses memory ICs to retain information. Memory serves two very important uses in a computer. First, memory ICs provide the computer's *working storage*—where programs are stored while the system executes its instructions. Working memory allows the CPU to access current instructions and hold variables developed during run-time. For example, a program must be loaded from some other mass-storage device into working memory before the CPU can run the program. Most computers offer a base of 640K of available memory, and 2Mb or more of additional memory that can be accessed by the running program. Working memory is typically *temporary*—that is, its contents are only valid so long as computer power is available. If the computer is turned off or power should fail, the contents of working memory are lost. When power is restored, the program has to be reloaded and run from scratch.

Second, memory ICs are used to hold the computer's power-on self-test (POST) and basic input/output system (BIOS) routines. The POST is invoked to test and initialize the computer during startup. BIOS is a set of short routines that let the computer handle its key operations. BIOS routines can be called by the computer's operating system (OS) or applications program. BIOS memory is *permanent*—the IC retains its contents even when power is turned off. Permanent memory guarantees that the routines will be immediately available whenever the system is on. Because memory ICs operate directly with electronic signals, an IC provides very high performance with access times lower than 200 nanoseconds (ns). Memory devices are detailed in chapter 5.

Memory cards

Memory ICs have come a long way in the last decade. Today, several megabytes can be stored with only a few ICs. High capacity, fast speed and moderately low power requirements have created a new demand for PC card mass-storage (also called memory cards). A memory card is basically a bank of temporary or permanent memory ICs which are self-contained in a credit card-size module .

There are now a substantial number of memory card designs, but the choice of temporary or permanent memory type depends on the particular card's intended applications. Laptop/notebook, palmtop, and pen-based computer systems are beginning to integrate memory cards as standard equipment. Card capacities range from several hundred kilobytes to 10Mb or more. Chapter 8 presents a detailed discussion of memory card types, interfaces, and troubleshooting techniques.

Floppy disk drives

Magnetic storage is nothing new to computer systems. Reel-to-reel tape and magnetic drum storage systems have been used for decades with old mainframe computers. While reel and drum storage are obsolete today, the principles and characteristics of magnetic storage technology continue to be refined. The floppy disk drive system is one of the most popular and enduring mass-storage systems. Floppy drives are not fast (with access times on the order of milliseconds) and they cannot store huge volumes of information (up to 1.44Mb), but the medium itself is removeable and very inexpensive.

Floppy drives existed before IBM's entry into the personal computer industry, but the phenomenal success of IBM's XT catapulted the floppy drive into standardization. With standard drives and diskettes, software manufacturers found a perfect medium for distributing commercial software packages. Computer users could also transfer files between machines in a quick and easy fashion. There is little doubt that the universal appeal and convenience of floppy drives, combined with the rapid introduction of utility software (i.e., spreadsheets and word processors) were key factors in the rapid acceptance of personal computers—not to mention the birth of the commercial software industry.

Not long after 5.25" (13.34 cm) floppy drives became established, 3.5" (8.89 cm) drives made their debut. In spite of their smaller physical size and simplified mechanics, 3.5" drives could fit more information on a disk than their 5.25" predecessors. Both drive sizes are still commonly used today, in both normal- (or double-) density and high-density versions. Chapter 6 shows you the components, technologies, and troubleshooting techniques needed to repair 5.25" and 3.5" floppy disk drives.

Hard disk drives

Of all the peripheral devices developed for personal computers over the last decade, few have been embraced as completely as the hard disk drive. Hard drives have rapidly evolved from an expensive luxury into an absolute necessity. Most serious application programs today require so much storage space for interrelated programs and files that it would literally be impossible to run such programs from the floppy drive alone. Hard drives utilize all of the magnetic recording principles that floppy drives do, but hard drives have been optimized and refined to offer startling performance and storage capacity that are orders of magnitude above what a floppy drive can provide.

Hard disks are perhaps the most adept of today's mass-storage devices. They provide megabytes (often hundreds of megabytes) of capacity for programs and data. In only a few moments, the drive is able to access and read (or write) the equivalent of a textbook or novel. Fast hard drive operation can actually make your entire system appear to operate faster. This is not a bad track record for devices that are now smaller than a deck of playing cards and that use less power than most night lights. Chapter 7 explains hard drive technology and troubleshooting in detail.

Tape drives

Tape systems are another type of magnetic mass-storage system designed exclusively for creating a backup copy of your entire hard disk. True, you could back up your hard disk onto floppy disks, but it would require dozens of floppy disks to completely back up today's large hard drives. Also, the tedium and inconvenience of diskette swapping can lead to wasteful operator errors. Tape drives can copy the contents of your hard drive onto a single, high-capacity cassette. It has been said that a tape cartridge is the floppy disk in an age of megabytes.

There are a few disadvantages to tape drive systems. They have changed very little in principle since the days of reel-to-reel tapes. A tape drive is a painfully slow device—partly because of the nature of magnetic tape technology, and partly because of the huge volume of data that must be transferred. Tapes are also *sequential* storage devices, so you cannot back up or restore a single file or files at random. You must start from the beginning and save (or restore) everything at once—it's usually an all or nothing proposition.

As distasteful as it might be to purchase and use a tape drive system, the ability to back up and protect a large volume of data on a regular basis is remarkably important (especially in a business environment). Backup is protection against the many ills that can plague a hard drive. The proven integrity and reliability of a tape backup has ensured that tape drives will be around for quite some time. Chapter 9 deals with the mechanisms and troubleshooting of tape drive systems.

Optical drives

Optical storage techniques are fairly new in the computer industry. By using beams of coherent (laser) light, digital information can be deciphered from reasonably simple plastic disks. While optical storage is not yet as fast as magnetic hard drives or solid-state electronics, CD-ROMs and companion products such as Write Once Read Many (WORM), rewritable optical, and floptical (magneto-optical) drives offer roughly 10 times more storage capacity than comparable magnetic storage media. Capacities of 500Mb to 1Gb or more is not uncommon. Data integrity is rated to last for centuries with some optical media—much longer than even the best magnetic media. Ruggedness is another key concern. After all, there is no need for low-flying read/write heads, and there is no contact between the head and media. Even if the media surface becomes slightly damaged, optical systems can look past many surface imperfections.

With such high data capacity and inherently reliable operation, optical mass-storage systems such as CD-ROM drives will eventually become as integral to normal computer operations as the hard drive. Chapter 10 explains optical drive technology and presents a series of troubleshooting procedures.

2
Typical components

Before taking on any type of repair, it is important that you understand the components you will encounter (Fig. 2-1). You must know what the various components look like, what they do, and how they are marked and rated. Fundamental component knowledge lets you understand just what you are looking at when your mass-storage device is finally apart, and helps you find your way around its circuitry easily. Component knowledge also lets you spot obvious defects such as burns or cracks. This chapter includes discussions of both conventional (or *through-hole*) components and surface-mount devices.

The chapter is not intended to provide a detailed background in electronics theory. Rather, it provides you with the essential characteristics and principles associated with the common components used in drives and memory systems. If you have questions, or need more information, feel free to contact the author directly or refer to any one of the many fine books that are available on electronics theory.

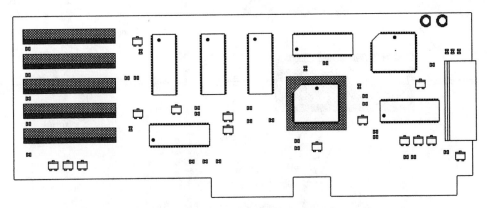

2-1   Components on a typical expansion board.

Passive components

In electronic terms, *passive* components are those components that store or dissipate a circuit's energy in a known, controlled fashion. Resistors, capacitors, and inductors all fall within this group. The term "passive" is used to indicate that such parts serve little practical purpose by themselves—you certainly could not form a CD-ROM or floppy disk drive with resistors, capacitors, and inductors alone. Passive components are used to set up circuit conditions for semiconductor-based parts such as diodes, transistors, and (primarily) integrated circuits.

Resistors

All resistors serve a single purpose—to dissipate power in a controlled fashion. Resistors appear in many circuits, but they are almost always used for such purposes as voltage division or current limiting. Resistors dissipate power by presenting a resistance to the flow of current. Wasted energy is then shed by the resistor as heat. In electronic circuits, so little energy is wasted by resistors that virtually no temperature increase is detectable. In high-energy circuits such as power supplies or amplifiers, however, resistors can shed substantial amounts of heat. The basic unit of resistance is the *ohm*, but you will see resistance also presented as kilohms (thousands of ohms) or megohms (millions of ohms). The symbol for resistance is the Greek symbol omega (Ω).

A classic carbon-composition resistor is shown in Fig. 2-2. Two metal leads are inserted into a molded body containing a packed carbon filling. Because it is much harder for electrons to pass through carbon than through copper, the carbon filling provides resistance to the flow of current. By varying the composition of the carbon filling, the value of resistance can be altered within a range from .1 ohm to 20 MΩ. Unfortunately, carbon resistors suffer from relatively poor tolerance ($\pm10\%$ or worse), and they are large in comparison to newer resistors.

Carbon-film resistors, as shown in Fig. 2-3, have largely replaced carbon-composition resistors in most circuits requiring through-hole resistors. Instead of carbon filling, a very precise layer of carbon film is applied to a thin ceramic tube.

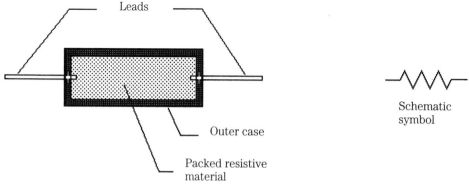

2-2   A carbon-composition resistor.

The thickness of this coating affects the amount of resistance: thicker coatings yield lower levels of resistance, and vice versa. Metal leads are attached by caps at both ends, and the entire finished assembly is dipped in epoxy or ceramic. Carbon film resistors are generally more accurate than carbon composition resistors, because a high-purity resistive film can be deposited with great precision during manufacture.

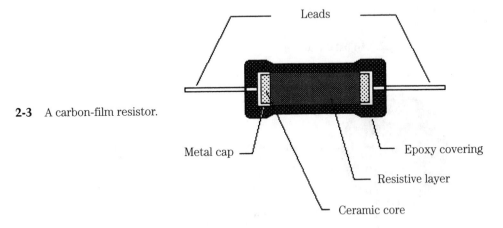

2-3   A carbon-film resistor.

A surface-mount resistor is illustrated in Fig. 2-4. As with carbon-film resistors, surface-mount resistors are formed by depositing a layer of resistive film onto a thin ceramic substrate. Metal tabs are attached at both ends of the wafer. Surface-mount resistors are soldered directly on the top or bottom sides of a printed circuit board instead of using leads to penetrate the PC board. Surface-mount resistors are incredibly small devices (only a few square millimeters in area), yet they offer very tight tolerances. Such small resistors are used extensively in high-volume electronic manufacturing.

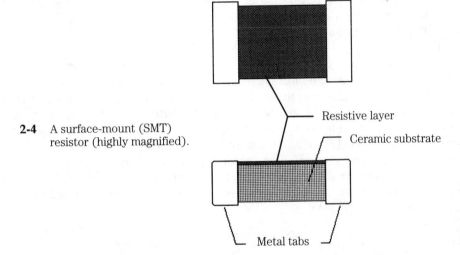

2-4   A surface-mount (SMT) resistor (highly magnified).

Adjustable resistors, known as *potentiometers* or *rheostats,* are usually employed to adjust voltage, current, or some other circuit operating parameter. As shown in Fig. 2-5, a typical potentiometer consists of a movable metal wiper resting on a layer of resistive film. Although the total resistance of the film, end-to-end, remains unchanged, resistance between either end and the wiper blade varies as the wiper is moved. There are two typical types of adjustable resistor: knob-type, where the wiper is turned clockwise or counter-clockwise using a rotating metal shaft, or slide-type, where the wiper is moved back and forth in a straight line.

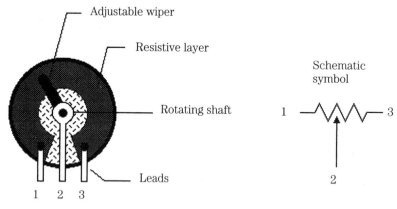

2-5   An adjustable resistor.

In addition to value and tolerance, resistors are also rated in terms of their power handling capacity. Power is normally measured in watts (W), and is dependent on the amount of current (I) and voltage (V) applied to the resistor as given by Ohm's law: P = I x V. Resistors are typically manufactured in 1/16, 1/8, 1/4, 1/2, 1, 2, and 5 W, in order to handle a variety of power conditions. Mass-storage systems rarely need resistors larger than 1/8 W. Size is directly related to power dissipation ability, so larger resistors are generally able to handle larger amounts of power than a smaller resistor of the same value.

Failures among potentiometers usually take the form of intermittent connections between the wiper blade and resistive film. Remember that film wears away as the wiper moves back and forth across it. Over time, enough film can wear away at certain points so that the wiper does not make good contact. This can cause many types of erratic or intermittent operation. Fortunately, it is rarely (if ever) necessary to continually adjust circuit parameters away from factory calibration settings, so it is unlikely that adjustable resistors will wear out. Dust and debris can collect in them, though, and cause intermittent operation when adjustment is needed. You can try cleaning an intermittent potentiometer with a high-quality electronic contact cleaner. If that doesn't correct the problem, the potentiometer or rheostat should be replaced.

Reading resistors

Every resistor is marked with its proper value. Marking allows resistors to be identified on sight and compared versus schematics or part layout drawings. Now that you know what resistors look like, you should be able to identify their value without relying on test equipment. There are three ways to mark a resistor: explicit marking, color coding, and numerical marking. It is important to understand all three types, because older storage circuits use resistors with a mix of marking schemes.

Explicit marking is just as the name implies—the actual value of the component is written onto the part. Large, ceramic resistors often use explicit markings. Their long, rectangular bodies are usually large enough to hold clearly printed characters.

Color coding has long been a popular marking scheme for carbon composition and carbon film resistors that are too small to hold explicit markings. The twelve colors used in color coding are shown in Table 2-1. The first ten colors (black through white) are used as *value* and *multiplier* colors. Silver and gold colors serve as *tolerance* indicators.

Table 2-1. Standard resistor color code

Color	Value	Multiplier	
Black	0	1	
Brown	1	10	
Red	2	100	
Orange	3	1000	
Yellow	4	10,000	
Green	5	100,000	
Blue	6	1,000,000	
Violet	7	...	
Grey	8	...	
White	9	...	
Silver	...	...	10% tolerance
Gold	...	...	5% tolerance

The color code approach uses a series of up to five colored bands as illustrated in Fig. 2-6. Band one is always located closest to the edge of the resistor. Bands one and two are the value bands, and band three is the multiplier. A fourth band, if present, will be silver or gold to indicate the resistor's tolerance. On rare occasions, you might encounter a fifth band which indicates the reliability of a resistor; this is used only for military/aerospace-grade resistors.

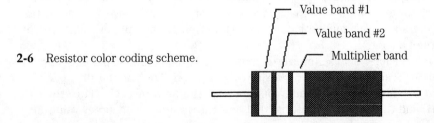

2-6 Resistor color coding scheme.

The color coding sequence is read as *band 1 band 2 x band 3*. For example, suppose the resistor of Fig. 2-6 is marked with a color sequence of brown, black, and red. You can see from Table 2-1 that brown corresponds to 1, black to 0, and red to 100 (because the red band occupies the *multiplier* position). The sequence is read as 10 x 100, or 1000 Ω (1 kΩ). If the first three color bands of a resistor are red, red, and orange, the resistor is read as 22 x 1000, or 22,000 Ω (22 kΩ).

When a fourth color band is present, it shows the resistor's tolerance. A gold band represents an excellent tolerance of ±5% of rated value. A silver band represents a fair tolerance of ±10%, and no tolerance band indicates a poor tolerance of ±20%. When a faulty resistor must be replaced, it should be replaced with resistor of equal or better tolerance whenever possible.

Color-coded resistors are rapidly being replaced by surface-mount (SMT) resistors. Surface-mount resistors are far too small for color coding. Instead, a three digit numerical code is used (you might need a small magnifying glass to read the digits). Each digit corresponds to the first three bands of the color code as shown in Fig. 2-7. The first two numbers are *value* digits, and the third number is the *multiplier*. The multiplier digit indicates how many places to the right the value's decimal place must be shifted. For example, a numerical code of 102 denotes a value of 10 with 2 zeros added on, making the number 1000 (1 kΩ). A marking of 331 would be read as 330 Ω, and so on.

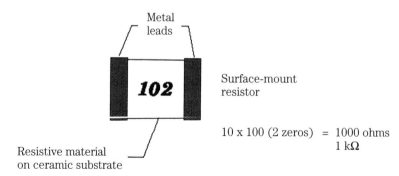

2-7 Resistor numerical markings.

Capacitors

Capacitors are devices that store energy in the form of an electrical charge. By themselves, capacitors have little practical use, but the capacitor principle has important applications when combined with other components in filters, timing circuits, and power supplies. Capacitance is measured in *farads* (F). In actual practice, a farad is a very large amount of capacitance, so most capacitors are measured using the microfarad (μF, or millionths of a farad) and picofarad (pF, or millionths of a millionth of a farad).

In principle, a capacitor is little more than two conductive plates separated by an insulator (called a *dielectric*) as shown in Fig. 2-8. The amount of capacitance provided by this type of assembly depends on the area of each plate, their distance apart, and the dielectric material that separates them. Even larger values of capaci-

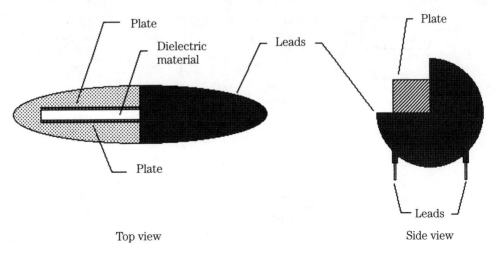

Plate

Dielectric
material

Leads

Plate

Plate

Plate

Leads

Top view

Side view

2-8 Cutaway view of a simple plate capacitor.

tance can be created by rolling up a plate/dielectric assembly and housing it in a cylinder.

When voltage is applied to a capacitor, electrons flow into it until it is fully charged. At that point, current stops flowing (even though voltage might still be applied), and voltage across the capacitor equals its applied voltage. If applied voltage is removed, the capacitor tends to retain the charge of electrons deposited on its plates. Just how long it can do this depends on the specific materials used to construct the capacitor, as well as its overall size. Internal resistance through the dielectric material eventually bleeds off any charge. For the purposes of this book, however, all you really need to remember is that capacitors are built to store electrical charge.

There are two types of capacitors that you should be familiar with. These can be categorized as *fixed* and *electrolytic*. A selection of capacitor types is illustrated in Fig. 2-9. Fixed capacitors are nonpolarized devices—they can be inserted into a circuit regardless of their lead orientation. Many fixed capacitors are assembled as small wafers or disks. Each conductive plate is typically aluminum foil. Common dielectrics include paper, mica, and various ceramic materials. The complete assembly is then coated in a hard plastic, epoxy, or ceramic housing to keep out humidity. Larger capacitors can be assembled into large, hermetically sealed canisters. Fixed capacitors are also used extensively in a surface-mount form.

Electrolytic capacitors are polarized components—they must be inserted into a circuit in the proper orientation with respect to the applied signal voltage. Tantalum capacitors are often found in a dipped (or *teardrop*) shape, or as small canisters. Aluminum electrolytic capacitors are usually used in general-purpose applications where polarized devices are needed. The difference between fixed and electrolytic capacitors is primarily in their materials, but the principles and purpose of capacitance remain the same.

Capacitors are often designated as *axial* or *radial* devices. This simply refers to the capacitor's particular lead configuration. When both leads emerge from the same

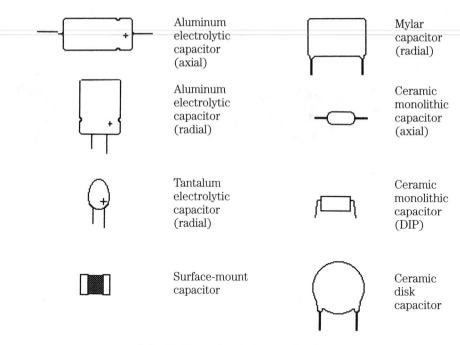

Aluminum
electrolytic
capacitor
(axial)

Mylar
capacitor
(radial)

Aluminum
electrolytic
capacitor
(radial)

Ceramic
monolithic
capacitor
(axial)

Tantalum
electrolytic
capacitor
(radial)

Ceramic
monolithic
capacitor
(DIP)

Surface-mount
capacitor

Ceramic
disk
capacitor

2-9   Outlines of various capacitor types.

end of the capacitor, the device is said to be radial. If the leads emerge from either side, the capacitor is known as axial.

Surface-mount capacitors are usually fixed ceramic devices using a dielectric core capped by electrodes at both ends. If an electrolytic capacitor is needed, a surface-mount tantalum device is typically used. Although the construction of a surface-mount tantalum capacitor differs substantially from a ceramic surface-mount capacitor, they both appear very similar to the unaided eye. All polarized capacitors are marked with some type of polarity indicator.

Like resistors, most capacitors tend to be rugged and reliable devices. Because they only store energy (not dissipate it), it is virtually impossible to burn them out. Capacitors can be damaged or destroyed by exceeding their working voltage (WV) rating, or by reversing the orientation of a polarized device. This can occur if a failure elsewhere in a circuit causes excessive energy to be applied across a capacitor, or if you should install a new electrolytic capacitor incorrectly.

Reading capacitors

Like resistors, all capacitors carry markings that identify their value. Once you understand the markings, you will be able to determine capacitor values on sight. Capacitors are typically marked in three ways: color coding, explicit marking, and numerical codes.

Color-coded capacitors use a color marking scheme very similar to resistor color codes. The first two colors represent a value, while a third color indicates a multiplier. Today, however, color-coded capacitors are rarely used in high-volume electronic manufacturing, so this book will not discuss color coding further. Color coded capacitors have largely been replaced by explicit markings and numerical codes, but you should be aware that older capacitors might carry a color code.

Explicit marking is used with capacitors that are physically large enough to carry their printed value. Larger ceramic disk, mylar, and electrolytic capacitors have plenty of surface area to hold readable markings. Note that all polarized capacitors, regardless of size, must show which of their two leads are positive or negative. Be certain to pay close attention to polarizer markings whenever you are testing or replacing capacitors.

Small, nonpolarized capacitors and many sizes of surface-mount capacitors now make use of numerical coding schemes. The pattern of numerical markings is easy to follow, because it is similar to the marking technique used with resistors. A series of three numbers is used: the first two numbers are the value digits, while the third number is the multiplier digit (how many zeros are added to the value digits). Capacitor numerical marking is illustrated in Fig. 2-10.

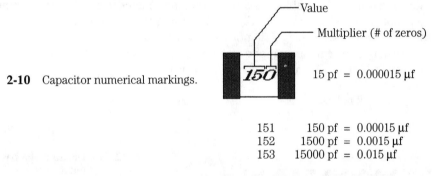

2-10 Capacitor numerical markings.

151	150 pf = 0.00015 µf
152	1500 pf = 0.0015 µf
153	15000 pf = 0.015 µf

Almost all capacitor numerical markings are based on picofarad measurements. Thus, the capacitor marked 150 would be read as a value of 15 with no zeros added (or 15 pF). A marking of 151 would then be 15 with one 0 added, or 150 pF. The marking 152 would be 15 with two 0s added, or 1500 pF, and so on. A marking of 224 would be 22 with four 0s (or 220,000 pF). As you see, the decimal place is always shifted to the right.

Although this marking system is based on picofarads, every value can be expressed as microfarads (µF) by dividing the pF value by 1 million. For example, a 15 pF capacitor could also be called a 0.000015 µF capacitor:

$$\frac{15 \text{ pF}}{1,000,000 \text{ pF/µF}} = 0.000015 \text{ µF}$$

Of course, there is no advantage in marking such a small capacitor in the µF range when 15 pF is such a convenient value, but the conversion is a simple one. The 15000 pF capacitor could also be shown as 0.015 µF:

$$\frac{15000 \text{ pF}}{1,000,000 \text{ pF/µF}} = 0.015 \text{ µF}$$

Capacitors with large picofarad values are often expressed more effectively as microfarads. To confirm your estimates, you can measure the capacitor with a capacitance meter.

Inductors

Inductors are also energy storage devices. But unlike capacitors, inductors store energy in the form of a magnetic field. Before the introduction of integrated circuits, inductors served a key role with capacitors in the formation of filters and resonant (or tuned) circuits. While advances in solid-state electronics have rendered inductors virtually obsolete in traditional applications, they remain invaluable for high-energy circuits such as power supplies. Inductors are also used in transformers, motors, relays, and solenoids. Inductance is measured in *henries* (H), but smaller inductors can be found in the millihenry (mH) or microhenry (µH) range.

An inductor is little more than a simple length of wire. Basic electrical laws state that a magnetic field is produced whenever current is passed through a conductor. However, the inductance generated by a single strand of wire is rarely significant enough to be useful. To establish useful levels of inductance, a conductor is wrapped in the shape of a coil as shown in Fig. 2-11. Coiling the inductor concentrates the magnetic field and causes magnetic poles to form. To concentrate the magnetic field even further, the coil can be wrapped around a *permeable core*. A permeable core is any material which can be magnetized, such as iron or steel.

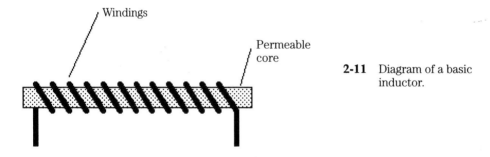

Windings

Permeable core

2-11   Diagram of a basic inductor.

Coils are available in many shapes and sizes, as shown in Fig. 2-12. The particular size and shape depend on the amount of energy that must be stored, and the magnetic characteristics that are desired. Larger coils are typically used in power supplies or ac adaptors. Small coils are available in surface-mount or leaded packages to serve in surge suppression and dc-dc converter circuits.

A *transformer* is actually a combination of inductors all working in tandem. As Fig. 2-13 illustrates, it is composed of three important elements: a *primary* (or input) winding, a *secondary* (or output) winding, and a *core* structure of some type. Transformers are used to alter (or transform) ac voltage and current levels in a circuit, as well as to isolate one circuit from another. An ac signal is applied to the primary winding. Because the magnitude of this input signal is constantly changing, the magnetic field it generates fluctuates as well. When this fluctuating field intersects the secondary coil, another ac signal is created (or *induced*) across it. This principle is known as *magnetic coupling*. Any secondary ac signal duplicates the original

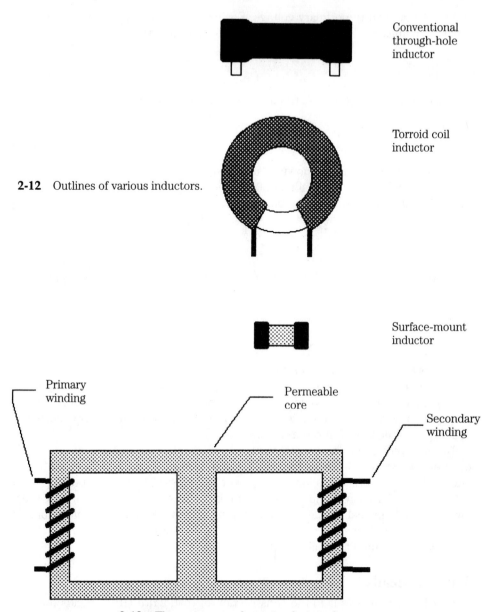

Conventional
through-hole
inductor

Torroid coil
inductor

2-12 Outlines of various inductors.

Surface-mount
inductor

Primary
winding

Permeable
core

Secondary
winding

2-13 Three common elements of a transformer.

signal. Primary and secondary windings are often wound around the same core structure, providing efficient magnetic coupling from primary to secondary.

The actual amount of voltage and current induced on a secondary coil depends on the ratio of the number of primary windings to the number of secondary windings. This relationship is known as the *turns ratio*. If the secondary coil contains more windings than the primary coil, then the voltage induced across the secondary coil will be greater than the primary voltage. For example, if the transformer has 1000 primary windings and 2000 secondary windings, the turns ratio is:

$$\frac{1000}{2000} \quad X \quad \frac{1}{2}$$

With 10 Vac applied to the primary, the secondary outputs roughly 20 Vac:

$$\frac{10 \text{ Vac}}{\frac{1}{2}} \quad = \quad 20 \text{ Vac}$$

Such an arrangement is known as a *step-up* transformer. If the situation were reversed where the primary coil had 2000 windings with 1000 windings in the secondary, the turns ratio would then be:

$$\frac{2000}{1000} \quad X \quad \frac{2}{1}$$

If 30 Vac were now applied to the primary, the secondary output would be 15 Vac:

$$\frac{30}{\frac{2}{1}}$$

This is known as a *step-down* transformer.

Current is also stepped in a transformer, but *opposite* to the proportion of voltage steps. If voltage is stepped down by the factor of a turns ratio, current is stepped up by the same factor. This relationship ensures that power out of a transformer is about equal to the power into the transformer.

Because inductors are energy storage devices, they should not dissipate any power by themselves. However, the wire resistance in each coil, combined with magnetic losses in the core, can allow some power to be lost as heat. Heat buildup is the leading cause of inductor failure. Long-term exposure to heat can eventually break down the tough enamel insulating each winding and cause a short circuit. Short circuits lower the coil's overall resistance, causing it to draw even more current. Breakdown accelerates until the coil is destroyed.

Magnetic heads

Another key use of coils is in the construction of read/write (R/W) heads for magnetic storage media. As you can see in Fig. 2-14, an R/W head consists of little more than a fine wire coiled around part of a small permeable core. For such a simple application, R/W heads are probably one of the most critical parts of any magnetic storage system (including floppy, hard, and tape drives).

If no current is applied to the head coil, no magnetic field is produced in the coil, and no flux is generated in the head assembly. When current is applied to the head coil from a driving circuit, a magnetic field is produced by the coil. The direction of

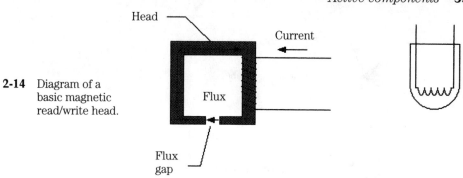

2-14 Diagram of a basic magnetic read/write head.

the magnetic field causes a path of magnetic flux in the head, and results in a powerful concentration of magnetic flux at the head's air gap. If the direction of current is reversed, the coil's magnetic field orientation also reverses. This reversal also reverses the flux path in the head assembly (and across the air gap). The flux produced across a head's air gap is deposited (or *written*) to the disk or tape.

A magnified head can also receive (or *read*) previously recorded binary flux information from magnetic media. When a head passes over recorded media, the flux patterns previously recorded intersect with the head's air gap. This produces a corresponding flux path in the head assembly which, in turn, generates a current in the head coil which is detected and processed by a receiving circuit. A flux bit in one direction would produce a current signal in one polarity, while an opposing flux bit would produce a current signal in reverse polarity. Receiving circuits in the drive convert the signal into corresponding logic bits. You will see much more about magnetic mass-storage in chapters 7, 8, and 9.

Active components

Diodes, transistors, and integrated circuits comprise a much broader and more powerful group of *active* components. Such components are referred to as active because each part actually *does* something. Active components use a circuit's energy to accomplish specific, practical functions. The next part of this chapter provides an overview of the active components you will find in mass-storage systems, and describes their capabilities.

Diodes

The classic *diode* is a two-terminal semiconductor devices that allows current to flow in one direction only—not in the other. This one-way property is known as *rectification*. Diodes are available in a wide array of case styles, as shown in Fig. 2-15. The size and materials used in a diode's case depend on the amount of current that must be carried. Glass cased diodes, usually made with silicon, are generally used for low-power (or *small signal*) applications. Plastic- or ceramic-cased diodes are typically employed for low or medium power applications like power supplies, circuit isolation, or inductive flyback protection. Diodes are also available in small surface-mount packages. A diode has two terminals. The *anode* is its positive terminal, and

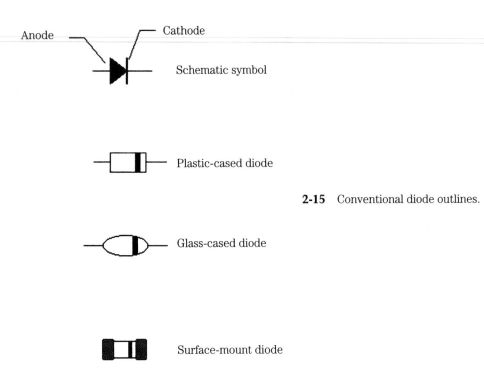

Anode   Cathode

Schematic symbol

Plastic-cased diode

2-15 Conventional diode outlines.

Glass-cased diode

Surface-mount diode

the *cathode* is its negative terminal. Note that a diode's cathode is always marked with a solid stripe or bar.

Whenever you deal with diodes (regardless of the case size or style), you should be concerned with two major diode specifications: forward current (I_F) and peak inverse voltage (PIV). Choose replacement diodes with I_F and PIV values that closely match the part to be replaced. When a silicon diode is forward biased as shown in Fig. 2-16, the diode develops a constant voltage drop of about .6 Vdc. The remainder of applied voltage drops across the current limiting resistor. Because a diode dissipates power, it is important to choose a current-limiting resistor that restricts forward current to a safe level—otherwise, the diode might be destroyed by excess heat.

A reverse-biased diode, such as the one shown in Fig. 2-17, acts almost like an open switch—no current is allowed to flow in the circuit. This also demonstrates the essential principle of rectification: diode current flows in only one direction. Whatever voltage is applied across the diode will appear across it. Even if the reverse voltage level were increased, the diode would not conduct. However, there are limits to the amount of reverse voltage that a diode can withstand. The limit is called PIV. If reverse voltage exceeds PIV, the diode junction can rupture and fail as either an open or short circuit. Typical PIV ratings can easily exceed 200 volts.

While rectifier diodes are not meant to be operated in the reverse-biased condition, the *zener* diode is a special type designed exclusively for reverse biasing. Figure 2-18 illustrates a common zener diode circuit. Notice the unique schematic symbol used for zener diodes. When applied voltage is below the zener's *breakdown*

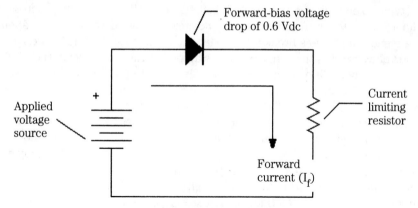

2-16 Forward-biased diode circuit.

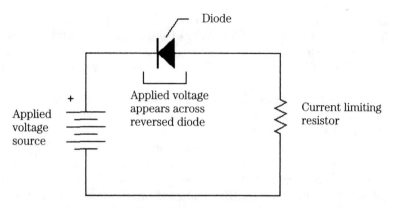

2-17 Reverse-biased diode circuit.

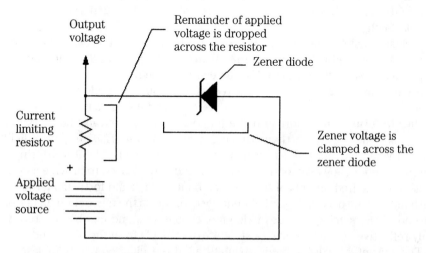

2-18 Zener diode voltage clamping circuit.

voltage (typical zener diodes operate at 5, 6, 9, 1 2, 15, or 24 Vdc), voltage across the zener diode equals the applied voltage, and no current flows in the diode. As applied voltage exceeds the zener's breakdown voltage, current begins to flow through the diode and voltage across the zener remains clamped at the zener's level (i.e., 5, 6, 9, 12 Vdc, etc.). Any additional applied voltage is then dropped across the current-limiting resistor. As long as applied voltage exceeds the zener's breakdown voltage, zener voltage remains constant. This *zener action* makes zener diodes perfect as simple regulators, and is the basis for most methods of linear voltage regulation.

It is virtually impossible to differentiate between rectifier and zener diodes by their outward appearance—both types appear identical in every way. The only ways you can tell them apart are to look up the particular device in a cross-reference manual, look at the part's representation in a schematic, or look at the device's silk screening on its PC board. Rectifier diodes are typically labeled with a "D" prefix (e.g., D32, D27, or D3), but zener diodes often use "Z" or "ZD" prefixes (e.g., ZD5 or ZD201).

Similarly, it is impossible to discern a faulty diode simply by looking at it, unless the diode has been destroyed by some type of sudden, severe overload. Such overloads are virtually nonexistent in computer circuitry, so you must use test instruments to confirm a diode's condition. Test instruments are discussed in the next chapter.

In all semiconductor devices, electrons must bridge a semiconductor junction during operation. By modifying the construction of a junction and encapsulating it inside a diffuse plastic housing, electrons moving across a junction liberates photons of visible (or infrared) light. This is the basic principle behind light-emitting diodes (LEDs). An LED is shown in Fig. 2-19. Notice that an LED is little more than a diode—the wavy arrows indicate that light is moving away from the device. Altering the chemical composition of an LED's materials alters the wavelength of emitted light (e.g., yellow, orange, red, green, blue, infrared, etc.). Like ordinary diodes, LEDs are intended to be forward-biased, but LED voltage drops are higher (.8 to 3.5 Vdc), and LEDs often require 10 to 35 mA of current to generate the optimum amount of light.

A close cousin to the LED is the *laser diode* (LD) which is used extensively as a signal source in optical and magneto-optical storage systems. If you intend to work on optical drives at all, you should be familiar with the LD.

A laser diode is generally constructed using gallium arsenide (GaAs) instead of silicon. Both positive (P) and negative (N) semiconductor materials are brought together to form a fairly normal diode junction as illustrated in Fig. 2-20, but the junction is somewhat wider than ordinary diodes. Like an LED, photons of light are liberated when current passes through the diode. Instead of light scattering away from the junction, however, both ends of the diode are cleaved to provide a mirrored effect to the excited photons. Photons then bounce back and forth along the diode's length until lasing occurs. Laser light energy overcomes the mirror and exits from either end of the semiconductor diode chip, though one end can be covered with a highly reflective coating so that most light exits the LD from the other end.

The output of a laser diode exhibits all three characteristics of laser light: *monochromicity* (only one wavelength of light is generated), *coherency* (light

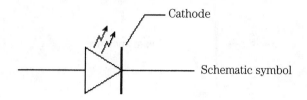

Cathode

Schematic symbol

2-19 LED schematic and outline diagrams.

Large outline diagram

Cathode mark

Small outline diagram

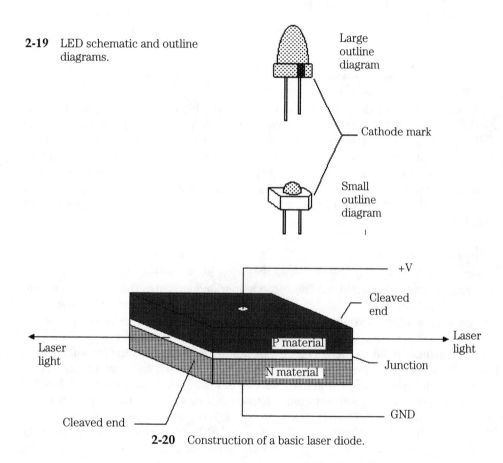

+V

Cleaved end

Laser light

P material

Laser light

Junction

N material

Cleaved end

GND

2-20 Construction of a basic laser diode.

waves are in phase with one another), and *low divergence* (light tends to stay in a straight line instead of spreading out). Because of their low efficiency, you usually find laser diode assemblies mounted into some type of heat sink or metal chassis.

Laser diodes often incorporate a *photodiode detector,* as shown in Fig. 2-21. A photodiode is stimulated by a small portion of laser light to act as a sensor in the laser diode assembly. The photodiode operates in two modes: the *photovoltaic mode* and the *photoconductive mode.* In the photovoltaic mode, a photodiode generates a voltage when exposed to the proper wavelength of light—rather like a solar

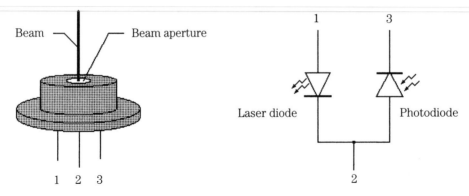

2-21 Diagram and schematic symbol of a laser diode.

cell. When a laser diode and a photodiode are coupled together, the photodiode is optimized to detect the laser's output wavelength. In the photoconductive mode, an external voltage is applied across the photodiode which then acts as a variable resistor whose value is inversely proportional to the laser power. In this way, a photodiode can provide a somewhat linear indication of the laser diode's output power. Note the schematic symbols for laser diodes and photodiodes. The advantage to using photodiodes as detectors is their very quick response time to changes in light conditions.

Diode markings

All diodes carry two very important markings, as shown in Fig. 2-22: the part number and the *cathode marking*. The cathode marking indicates the cathode (or negative) diode lead. Because diodes are polarized devices, it is critical that you know which lead is which. Otherwise, an incorrectly replaced diode can cause a circuit malfunction.

Unlike passive components, diode part numbers contain no tangible information on a diode's performance specifications or limits. Instead, the part number is an index or reference number which allows you to look up the particular specification in a manufacturer's or cross-reference data book. Classic diode part numbers begin with the prefix "1N," followed by one to four digits. The "1N" prefix is used by the Joint Electron Devices Engineering Council (JEDEC) in the United States to denote

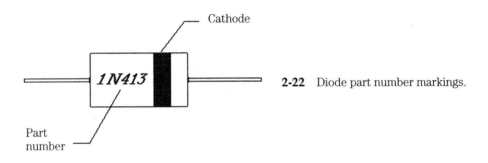

2-22 Diode part number markings.

devices with one semiconductor junction (diodes). Typical Japanese diode part numbers begin with the prefix "1SS," where "SS" indicates "small-signal."

Of course, you will probably encounter diodes with many unique and arcane markings. Fortunately, there are many clues to guide you along. Your first clue is the white (or gray) cathode band. At least you can identify the part as a diode. The second identifier is the silk screen lettering on the PC board. Diodes are usually assigned "D" or "ZD" numbering prefixes to denote a rectifier diode or a zener diode. Once you are confident that you have identified a diode, use a cross-reference index to look up the suspect part's replacement or equivalent. The specifications you find for the equivalent part in a cross-reference manual will closely (if not exactly) match those for the original part. There are many semiconductor cross-references available.

Transistors

A transistor is a three-terminal semiconductor device whose output signal is directly controlled by its input signal. With passive components, a transistor can be configured to perform either amplification or switching tasks. There isn't enough room in this book to discuss the theory and characteristics of transistors, but it is important that you know the most important concepts of transistors, and understand their various uses.

There are two major types of transistors: bipolar transistors and field-effect transistors. Bipolar transistors are common, inexpensive, general-purpose devices that can be made to handle amplification and switching tasks with equal ease. The three leads of a bipolar transistor are the base, the emitter, and the collector. In most applications, the *base* serves as the transistor's input—that is where the input signal is applied. The *emitter* is typically tied to ground (usually through one or more values of resistance), and the *collector* provides the output signal. The transistor can also be configured so that the input signal is supplied to the collector, the base is grounded, and the output appears on the emitter.

There are two types of bipolar transistor: negative-positive-negative (npn) and positive-negative-positive (pnp). For an npn transistor, base voltage must be positive with respect to the emitter. As base voltage increases, the transistor is turned on and current begins to flow from collector to emitter. As base voltage increases further, the transistor continues to turn on and allows more current into the collector, until the transistor finally *saturates*. A saturated transistor cannot be turned on any further. A pnp transistor requires a negative base voltage (with respect to the emitter) in order to cause the transistor to turn on and conduct current. As base voltage becomes more negative, the transistor turns on more and more until it saturates. By far, npn transistors are more commonly used today as discrete components in mass-storage circuits.

A simple, low-power bipolar transistor amplifier arrangement is illustrated in Fig. 2-23. Resistors are used to set up the voltage and current conditions that the transistor needs in order to function as a *linear amplifier*. Initial voltage and current setup is known as *biasing* the transistor. The term "linear" indicates that the output signal is a larger duplicate of the input signal. Capacitors at the input and

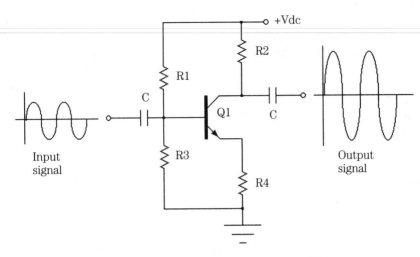

2-23 Diagram of a bipolar transistor amplifier.

output prevent dc voltages from entering the amplifier and offsetting its bias levels—only ac signals are allowed to pass.

When a bipolar transistor is used in a switching circuit (also known as a *driver circuit*), the arrangement is often somewhat simpler, as shown in Fig. 2-24. Unlike a transistor amplifier whose output signal varies in direct proportion to its input, a switching circuit is either on or off—very much like a mechanical switch. Electronic circuits make extensive use of switching circuits in order to operate LEDs or piezoelectric buzzers. Motors in most mechanical drive systems such as floppy drives are switched using transistor driving circuits.

The typical switching circuit uses a digital signal from an IC as the control signal. When the control signal is at a logic 0, the transistor (and its load) remains off. When a logic 1 signal is supplied to the driver, the transistor saturates. Current flows through the load, into the collector, through the transistor to the emitter, then to ground. A base resistor is added to limit current into the base from the signal source.

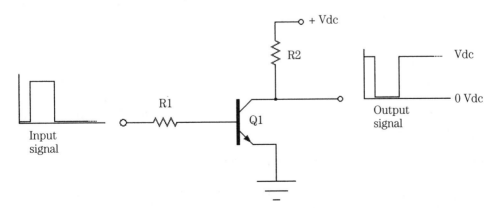

2-24 Diagram of a bipolar transistor switch.

An additional resistor might be needed in the collector circuit to limit current if the load is too large.

Phototransistors are a unique variation of bipolar transistors. Instead of an electrical signal being used to control the transistor, photons of light provide the base signal. Light enters the phototransistor through a clear quartz or plastic window on the transistor's body. Light that strikes the transistor's base liberates electrons that become base current. The more light that enters the phototransistor, the more base current that is produced, and vice versa. While phototransistors can be operated as linear amplifiers, they are most often found in switching circuits that detect the presence or absence of light.

Although phototransistors can detect light from a wide variety of sources, normally an LED is used to supply a known, constant light source. When a phototransistor and LED are matched together in this way, an *optocoupler* (or *optoisolator*) is formed, as shown in Fig. 2-25. Notice the new schematic symbol for a phototransistor. The wavy lines indicate that light is entering at the base. Optocouplers are used in floppy drives to detect the presence or absence of a disk's write-protect notch, and to detect whether the drive door is closed. Optocouplers can also be fabricated together on the same integrated circuit to provide circuit isolation.

Bold

2-25 Diagram of an optocoupler.   LED source

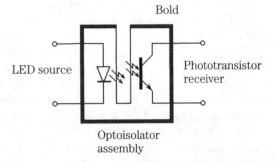

Phototransistor
receiver

Optoisolator
assembly

Field-effect transistors (FETs) are constructed in a radically different fashion from bipolar transistors. Although FETs make use of the same basic materials and can operate as either amplifiers or switches, they require biasing components of much higher value to set the proper operating conditions. FETs are either N-channel or P-channel devices, as shown in Fig. 2-26. The difference in transistor types depends on the materials used to construct the particular FET. A FET has three terminals: a *source*, a *gate*, and a *drain*. These leads correspond to the emitter, base, and collector of a bipolar transistor. The gate is typically used for the input or control signal. The source is normally tied to ground (sometimes through one or more values of resistance), and the drain supplies the output signal.

When no voltage is applied to an FET's gate, current flows freely from drain to source. Any necessary current limiting must be provided by inserting a resistor in series into the drain or source circuit. By adjusting the control voltage at the gate, current flow in the drain and source can be controlled. For an N-channel FET, control voltage must be a negative voltage. As gate voltage is made more negative, channel current is restricted further until it is cut off entirely. For a P-channel FET, a

N-channel FET   P-channel FET

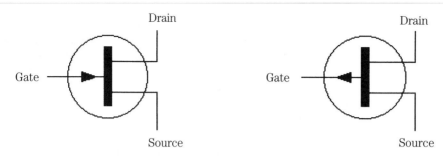

2-26   Schematic symbols for field-effect transistors (FETs).

positive control voltage is needed. Higher positive gate voltage restricts channel current further until the channel is cut off.

A variation of the FET is the metal-oxide semiconductor FET (MOSFET). It is unlikely that you will ever encounter discrete MOSFET devices except in high-power circuits, but many sophisticated digital integrated circuits make extensive use of MOSFETs. One of the few undesirable characteristics of FETs (and MOSFETs) is their sensitivity to damage by electrostatic discharge (ESD). You will learn about ESD in chapter 4.

There is a variety of electrical specifications that describe the performance and characteristics of particular transistors. When you discover that a transistor must be replaced, it is always wise to use an exact replacement part. That way, you can be assured that the replacement part behaves as expected. Under some circumstances, however, an exact replacement part might take too long to obtain, or might not be available. You can then use manufacturer's or cross-reference data to locate substitute parts with specifications similar to the original part. Keep in mind that substituting one part with a different part—even when specifications are very similar—can have an unforeseeable impact on the circuit. Do not attempt to use "close" replacement parts unless you have a keen understanding of transistor principles and specifications.

Transistors are available in a wide variety of case styles and sizes, depending on the amount of power that must be handled. Figure 2-27 illustrates a selection of five popular case styles. Low-power, general-purpose devices are often packaged in the small, plastic TO-92 cases. The TO-18 metal case is also used for low-power devices, but the TO-18 shown houses a phototransistor. Note the quartz window on the case top which allows light to enter the device. For regular transistor applications, the TO-18 "top hat" case is all metal.

Medium-power transistors use the larger plastic TO-128 or TO-220 cases. The TO-128 uses a thin metal heat sink molded into the top of the device. TO-220 cases use a large metal mounting flange/heat sink located directly behind the plastic case. The flange provides mechanical strength, as well as a secure thermal path for an external heat sink. The all-metal TO-3 case (not shown) is used for high-power transistors. Two mounting holes are provided to bolt the device to a chassis or external

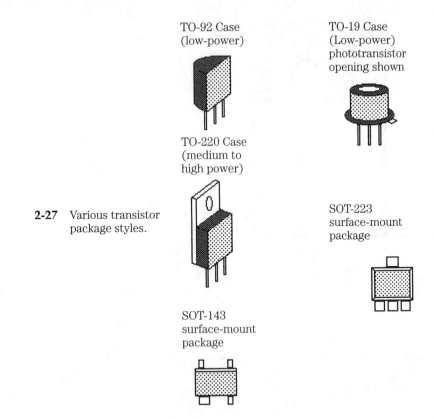

TO-92 Case
(low-power)

TO-19 Case
(Low-power)
phototransistor
opening shown

TO-220 Case
(medium to
high power)

2-27 Various transistor
package styles.

SOT-223
surface-mount
package

SOT-143
surface-mount
package

heat sink. As a general rule, case size is proportional to the power capacity of the transistor.

Transistors can also be manufactured in surface-mount cases. Two typical surface-mount small-outline transistor (SOT) case styles are shown in Fig. 2-27. Due to their small size, SMT transistors cannot dissipate very much power, but they are ideal for small, low-power systems such as mobile computers.

Transistor markings

As shown in Fig. 2-28, a transistor's part number is merely an index or reference number that allows you to look up the part's equivalent components or specifications in a data book or cross-reference manual. The number itself contains no useful information about the part's actual performance characteristics or limits. Classic bipolar transistor part numbers begin with the prefix "2N," followed by up to five digits. The "2N" prefix is used by JEDEC in the United States to denote devices with two semiconductor junctions. Classical Japanese transistor part numbers begin with any of four prefixes: "2SA" (high-frequency pnp transistor), "2SB" (low-frequency pnp transistor), "2SC" (high-frequency npn transistor), and "2SD" (low-frequency npn transistor). JEDEC uses the prefix "3N" to denote FETs or Junction FETs (JFETs). The prefixes "2SJ" (p-channel JFET), "2SK" (n-channel JFET), and "3SK" (n- or p-channel MOSFETs) have been used in Japan.

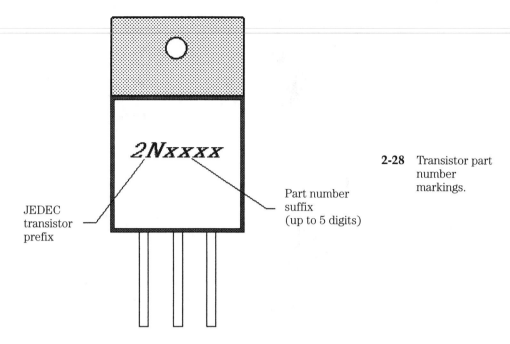

JEDEC
transistor
prefix

Part number
suffix
(up to 5 digits)

2-28 Transistor part
number
markings.

You will also encounter a great many transistors with arcane or non-standard markings. In almost all cases, you can identify replacement transistors and look up performance specifications using manufacturer's data or a cross-reference guide. Although the specifications found in a cross-reference guide are for the replacement parts, they generally match the original part's specifications very closely.

As with diodes, transistors rarely show any outward signs of failure unless they have melted or shattered from an extreme overload. You generally must use test equipment to identify faulty transistors. Testing can be accomplished by measuring the device while the circuit is running, or removing the device from the circuit and measuring its characteristics out of circuit.

Integrated circuits

Integrated circuits (ICs) are by far the most diverse and powerful group of electronic components that you will ever deal with. They have rapidly become the fundamental building blocks of modern electronic circuits. Amplifiers, memories, microprocessors, digital logic arrays, oscillators, timers, regulators, and a myriad of other complex functions can all be manufactured as ICs. Circuits that only a decade ago would have required an entire PC board in a desktop computer are now being fabricated entirely on a single IC.

Although you can often approximate the complexity (and importance) of an integrated circuit from the number of pins that it has, it is virtually impossible to predict precisely what an IC does just by looking at it. You need a schematic of the circuit or manufacturer's data of a particular IC in order to determine what the IC does.

Every integrated circuit—whether analog or digital—is composed largely of microscopic transistors, diodes, capacitors, and resistors which are fabricated onto an IC die. Many capacitors and inductors cannot be fabricated on ICs, so conventional parts can be attached to an IC through one or more external leads. A large number of mass-storage systems are almost entirely digital systems. That is, most of the ICs are designed to work with binary signals. The microprocessor, memory, and most of the controller ICs are digital logic components. Other ICs, however, are intended to work with analog signal levels. Serial communication ICs, display driver ICs, and disk driver ICs are only some of the analog devices that you might find.

A *logic gate* is a circuit which produces a binary result based on one or more binary inputs. A single integrated circuit can hold as few as one logic gate, or thousands of logic gates, depending on the complexity of the particular IC. There are eight basic types of logic gates: AND, OR, NAND, NOR, INVERTER, BUFFER, XOR (exclusive OR), and XNOR (exclusive NOR). Each gate uses its own particular logic symbol as shown in Fig. 2-29. Beside each symbol is the *truth table* for the particular gate. A truth table illustrates the gate's output for every possible combination of inputs. For the sake of simplicity, no more than two inputs are shown, but individual gates can have four, eight, or more inputs.

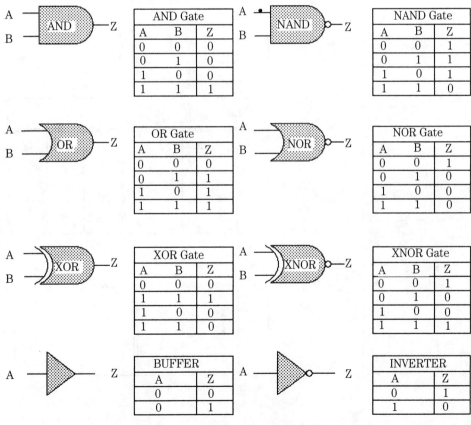

2-29 A comparison of basic logic gates.

Flip-flops are slightly more involved than general-purpose gates, but they are such flexible logic building blocks that they are usually considered to be logic gates. In the simplest sense, flip-flops are memory devices, because they can "remember" the various logic states in a circuit. Flip-flops are also ideal for working with logical sequences. You often find flip-flops used around counter-timer circuits. There are three classic variations of flip-flops, as shown in Fig. 2-30: the D flip-flop, the SR flip-flop, and the JK flip-flop. Each flip-flop is shown with its corresponding truth table.

The SR flip-flop is rarely used alone in digital designs because it is *asynchronous*—outputs can change as soon as inputs change. Small computers rely on *synchronous* circuits, so unexpected or untimed changes in device outputs cannot be tolerated. The D and JK type flip-flops utilize a clock (or CLK) input along with data input. As a result, inputs can change at will, but the outputs will only change

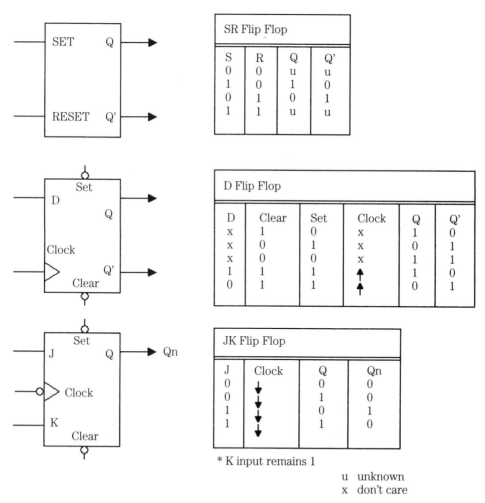

SR Flip Flop

S	R	Q	Q'
0	0	u	u
1	0	1	0
0	1	0	1
1	1	u	u

D Flip Flop

D	Clear	Set	Clock	Q	Q'
x	1	0	x	1	0
x	0	1	x	0	1
x	0	0	x	1	1
1	1	1	↑	1	0
0	1	1	↑	0	1

JK Flip Flop

J	Clock	Q	Qn
0	↓	0	0
0	↓	1	0
1	↓	0	1
1	↓	1	0

* K input remains 1

u   unknown
x   don't care

2-30   A comparison of basic flip-flops.

when prompted by a synchronizing clock pulse. D flip-flops are often used to help manage the flow of data along data busses—one flip-flop is used for each data bit.

As you look over the symbols in Figs. 2-29 and 2-30, notice that some of the inputs have a *bubble* at the device. Whenever you see a bubble, it indicates negative logic. In conventional Boolean logic, a "true" signal indicates an "on" condition, or the presence of a voltage. In negative logic, a "true" signal is "off," and voltage is absent. This concept is extremely important in troubleshooting so that you do not confuse a correct signal for an erroneous signal.

Some flip-flops are also equipped with master override inputs. When the *set override* becomes true, the Q output becomes true immediately regardless of the input or clock condition. If the Q output was true before set is activated, it remains true. If Q was false, it immediately becomes true. The other master override is *reset*. When reset becomes true, the Q output becomes false immediately. Keep in mind that set and reset can never be made true simultaneously.

The vast majority of logic components used in today's small computers contain so many gates that it would be impossible to show them all on a schematic diagram. Current microprocessors, gate arrays, and application-specific ICs (ASICs) can each contain thousands of gates. To simplify schematics and drawings, most highly integrated ICs are shown only as generic logic blocks that are interconnected to one another.

Every logic IC requires a power source in order to operate. At least one positive voltage source (Vcc) must be applied to the IC. The IC must also be grounded with respect to the source voltage. An IC's ground pin is usually labeled Vss or GND. Since the days of the first logic ICs, supply voltage has been a standard of +5 Vdc. Using a +5 Vdc source, logic 1s are interpreted as +2.4 Vdc or higher, and logic 0s are considered to be +0.8 Vdc or lower. The transistor circuitry within each logic gate provides outputs at these levels. If +5 Vdc is not supplied to the IC, it functions erratically (if at all). If more than +6 Vdc is forced into the IC, excess power dissipation will destroy the IC.

Over the last few years, conventional +5 Vdc logic is being replaced by a new class of *low-voltage* digital logic devices. Instead of +5 Vdc Vcc, +3.0 to +3.3 Vdc is used. Logic 1s and 0s remain unchanged. There are advantages to low-voltage logic that are appealing to electronics designers. Less voltage results in lower power dissipation for each IC, so power consumption is reduced. Battery life is significantly improved; you can operate longer on each battery charge. Also, lower voltage causes less stress on each transistor, so ICs can continue to pack more functions and features into new devices without fear of overheating the device. Your new notebook or palmtop is probably using at least some low-voltage components right now. Chapter 3 shows you how to measure conventional and low-voltage logic signals. Low-voltage logic will be mentioned throughout the remainder of this book.

Integrated circuits are manufactured in a staggering array of package styles. Older package styles such as the dual in-line package (DIP) and single in-line package (SIP) are intended for printed circuits using conventional through-hole assembly techniques. Through-hole assembly requires that a component be inserted so that its leads protrude through the PC board. The leads are soldered into place where each lead protrudes. However, the push to pack increasingly more-powerful

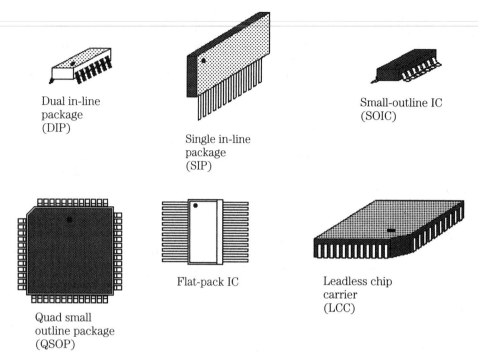

Dual in-line
package
(DIP)

Single in-line
package
(SIP)

Small-outline IC
(SOIC)

Quad small
outline package
(QSOP)

Flat-pack IC

Leadless chip
carrier
(LCC)

2-31 Various IC package diagrams.

ICs onto smaller PC boards has given rise to an overwhelming number of surface-mount IC package styles. Figure 2-31 shows a small sampling of typical package styles.

One of the key advantages of surface-mount packages is that components can be soldered onto both sides of a PC board—thus, almost doubling the amount of available PC board area. The small outline IC (SOIC) design appears very similar to a DIP, but the SOIC is significantly smaller, and its flat (or gull-wing shaped) pins are spaced together very closely. The very small outline package (VSOP) and the quad small outline package (QSOP) are designed to package complex ICs into extremely small packages with leads on two or four sides. Quad packages are also square (instead of rectangular) with pins on all four sides. Small outline J-lead (SOJ) packages replace regular gull-wing leads with leads that are bent down and under the device in a J shape.

Flat packs tend to be large, square ICs used primarily for more sophisticated functions such as microprocessors and specialized controllers. A quad flat pack (QFP) and a thin quad flat pack (TQFP) offer as many as 100 pins (25 pins per side). TQFPs are handy in extremely tight spaces where regular QFPs might get in the way of other assemblies. Chip carriers are either leaded (with leads) or unleaded (without leads). Leadless chip carriers (LCCs) provide exposed contacts that require the use of a chip carrier socket to guarantee proper connections. Plastic leaded chip carrier (PLCC) packages offer J-shaped pins that can either be surface mounted directly to a PC board, or inserted into a chip carrier socket. The pin grid array

(PGA) is the most sophisticated packaging scheme in use today. PGAs can provide hundreds of leads on an IC. Sophisticated microprocessors such as Intel's 80486 are packaged in PGAs exceeding 150 pins. PGAs also require the use of sockets to ensure proper contact for all pins. Extreme care must be taken to prevent damage to pins when inserting and extracting PGAs.

It is rare for any type of IC to show outward signs of failure, so it is very important that you carefully check suspect ICs using appropriate test equipment and data while the IC is actually operating in the system. Gather all the information you can about an IC before replacing it, because IC replacement always carries an element of risk. You risk damage to the PC board during IC removal, and damage to the new IC during installation.

Electromechanical components

Electromechanical (EM) components are relatively specialized components that use electrical energy to produce and deliver mechanical force. EM components in mass-storage devices are large in size and have relatively high power requirements. You should be familiar with two of the fundamental EM components that you might encounter: motors and solenoids.

Motors

Motors are an absolutely essential part of every floppy drive and hard drive ever produced. Both types of drives are used to store digital information which is held on small disks coated with layers of magnetic material. A motor is required to spin these disks. A floppy disk must be rotated at 300 RPM, while a set of hard disk platters must spin at 3600 RPM. A floppy drive also requires another motor to move the read/write heads to various recording tracks along the disk's radius.

All motors convert electrical energy into rotating mechanical force. In turn, that force can be distributed to the proper mechanism (e.g., head positioning mechanics or disk spindle). A *dc motor* is typically used to spin disks at a constant speed. Figure 2-32 illustrates the schematic symbol for a dc motor. Direct current is applied to a series of powerful coils wrapped around a motor shaft (called a *rotor*), which is free to turn. The rotor is mounted within an array of opposing permanent magnets (known as the *stator*). When dc is applied, a strong magnetic field is produced in the rotor coils. The induced fields oppose the fields of the permanent magnets. It is this force of opposition which causes the rotor to turn. The dc motor speed is adjusted by varying voltage and current to the armature. Voltage connections to the rotor coils are made through a series of slip rings and contact brushes.

2-32 Schematic symbol for a dc motor.

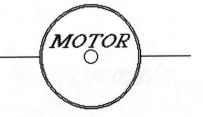

While dc motors are good for maintaining a constant speed, they are poor for precise positioning applications. A *stepping motor* (or *steppe*) is used to handle positioning. A stepper is constructed similarly to an ac induction motor. Steppers use a series of permanent magnets built into a rotating shaft, while sets of small individual coils are positioned about the stationary frame. By powering sets of coils in sequence, the rotor can be made to turn at known increments. Each driver signal is a square wave, so the rotor jumps (or steps) quite accurately and remain fixed in its new position for as long as its driver signals maintain their conditions. For example, a typical stepper can achieve a resolution of 1.8 degrees per step. That means the motor must make 200 steps to complete one full revolution. Figure 2-33 shows a schematic symbol for a stepping motor.

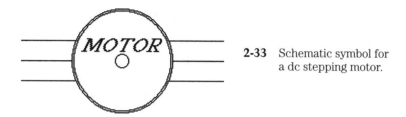

2-33 Schematic symbol for a dc stepping motor.

Stepping motors are ideal for precise positioning. Because the motor moves in known angular steps, the rotor shaft can be rotated to any position simply by applying the appropriate number of electrical driving pulses. Suppose your motor has to turn 180 degrees. If each motor step equals 1.8 degrees, control circuitry would need to produce 100 pulses to turn the rotor exactly the prescribed amount. In floppy drives, stepper motor rotation is converted into linear motion for read/write head positioning.

Solenoids

A solenoid is virtually identical to an ordinary coil as shown in Fig. 2-34, but the coil is wrapped around a hollow tube, and a permeable object (called a *plunger*) is placed into the tube. With no power applied, the plunger rests within its tube. A spring or similar return mechanism is attached to the plunger. When current is applied to the solenoid coil, the plunger becomes magnetized. Magnetic force pushes the plunger out of the tube. The return mechanism keeps the plunger from simply flying away. Plunger motion is used to engage or disengage mechanical linkages that are encountered in mass-storage systems. When energizing current is removed, the spring draws the plunger back to rest within its tube.

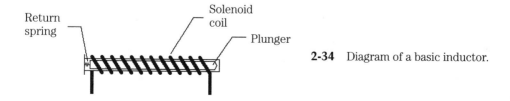

2-34 Diagram of a basic inductor.

3
Tools and
test equipment

You need a set of basic tools and test equipment before trying to tackle a storage system repair (Fig. 3-1). Test equipment measures important circuit parameters such as voltage, current, resistance, capacitance, and semiconductor junction conditions. Other test devices let you follow logic conditions and view complex waveforms at critical points in the circuit. This chapter introduces the background and testing methods for multimeters, component checkers, logic probes, and oscilloscopes. It also gives you an advance look at some of the more specialized test instruments that you might encounter in mass-storage repair.

3-1 An Iomega Bernoulli MultiDisk storage system.

Tools and materials

If you don't have a well-stocked toolbox yet, now is the time to consider the things you need. Before you begin a repair, gather a set of small hand tools and some inexpensive materials. Never underestimate the value of having the proper tools—they often make or break your repair efforts.

Hand tools

Hand tools are primarily used to disassemble and reassemble equipment housings, enclosures, mounting brackets, and expansion card rail guides. It isn't necessary to stock top-quality tools, but your tools should be of the proper size and shape to do the job. Because many of today's computers and peripheral devices are extremely small and tightly packaged assemblies, you should select tools that are small and thin whenever possible.

Screwdrivers should be the first item on your list. Computer assemblies are generally held together with small or medium-size Phillips screws. Once you remove the outer housing, you will find that most other internal parts are also held in place with Phillips screws. Consider obtaining one or two small and one medium Phillips screwdrivers. You almost never need a large screwdriver. Each screwdriver should be about 10.16 cm (4") to 15.24 cm (6") long, with a wide handle for a good grip. Jeweler's screwdrivers are recommended for very fine or delicate assemblies. Round out your selection of screwdrivers with one small and one medium slotted (flat blade) screwdriver. You won't use them as often as Phillips screwdrivers, but they can come in handy.

There are three specialized types of screw heads that you should be aware of. *Allen screws* use a hexagonal hole instead of a slotted or Phillips head. *Torx screws* and *spline screws* use specially shaped holes that accept only the corresponding size and shape of screwdriver. It is a good idea to keep a set of small hex keys on hand, but you rarely find specialized screw heads. Torx and spline screws are almost never encountered.

Wrenches are used to turn hex-shaped bolt heads or nuts. There are not many instances where you need to remove nuts and bolts, but an inexpensive set of small electronics-grade open-ended wrenches is recommended. A small adjustable wrench can also be used.

Needlenose pliers (Fig. 3-2) are valued additions to your toolbox. Not as bulky and awkward as ordinary mechanic's pliers, needlenose pliers can be used to grip or bend both mechanical and electronic parts. Needlenose pliers can also serve as heat sinks when soldering and soldering (chapter 4 discusses these operations in more detail). Obtain both short- and long-nose versions. Short nose pliers make great heat sinks, and can grasp parts securely. Long nose pliers are excellent for picking up and grasping parts lost in the tight confines of a computer or peripheral. Any needlenose pliers you buy should be small, good-quality, electronics-grade tools.

Diagonal cutters (Fig. 3-3) are also an important part of your tool collection. Cutters are used to cut wire and component leads when working with computer electronics. You need only one set of cutters, but it should be a small, high-quality,

Cooper Tools

3-2   Needlenose pliers.

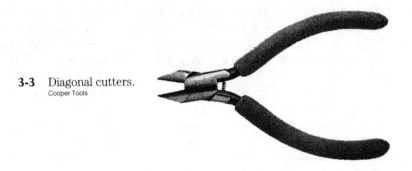

3-3 Diagonal cutters.
Cooper Tools

electronics-grade tool. Cutters should also have a low profile and a small cutting head to fit in tight spaces. You should never use cutters to cut plastic, metal, or PC board material.

Also add a pair of tweezers to your tool kit. The tweezers should be small, long, and made from antistatic plastic material. Metal tweezers should not be used, in order to prevent an accidental short circuit or a shock hazard if they come into contact with operating circuitry. Metal tweezers can also conduct potentially damaging static charges into sensitive ICs.

Soldering tools

You need a good general-purpose soldering iron to repair your small computer's circuitry (Fig. 3-4). A low-wattage (20 to 25 W) iron with a fine tip is usually best. You can obtain a good soldering iron from any local electronics store. Most soldering irons are powered directly from ac, and these are fine for general touch-ups and heavier work. However, you should consider a dc-powered or gas-fueled iron for desoldering delicate, static-sensitive ICs. No matter what iron you buy, try to ensure that it is recommended as static-safe.

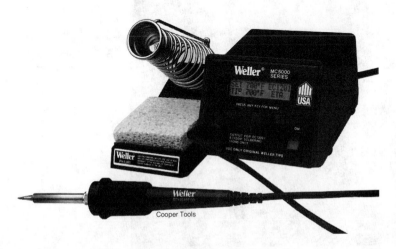

Cooper Tools

3-4 A Weller MC5000 soldering station.

Note: The soldering iron absolutely must have its own metal stand. Never, under any circumstances, allow a soldering iron to rest on a counter or tabletop unattended. The potential for nasty burns or fire is simply too great. Keep a wet sponge handy to periodically wipe the iron's tip. Invest in a roll of good electronics-grade rosin-core solder.

Desoldering tools are necessary to remove faulty components and wires. Once the solder joint is heated with the soldering iron, a desoldering tool can remove the molten solder to free the joint. A *solder vacuum* uses a small, spring-loaded plunger mounted in a narrow cylinder. When triggered, the plunger recoils and generates a vacuum which draws up any molten solder in the vicinity. *Solder wick* is little more than a fine copper braid. By heating the braid against a solder joint, molten solder wicks up into the braid through capillary action. These conventional desoldering tools are most effective on through-hole components.

Surface-mount components can also be desoldered with conventional desoldering tools, but there are more efficient techniques for these parts. Specially shaped desoldering tips (Fig. 3-5) can ease surface-mount desoldering by heating all of the component's leads simultaneously. Powered vacuum pumps (Fig. 3-6) can also be used to remove molten solder much more thoroughly than spring-loaded versions.

Other tools

A hand-held, battery-powered vacuum cleaner helps with routine maintenance operations. Periodically removing dust and debris from your keyboard can prevent

3-5 A surface-mount desoldering tip.

PACE, Inc.

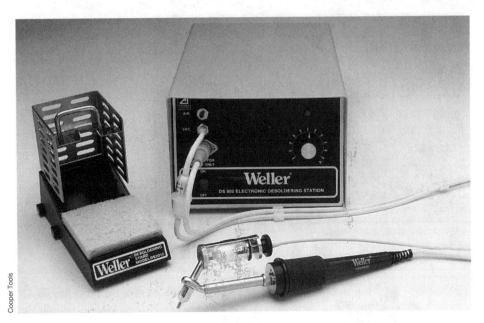

Cooper Tools

3-6 A Weller DS800 vacuum desoldering station.

intermittent key operation. You should also brush or vacuum any dust that accumulates in your computer's vent holes; this helps to keep computers and peripherals running cooler.

Most computer systems now use surface-mount ICs and components, so you rarely have need of IC inserters and extractors. The exceptions to this rule are plastic leaded chip carriers (PLCCs) and pin grid arrays (PGAs). Once a PLCC or PGA has been inserted into its socket, there is virtually no way to remove it without a specialized extraction tool. The extractor tool's tips either grasp the PGA ICs edges directly, or are inserted into slots at either set of opposing corners on the PLCC socket. Squeeze the extractor gently to push the tips under the IC, then wiggle the IC to pull it free. Once an IC is free, be certain to keep it on an antistatic mat, or on a piece of antistatic foam.

You will also need a selection of appropriate test clips. Test clips fit over ICs of virtually every description, allowing you to attach test leads for hands-free testing. Figure 3-7 shows a simple PLCC test clip for 32-pin PLCC ICs. The clip is squeezed gently and pushed over the IC. Spring action then holds the clip in place. You can place logic analyzer or oscilloscope leads on the bare pins available from the clip. Figure 3-8 shows somewhat larger test clips designed to fit quad flat pack (QFP) ICs. The exact size of a test clip varies with the number of pins and pin spacing (pitch) of the particular IC under test .

Additional test clip types are illustrated in Figs. 3-9 and 3-10. Notice that each clip is force-fitted over the corresponding IC, and each test pin is firmly attached to a small PC board on the clip. Fixed pin positioning such as this allows ribbon cables to connect ICs to test systems or emulator modules.

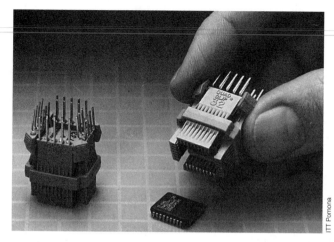

3-7   A PLCC test clip.

3-8   A quad flat pack
(QFP) test clip.
ITT Pomona

3-9   A PQFP "wide body"
test clip.

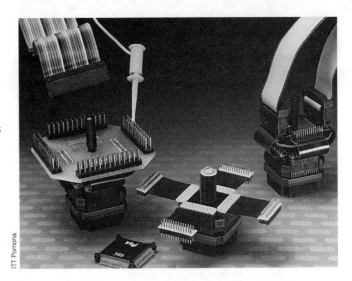

3-10 Flexible test clips for QFP testing.

ITT Pomona

Your tool kit should always have a supply of antistatic materials to help prevent accidental damage to expensive electronics. An antistatic wrist strap connects your body to ground in order to remove any static charge buildup from your body. When working with PC boards and ICs, use antistatic foam to hold ICs and antistatic bags to hold PC boards. Avoid styrofoam and other plastics that hold static charges. You might also invest in an antistatic mat, which rolls out onto a desk or workbench and connects to ground. An antistatic mat allows you to place delicate PC boards and chassis on your workbench while you work with them.

Keep an assortment of solid and stranded hookup wire in your toolbox. Wire should be between 18 to 24 AWG (gauge)—preferably above 20 AWG. Heat-shrink tubing is another handy material for your repairs. Tubing can be cut to length as needed, then positioned and shrunk to insulate wire splices and long component leads. You can buy a special heat gun to shrink the tubing, but an ordinary blow dryer for hair usually works just as well. When heating tubing, be certain to direct hot air away from ICs and PC boards.

Multimeters

Multimeters are by far the handiest and most versatile pieces of test equipment that you will use (Fig. 3-11). If your toolbox doesn't already contain a good-quality multimeter, now would be a good time to purchase one. Even the most basic digital multimeters are capable of measuring resistance, ac and dc voltage, and ac and dc current. For under $150, you can buy a digital multimeter that includes handy features like a capacitance checker, a frequency meter, an extended current measuring range, a continuity buzzer, and even a diode and transistor checker. These are features that help you not only in computer and peripheral repairs, but in many other types of electronic repairs as well. Digital multimeters are easier to read, more tolerant of operator error, and more precise then their analog predecessors.

3-11   A B+K Model 2707 multimeter.

Meter setup

For most multimeters, there are only three considerations during setup and use. First, turn the meter on. Unlike analog multimeters, digital multimeters require power to operate liquid crystal or LED displays. Make sure that you turn meter power off again when you are done, in order to conserve battery life. Second, set the meter to its desired *function* or *mode*. The function might be frequency, voltage, capacitance, resistance, etc., depending on the particular physical parameter that you wish to measure.

Finally, select the meter's *range* for the selected function. Ideally, you should choose the range that is nearest to, but above, the level you expect to measure. For example, to measure a 9 Vdc transistor battery, you would set your meter to the dc voltage function, then set the range as close to (but greater than) 9 Vdc as possible. If your meter's voltage ranges are .2 Vdc, 2 Vdc, 20 Vdc, and 200 Vdc, the 20 Vdc range is the best choice.

If you are unsure about which range to use, start by choosing the highest possible range. Once you take some measurements and get a better idea of the actual reading, you can then adjust the meter's range to achieve a more precise reading. If your reading exceeds the meter's current range, an *overrange warning* is displayed until you increase the meter's range above the measured value. Some digital multimeters can automatically select the appropriate range setting once a signal is applied.

Checking test leads

It's usually a good idea to check the integrity of the meter's test leads from time to time. Because test leads undergo a serious amount of tugging and general abuse, you should confirm that the probes are working as expected. There are few experiences more frustrating than to invest time and money replacing parts that your meter suggested were faulty, only to discover that the meter's leads had an internal fault.

To check your probes, set your meter to the resistance function and select the lowest scale (e.g., 0.1 Ω). You will see an overrange condition—this is expected when setting up for resistance measurements. Check to be sure that both test probes are inserted into the meter properly, then touch the probe tips together. The resistance reading should drop to about 0 Ω to indicate that your meter probes are intact. If you do not see roughly 0 Ω, check your probes carefully. After you've proven out your test probes, return the multimeter to its original function and range so you can continue testing.

You might see other terms related to multimeter testing. *Static tests* are usually made on components (either in or out of a circuit) with power removed. Resistance, capacitance, and semiconductor junction tests are all static tests. *Dynamic tests* typically examine circuit conditions, so power must be applied to the circuit, and all components must be in place. Voltage, current , and frequency are the most common dynamic tests.

Measuring voltage

Every signal in your small computer has a certain amount of voltage associated with it. By measuring signal voltages with a multimeter or other test instrument, you can usually make a determination as to whether or not the signal is correct. Supply voltages which provide power to your circuits can also be measured to ensure that components are receiving enough energy to operate. Voltage tests are the most fundamental (and the most important) dynamic tests in electronic troubleshooting.

Multimeters can measure both dc voltages (marked dcV or Vdc) and ac voltages (marked acV or Vac) directly. Remember that all voltage measurements are taken in parallel with the desired circuit or component. Never interrupt a circuit and attempt to measure voltage in series with other components. Any such reading would be meaningless, and your circuit probably will not even function.

Follow your setup guidelines and configure your meter to measure ac or dc voltage as required, then select the proper range for the voltages you are measuring. If you are unsure what range to use, always start with the largest possible range. An autoranging multimeter sets its own range once a signal is applied. Place your test leads across (in parallel with) the circuit or part under test (PUT) as shown in Fig. 3-12, then read voltage directly from the meter's digital display. Direct current voltage readings are polarity-sensitive, so if you read +5 Vdc and reverse the test leads, you will see a reading of –5 Vdc. Alternating current voltage readings are not polarity-sensitive.

Measuring current

Most general-purpose multimeters allow you to measure ac current (marked acA or Iac) and dc current (marked dcA or Idc) in an operating circuit, although there are typically fewer ranges to choose from. As with voltage measurements, current is a dynamic test, so the circuit or component being tested must be under power. **Note:** Current must be measured in series with a circuit or component.

Unfortunately, inserting a meter in series is not always a simple task. In many cases, you must interrupt a circuit at the point you wish to measure, then connect

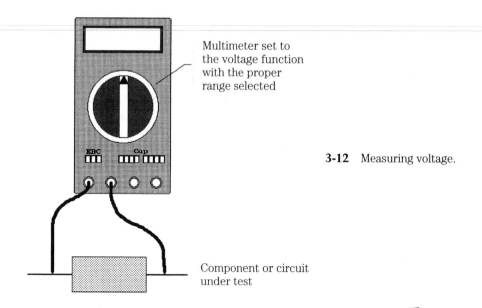

Multimeter set to
the voltage function
with the proper
range selected

3-12   Measuring voltage.

Component or circuit
under test

the test leads across the break. While it might be quite easy to interrupt a circuit, remember that you must also put the circuit back together, so use care when choosing a point to break. Never attempt to measure current in parallel across a component or circuit. Current meters, by their very nature, exhibit a very low resistance across their test leads (often below .1 Ω). Placing a current meter in parallel can cause a short circuit across a component that can damage the component, the circuit under test, or the meter itself.

Set your multimeter to the desired function (dcA or acA) and select the appropriate range. If you are unsure about the proper range, set the meter to its largest possible range. It is usually necessary to plug your positive test lead into the "Current Input" jack on the multimeter. Unless your multimeter is protected by an internal fuse (which most meters are), its internal current measurement circuits can be damaged by excessive current. Make sure that your meter can handle the maximum amount of current you are expecting.

Turn off all power to a circuit before inserting a current meter. Deactivation prevents any unpredictable or undesirable circuit operation when you actually interrupt the circuit. If you wish to measure power supply current feeding a circuit, as in Fig. 3-13, break the power supply line at any convenient point, insert the meter carefully, then reapply power. Read current directly from the meter's display. This procedure can also be used for taking current measurements within a circuit.

Measuring frequency

Some multimeters offer a frequency counter (marked "f" or "Hz") that can read the frequency of a sinusoidal signal. The ranges that are available depend on your particular meter. Simple hand-held meters can often read up to 100 kHz, while bench-top models can handle 10 MHz or more. Frequency measurements are dynamic readings made with circuit power applied.

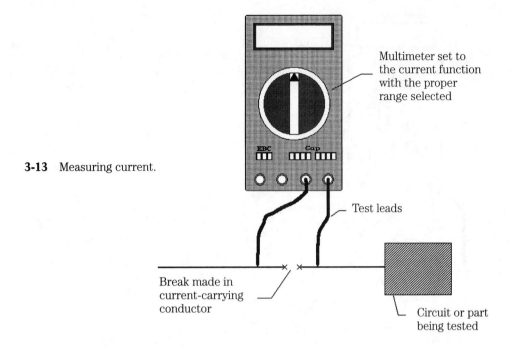

Multimeter set to
the current function
with the proper
range selected

3-13 Measuring current.

Test leads

Break made in
current-carrying
conductor

Circuit or part
being tested

Set your multimeter to its frequency counter function and select the appropriate range. Again, select the highest possible range if you aren't sure which range to use. Place the test leads in parallel across the component or circuit to be tested as shown in Fig. 3-14, and read frequency directly from the meter's display. An autoranging multimeter selects the proper range after the signal is applied.

Analog frequency measurements have little practical use in computer repair, because most signals you encounter are square instead of sinusoidal. Square waves usually yield false readings unless the meter is designed specifically for square-wave readings. A digital frequency counter and an oscilloscope can be used to measure square waves instead.

Measuring resistance

Resistance (ohms) is the most common static measurement that your multimeter performs. This function is handy not only for checking resistors themselves, but for checking other resistive elements like wires, solenoids, motors, connectors, and some basic semiconductor components. Resistance is a static test, so all power to the component or circuit must be removed. It is usually necessary to remove at least one component lead from the circuit to prevent interconnections with other components from causing false readings.

Ordinary resistors, coils, and wires can be checked simply by switching to the resistance function (often marked "Ohms" or Ω) and selecting the appropriate range. Autoranging multimeters select the proper range after the meter's test leads are connected. Many multimeters can reliably measure resistance up to about 20 MΩ. Place the test leads in parallel across the component as shown in Fig. 3-15, and read

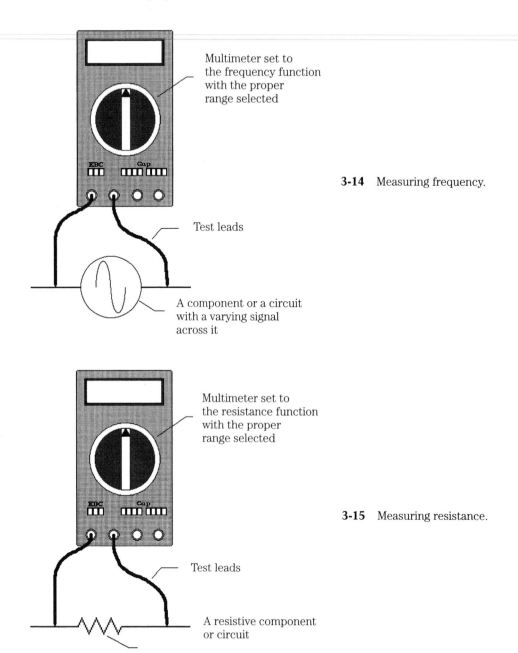

Multimeter set to
the frequency function
with the proper
range selected

3-14 Measuring frequency.

Test leads

A component or a circuit
with a varying signal
across it

Multimeter set to
the resistance function
with the proper
range selected

3-15 Measuring resistance.

Test leads

A resistive component
or circuit

resistance directly from the meter's display. If resistance exceeds the selected range, the display indicates an overrange (or infinite resistance) connection.

Continuity checks are made to ensure a reliable, low-resistance connection between two points. For example, you could check the continuity of a cable between two connectors to ensure that both ends are connected properly. Set your multimeter to a low resistance scale, then place your test leads across both points to measure. Ideally, good continuity should be about 0 Ω. Continuity tests can also be taken to show that a short circuit has not occurred between two points.

Measuring capacitors

There are two methods of checking a capacitor using your multimeter: *exact measurement* and *quality check*. The exact measurement test determines the actual value of a capacitor. If the reading is close to the value marked on the capacitor, you know the device is good. If not, the device is faulty and should be replaced. Exact measurement requires that your multimeter be equipped with a capacitance checker. If your meter does not have a capacitance checker, you can measure a capacitor directly on any other type of specialized component checker, such as the B+K Precision Model 390 Test Bench shown in Fig. 3-16. You could also use your multimeter to perform a simple quality check of a suspect capacitor.

3-16   A B+K Model 390 multimeter.

Capacitor checkers, whether built into your multimeter or part of a stand-alone component checker, are extremely simple to use. Turn off all circuit power. Set the function to measure capacitors, select the range of capacitance to be measured, then place your test probes in parallel across the capacitor to be measured. You should remove at least one of the capacitor's leads from the circuit being tested, in order to prevent the interconnections of other components from adversely effecting the capacitance reading. In some cases, it might be easier to remove the suspect part entirely before measuring it. Some meters provide test slots that let you insert the component directly into the meter's face. Once in place, you can read the capacitor's value directly from the meter display.

If your multimeter is not equipped with an internal capacitor checker, you can still use the resistance ranges of your meter to approximate a capacitor's quality. This type of check provides a "quick and dirty" judgment of whether the capacitor is good or bad. The principle behind this type of check is simple: all meter ranges use an internal battery to supply current to the component under test. When that current is applied to a working capacitor as shown in Fig. 3-17, it causes the capacitor to charge. Charge accumulates as the meter is left connected. When first connected, the uncharged capacitor draws a healthy amount of current, which reads as low resistance. As the capacitor charges, its rate of charge slows down and less and less current is drawn as time goes on, resulting in a gradually increasing resistance level. Ideally, a fully charged capacitor stops drawing current—this results in an over-range, or infinite resistance display. When a capacitor behaves in this way, it is probably good.

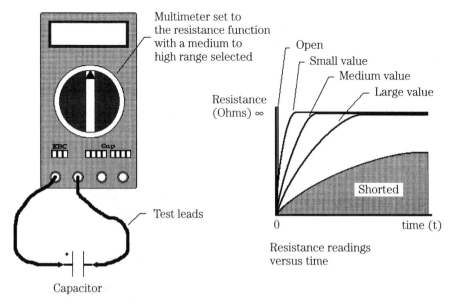

3-17   Measuring the quality of a capacitor using the multimeter resistance function.

Understand that you are not actually measuring resistance or capacitance here, but only the profile of a capacitor's charging characteristics. If the capacitor is extremely small (in the picofarad range), or is open-circuited, it will not accept any substantial charge, so the multimeter reads infinity almost immediately. If a capacitor is partially (or totally) short-circuited, it will not hold a charge, so you might read 0 Ω, or resistance might climb to some value below infinity and remain there. In either case, the capacitor is probably defective. If you doubt your readings, check several other capacitors of the same value and compare readings. Be sure to make this test on a moderate to high resistance scale. A low resistance scale might over-range too quickly to achieve a clear reading.

Diode checks

Many multimeters provide a special diode resistance scale for checking the static resistance of common diode junctions. Because working diodes only conduct current in one direction, the diode check lets you determine whether a diode is open- or short-circuited. Remember that diode checking is a static test, so all power must be removed from the part under test. Before making measurements, be certain that at least one of the diode's leads have been removed from the circuit. Isolating the diode prevents interconnections with other circuit components from causing false readings.

Select the "Diode" option from your multimeter's resistance functions. You generally do not have to bother with a range setting while in the diode mode. Connect your test leads in parallel across the diode in the forward-bias direction as shown in Fig. 3-18. A working silicon diode should exhibit a static resistance between about 450 and 700 Ω, which reads directly on the meter's display. Reverse the orientation of your test probes to reverse-bias the diode as in Fig. 3-19. Because a working diode does not conduct at all in the reverse direction, you should read infinite resistance.

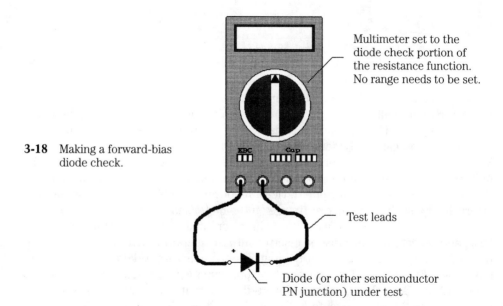

Multimeter set to the diode check portion of the resistance function. No range needs to be set.

3-18 Making a forward-bias diode check.

Test leads

Diode (or other semiconductor PN junction) under test

A short-circuited diode exhibits a very low resistance in both the forward and reverse-biased directions. This indicates a shorted semiconductor junction. An open-circuited diode exhibits very high resistance (usually infinity) in both its forward and reverse-biased directions. A diode that is opened or shorted must be replaced. If you feel unsure how to interpret your measurements, test several other comparable diodes and compare readings.

Transistor checks

Transistors are slightly more sophisticated semiconductor devices that can be tested using the transistor checking function on your multimeter or component checker. Transistor junctions can also be checked using a multimeter's diode checking function. The following procedures show you both methods of transistor checking.

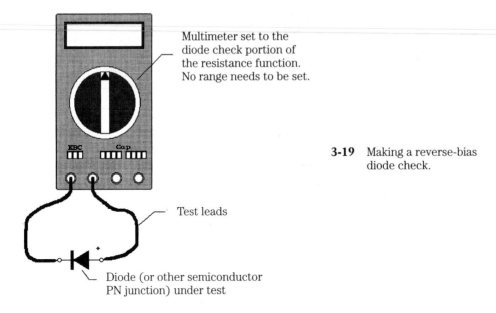

Multimeter set to the
diode check portion of
the resistance function.
No range needs to be set.

Test leads

Diode (or other semiconductor
PN junction) under test

3-19 Making a reverse-bias
diode check.

Some multimeters feature a built-in transistor checker that measures a bipolar transistor's gain (called "beta" or "hfe") directly. By comparing measured gain to the gain value specified in manufacturer's data (or measurements taken from other identical parts), you can easily determine whether the transistor is operating properly. Multimeters with a transistor checker generally offer a test fixture right on the meter's face. The fixture consists of two three-hole sockets—one socket for npn devices, and another hole for pnp devices. If your meter offers a transistor checker, insert the transistor into the test fixture on the meter's face.

Because all bipolar transistors are three-terminal devices (having an emitter, base, and collector), they must be inserted into the meter in their proper lead orientation in order to obtain a correct reading. The manufacturer's data sheet for a transistor identifies each lead and tell you the approximate gain reading that you should expect to see. Once the transistor is inserted properly in the correct socket, you can read gain directly from the meter's display.

Set the meter to its transistor checker function. You should not have to worry about selecting a range when checking transistors. Insert the transistor into its test fixture. An unusually low reading (or zero) suggests a short-circuited transistor, while a high (or infinite) reading indicates an open-circuited transistor. In either case, the transistor is probably defective and should be replaced. If you are uncertain of your readings, test several identical transistors and compare your readings.

If your particular multimeter or parts tester offers only a diode checker, you can approximate the transistor's condition by measuring its semiconductor junctions individually. Figure 3-20 illustrates the transistor junction test method. Although structurally different from conventional diodes, the base-emitter and base-collector junctions of bipolar transistors behave just like diodes. As a general rule, you should remove the transistor from its circuit to prevent false readings caused by other inter-

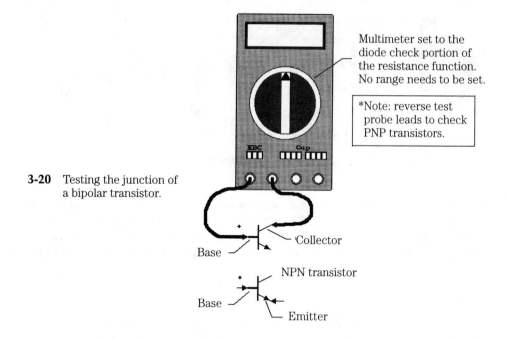

Multimeter set to the
diode check portion of
the resistance function.
No range needs to be set.

*Note: reverse test
probe leads to check
PNP transistors.

3-20 Testing the junction of
a bipolar transistor.

Base

Collector

NPN transistor

Base

Emitter

connected components. Junction testing is also handy for all varieties of surface-mount transistors, which do not fit into conventional multimeter test sockets.

Set your multimeter to the diode resistance function. If the suspect transistor is npn type (manufacturer's data or a corresponding schematic symbol will tell you), place the positive test lead at the transistor's base, and the negative test lead on the transistor's emitter. This test lead arrangement should forward-bias the transistor's base-emitter junction and result in a normal amount of diode resistance (450 to 700 Ω). Reverse the test leads across the base-emitter junction. The junction should now be reverse-biased, showing infinite resistance. Repeat this entire procedure for the base-collector junction.

If the suspect transistor is the pnp type, the placement of your test leads should be the reverse of those described in the preceding paragraph. In other words, a junction that is forward-biased in an npn transistor is reverse-biased in a pnp device. To forward-bias the base-emitter junction of a PNP transistor, place the positive test lead on the emitter, and the negative test lead on the base. The same concept holds true for the base-collector junction.

Once both junctions are checked, measure the diode resistance from collector to emitter. You should read infinite resistance in both test lead orientations. Although there should be no connection from collector to emitter while the transistor is unpowered, a short circuit can sometimes develop during a failure.

If any of your junctions read an unusually high (or infinite) resistance in both directions, the junction is probably open-circuited . An unusually low resistance (or 0 Ω) in either direction suggests that the junction is short-circuited. Any resistance below infinity between the collector and emitter suggests a damaged transistor. In any case, the transistor should be replaced. The B+K Model 540 Component

3-21 A B+K Model 540
Component Tester.

B+K Precision

Checker displays the dynamic performance of bipolar and field effect transistors as a graphic representation on a CRT (Fig. 3-21). By observing the graphic curve characteristic of each unique transistor, you can determine whether or not the device is faulty. Some graphic analyzers also provide an output that allows the curve to be plotted or printed for future reference.

IC checks

There are very few conclusive ways to test integrated circuits without resorting to complex logic analyzers and expensive IC testing equipment. Because ICs are so incredibly diverse, there is no single universal test that pinpoints every possible failure. The one IC testing technique that appears to find a large percentage of IC faults is the *comparison approach*. By comparing the performance of a suspect IC against that of a known good (or *reference*) IC, any differences can be quickly identified and reported. The B+K Precision Model 541, shown in Fig. 3-22, is an IC comparator capable of checking DIP ICs with up to 40 pins. A reference IC is inserted in the left socket, while the suspect component is placed in the right socket. Each IC pin is signalled individually by selecting the corresponding button along the tester's front. Although the testing process is somewhat redundant, you can be fairly confident in the test results.

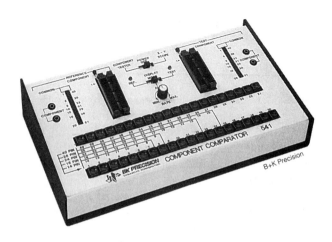

3-22 A B+K Model 541
Component
Comparator.

B+K Precision

You can also make use of *IC service charts* (sometimes called *service checkout charts*). IC service charts show the logic (or voltage) level for each pin of an IC. By checking the actual state of each pin against the chart, you can often identify faulty devices. You will see more about using IC service charts later in the book.

Circuit analyzer

If you are a technician or you work in a professional computer repair environment, it might be faster and more helpful to test components while they are still inserted in the circuit, or even test the entire circuit. Circuit analyzers such as the Model 545 from B+K Precision (Fig. 3-23) use an *impedance signature test* technique. An impedance signature is obtained by applying a very low-current sine wave signal across a component or circuit, then displaying the voltage-to-current (VI) curve on a CRT or flat-panel display. Every component or circuit offers a unique, repeatable VI curve, so any differences at all are easily recognized. The Model 545 has two input channels, which allows the suspect component or circuit to be compared against another, known-good reference.

3-23 A B+K Model 545 Circuit Analyzer.

The displays illustrated in Fig. 3-24 show the typical output of a circuit analyzer. Test systems such as the Model 545 can test resistors, capacitors, inductors, diodes (and diode bridges), LEDs, zener diodes, bipolar transistors, FETs, optoisolators, and SCRs. It is also interesting to note that the analyzer also tests simple analog and digital ICs, as well as a broad array of components in combination. The B+K analyzer offers a serial communication interface that allows displayed images to be downloaded to any computer or printer. While the actual testing procedures are different for each type of system, a circuit analyzer is a powerful addition to your professional test bench.

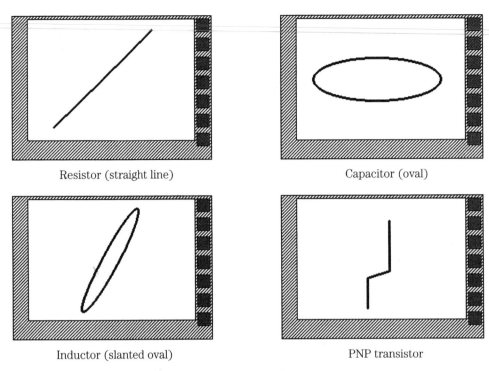

Resistor (straight line)   Capacitor (oval)

Inductor (slanted oval)   PNP transistor

3-24   Typical circuit analyzer traces.

Logic probes

One problem with multimeters is that they do not relate very well to the fast-changing signals found in digital logic circuits. A multimeter can certainly measure whether a logic voltage is on or off, but if that logic signal changes quickly (e.g., a clock or bus signal), a dc voltmeter only shows the average signal. A logic probe is little more than an extremely simple voltage sensor, but it can precisely and conveniently detect digital logic levels, clock signals, and digital pulses. Some logic probes can operate at speeds greater than 50 MHz.

A logic probe, shown in Fig. 3-25, is perhaps the simplest and least expensive test instrument that you will ever use, but it provides valuable and reliable information when you are troubleshooting digital logic circuitry. Logic probes are usually powered from the circuit under test, and they must be connected into the common (ground) of the circuit being tested to ensure a proper reference level. Attach the probe's power lead to any logic supply voltage source in the circuit. Logic probes are capable of working from a wide range of supply voltages (typically +4 to +18 Vdc).

Reading the logic probe

Logic probes use a series of LED indicators to display the measured condition: a logic "high" (or 1), a logic "low" (or 0), or a "pulse" (or clock) signal. Many models offer a switch that allows the probe to operate with two common logic families: TTL

3-25 A typical
logic probe.

or CMOS. You sometimes find TTL and CMOS devices mixed in the same circuit, but one type usually dominates.

In order to use a logic probe, touch its metal tip to the desired IC or component lead. Be certain that the point you wish to measure is, in fact, a logic point—high voltage signals can damage your logic probe. The logic state is interpreted by a few simple gates within the probe, then displayed on the appropriate LED (or combination of LEDs). Table 3-1 illustrates the LED sequences for one particular type of logic probe. By comparing the probe's measurements to the information contained in an IC service chart or schematic diagram, you can determine whether or not the signal (or suspect IC) is behaving properly.

Table 3-1. Typical logic probe LED patterns

Input signal		HI LED	LO LED	PULSE LED
Logic "1"	TTL or CMOS	ON	OFF	OFF
Logic "0"	TTL or CMOS	OFF	ON	OFF
Bad logic level or open circuit		OFF	OFF	OFF
Square wave	<200 kHz	ON	ON	BLINK
Square wave	>200 kHz	ON/OFF	ON/OFF	BLINK
Narrow "high" pulse		OFF	ON/OFF	BLINK
Narrow "low" pulse		ON/OFF	OFF	BLINK

Logic probes and service charts

Although the logic probe can provide an array of very useful information about the various conditions of digital circuits, such information is difficult to interpret unless you have something to compare your readings against. After all, how do you know if a signal is right or wrong if you don't know what it's supposed to be in the first place? A *service chart* supplies that reference information for comparison. Commercial service data such as the information available from Howard W. Sams & Co. typically contains comprehensive service chart listings.

Table 3-2. Sample service chart

Integrated Circuit Service Chart				
IC Part Number: _SN 7400_			IC Number: _U29_	
IC Function: _Quad. 2 INPUT NAND GATE_				

IC Pin	Logic Cond.	Voltage	I/O	Descriptions and Notes
1	0	0.3	I	GATE 1
2	1	3.8	I	"
3	1	4.2	O	"
4	0	0.2	I	GATE 2
5	0	0.2	I	"
6	1	4.6	O	"
7	VSS (GND)	0v	—	GROUND
8	PULSE	~2.6	O	GATE 3
9	PULSE	~2.3	I	"
10	1	4.3	I	"
11	0	0.1	O	GATE 4
12	1	4.2	I	"
13	1	4.4	I	"
14	Vcc (+Vdc)	+5v	—	+Vcc SUPPLY VOLTAGE

Table 3-2 shows a simple service chart for a single IC. For each IC pin, you will find an average dc voltage reading, a description of the pin as an input or output, and logic probe conditions. By supplying both types of readings, you can use either a voltmeter or a logic probe to check the IC. Also note that each chart is made under defined circuit conditions (e.g., standing idle at the DOS prompt, during hard drive access, etc.).

When your readings match the levels shown in a service chart, you can assume that the IC is operating properly, and then move on to check another IC. When you find an IC output that is incorrect, the IC generating the output might well be defective. If you find an IC input that is incorrect, the IC accepting the input could be faulty, but make sure to check the IC(s) providing the questionable signal before changing the suspect IC outright. Remember that troubleshooting is an analysis of cause and effect relationships—in order to correct the effect, you must correct the cause.

What happens when you do not have a service chart to compare your readings against? There is no simple answer to this problem, but you usually have three options. First, you can take a proactive roll in troubleshooting and develop your own service charts. This would require you to disassemble your machine before it fails and make a complete set of measurements. You could then keep your measurements tucked away until you need them. The second approach is to use common sense in conjunction with a schematic or service data. Does a particular reading make sense? For example, if you see pulse activity on every data bus line but one, chances are an IC is freezing the suspect data line. Experience will teach you which signal readings are right and wrong. Finally, you could forego troubleshooting to the component level altogether and simply replace to the module or subsystem level (i.e., replace power supplies, LCD assemblies, or motherboards).

Reading low-voltage logic

For many years now, conventional digital logic ICs have been powered by a standard supply voltage of +5 Vdc. However, the +5 Vdc standard is quickly being replaced by a new, low-voltage standard: +3.3 Vdc. A lower supply voltage means that ICs draw significantly less power. For battery powered equipment, this means fewer battery changes and longer charge life. With ICs running at around +3 volts, what happens to logic signal levels?

Fortunately, the family of new 3-volt ICs still operate within the accepted conventions of 5-volt logic levels. For example, a 5-volt logic IC provides a minimum logic 1 output of +2.4 Vdc, and a maximum logic 0 output of +0.4 Vdc, while accepting a minimum logic 1 input of +2.0 Vdc and a maximum logic 0 input of +0.8 Vdc. The new 3-volt logic "rides the rails" by providing a logic 1 at about +3.0 Vdc and a logic 0 of roughly 0 Vdc, yet it accepts a minimum logic 1 input of +2.0 Vdc and a maximum logic 0 input of +0.8 Vdc. As you can see, the two logic families use compatible logic levels. The only problem arises when a logic 1 from a 5-volt gate (which can be as high as +4.9 Vdc) drives a 3-volt logic input. When an input voltage exceeds supply voltage in this way, the low-voltage logic can be damaged. Low-voltage logic designers working hard to overcome this voltage incompatibility problem. The relationship of logic levels to voltage levels is illustrated graphically in Fig. 3-26.

When troubleshooting, be aware that the smallest computers (e.g., notebook, palmtop, and pen computers) probably utilize at least a few—and possibly all—low-voltage logic components. Desktop systems, on the other hand, are only now beginning to use low-voltage logic. Because the logic levels are at least compatible in principle, your logic probe should be able to provide correct readings as long as it is being powered and grounded correctly.

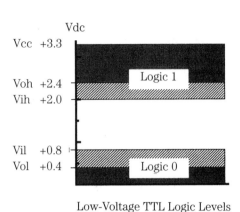

Vdc

Vcc +5.0	
Voh +2.4	Logic 1
Vih +2.0	
Vil +0.8	
Vol +0.4	Logic 0

Conventional TTL Logic Levels

Vdc

Vcc +3.3	
Voh +2.4	Logic 1
Vih +2.0	
Vil +0.8	
Vol +0.4	Logic 0

Low-Voltage TTL Logic Levels

3-26   A graphic comparison of +5 volt and low-voltage logic levels.

Oscilloscopes

Oscilloscopes offer a tremendous advantage over multimeters and logic probes. Instead of reading signals in terms of numbers or lighted indicators, an oscilloscope shows voltage versus time on a graphical display. Not only can you observe ac and dc voltages, but oscilloscopes enable you to watch any other unusual signals occur in real time. When used correctly, an oscilloscope allows you to witness signals and events occurring in terms of microseconds or less. If you have used an oscilloscope (or seen one used), then you probably know just how useful they can be. Oscilloscopes such as the one shown in Fig. 3-27 might appear overwhelming at first, but many of their operations are similar regardless of model.

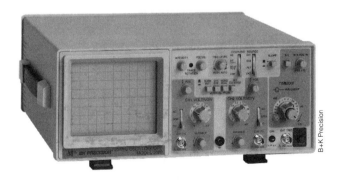

3-27   A B+K Model 2160 oscilloscope.

Oscilloscope start-up procedure

Before taking any measurements, a clear, stable trace must be obtained. If a trace is not already visible, make sure that any CRT screen storage modes are turned off, and that trace intensity is turned up to at least 50%. Set trace triggering to its automatic mode and adjust the horizontal and vertical offset controls to the center of their ranges. Be sure to select an internal trigger source from the channel your probe is plugged in to, then adjust the trigger level until a stable trace is displayed. Vary the vertical offset if necessary to center the trace in the CRT.

If a trace is not yet visible, use the *beam finder* to reveal the beam's location. A beam finder compresses the vertical and horizontal ranges to force a trace onto the display. This gives you a rough idea of the trace's relative position. Once you have moved the trace into position, adjust the focus and intensity controls to obtain a crisp, sharp trace. Keep intensity at a moderately low level to improve display accuracy and preserve the CRT phosphors.

Your oscilloscope should be calibrated to its probe before use. A typical oscilloscope probe is shown in Fig. 3-28. Calibration is a quick and straightforward operation which requires only a low-amplitude, low-frequency square wave. Many models have a built-in calibration signal generator (usually a 1 kHz, 300 mV square wave with a duty cycle of 50%). Attach your probe to the desired input jack, then place the probe tip across the calibration signal. Adjust the horizontal (TIME/DIV) and vertical (VOLTS/DIV) controls so that one or two complete cycles are clearly shown on the CRT.

Observe the visual characteristics of the test signal as shown in Fig. 3-29. If the square wave's corners are rounded, there might not be enough probe capacitance (sometimes denoted with the label "Cprobe"). Spiked square wave corners suggest too much capacitance in the probe. Either way, the scope and probe are not matched properly. You must adjust the probe capacitance to establish a good electrical

3-28 A B+K Model PR-46 oscilloscope probe.

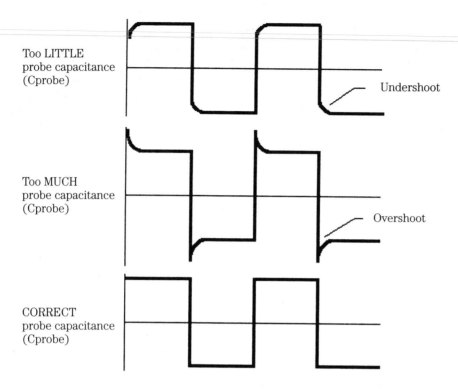

Too LITTLE
probe capacitance
(Cprobe)

Undershoot

Too MUCH
probe capacitance
(Cprobe)

Overshoot

CORRECT
probe capacitance
(Cprobe)

3-29 A comparison of typical oscilloscope probe calibration signals.

match—otherwise, signal distortion results during your measurements. Slowly adjust the variable capacitance of your probe until the corners shown on the calibration signal are as square as possible. If you are not able to achieve a clean square wave, try a different probe.

Voltage measurements

The first step in any voltage measurement is to set the normal trace (called the *baseline*) where you want it. Normally, the baseline is placed along the center of the graticule during start-up, but it can be placed anywhere along the CRT so long as the trace is visible. To establish a baseline, switch your input coupling control to its ground position. Grounding the input disconnects any existing input signal and ensures a zero reading. Adjust the vertical offset control to shift the baseline wherever you want the zero reading to be (usually in the display center). If you have no particular preference, simply center the trace in the CRT.

To measure dc, set your input coupling switch to its dc position, then adjust the VOLTS/DIV control to provide the desired amount of sensitivity. If you are unsure which sensitivity is appropriate, start with a very low sensitivity (a large VOLTS/DIV setting), then carefully increase sensitivity (reduce the VOLTS/DIV setting) after the input signal is connected. This procedure prevents a trace from simply jumping off the screen when an unknown signal is first applied. If your signal does leave the visible portion of the display, you can reduce the sensitivity (increase the VOLTS/DIV setting) to make the trace visible again.

For example, suppose you are measuring a +5 Vdc power supply output. If VOLTS/DIV is set to 5 VOLTS/DIV, each major vertical division of the CRT display represents 5 Vdc, so your +5 Vdc signal should appear 1 full division above the baseline:

5 VOLTS/DIV x 1 DIV = 5 Vdc

as shown in Fig. 3-30. At a VOLTS/DIV setting of 2 VOLTS/DIV, the same +5 Vdc signal would now appear 2.5 divisions above the baseline:

2 VOLTS/DIV x 2.5 DIV = 5 Vdc

If the input signal is a negative voltage, the trace appears below the baseline, but it is read the same way.

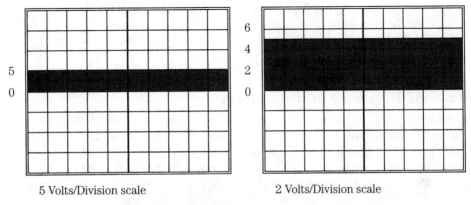

5 Volts/Division scale   2 Volts/Division scale

3-30   Measuring dc voltages with an oscilloscope.

Alternating current signals can also be read directly from the oscilloscope. Switch the input coupling control to its "ac" position, then set a baseline just as you would for dc measurements. If you are unsure about how to set the vertical sensitivity, start with a low sensitivity (a large VOLTS/DIV setting), then slowly increase the sensitivity (reduce the VOLTS/DIV setting) when the input signal is connected. Keep in mind that ac voltage measurements on an oscilloscope do not match ac voltage readings on a multimeter. An oscilloscope displays instantaneous peak values for a waveform, while ac voltmeters measure in terms of RMS (root mean square) values. To convert a peak voltage reading to RMS, divide the peak reading by 1.414. Another limitation of multimeters is that they can only measure sinusoidal ac signals. Square, triangle, or other unusual waveforms are interpreted as an average value by a multimeter.

When actually measuring an ac signal, it might be necessary to adjust the oscilloscope's trigger level control to obtain a stable (still) trace. As Fig. 3-31 illustrates, signal voltages can be measured directly from the display. For example, the sinusoidal waveform of Fig. 3-31 varies from –10 to +10 V. If oscilloscope sensitivity were

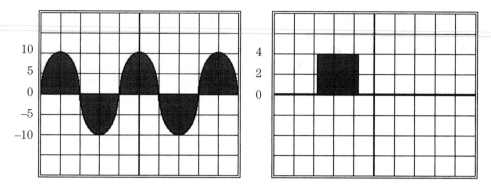

3-31 Measuring ac voltages with an oscilloscope.

set to 5 VOLTS/DIV, signal peaks would occur 2 divisions above and 2 divisions below the baseline. Because the oscilloscope provides peak measurements, an ac voltmeter would show the signal as:

$$\frac{10}{1.414} = 7.07 \text{ VRMS}$$

Time and frequency measurements

An oscilloscope is an ideal tool for measuring critical parameters such as pulse width, duty cycle, and frequency. The horizontal sensitivity control (TIME/DIV) comes into play with time and frequency measurements. Before making any measurements, you must first obtain a clear baseline as you would for voltage measurements. When a baseline is established and a signal is finally connected, adjust the TIME/DIV control to display one or two complete signal cycles.

Typical period measurements are illustrated in Fig. 3-32. With VOLTS/DIV set to 5 ms/DIV, the sinusoidal waveform shown repeats every 2 divisions. This represents a period of 10 ms:

5 ms/DIV x 2 DIV = 10 ms

Because frequency is simply the reciprocal of time, it can be calculated by inverting the time value. A period of 10 ms would represent a frequency of 100 Hz:

$$\frac{1 \text{ s}}{10 \text{ ms}} = 100 \text{ Hz}$$

This also works for square waves and regularly repeating nonsinusoidal waveforms. The square wave shown in Fig. 3-32 repeats every 4 divisions. At a TIME/DIV setting of 1 ms/DIV, its period would be 4 ms. This corresponds to a frequency 250 Hz:

$$\frac{1 \text{ s}}{4 \text{ ms}} = 250 \text{ Hz}$$

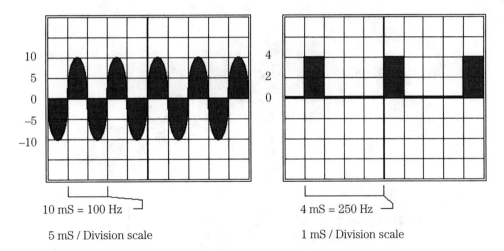

3-32 Measuring time on an oscilloscope.

Instead of measuring the entire period of a pulse cycle, you can also read the time between any two points of interest. For the square wave of Fig. 3-32, you could read the pulse width to be 1 ms. You could also read the low portion of the cycle as a duration of 3 ms (added together for a total signal period of 4 ms). A signal's *duty cycle* is simply the ratio of a signal's ON time to its total period expressed as a percentage. For example, a square wave that is ON for 2 ms and OFF for 2 ms would have a duty cycle of 50%:

$$\frac{2 \text{ ms}}{2 \text{ ms} + 2 \text{ ms}} \times 100\% = 50\%$$

For an ON time of 1 ms and an OFF time of 3 ms, the duty cycle would be 25%:

$$\frac{1 \text{ ms}}{1 \text{ ms} + 3 \text{ ms}} \times 100\% = 25\%$$

Logic analyzers

As useful and flexible as an oscilloscope can be, there are many circumstances when it would be helpful to evaluate a selection of digital signals simultaneously, so that logic signals can be compared in terms of state (1s and 0s) and timing relationships. A logic analyzer is a powerful analytical tool that can represent digital information in terms of waveform timing, ASCII characters, or binary and hexadecimal patterns. Many logic analyzers can record their readings on a printer, or record to a floppy disk or solid-state memory card for further evaluation. While most logic analyzers are sophisticated, stand-alone pieces of test equipment, there is a growing number of PC-based analyzers that can be run through an ordinary desktop computer (Fig. 3-33). PC-based analyzers often lack the "bells and whistles" found in stand-alone units, but are well suited for basic, budget-conscious repair shops. Logic analyzers

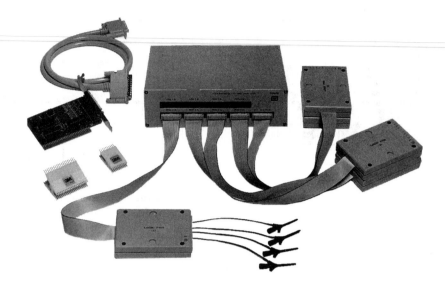

3-33   A computer-based logic analyzer system. Link Computer Graphics, Inc.

are extremely effective at studying computer bus operations, so you can locate problems in core logic.

Because of the setup complexity and operating variations between logic analyzers, it is impossible to describe them adequately in only a few book pages. Manufacturer's guides and owner's manuals should tell you everything you need to know. For the moment, you should realize that a logic analyzer is an important troubleshooting tool that can speed your repairs of microprocessor-based systems such as computers or computer peripherals.

4
Service guidelines

Electronic troubleshooting is a unique pursuit—an activity that falls somewhere between art and science. Your success depends not only on the right documentation
and test equipment, but on intuition and a thorough, careful troubleshooting approach. This chapter shows you how to evaluate and track down problems in your
small computer, and how to locate technical data. It also offers a series of service
guidelines that can ease your work (Fig. 4-1).

4-1 A Hewlett-Packard Kitty
Hawk hard drive.

The troubleshooting process

Regardless of how complex your particular computer or peripheral device might be,
a dependable troubleshooting procedure can be broken down into four basic steps,
as illustrated in Fig. 4-2:

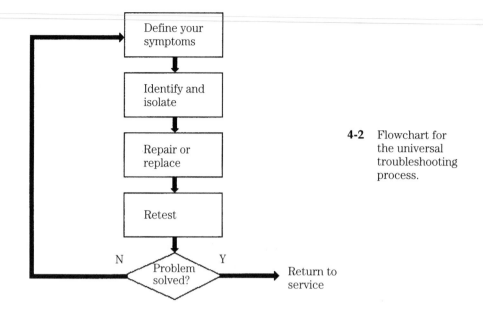

4-2 Flowchart for the universal troubleshooting process.

1. Define your symptoms.
2. Identify and isolate the potential source (or location) of your problem.
3. Repair or replace the suspected component or assembly.
4. Retest the unit thoroughly to be sure that you have solved the problem. If you have not solved the problem, start again from step 1.

This is a universal procedure that you can apply to any type of troubleshooting —not just troubleshooting for computer equipment.

Define your symptoms

Sooner or later, your floppy drive, tape backup, or other storage device is going to break down. In many cases, the cause might be as simple as a loose wire or connector, or as complicated as an IC failure. Before you open your toolbox, you must have a firm understanding of all the symptoms. Think about the symptoms carefully. Is the disk or tape inserted properly? Is the power or access LED lit? Does this problem occur only when the computer is tapped or moved? Recognizing and understanding all the symptoms makes it much easier to trace a problem to the appropriate assembly or component.

Take the time to write down as many symptoms as you can. This note-taking might seem tedious at first, but once you have begun your repair, a written record of symptoms and circumstances helps keep you focused on the task at hand. It also helps to jog your memory if you must explain the symptoms to someone else at a later date. As a professional troubleshooter, you must often log problems or otherwise document your activities anyway.

Identify and isolate

Before you try to isolate a problem within a piece of computer hardware, you must first be sure that it is the equipment itself that is causing the problem. In many circumstances, this is fairly obvious, but there might be situations that appear ambiguous (e.g., there is no power, no DOS prompt, etc.). Always remember that storage devices work because of an intimate mingling of hardware and software. A faulty or improperly configured piece of software can cause confusing system errors.

When you are confident that the failure lies in your system's hardware, you can begin to identify possible problem areas. Start your search at the subsection level. The troubleshooting procedures throughout this book guide you through the major sections of today's popular storage systems, and aid you in deciding which subsection might be at fault. When you have identified a potential problem area, you can begin the actual repair process, and possibly even track the fault to a component level.

Repair or replace

Once you have an understanding of what is wrong and where to look, you can begin the actual repair process that you feel will correct the symptoms. Most storage devices are a healthy mix of both electronic circuitry and electromechanical devices, so most procedures require the exchange of electronic or electromechanical parts. As a general rule, all procedures should be considered important and should be followed carefully.

Parts are usually classified as components or subassemblies. A *component part* is the smallest possible individual part that you can work with. Components serve many different purposes in a small computer. Resistors, capacitors, transformers, motors, and integrated circuits are just a few types of component parts. Components contain no serviceable parts within themselves—a defective component must be replaced. A *subassembly* can be composed of many individual components. Unlike components, subassemblies serve a single specific purpose in a storage device (e.g., a read/write head amplifier PC board), but it can usually be repaired by locating and replacing any faulty components. Note that it is always acceptable to replace a defective subassembly with a new one, but it really depends on how much time and effort you are willing (or able) to commit to the repair.

Mail-order component companies listed at the back of this book can provide you with general-purpose electronic components and equipment to aid in your repair. Most send along their complete catalog or product listing at your request. Keep in mind, however, that computers and their peripheral devices make extensive use of specialized integrated circuits and physical assemblies. For specialized parts, you often have to deal directly with the manufacturer. Going to a manufacturer is always somewhat of a calculated risk—they might choose to do business only with their affiliated service centers, or simply refuse to sell parts to consumers outright. If you find a manufacturer willing to sell you parts, you should know the exact code or part number used by that manufacturer. This is often available within the manufacturer's technical data, if you have it. Keep in mind that many manufacturers are ill-equipped to deal directly with individual consumers, so be patient, and be prepared to make several different calls.

During a repair, you might reach a roadblock that requires you to leave your equipment for a day or two (maybe longer). Make it a point to reassemble your system as much as possible before leaving it. Gather any loose parts in plastic bags, seal them shut, and mark them clearly. If you are working with electronic circuitry, make sure to use good-quality antistatic boxes or bags for storage. Partial reassembly (combined with careful notes) helps you remember how the unit goes together later on.

Retest

When a repair is finally complete, the system must be reassembled carefully before testing it. Guards, housings, cables, and shields must be restored before final testing. If symptoms persist, you have to reevaluate the symptoms and narrow the problem to another part of the equipment. If normal operation is restored (or greatly improved), test the computer's various functions. When you verify that your symptoms have stopped during actual operation, the equipment can be returned to service.

Don't be discouraged if the equipment still malfunctions. Simply walk away, clear your head, and start again by defining your current symptoms. Never continue with a repair if you are tired or frustrated—tomorrow is another day. Even the most experienced troubleshooters get overwhelmed from time to time. You should also realize that there might be more than one bad part to deal with. Remember that storage devices are just a collection of assemblies, and each assembly is a collection of parts. Normally, everything works together, but when one part fails, it can cause one or more interconnected parts to fail as well. When repairing to the component level, be prepared to make several repair attempts before the computer is repaired completely. Experience will show you which shortcuts are most effective.

Technical information

Information is perhaps your most valuable tool when repairing any piece of electronic equipment. Highly involved electronic troubleshooting generally requires a complete set of schematics and a parts list. Some peripheral manufacturers do sell technical information for their products (or at least their older products). Tandy Corporation (Radio Shack), Sony, Teac, and Sharp are just a few manufacturers that make their technical data available to consumers and independent technicians. Contact the manufacturer's literature or customer service department for specific data prices and availability. Be sure to request a *service manual* or *maintenance manual*, not an owner's or user's manual.

If you obtain technical information, it is strongly recommended that you have the data on hand before starting your repair. Service manuals often contain important information on custom or application-specific integrated circuits (ASICs) used in the equipment that you cannot obtain elsewhere.

Static electricity

As with any type of electronic troubleshooting activity, there is always a risk of further damage being caused to equipment accidentally during the repair process. With sophisticated computer electronics, that damage hazard comes in the form of *electrostatic discharge* (ESD), which can destroy sensitive electronic parts.

If you have ever walked across a carpeted floor on a cold, dry winter day, you have probably experienced the effects of ESD firsthand when you reached for a metal object (such as a door knob). Under the right conditions, your body can accumulate static charge potentials that exceed 20,000 V.

When you provide a conductive path for electrons to flow, that built-up charge rushes away from your body at the point closest to the metal object. The result is often a brief, stinging shock. Such a jolt can be startling and annoying, but it is generally harmless to people. Semiconductor devices, on the other hand, are highly susceptible to real physical damage from ESD when you handle or replace circuit boards and integrated circuits. This section introduces you to static electricity and show you how to prevent ESD damage during your repairs.

Static formation

When two dissimilar materials are rubbed together (such as a carpet and the soles of your shoes), the force of friction causes electrons to move from one material to another. The excess (or lack) of electrons cause a charge or equal but opposite polarities to develop on each material. Because electrons are not flowing, there is no current, so the charge is said to be *static*. However, the charge does exhibit a voltage potential. As materials continue to rub together, their charge increases—sometimes to potentials of thousands of volts.

In humans, static charges are often developed by normal, everyday activities such as combing hair. Friction between the comb and your hair causes opposing charges to develop. Sliding across a vinyl car seat, pulling a sweater on or off, or taking clothes out of a dryer are just some of the ways static charges can develop in the body—it is virtually impossible to avoid. ESD is more pronounced in winter months because dry (low-humidity) air allows a greater accumulation of charge. In the summer, humidity in the air tends to bleed away (or short circuit) most accumulated charges before they reach shock levels that you can feel. Regardless of the season, though, ESD is always present to some degree, and always a danger to sensitive electronics.

Device damage

ESD poses a serious threat to most advanced ICs. ICs can easily be destroyed by static discharge levels of just a few hundred volts—well below your body's ability to even feel a static discharge. Static discharge at sufficient levels can damage bipolar transistors, transistor-transistor logic (TTL) gates, emitter-coupled logic (ECL) gates, operational amplifiers (op-amps), silicon-controlled rectifiers (SCRs), and junction field-effect transistors (JFETs), but certainly the most susceptible

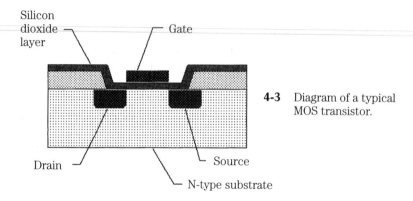

Silicon dioxide layer

Gate

4-3 Diagram of a typical MOS transistor.

Drain

Source

N-type substrate

components to ESD are those ICs fabricated using metal-oxide semiconductor (MOS) technology. A typical MOS transistor is shown in Fig. 4-3.

The MOS family of devices (PMOS, NMOS, HMOS, CMOS, etc.) has become the cornerstone of high-performance ICs such as memories, high-speed logic and microprocessors, and other advanced components that can be found in today's small computers. Typical MOS ICs can easily fit over 500,000 transistors onto a single IC die. Every part of these transistors must be made continually smaller to keep pace with the constant demand for ever-higher levels of IC complexity. As each part of the transistor shrinks, however, its inherent breakdown voltage drops, and its susceptibility to ESD damage escalates.

A typical MOS transistor breakdown is illustrated in Fig. 4-4. Notice the areas of positive and negative semiconductor material which forms its three terminals: source, gate, and drain. The gate is isolated from the other parts of the transistor by a thin film of silicon dioxide (sometimes called the *oxide layer*). Unfortunately, this layer is extremely thin. High voltages, like those from electrostatic discharges, can easily overload the oxide layer, resulting in a puncture through the gate. Once this happens, the transistor (and therefore the entire IC) is permanently defective and must be replaced.

Controlling static electricity

Never underestimate the importance of static control during your repairs. Without realizing it, you could destroy a new IC or circuit board before you even have the chance to install it—and you might never even know that static damage has occurred. All it takes is the careless touch of a charged hand or a loose piece of clothing. Take the necessary steps to ensure the safe handling and replacement of your sensitive (and expensive) electronics.

One way to control static is to keep charges away from boards and ICs to begin with. This is often accomplished as part of a device's packaging and shipping container. ICs are typically packed in a specially-made conductive foam. Carbon granules are compounded right into the polyethylene foam to achieve conductivity (about 3000 Ω per centimeter). Foam support helps to resist IC lead bending, absorb vibrations, and keeps every lead of the IC at the same potential (known as *equipotential bonding*). Conductive plastics are used to manufacture antistatic boxes as

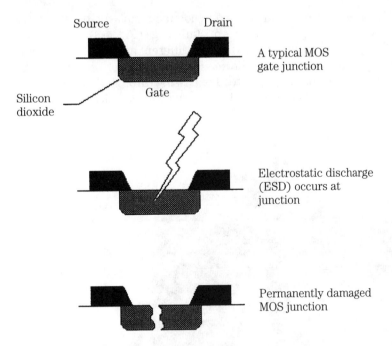

4-4   The sequence of electrostatic breakdown in a MOS device.

shown in Fig. 4-5. Antistatic boxes can be used with or without conductive foam. Conductive foam and antistatic boxes are reusable, so you can insert ICs for safe keeping, then remove them as needed. You can purchase conductive foam from most electronics retail stores.

4-5   Antistatic boxes.

Circuit boards are normally held in conductive plastic bags that dissipate static charges before damage can occur. Antistatic bags (Fig. 4-6) are made up of different material layers—each material exhibiting different amounts of conductivity. The bag acts as a *faraday cage* for the device it contains. Electrons from an ESD dissipate along the bag's surface layers instead of passing through the bag wall to its contents. Antistatic bags are also available through many electronics retail stores.

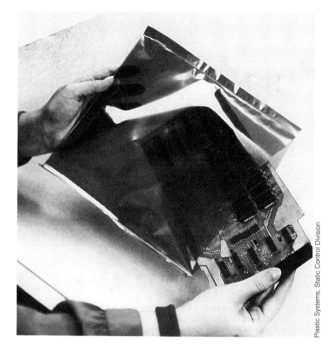

4-6 An anti-static bag.

Plastic Systems, Static Control Division

Whenever you work with sensitive electronics, you should dissipate charges that might have accumulated on your body. A conductive fabric wrist strap (Fig. 4-7) which is soundly connected to an earth ground slowly bleeds away any charges from your body. Avoid grabbing hold of a ground directly. Although this discharges you, it can result in a nasty jolt if you have picked up a large electrostatic charge.

Even the action of wiping a plastic cabinet or video monitor can produce a large electrostatic field. Antistatic chemical agents added to lint-free cleaning wipes (Fig. 4-8) allow cleaning to be performed without the fear of excessive ESD accumulation. Wipes are typically pretreated and sealed in small pouches for convenience.

Work surfaces must also be as static free as possible. This is very important. When circuit boards or chassis are removed from their systems and brought to your workbench, use an antistatic mat (Fig. 4-9) to protect the delicate electronics. The antistatic mat is essentially a conductive layer that is unrolled onto desks or benches, and it connects to earth ground just like the wrist strap.

There are instruments that can be used to measure the level of electrostatic fields on any surface or object. Electrostatic meters (Fig. 4-10) are relatively inexpensive and easy to use—you simply bring the meter within an inch or so of the item

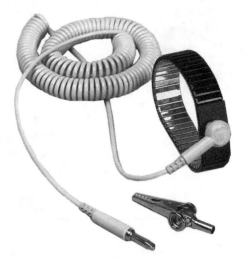

4-7   An antistatic wrist strap.
Plastic Systems, Static Control Division

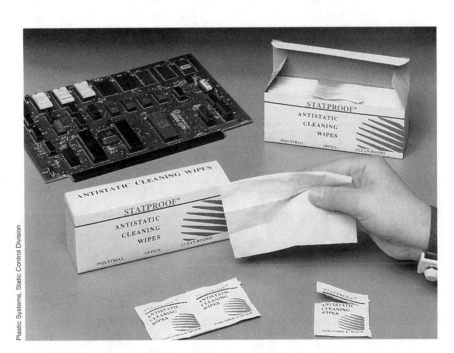

Plastic Systems, Static Control Division

4-8   Antistatic chemical wipes.

to be measured, press the "Read" button, and read the static level in kV (thousands of volts) directly from the meter display. Electrostatic meters are generally powered by one or more AA-type batteries.

Remember to make careful use of your static controls. Keep ICs and circuit boards in their antistatic containers at all times. Never place parts onto or into synthetic materials (such as nonconductive plastic cabinets or fabric coverings) that

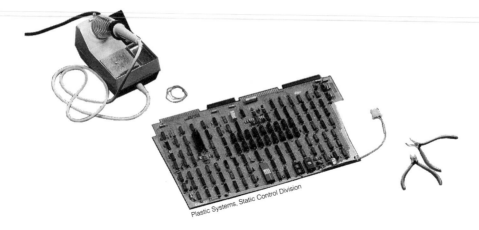

4-9 An antistatic work surface mat.

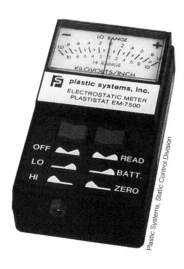

4-10 An electrostatic field meter.

could hold a charge. Handle static sensitive parts carefully. Avoid touching IC pins if at all possible. Be sure to use a conductive wrist strap and mat connected to a reliable earth ground.

Electricity hazards

No matter how harmless your storage device might appear, always remember that potential shock hazards exist. Although internally mounted storage devices operate from dc voltages produced by the computer, external storage devices are sometimes powered by ac line voltage. When an ac-powered storage device is disassembled, there can be several locations where live ac voltage is exposed and easily accessible. Electronic equipment operates from 120 Vac at 60 Hz. Many European countries use

240 Vac at 50 Hz. When this type of voltage potential establishes a path through your body, it can cause a flow of current that might be large enough to stop your heart. Because it only takes about 100 mA to trigger a cardiac arrest, and a typical power supply fuse is rated for 1 or 2 A, fuses and circuit breakers do not protect you.

It is your skin's resistance that limits the flow of current through the body. Ohm's law states that for any voltage, current flow increases as resistance drops (and vice versa). Dry skin exhibits a high resistance of several hundred thousand ohms, while moist, cut, or wet skin can drop to only several hundred ohms. This means that even comparatively low voltages can produce a shock if your skin resistance is low enough.

Take the following steps to protect yourself from injury:

- Keep the device under repair unplugged (not just turned off) as much as possible during disassembly and repair. When you must perform a service procedure that requires power to be applied, plug the supply into an isolation transformer just long enough to perform your procedure, then unplug it again. This makes the repair safer for you, as well as for anyone else that might happen along.
- Whenever you must work on a power supply, try to wear rubber gloves. These insulate your hands just like insulation on a wire. You might think that rubber gloves are inconvenient and uncomfortable, but they are far better than the inconvenience and discomfort of an electric shock. Make it a point to wear a long-sleeved shirt with sleeves rolled down and buttoned—this insulates your forearms.
- If rubber gloves are absolutely out of the question for one reason or another, remove all metal jewelry and work with one hand behind your back. The metals in your jewelry are excellent conductors. Should your ring or watchband hook onto a live ac line, it can conduct current directly to your skin. By keeping one hand behind your back, you cannot grasp both ends of a live ac line to complete a strong current path through your heart.
- Work dry—do not work with wet hands or clothing. Do not work in wet or damp environments. Make sure that any nearby fire extinguishing equipment is suitable for electrical fires.
- Treat electricity with tremendous respect. Whenever electronic circuitry is exposed (especially power supply circuitry), a shock hazard exists. Remember that it is the flow of current through your body, not the voltage potential, that can injure you. Insulate yourself as much as possible from any exposed wiring.

Conventional soldering technology

Soldering is the most commonly used method of connecting wires and components within an electrical or electronic circuit (Fig. 4-11). Metal surfaces (in this case, component leads, wires, or printed circuit boards) are heated to high temperatures, then joined together with a layer of compatible metal in its molten state. When performed correctly with the right materials, soldering forms a lasting, corrosion-proof, inter-molecular bond that is mechanically strong and electrically sound. All that is required is the appropriate soldering iron and electronics-grade (called *60/40*) solder. This section explains the tools and techniques for both regular and surface-mount soldering.

4-11 Soldering on a surface-mount PC board.

PACE, Inc.

Background

By strict definition, *soldering* is a process of bonding metals together. There are three distinct types of soldering: *brazing, silver soldering,* and *soft soldering.* Brazing and silver soldering are used when working with hard or precious metals; soft soldering is the technique of choice for electronics work.

In order to bond wires or component leads, which are typically made of copper, a third metal must be added while in its molten state. The bonding metal is known simply as solder. Several different types of solder are available to handle each soldering technique, but the chosen solder must be compatible with the metals to be bonded—otherwise, a bond will not form. Lead and tin are two common and inexpensive metals that adhere very well to copper. However, neither metal by itself has the strength, hardness, and melting point characteristics to make them practically useful. Therefore, lead and tin are combined into an alloy. A ratio of approximately 60% tin and 40% lead yields an alloy that offers reasonable hardness, good pliability, and a relatively low melting point that is ideal for electronics work. This is the solder that must be used.

While solder adheres very well to copper, it does not adhere well at all to the natural oxides that form on a conductor's surface. Even though conductors might appear clean and clear with the unaided eye, some amount of oxidation is always present. Oxides must be removed before a good bond can be achieved. A resin cleaning agent, called *flux,* can be applied to conductors before soldering. Resin is chemically inactive at room temperature, but it becomes extremely active when heated to soldering temperatures. Activated flux bonds with oxides and strips them away from copper surfaces. As a completed solder joint cools, residual resin also cools and returns safely to an inactive state.

Never, under any circumstances, should you use an acid- or solvent-based flux to prepare conductors. Acid fluxes can clean away oxides as well as resin, but acids and solvents remain active after the joint cools. Over time, active acid flux continues to dissolve copper wires and eventually causes a circuit failure. Resin flux can be purchased as a paste that is brushed onto conductors before soldering, but most electronic solders have a core of resin manufactured right into the solder strand itself. Prefabricated flux eliminates the mess of flux paste, and cleans the joint as solder is applied. The paste solder used in surface-mount soldering usually contains chemical agents.

Irons and tips

A soldering iron is little more than a resistive heating element built into the end of a long steel tube as shown in the cross-sectional diagram of Fig. 4-12. When voltage is applied to the heater, it warms the base of a metal tip. Any heat conducted down the cooldown tube (toward the handle) is dissipated harmlessly to the surrounding air. This keeps the handle temperature low enough to hold comfortably. Even the larger professional soldering stations (Fig. 4-13) use this approach.

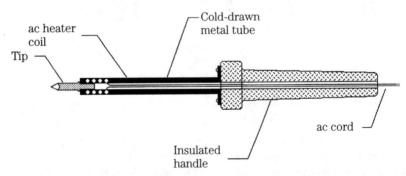

4-12   Cross-sectional diagram of a simple soldering iron.

4-13   An adjustable temperature soldering station.

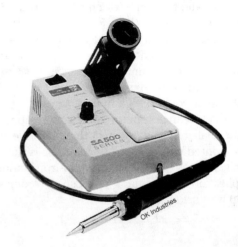

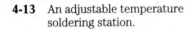

Although some heat is wasted along the cooldown tube, most heat is channeled into a soldering tip similar to the one shown in Fig. 4-14. Tips generally have a core of solid copper that is plated with iron. The plated core is then coated with a layer of nickel to stop high-temperature metal corrosion. The entire assembly (except for the tip's very end) is finally plated with chromium which gives a new tip its shiny chrome appearance. A chromium coating renders the tip *non-wettable*—solder does not stick to it. Because solder must stick at the tip's end, the end is plated with tin. A tin coating (a basic component of solder) makes the tip *wettable* so that molten solder does adhere. Tips can be manufactured in a wide variety of shapes and sizes to handle different soldering tasks. Before you can select the best tip for the job, you must understand ideal soldering conditions.

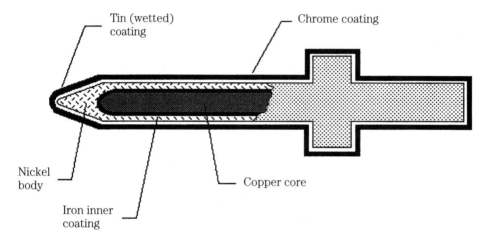

4-14   Cross-sectional diagram of a typical soldering iron tip.

The very best soldering connections are made within only a narrow window of time and temperature. A solder joint heated between 260° to 288°C (500° to 550°F) for one to two seconds makes the best connections. You should select a soldering iron wattage and tip shape to achieve these conditions. For very precise work, use a tip temperature sensor (Fig. 4-15) to verify the tip's actual temperature. The purpose of the soldering iron is not to melt solder—instead, a soldering iron is supposed to deliver heat to a joint, and the joint should melt the solder. A large solder joint (with larger or more numerous connections) requires a larger iron and tip than a small joint (with fewer or smaller connections). If you use a small iron to heat a large joint, the joint could dissipate heat faster than the iron can deliver it, so the joint might not reach an acceptable soldering temperature. Conversely, using a large iron to heat a small joint can overheat the joint. Overheating can melt wire insulation and damage printed circuit board traces. This is the reason why temperature-controlled soldering stations (Fig. 4-16) or multi-iron stations are so popular. Match wattage to the application. Most general-purpose electronics work can be accomplished using a 25 to 30 watt soldering iron.

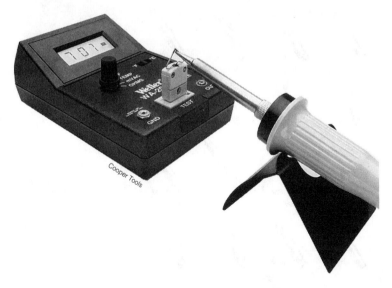

4-15 A soldering iron tip temperature sensor.

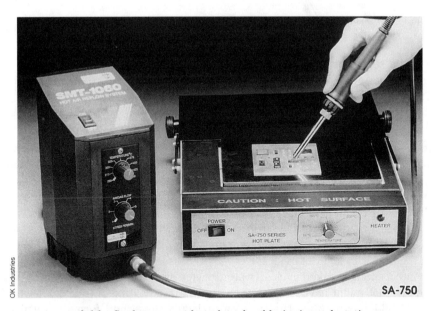

4-16 Surface-mount hot-plate desoldering/rework station.

Because the end of a tip actually contacts the joint to be soldered, the tip's shape and size can assist heat transfer greatly. When heat must be applied across a wide area, such as a wire splice, a wide area tip should be used. A screwdriver or "flat-blade" tip is a good choice. If heat must be directed with pinpoint accuracy for small, tight joints or printed circuits, a narrow blade or conical tip is best. Figure 4-17

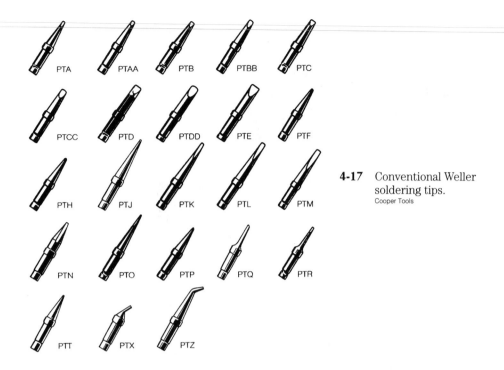

PTA PTAA PTB PTBB PTC

PTCC PTD PTDD PTE PTF

PTH PTJ PTK PTL PTM

4-17 Conventional Weller soldering tips.
Cooper Tools

PTN PTO PTP PTQ PTR

PTT PTX PTZ

illustrates a selection of conventional Weller soldering iron tips, and Fig. 4-18 shows a selection of surface-mount tips. More information on surface-mount soldering is presented later in this chapter.

Soldering

Always keep your soldering iron parked in a secure holder while it is on. Never allow a hot iron to sit freely on a tabletop or on anything that might be flammable. **Note:** Make it a rule always to wear safety glasses when soldering. Active resin or molten solder can easily flick off the iron or joint and do permanent damage to your eyes.

Give your iron plenty of time to warm up. Five minutes of warming time is usually adequate, but small-wattage irons (or irons with larger tips) might need more time. Once the iron is at its working temperature, you should coat the wettable portion of the tip with a layer of fresh solder—a process known as *tinning* the iron. Rub the tip into a sponge soaked in clean water to wipe away any accumulations of debris and carbon that might have formed, then apply a thin coating of fresh solder to the tip's end. Solder penetrates the tip to a molecular level and forms a cushion of molten solder that aids in heat transfer. Re-tin the iron whenever its tip becomes blackened—perhaps every few minutes, or after several joints.

It is often helpful to tin each individual conductor before actually making the complete joint. To tin a wire, prepare it by stripping away 3/16" to 1/4" of insulation. As you strip insulation, be sure not to nick or damage the conductor. Heat the exposed copper for about a second, then apply solder into the wire—not into the iron. If the iron and tip are appropriate, solder should flow evenly and smoothly into

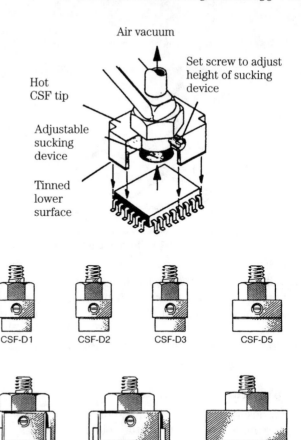

Air vacuum

Set screw to adjust
height of sucking
device

Hot
CSF tip

Adjustable
sucking
device

Tinned
lower
surface

4-18 Desoldering tips for
quad flat pack ICs.
Cooper

CSF-D1   CSF-D2   CSF-D3   CSF-D5

CSF-Q1   CSF-Q2   CSF-D4

the conductor. Apply just enough solder to bond each of a stranded wire's exposed strands. You will find that conductors heat faster and solder flows better when all parts of a joint are tinned in advance.

Making a complete solder joint is just as easy. Bring together each of your conductors as necessary to form the joint. For example, if you are soldering a component into a printed circuit board, insert the component's leads into the proper PC board holes. Place the iron against all conductors to be heated at the joint. For a printed circuit board, heat the printed trace and component lead together (Fig. 4-19). After about one second, flow solder gently into the hot conductors—not the iron. Be sure that solder flows cleanly and evenly into the joint. Apply solder for another one or two seconds, then remove both solder and iron. **Note:** Do not attempt to touch or move the joint for several seconds. Wait until the solder cools and sets. If the joint requires additional solder, reheat the joint and flow in a bit more solder.

You can identify a good solder joint by its smooth, even, silver-gray appearance. Any charred or carbonized flux on the joint indicates that your soldering temperature is too high, or that heat is being applied for too long. Remember that solder

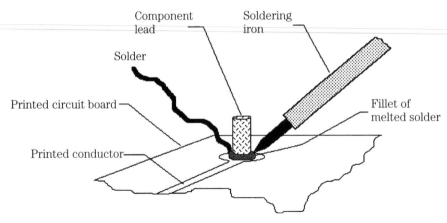

4-19 Forming a basic solder connection.

cannot flow unless the joint is hot. If the joint is not hot, the solder cools before it bonds. The result is a rough, built-up, dull gray or blackish mound that does not adhere to the joint very well. This is known as a *cold* solder joint. A cold joint can often be corrected by reheating the joint properly and applying fresh solder. If you are uncomfortable with soldering techniques, you should practice on scrap wire or PC boards until you become proficient.

Conventional desoldering

When desoldering an electronic connection, you must remove the intermolecular bond that has formed during the soldering process. In reality, however, this is virtually impossible to achieve completely. The best that you can hope for is to remove enough solder to gently break the connection apart without destroying the component or damaging the associated PC trace. Desoldering is essentially a matter of removing as much solder as possible—the more solder, the better.

You will find that some connections are very easy to remove. For instance, a wire inserted into a printed circuit board can be removed easily just by heating the joint and gently withdrawing the wire from its hole once solder is molten. Use extreme caution when desoldering wires and components. Leads and wires under tension can spring free once solder is molten. A springing wire can launch a bead of hot solder into the air. Again, always use safety glasses or goggles to protect your eyes from flying solder.

Desoldering other types of connections, such as through-hole components, is more difficult. When desoldering a part with more than one wire, it is virtually impossible to heat all of its leads simultaneously while withdrawing the part. As a result, it becomes necessary to remove as much solder as possible from each lead, then gently break each lead free as shown in Fig. 4-20. Grab hold of each lead with a pair of needlenose pliers and wiggle the lead back and forth gently until it breaks free. Solder can be removed using regular desoldering tools such as a solder vacuum or solder wick, as illustrated in Fig. 4-21.

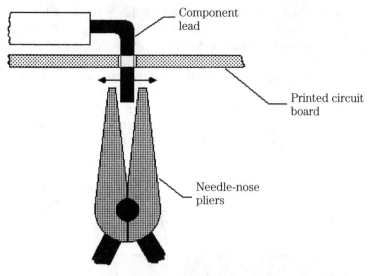

4-20 Breaking a stubborn through-hole solder connection.

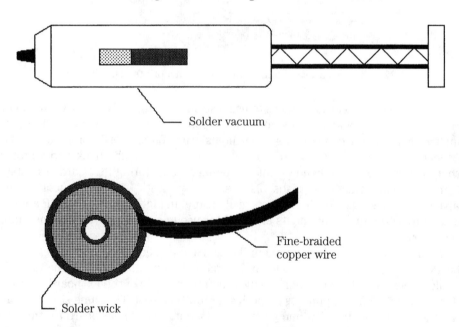

4-21 Conventional desoldering tools.

Surface-mount soldering technology

Conventional printed circuits make use of through-hole components. Leaded parts are inserted on one side of the PC board, while their leads are soldered to printed wiring traces on the other side. Through-hole PC board assembly has been the premier method of circuit mass-production since the 1960s, and will likely remain a force in PC board production for many years to come. With the ever-increasing need to pack more circuitry into less board space, through-hole circuit assembly is rapidly being replaced by a technique called surface-mount (SMT) fabrication. A surface-mount PC board uses specially miniaturized components that are mounted and soldered to one side of the PC board only (Fig. 4-22). There are no leads to protrude through the board. In the last few years, just about every electronic component has become available in one or more SMT package versions. While SMT assemblies are growing in popularity, it is not uncommon to find *hybrid assemblies*, which contain both SMT and through-hole components

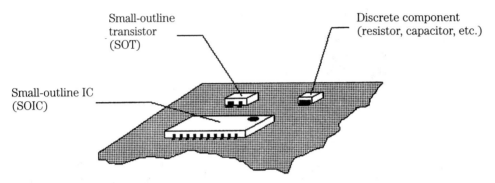

4-22   View of surface-mount components on a printed circuit board.

There are many real advantages to using surface-mount PC boards. Components are changed significantly. For example, SMT components are cheaper, lighter, and smaller than leaded components—this holds true for all SMT components. The absence of long leads allows SMT components to resist high shock and vibration (there is also no need to bend or cut component leads during PC board assembly). Removing long component leads also reduces parasitic circuit inductance and capacitance, making SMT circuits especially useful in high-frequency or RF applications. Surface-mount components are ideal for use in automatic PC board assembly machinery.

Such broad changes in component design have had equally important effects on the PC boards themselves. Smaller individual components allow PC boards to be smaller. Because SMT components only attach to one side of the PC board, it is possible to mount SMT components on both sides of the board. The same size PC board can, therefore, hold twice as many SMT components as a similar board for through-hole components. PC board materials are exactly the same for SMT circuits—no special board materials are needed. Eliminating through-hole components also eliminates the many plated through-holes that are needed to connect component leads to the board. Reduced drilling and plating can cut manufacturing costs even further.

The next portion of this chapter presents the details of SMT circuit fabrication and desoldering techniques. You should take the time to understand SMT concepts and fabrication because they are used in so many of today's consumer electronic products—especially computers and peripherals.

SMT circuit fabrication

Before any soldering can be performed, all surface-mount components must be placed on the PC board. The process is called *populating* the board. Automated placement equipment grabs each needed part from a supply roll or stack, then attaches each part in its correct orientation. Just how each part is attached depends upon where the component must be placed, and what type of soldering will be performed.

The *wave soldering* process is shown in Fig. 4-23. As you see, the PC board must be inverted (components on the bottom) during soldering. The board is then passed through a heating chamber, and a small wave of molten solder (about 240° to 260°C) is circulated onto the board. Molten solder adheres to the exposed metals in the components and PC board lands—this solders the part into place. The board is allowed to cool slowly and can then be tested. Components are then added to the other side, and the wave soldering process is repeated. Notice that SMT parts that are inverted must be glued into place before soldering. Wave soldering is popular because it is the process used with through-hole assemblies. In fact, any necessary through-hole components can be added and wave soldered along with the SMT parts. Gluing is accomplished automatically during assembly, but there are manual dispensing machines for prototype or repair work (Fig. 4-24).

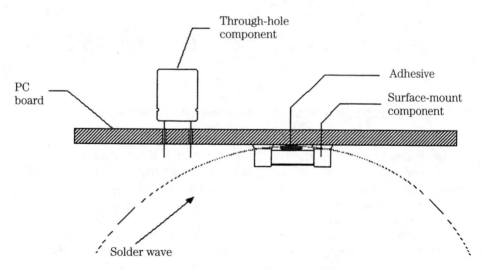

4-23   An example of surface-mount wave soldering.

Reflow soldering is illustrated in Fig. 4-25. In the reflow technique, a soft solder paste is applied to the PC board contact points by sweeping a layer of paste over a predefined solder mask—rather like silk screening. The mask is then removed, leaving solder paste in the appropriate locations. Automated placement equipment positions each part on top of the solder paste. The paste offers a light adhesive action which holds the parts in place. The populated PC board, with components still upright is heated quickly and exposed to soldering temperatures. Soldering heat is

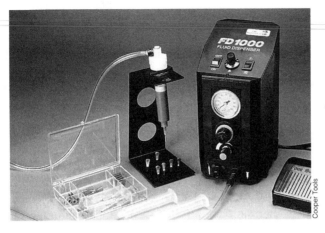

4-24 A fluid/adhesive dispenser.

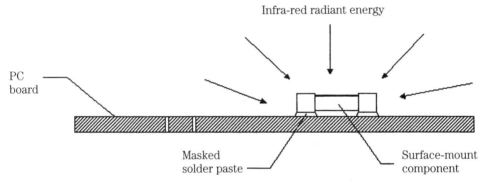

Infra-red radiant energy

PC board

Masked solder paste

Surface-mount component

4-25 An example of surface-mount reflow soldering.

typically provided by passing the board through a field of superheated gas vapor (called *vapor phase reflow*), or by exposing the board to the energy of infrared heating lamps (called *infrared reflow*). Heat melts the solder paste, which effectively solders each component to its appropriate trace.

Of course, you can also solder a surface-mount component manually with conventional soldering techniques. Keep in mind, however, that SMT parts and PC traces are small, delicate items that are incapable of shedding the direct heat applied from a soldering iron. If you are not extremely careful with soldering time and temperature, you can easily destroy the component, damage the delicate PC board, or both. Use the lowest power possible for your soldering iron (i.e., 12 to 20 W). Use a very fine tip, and apply heat for only the absolute minimum period of time. Let each joint cool thoroughly before moving onto the next one.

Surface-mount desoldering

During a repair, you can use a conventional, low-wattage soldering iron to install replacement parts one lead at a time. Desoldering SMT components, however, is a delicate and intricate task. As with conventional desoldering, it is virtually impossible to remove every molecule of solder from two mated surfaces. Even with the best solder wick or solder vacuum, a part will remain lightly bonded to its PC traces. You cannot heat and withdraw individual component leads, and any attempt to pull a part from the board will certainly damage the PC traces. Surface-mount desoldering presents some unique and perplexing problems for troubleshooters.

The only truly effective way to desolder an SMT component is to use a soldering pencil fitted with a surface-mount desoldering tip (Fig. 4-26). SMT tips are designed to heat every joint of a part simultaneously (instead of conventional tips that direct heat to only one joint at a time). By heating all of the joints at once, the part comes free and can be withdrawn from the board cleanly with a small vacuum nozzle or tweezers. You can also "sweep" the freed part right off the board in one quick motion, then clean up any residual solder with conventional desoldering tools.

4-26   SMT desoldering with an SOIC tip.

Figure 4-27 shows a dual soldering station with a "tweezer" iron and quad flat pack (QFP) iron. **Remember:** Always wear safety glasses when soldering or desoldering. Some full-featured solder rework stations offer an adjustable temperature control, along with a vacuum attachment for solder or component removal. Keep in mind that most SMT tips are physically much larger than conventional tips, and consequently need more power (25 to 35 W) to achieve temperatures that can melt solder. If you are outfitting to perform SMT repairs, it is worthwhile to invest in a solder station and tip set designed for SMT work. For the budget-conscious enthusiast, a hand-held soldering pencil can be fitted with SMT tips for relatively little money.

There is a large selection of SMT desoldering tips to choose from, based on the type of SMT device that you must remove. Figure 4-28 shows a close-up view of a hot-air SMT tip with a built-in vacuum nozzle. Hot air is used to melt the solder at each QFP lead. When solder is molten, the IC is withdrawn from the PC board by a small vacuum line within the iron.

4-27 Desoldering equipment for SMT rework.

OK Industries

4-28 A QFP desoldering tip.

PACE, Inc.

Printed circuits

In the very early days of consumer electronics, circuit assemblies were manufactured by hand on bulky metal frames. Each component was then wired together by hand. If you have ever seen a chassis from an old tube-driven television or radio, you have seen this type of construction. Eventually, the cost of hand-building electronic chassis became very high. A new technique was introduced that used photographic processes to print wiring patterns onto copper-clad boards. Excess copper was then chemically stripped away leaving only the desired wiring patterns. Parts could then be inserted and soldered quickly, easily, and accurately.

Before long, manufacturers realized that these *printed circuits* appeared more uniform, were easier to inspect and test, required much less labor to assemble, and were lighter and less bulky than metal chassis assembly. Today, virtually all electronic equipment incorporates some type of printed circuit board. The size and complexity of the board depends largely on the particular circuit's job. This section describes the major types of printed circuit boards that you might encounter, and presents a selection of PC board troubleshooting and repair techniques.

Types of printed circuits

Printed circuits are available as *single-sided, double-sided,* and *multilayer boards.* Computer equipment typically uses multilayer boards. Each type of board can hold both surface-mount and through-hole components. Single-sided PC boards are the simplest and least expensive type of printed circuit. Copper traces are etched only on one side of the board. Holes can then be drilled through the board to accommodate component leads if necessary. Through-hole components are inserted from the blank side of the board (the "component" side) so that their leads protrude on the copper trace side (the "solder" side). Component leads can then be soldered to their copper traces to complete the printed circuit. Single-sided PC boards support SMT components.

When circuits become too complex to route all traces on one side of the PC board, traces can be etched onto both sides of a printed circuit. This is called a double-sided PC board. Electrically conductive, plated holes are used to interconnect both sides of the board as needed. Such plated holes are also used to hold through-hole component leads. Solder conducts up the plated hole through capillary action and ensures that a component lead is properly connected to both sides of the board—this allows the board to be soldered from one side only during manufacture. However, desoldering leads in plated holes can become somewhat difficult because solder adheres all the way through the hole. All internal solder must be removed before a lead can be withdrawn. If you pull out a wire or component lead before solder is removed, you stand a good chance of ripping the plating right out of the hole. Double-sided PC boards are excellent for SMT components, because components can be soldered on both sides of the board.

Even more complex circuit designs can be fabricated on multilayer PC boards. Not only do you find traces on both external sides of the PC board, but there can be even more layers of etched traces sandwiched and interconnected between these two faces, with each layer separated by a thin insulating layer. As with double-sided boards, multilayer boards use plated through-holes to hold component leads, and bond various layers together.

Typical printed circuits use etched copper traces on a base material of paper-based phenolic or epoxy. Other printed circuits incorporate a base of glass-fabric epoxy, or some similar plastic-based substance. These materials offer a light, strong, rigid base for printed circuits.

A fourth (but less commonly used) type of printed circuit is known as the *flexible printed circuit*. Copper traces are deposited onto a layer of plastic. Traces can be included on both sides of this base layer to form a single or double-sided circuit. Traces are then covered by an insulating layer of plastic. Using alternate layers of copper traces and flexible insulation, it is possible to form multilayer flexible printed circuits.

Flexible circuits have the ability to fold and conform to tight or irregular spaces. As a result, flexible circuits are often used as wiring harnesses—that is, components are placed as needed, then a flexible circuit is inserted and attached by screws or solder to interconnect each component. Individual components are rarely soldered to a flexible PC as they are with a rigid PC board.

Printed circuit repairs

Printed circuits are generally very reliable structures, but physical abuse can easily damage the rigid phenolic or glass base, as well as any printed traces. If damage occurs to a PC board, you should know what signs of damage to look for, and what steps you can take to correct any damage. There are four general PC board problems that you should know about: lead failure, printed trace break, board cracks, and heat damage.

Lead failure   Normally a good solder joint holds a wire or component lead tightly into its connection on a PC board. However, if that wire or connection is suddenly placed under a lot of stress, the solder joint can fail partially or completely, as shown in Fig. 4-29. Stress can be applied with sudden, sharp movements such as dropping or striking the computer.

Lead failure is not always an obvious problem unless the lead or wire is away from its PC land entirely. If the conductor is still making contact with the PC board, its electrical connection might be broken or intermittent. You can test an intermittent connection by exposing the PC board, then gently tapping on the board or suspect conductor. By tapping different areas of the board, it is possible to focus on an intermittent connection in the area which is most sensitive to the tapping. You can also test suspected intermittent connections by gently wiggling wires or component leads. The component or conductor most sensitive to the touch is probably the one that is intermittent.

Another case of lead failure can occur on double-sided or multilayer PC boards during desoldering. Various layers are connected together by plated holes. Through-hole component leads are typically soldered into plated through-holes. If you pull out a conductor without removing all of the solder, you can rip out part or all of the hole's plating along with the conductor. When this happens, the electrical integrity at that point of the PC board is broken.

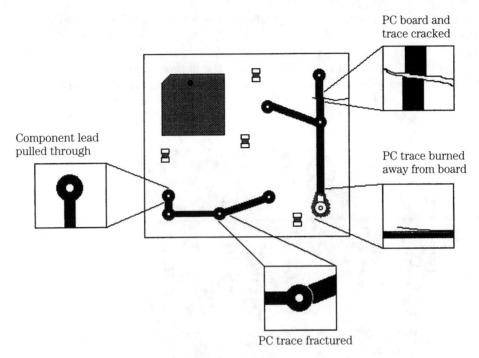

4-29 Four typical PC board problems.

For double-sided PC boards, this can often be corrected by resoldering the new component lead on both sides of the PC board. There is usually enough exposed copper on the component side to ensure a reasonable solder fillet. Unfortunately, there is no reliable way to solder a new lead to each layer of a multilayer board. As a result, a damaged through-hole on a multilayer board might be beyond repair, and the board must be replaced.

The best way to avoid damaging a plated through-hole is to heat a joint while removing the lead simultaneously. Grasp the lead with a pair of needlenose pliers while heating the joint. When solder is molten, gently pull out the component lead. You can then safely clean up any residual solder with conventional desoldering tools. **Note:** Never grasp the component lead with your bare fingers. The entire lead reaches soldering temperatures almost immediately. Always wear safety glasses when soldering or desoldering.

Printed trace break   Another common problem that takes place in printed circuits is known as a trace break. This can also be the result of a physical shock or sudden impact to the PC board. In this case, a portion of the printed trace (usually where a solder pad meets the remainder of the trace) can suffer a fine, hairline fracture that results in an open or intermittent circuit. What makes this particular problem especially difficult is that a trace break can be almost impossible to see upon visual inspection. You must often wiggle each solder pad until you find the fractured connection. Large, heavy components, such as transformers or relays, are often prime candidates for trace breaks, so start your search there.

Do not attempt to create a bridge of solder across the break, or jumper directly across the fracture. Solder does not adhere well to the chemical coatings often used with PC boards, so such quick fixes rarely last long. In order to correct a printed trace break, you should desolder and remove the broken portion of the trace, then solder a jumper wire between two associated component leads—do not solder directly to the printed trace. You can also use the materials in commercial PC board repair packages such as the CIR-KIT PC repair kit from PACE, Inc. (Fig. 4-30).

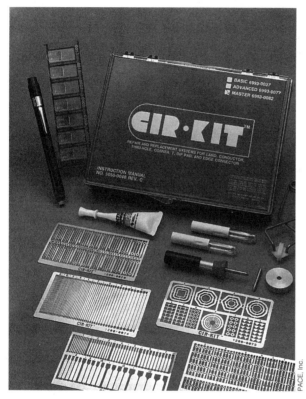

4-30 A circuit board repair kit.

Board cracks   Under extreme conditions, the phenolic or glass-epoxy circuit board itself can actually crack. This is not unusual for equipment that has been dropped or abused. When a crack occurs, the course of the crack can sever one or more printed traces. Luckily, board cracks are fairly easy to detect on sight. By following the crack, it is a simple matter to locate any severed traces on the board surface.

As with trace breaks, the best, most reliable method of repairing broken traces is to solder a wire jumper between two associated solder pads or component leads. Never try to make a solder bridge across a break. Solder does not adhere well to the chemicals used on many PC board traces, so such fixes do not last long. If the physical crack is severe, you might want to work a bit of good-quality epoxy adhesive into the crack to help reinforce the board. Multilayer PC boards cannot be repaired practically.

Heat damage   Printed copper traces are bonded firmly to the phenolic or glass-epoxy board underneath. When extreme heat is applied to the copper traces, however, it is possible to separate the copper trace from the board. This type of damage usually occurs during soldering or desoldering when concentrated heat is applied with a soldering iron.

The only real remedy for this type of damage is to carefully cut off that portion of the separated trace to prevent the loose copper from accidentally shorting out other components, and solder a wire jumper from the component lead to an adjacent solder pad or component lead.

5
Solid-state
memory devices

Solid-state memory faults constitute a large percentage of computer problems. Because memory ICs contain the program instructions and data needed for execution by a microprocessor, the loss of even one bit can have a catastrophic effect on the system. This chapter introduces some of the most important memory concepts, shows you a selection of IC configurations, and presents a series of troubleshooting techniques to help you track down and correct memory problems (Fig. 5-1). For a detailed discussion of notebook and laptop computer memory troubleshooting, refer to *Troubleshooting and Repairing Notebook, Palmtop, and Pen Computers: A Technician's Guide* (Windcrest/McGraw-Hill).

5-1 A 16 Mbit memory IC.

Texas Instruments, Inc.

Memory concepts

Before you jump into memory troubleshooting, you should understand the concepts behind memory device organization and operation. Memory devices have evolved rapidly along with microprocessors over the last decade or so. Such intense evolution has resulted in an amazingly diverse selection of devices that are tailored to optimize almost any computer system. In spite of this diversity, however, the basic concepts and operations of solid-state memory are virtually universal. Let's start at the beginning.

Storage cells

Memory ICs store programs and data as a long series of binary 1s and 0s, where 1 represents the presence of a signal voltage, and 0 represents the absence of a signal voltage. Because each bit represents a voltage level, the voltage must be stored in an electronic circuit. Each circuit is known as a *storage cell*. The contents of storage cells can be copied to a bus or other waiting device (known as *reading*). Some storage cells also allow new signal levels to be copied in from external bus signals (called *writing*). The exact structure and construction of a storage cell depends on the characteristics of the particular memory device. By combining storage cells into arrays, as shown in Fig. 5-2, memory circuits can be created to hold many millions of bits. Storage cell arrays are fabricated on small silicon wafers as integrated circuits. There are typically six broad types of storage cells in use today: SRAM, DRAM, ROM, PROM, EPROM, and EEPROM. Any computer can contain several of these memory types. The following sections present an overview of memory types, and chapter 8 covers these types in more detail.

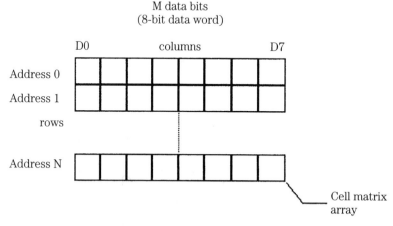

5-2 A typical storage cell array.

RAM vs. ROM

The two common threads that run through each memory type are the acronyms RAM and ROM. *Random-access memory* (RAM) devices are somewhat misnamed, because all memory ICs can be accessed randomly. The term "read/write memory" is more descriptive, but RAM is a traditional label that is difficult to overcome. There are two characteristics that define a RAM device. First, RAM storage cells can be both read from and written to, so the contents can be altered at will. Second, RAM devices are *volatile*—that is, a constant supply of power is required to sustain RAM contents. If power fails or the computer is turned off, RAM contents are lost. RAM is ideal for holding the loaded programs and data needed by the computer during execution.

The alternative type of memory is *read-only memory* (ROM). ROM storage cells can only be read during normal computer operation (although EEPROM devices can be electrically erased and rewritten while in the computer). ROM devices are also *nonvolatile*, so ROM cells retain their contents when the system's power is off. These characteristics make ROM devices well suited for holding POST and BIOS programs that do not change.

Device types

Static RAM (SRAM) stores bits in cells that act like electronic switches. SRAM cells turn electricity on (logic 1) or off (logic 0) to reflect the cell's state. In practice, an SRAM cell is usually a flip-flop circuit that is preset (logic 1) or reset (logic 0) when written. The flip-flop stores the condition of the bit until it is altered by a subsequent write operation (or until power is removed). Once data is stored in an SRAM cell, it is retained indefinitely without any further interaction by the computer. Unfortunately, SRAM cells are physically large and consume a relatively large amount of power in active use. Today's SRAM ICs are generally limited to 256K.

Dynamic RAM (DRAM) stores bits in the form of electrical charges on incredibly small solid-state capacitors. A single MOS transistor is included with each capacitor to act as a switch or control element. The presence or absence of a charge defines whether the bit is a logic 1 or logic 0. By making each storage capacitor very small, charges can be added or withdrawn from a capacitor in only a few nanoseconds. Because each storage cell is extremely small and uses almost no current, storage density is exceptionally high, and power dissipation is very low.

Unfortunately, DRAMs are not nearly as simple to operate as SRAM devices. The electrical charges used to represent each bit condition have a life span of only a few milliseconds or so. After that, charge levels are irretrievably lost and memory is corrupted. To preserve the charge conditions in a DRAM, each cell must be periodically refreshed. It is because of this need for regular, active maintenance that these devices are called "dynamic." Refresh operation is covered later in this chapter.

Conventional ROM (or mask ROM) cells are nothing more than the absence (logic 1) or presence (logic 0) of a physical electrical connection. The precise pattern of 1s and 0s is specified by the purchaser and fabricated onto the ROM during its manufacture. Once a mask ROM IC is created, its contents can never be changed. Because no active circuitry is needed to store 1s and 0s, ROM ICs offer some of the highest storage densities available. ROM devices are also available in a number of other programmable versions (PROM, EPROM, and EEPROM). As with all types of ROM devices, mask ROM does not lose its contents when computer power is turned off.

Due to the time delays and expense of having ROMs manufactured, it is usually much faster and less expensive to "program" your own ROMs until their contents are proven and thoroughly debugged. *Programmable read-only memory* (PROM) ICs work very much like mask ROMs, in that logic levels are established by the presence of simple electrical connections. However, PROMs are manufactured with all possible connections in place (all logic 0s). A piece of equipment called a *PROM programmer* reads the program to be loaded from the computer and steps through each address. Each bit that must be a logic 1 is "zapped" with a high-voltage pulse which destroys that connection to form a logic 1. This process is called *burning* the PROM. Once a PROM is programmed, its contents cannot be cleared or rewritten.

Naturally, it is better to recycle memory devices instead of throwing them away over a single bit error. *Erasable PROMS* (EPROMS) are used to provide thousands of erase-rewrite cycles in a useful lifetime. EPROM bits are not stored as physical connections, but as electrical charges deposited onto the IC's substrate. Microscopic transistors detect the presence or absence of charge as a logic 1 or logic 0, respectively. Once a charge is deposited, it remains in place permanently.

To erase an EPROM, the semiconductor die holding the electrical charges must be excited by short-wavelength ultraviolet (UV) light. UV allows the charges to dissipate and return each EPROM storage cell to a "blank" condition. You can recognize EPROMs by the quartz or plastic window in the IC body. Note that sunlight and fluorescent light contain wavelengths that can erase EPROM data, so you should keep the erasure window covered with a piece of black tape or an adhesive label.

Removing an IC from a circuit in order to erase and reprogram it can be a very inconvenient (and potentially damaging) task. An *electrically erasable PROM* (EEPROM) is a modified version of the EPROM whose contents can be erased using electrical pulses instead of ultraviolet light. This approach allows blocks of addresses (not necessarily the entire device) to be erased and rewritten while the IC is still in the circuit. An EEPROM IC retains its contents when the system's power is off.

Elements of a memory IC

It takes much more than just a few storage cells to make a working memory IC. Memory ICs can be broken down into four segments: the storage array, the address buffer and decoding circuits, the data bus buffer circuits, and the control circuits. Each of these elements are very important to memory operation. Figure 5-3 illustrates these areas in a typical memory IC.

Storage cells must be organized into a two-dimensional *storage array* (or matrix) made up of rows and columns. This memory array is where information is actually stored. Depending on the type of cells used, there can be millions of cells in the array. However, additional circuitry is needed to select which cells in the array are active, to manage the data at those cells, and to control the flow of data into or out of the IC.

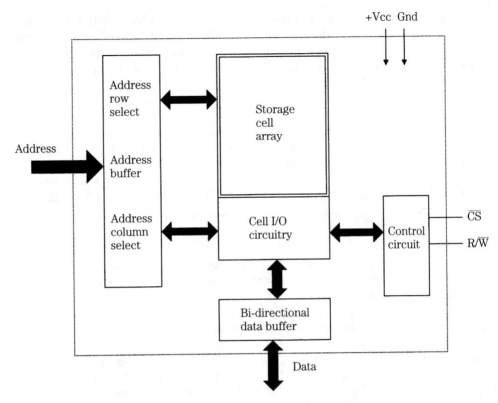

5-3 Block diagram of a simple RAM IC.

Address signals select the active cells. Once valid address signals are applied to the IC, address decoding circuitry enables the proper cells. Each address may select 1, 2, 4, 8, or 16 cells depending on the array's configuration and its address decoding circuitry. It is important to note that memory ICs are defined by their address/data organization. For example, a 16K IC can be organized in several ways:

- 16K x 1 bit (16,384 address locations with 1 bit per address)
- 4K x 4 bits (4096 addresses with 4 bits per address)
- 2K x 8 bits (2048 addresses with 8 bits per address)

and so on—but it is still a 16K IC. Today, most high-density memory ICs are provided with many address lines, but few bits per address. You will see later how individual ICs can be combined to provide a complete data bus. Knowledge of memory organization is vital if you must find ICs for replacement or upgrade. A schematic or block diagram of your system usually indicates memory size and organization. You can also determine memory size by locating the IC in a manufacturer's data or cross-reference book.

Once the desired cells are active, *control signals* determine how the IC responds to data. There are two common control signals: Chip Select ($\overline{CS}$) and Write Enable ($\overline{WE}$). The Write Enable signal is also referred to as Read/Write ($R/\overline{W}$). When the Chip Select is logic 1, the IC is disabled, so it does not interact with the data bus at all, regardless of what address is applied. In the disabled state, the IC's data lines are neither logic 1 or logic 0, but a high-impedance state that effectively "disconnects" the IC from the data bus . The Chip Select signal is handy for controlling multiple memory ICs that share the same bus.

When the Chip Select is logic 0, the IC is enabled. Data signals at the selected address can leave and enter the memory array normally. The Read/Write signal defines the direction of data flow. When the Read/Write signal is logic 1, data at the selected address leaves the IC through a data buffer—the IC is read. If the Read/Write signal is logic 0 (and the storage array uses RAM cells) data entering the IC is buffered and stored in the cells selected by the address signals—the IC is written. Address decoding, data buffering, and IC control must work together to operate the storage array.

Access time

In an ideal memory device, selected data would be instantly available at the IC's data lines. In the real world, however, there is always some finite amount of delay between the time when an address input is valid, and the time when selected data becomes valid at the data lines. This time delay is known as *access time*. Even though memory IC access time is measured in nanoseconds, it has a profound impact on the overall performance of your computer. Memory devices that are not fast enough to keep pace with the microprocessor can seriously impair performance and necessitate the use of *wait states*. DRAM components typically have the shortest access times, while EPROM and EEPROM devices have the longest access times.

Wait states

The importance of memory performance became evident in the early 1980s during the introduction of 80286-class machines (IBM ATs). Memory ICs of the day were unable to keep pace with the 80286, which led to serious system performance problems. Designers overcame this problem by slowing down the microprocessor during memory access. This was done by adding wait states, which cause the microprocessor to suspend its activities for one or more clock cycles. This allows slower memory to catch up. The number of wait states depends on the relationship between memory speed and microprocessor speed. Larger disparities require more wait states, and vice versa. Wait states are still used in some low-end computers today, but they are much more widely used in older computers.

Refresh operations

The electrical charges placed in each DRAM storage cell must be periodically replenished, or refreshed, every few milliseconds. Without refresh, DRAM data can be lost. In principle, refresh requires that each storage cell be read and rewritten to the memory array. This is typically accomplished by reading and rewriting an entire row of the array at one time. Each row of bits is sequentially read into the *sense/refresh amplifier* (part of the DRAM IC), which recharges the appropriate storage capacitors, then rewrites each row bit to the array. In operation, a row of bits is automatically refreshed whenever an array row is selected. Thus, the entire memory array can be refreshed by reading each row in the array every few milliseconds.

The key to refresh is in the way DRAMs are addressed. Unlike other memory ICs that supply all address signals to the IC simultaneously, a DRAM is addressed in a two-step sequence. The overall address is separated into a row (low) address and a column (high) address. Row-address bits are placed on the DRAM address bus first, and the row address select ($\overline{RAS}$) line is pulsed to logic 0 in order to multiplex the bits into the IC's address decoding circuitry. The low portion of the address activates an entire array row and causes each bit in the row to be sensed and refreshed. Logic 0s remain logic 0s, and logic 1s are recharged to their full value.

Column-address bits are then placed on the DRAM address bus, and the column address select ($\overline{CAS}$) is pulsed to logic 0. The column portion of the address selects the appropriate bits within the chosen row. If a read operation is taking place, the selected bits pass through the data buffer to the data bus. During a write operation, the read/write line must be logic 0, and valid data must be available to the IC before $\overline{CAS}$ is strobed. New data bits are then placed in their corresponding locations in the memory array.

Even if the IC is not being accessed for reading or writing, the memory array must still be refreshed to ensure data integrity. Fortunately, refresh can be accomplished by interrupting the microprocessor to run a refresh routine which simply steps through every row address in sequence (column addresses need not be selected for simple refresh). This row-only (or $\overline{RAS}$-only) refresh technique speeds the refresh process. Although refreshing DRAM every few milliseconds may seem like a constant aggravation, the computer can execute quite a few instructions before being interrupted for refresh. There are several other refresh techniques that can be used in DRAM systems, but they are not covered in this book.

Enhanced memory

Memory speed is directly related to your computer system's performance. Microprocessors constantly access system memory for instructions and data. If memory is not fast enough to keep up with the CPU, the wait states that must be added slow down the system and waste the potential power offered by today's new CPUs. A large portion of computer design has been directed toward improving memory performance. In some cases, memory technology has been modified and tweaked to supply enhanced performance in certain operating modes. In other cases, ordinary memory ICs are used in optimized circuit arrangements. The following sections introduce you to some of the memory enhancement techniques that might be used in your computer.

Page-mode RAM

One of the main objectives of memory is to keep wait states at zero. Having no wait states results in faster system performance. Page-mode RAM uses elements of both static and dynamic memory to reduce wait states. Page-mode RAM divides its total memory array onto subsections (called *pages*) of about 2K each. When data is repeatedly addressed from within the same page, memory can be accessed without wait states. When memory access must take place from a different page, wait states are added until the new page is accessed. The most efficient operation is achieved when page-to-page access is kept to a minimum. Using page-mode RAM can improve overall memory performance by up to 60%.

Banked memory

Another method of improving system memory performance is to *bank,* or *interleave,* the system RAM. Interleaved memory is similar to page-mode RAM because system performance is improved when sequential (contiguous) memory locations are read, but ordinary system RAM ICs can be used instead of page-mode RAM, and bank sizes can be on the order of megabytes.

System RAM is divided into two or four banks (or more). Sequential bits are held on successive banks (i.e, byte 1 is in bank 1, byte 2 is in bank 2, byte 3 is in bank 1, byte 4 is in bank 2, and so on) so the CPU steps from bank to bank. While the microprocessor is reading one bank, the alternate bank is cycling so that no waiting is required when the CPU reads again—thus, wait states can be eliminated as long as the next bits to be read are in an alternate bank. If data must be accessed out of order, wait states are inserted automatically until a new alternating sequence is running. Banked memory can improve system performance by up to 75% while still using standard memory ICs.

Video memory

The image you see on a computer's display is actually held in a small area of memory called *video RAM* (VRAM). VRAM acts as a frame buffer where a bit, byte, or several bytes are used to represent each element (or *pixel*) of the picture, depending on the screen mode. The display controller reads through video memory from 30 to 60 times each second and recreates (or *retraces*) the image specified in memory. The computer writes to VRAM in order to update the image being displayed.

However, ordinary memory ICs cannot be read and written simultaneously. The time delay caused by waiting for reading to finish before writing can begin is an annoying problem. Many video systems now use specialized VRAM ICs with two data paths—one for input and one for output. By using two independent data paths, the same memory location can be read and written simultaneously. The CPU writes updated image information to video memory at its own pace, and the video controller sequentially reads image data independently.

Memory cache

Caching is a memory speed enhancement technique used with today's highest-performance systems. A cache places a relatively small amount of very fast memory between the CPU and the bulk of on-line memory. A cache controller circuit keeps track of the microprocessor's memory access and tries to keep the cache filled with data that the CPU is most likely to need next. A *cache hit* occurs when the needed data is found in the cache—this data is accessed without wait states and system performance is enhanced. If the needed data is not in the cache, a *cache miss* occurs and data is accessed from system memory at normal speeds (including wait states). The cache is then refilled if necessary and the hit-or-miss access continues.

The size of a cache is the biggest overall performance factor. Most practical caches contain 8K to 128K. Of course, larger or smaller caches may be used, but small caches mean more cache misses (and lower overall system performance). Large caches certainly mean more cache hits, but the cost and physical size of additional memory becomes impractical. The microprocessor uses one of three methods to determine whether needed data is in the cache: *direct-mapped, full-associative,* and *set-associative.* This chapter does not detail these particular methods, but it is important for you to understand the nature and purpose of a memory cache.

Shadow memory

Whether you are considering the BIOS ROM on a computer's motherboard, or a ROM IC on an expansion board, all ROM devices are frustratingly slow. Access times often exceed several hundred nanoseconds. As a result, ROM access requires a large number of wait states, slowing down the system's performance. This problem is compounded because the routines stored in BIOS (especially the video BIOS ROM on the video board) are some of the most frequently accessed routines in a computer.

Beginning with the 80386-class computers, some designs employed a memory technique called *shadowing.* ROM contents are loaded into an area of fast RAM during system initialization, then the computer maps the fast RAM into memory locations used by the ROM devices. Whenever ROM routines must be accessed during run-time, information is taken from the shadow ROM instead of the actual ROM IC. The ROM performance can be improved by at least 300%.

Shadow memory is also useful for ROM devices that do not use the full available data bus width. For example, a 16-bit computer system may hold an expansion board containing an 8-bit ROM IC. The system would have to access the ROM twice to extract a single 16-bit word. If the computer is a 32-bit machine, the 8-bit ROM would have to be addressed four times to make a complete 32-bit word. You can imagine the hideous system delays that can be encountered. Loading the ROM to shadow memory in advance virtually eliminates such delays. Shadowing can usually be turned on or off through the system's setup routines.

Memory configurations

One memory IC alone cannot possibly begin to handle a system's memory requirements. In most cases, multiple memory ICs must be ganged together to provide the necessary amount of addresses and data bits to accommodate your system. Figure 5-4 illustrates a typical memory IC arrangement in a PC. There are 9 DRAM ICs (8 data bits and 1 parity bit). Each IC itself provides 4 Mbits of storage arranged as 4M x 1 bits (for PCs with a 16-bit data bus, 8 additional ICs would be needed). By addressing 9 ICs simultaneously, each IC can provide 1 bit of the data bus (plus a parity bit). IC1 provides D0, IC2 provides D1, IC3 provides D2, and so on. R/W, $\overline{\text{RAS}}$, $\overline{\text{CAS}}$, and $\overline{\text{CS}}$ signals can also drive each of the ICs simultaneously. A parity bit is added to each data byte as an error checking measure. There are two types of parity used in memory circuits: even and odd. For even parity, the parity bit is made logic

Address bus

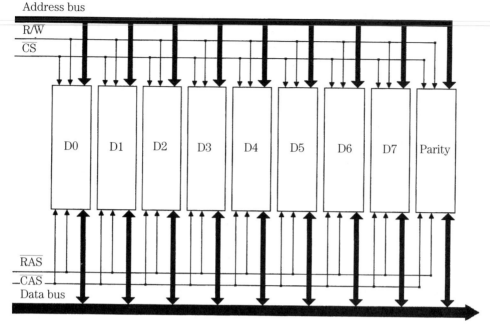

R/W
CS

| D0 | D1 | D2 | D3 | D4 | D5 | D6 | D7 | Parity |

RAS
—CAS
Data bus

5-4 An example of DRAM organization.

1 to make the total number of data bits even. For odd parity, the parity bit is made logic 1 to make the total number of data bits odd.

The chip select signal is generated by decoding the upper address lines to select the proper *address range* for these 9 ICs. For example, it takes 22 bits (2^{22}) to address 4 million locations, but computers often have 24 or more address lines. The uppermost two bits can be decoded into four 4Mb segments. In other words, the arrangement of Fig. 5-4 can be duplicated four times in the computer. The uppermost two address bits determine which of the four 4Mb segments is active, and the lower 22 address bits determine which location within any one 4Mb segment is active.

Of course, there are many possible combinations of memory ICs, but this gives you a general idea of how ICs can be arranged to provide substantial amounts of system memory. Computers typically supply several such memory blocks as a base configuration. Additional memory blocks can be added later in the form of SIMMs or memory cards.

Memory organization

The memory in your computer represents the result of evolution over several computer generations. Memory operation is handled by your system's microprocessor, so as CPUs have improved, memory-handling capabilities have improved as well. Today's microprocessors, such as the 80486 and Pentium, are capable of addressing more than 4Gb of system memory—well beyond the levels of contemporary software applications. Unfortunately, the early PCs were not nearly so powerful. Older PCs could only address 1Mb of memory due to limitations of the 8088 microprocessor.

Because backward compatibility is so important to computer users, the drawbacks and limitations of older systems had to be carried forward into newer computers instead of being eliminated. Newer systems overcome their inherent limitations by adding different classes of memory, along with the hardware and software to access the memory. This part of the chapter describes the three classic types of computer memory: conventional, extended, and expanded memory. It also describes high memory concepts. Note that these memory types have nothing to do with the actual ICs in your system, but rather with the way in which software uses the memory.

Conventional memory

Conventional memory is the traditional 640K assigned to the DOS Memory Area. The original PCs used microprocessors that could only address 1Mb of memory (called *real-mode* or *base memory*). Out of that 1Mb, portions of the memory must be set aside for basic system functions. BIOS code, video memory, interrupt vectors, and BIOS data are only some of the areas that require *reserved memory*. The remaining 640K is available to load and run an application, which can be any combination of executable code and data. The original PC only provided 512K for the DOS program area, but computer designers quickly learned that another 128K could be added to the DOS area while still retaining enough memory for overhead functions, so 512K became 640K.

Every IBM-compatible PC still provides a 640K base memory range, and most application programs continue to fit within that limit to ensure backward compatibility to older systems. However, the drawbacks of the 8088 CPU were soon apparent. More memory had to added to the computer for its evolution to continue. Yet, memory had to be added in a way that did not interfere with the conventional memory area.

Extended memory

The 80286 processor, introduced in IBM's PC/AT, was envisioned to overcome the 640K barrier by incorporating a *protected mode* of addressing. The 80286 can address up to 16Mb of memory in protected mode, while its successors (the 80386 and 80486) can handle 4Gb of protected-mode memory. Today, virtually all computer systems provide several Mb of this *extended memory*. Besides an advanced microprocessor, another key element for extended memory is software. Memory-management software must be loaded in advance for the computer to access its extended memory. Microsoft's DOS 5.0 provides an extended memory manager utility, but there are other off-the-shelf utilities as well.

Unfortunately, DOS itself cannot make use of extended memory. You can fill the extended memory with data, but the executable code comprising the program remains limited to the original 640K of base memory. Some programs written with *DOS extenders* can overcome the 640K limit, but the additional code needed for the extenders can make such programs slower and more inefficient. A DOS extender is essentially a software module containing its own memory-management code, which is compiled into the final application program.

The DOS extender loads a program in real-mode memory. After the program is loaded, it switches program control to the protected-mode memory. When the program in protected mode needs to execute a DOS (real-mode) function, the DOS extender converts protected-mode addresses into real-mode addresses, copies any necessary program data from protected- to real-mode locations, switches the CPU to real-mode addressing, and carries out the function. The DOS extender then copies any results (if necessary) back to protected-mode addresses, switches the system to protected-mode once again, and the program continues to run. This back-and-forth conversion overhead results in less than optimum performance compared to strictly real-mode programs.

Even with multiple megabytes of extended memory typically available, it is possible (but unlikely) that any one program will utilize all of the extended memory. Multiple programs that use extended memory must not attempt to utilize the same memory locations. If conflicts occur, a catastrophic system crash is almost inevitable. To prevent conflicts in extended memory, memory manager software can make use of three major industry standards; the Extended Memory Specification (XMS), the Virtual Control Program Interface (VCPI), or the DOS Protected-Mode Interface (PMI). This chapter does not detail these standards, but you should know where they are used.

Expanded memory

Expanded memory is another popular technique used to overcome the traditional 640K limit of real-mode addressing. Expanded memory differs from extended memory in the way memory is used. Instead of trying to address physical memory locations outside of the conventional memory range as extended memory does, expanded memory blocks are switched into the base memory range where the CPU can access it in real mode. The original expanded memory specification (called the Lotus-Intel-Microsoft, LIM, or EMS specification) used 16K banks of memory which were mapped into a 64K range of real-mode memory existing just above the video memory range. Thus, four "blocks" of expanded memory (out of a possible 8Mb) could be dealt with simultaneously in real mode.

Early implementations of expanded memory utilize special expansion boards that switch blocks of memory, but later CPUs that support memory mapping allow expanded memory managers (EMMs or LIMs) to supply software-only solutions for 80386- and 80486-based machines. At the time of this writing, EMS/LIM 4.0 is the latest version of the expanded memory standard. It handles up to 32Mb of memory. An expanded memory manager such as the DOS utility EMM386.EXE allows the extended memory sitting in your computer to emulate expanded memory. For most practical purposes, expanded memory is more useful than extended memory, because its ability to map directly to the real mode allows support for program multitasking.

To use expanded memory, programs must be written specifically to take advantage of the function calls and subroutines needed to switch memory blocks. Functions are completely specified in the LIM/EMS 4.0 standard.

High DOS memory

The upper 384K of real-mode memory is not available to DOS because it is dedicated to handling memory requirements of the physical computer system. This is called the *high DOS memory range*. However, even the most advanced PCs do not use the entire 384K, so there is often a substantial amount of unused memory existing in your system's real-mode range. Late model CPUs like the 80386 and 80486 can remap extended memory into the range unused by your system. Because this "found" memory space is not contiguous with your 640K DOS space, DOS application programs cannot use the space, but small independent drivers and TSRs can be loaded and run from this area. The advantage to using high DOS memory is that more of the 640K DOS range remains available for your application program. Memory management programs (such as the utilities found with DOS 5.0) are needed to locate and remap these memory blocks.

High memory

There is a peculiar anomaly that occurs with CPUs offering extended memory: they can access one segment (about 64K) of extended memory beyond the real-mode area. This capability arises because of the address line layout on late-model CPUs. As a result, the real-mode operation can access roughly 64K above the 1Mb limit. Like high DOS memory, this "found" 64K is not contiguous with the normal 640K DOS memory range, so DOS cannot use this high memory to load a DOS application, but device drivers and TSRs can be placed in high memory. DOS 5.0 is intentionally designed so that its 40K of code can be easily moved into this high memory area. With DOS loaded into high memory, an extra 40K or so is available within the 640K DOS range.

Memory devices

Another important aspect of memory troubleshooting is recognizing the packaging that contains memory ICs. Although memory circuits are all fabricated onto minute pieces of silicon wafer, each chip is hermetically sealed into a leaded container which allows the device to be handled and integrated into larger circuit assemblies. You will encounter several major classes of IC packaging: DIPs, SIPs, ZIPs, SIMMs, and memory cards. The package style used in a computer generally depends on the vintage of the system, so you should be familiar with each package type as shown in Fig. 5-5.

DIPs

Dual in-line packages (DIPs) are the oldest solid-state memory device package. They were used for the original IBM PC, XT, and AT classes of computer. DIPs are easy to handle, and can be inserted into IC sockets with very little skill. Many early computers provided empty expansion sockets on the motherboard to allow the addition of memory ICs (which were very expensive at the time). If you have ever worked on an older computer, you have probably seen the long rows of empty IC sockets in a central location on the motherboard, or on third-party memory expansion cards.

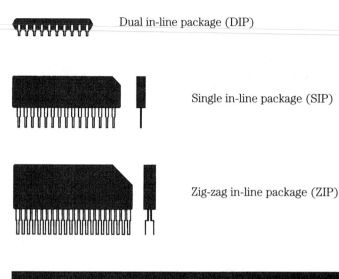

Dual in-line package (DIP)

Single in-line package (SIP)

Zig-zag in-line package (ZIP)

Single in-line
memory
module
(SIMM)

5-5   A comparison of memory packages.

Inserting a DIP is a simple matter of straightening its pins (DIP pins usually have a slight outward bend that is marginally wider than the socket), aligning pin 1 in the proper orientation, and gently pushing the IC into its socket without bending any of its pins in the process. If a pin is bent by accident, the IC is probably ruined. Removing a DIP can easily be accomplished by pulling the IC evenly out of its socket with an inexpensive DIP removal tool. You can also use a regular screwdriver blade to gently pry the IC up and out of its socket. Pry just a bit on alternating ends of the IC to keep the pins from bending. If you pry only one end of the IC out of its socket, the pins remaining in the socket will bend. Excessively bent leads will ruin the IC.

SIPs and ZIPs

As memory density increased and computer sizes decreased, other packaging techniques were employed for memory ICs. The *single in-line package* (SIP) has all of its pins along one edge of a vertically oriented container. The *zig-zag in-line package* (ZIP) also has its pins along one side of a vertically oriented container, but ZIPs overcome the pin spacing limitations of a SIP by staggering its pins in a zig-zag pattern. A ZIP can handle many more pins than a similarly sized SIP, so ZIPs were used more often for high-density memory in the later AT clones and early 80386-class PCs.

Like any DIP, SIPs and ZIPs are through-hole components that can either be hard-soldered into place during motherboard (or expansion module) assembly, or inserted into preexisting sockets during your upgrade. Unfortunately, SIPs and ZIPs never gained popularity because their single-edge design did not remain in sockets very well. Thermal heating and cooling tended to rock the ICs right out of their sockets.

SIMMs

Another reason for the demise of DIPs, SIPs, and ZIPs was the introduction and broad adoption of surface-mount ICs. It was no longer possible for users to expand memory by simply plugging in ICs because surface-mount ICs cannot be plugged in (except for PLCCs and PGAs, but they are not popular memory packages at this time). Surface-mount memory ICs are fabricated onto small printed circuit modules. These "memory modules" could then be plugged into corresponding receptacles on the motherboard. The *single in-line memory module* (SIMM) remains a popular device for later 80386-class and almost all 80486-class computers. SIMMs also make it cost-effective to create bulk modules—memory can be expanded by megabytes at a time instead of kilobytes. There are no pins to bend or break, and the module assembly can easily be clipped into place by plastic retainers. SIMMs are vertically oriented, so they take up a minimum amount of "real estate" on the motherboard.

SIMMs are relatively easy to install and remove. You need only be concerned with aligning the SIMM correctly and making sure it is evenly and completely inserted into its socket. No special tools are needed. To removing a SIMM, you simply unclip the module and pull it out of its socket. You must be careful not to accidentally snap or crack the module by squeezing it. **Note:** Always use an antistatic wrist strap and antistatic packaging when handling SIMMs. Refer to chapter 4 for more information on static electricity and ESD protection.

Memory cards

No matter whether you use a DIP, SIP, ZIP, or SIMM, there is one common requirement for their installation or removal—the computer must be disassembled. While disassembly may not be a problem for large, open desktop systems where you have easy access to the motherboard, small computers like laptops or notebooks are incredibly dense and complex assemblies. Notebook and subnotebook computer manufacturers have long sought to prevent casual disassembly by allowing memory modules like SIMMs to be added through prefabricated openings in the unit's housing.

The next step in the evolution of memory packaging was to place high-density memory devices into a small, slender enclosure—rather like a credit card. The card can then be plugged into the small computer. This convenience eliminates the need to disassemble the computer's housing. The *memory card* is designed with a standard connector scheme that allows cards from almost any manufacturer to operate in your system. As you will see in chapter 8, there are many different types and uses of memory cards, other than to simply expand your system's memory capacity. DRAM cards are very popular for adding memory to notebook and subnotebook computers, as well as other peripherals such as laser printers.

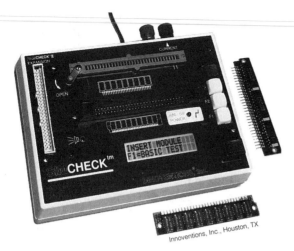

5-6 An Innoventions SIMCHECK memory module tester.

Innoventions, Inc., Houston, TX

5-7 A SIMCHECK adaptor for PS/2 modules.

Innoventions, Inc., Houston, TX

Innoventions, Inc., Houston, TX

5-8 An Innoventions Static RAM tester.

Memory troubleshooting

Armed with an understanding of basic memory concepts and packaging, we can now turn to memory troubleshooting. Ultimately, the objective of memory troubleshooting is to locate the defective memory module (or IC in older computers) and replace it. The trick is to locate the defective item. Every computer performs a check of its memory components when the computer is first activated, and continually checks the integrity of memory contents while in operation. If a memory problem exists or develops during operation, the computer is almost always able to identify the problem's location. It is then a matter of replacing the IC or module that resides in that location.

The problem commonly encountered in memory troubleshooting is that the translation from a hexadecimal address (shown in an error message) to an actual IC or SIMM is not straightforward. Every computer is designed a bit differently, and uses memory components of varying configurations. Even SIMMs are built slightly differently for each system model. Unless you have a memory map comparing address ranges with IC or SIMM slots for your particular machine, you must trouble-shoot memory on a trial-and-error basis. Isolation by substitution is the most common approach to memory repair.

Memory test equipment

If you are working in a repair shop, or plan to be testing a substantial number of memory devices, you should consider acquiring some specialized test equipment. A memory tester, such as the SIMCHECK from Innoventions, Inc. (Fig. 5-6), is a modular microprocessor-based system that can perform a thorough, comprehensive test of various SIMMs and indicate the specific IC that has failed (if any). The system can be configured to work with specific SIMMs by installing an appropriate adapter module like the one shown in Fig. 5-7. Intelligent testers work automatically, and show the progress and results of their examinations on a multiline LCD. This totally eliminates guesswork from memory testing.

Single ICs such as DIPs and SIPs can be tested using a single-chip plug-in module. The static RAM checker illustrated in Fig. 5-8 is another test bed for checking high-performance static RAM components in a DIP package. Both Innoventions test devices work together to provide a full-featured test system. Specialized tools can be an added expense—but no more so than an oscilloscope or other piece of useful test equipment. The return on your investment is less time wasted in the repair, and fewer parts to replace.

POST operations

When your computer is first turned on, it executes a power-on self-test (POST) routine. The POST is designed to test each of the computer's major subsections before attempting to load the disk operating system. POST inspects the microprocessor, video display, keyboard, memory, and any peripheral devices that may be detected. If a fatal error is detected before the video system is initialized, a series of audible beeps sound to indicate the problem. After the video system is initialized, any other error codes are displayed on the monitor. For the purposes of this chapter, your troubleshooting will rely on error codes generated by the POST.

System CMOS setup

The variables that define how your system is configured are typically held in roughly 64 bytes managed by the computer's real-time clock (RTC) IC. The RTC is a CMOS IC which requires very little power (microamperes) in order to maintain its contents. One or more small lithium cells can typically back up your RTC's setup information for several years.

Part of the CMOS setup includes entries for the amount of conventional and expansion memory available in the system. The system reads the amount of memory that should be available from CMOS memory and compares that amount to the memory that it finds during testing. When a memory error is indicated, your first step should be to check the variables in your CMOS setup. If the backup battery fails, the memory amounts listed in CMOS memory probably does not match the actual amount of installed memory, and a POST error occurs. Try entering the proper amount of memory and warm-booting the computer. If the error goes away, try replacing the backup battery. If the error remains (or the CMOS setup contents are correct), you should suspect a fault in one or more memory ICs.

Troubleshooting with XT error codes

It seems only fitting to start a review of memory problems with the original IBM PC/XT computer. In the "good old days" of personal computing when there were only one or two commercial computers on the market, there were few memory arrangements. POST could be written very specifically, and errors could be correlated directly to memory IC location. The POST routine in an XT's BIOS ROM is designed to identify the exact bank and bit where a memory error is detected, and display that information on the computer's monitor.

IBM PC/XT computers classify a memory (RAM) failure as error code 201. In actual operation, a RAM error would appear as XXYY 201, where XX is the bank, and YY is the bit where the fault is detected. An XT is built with four RAM banks—each with nine bits (parity plus eight bits). Table 5-1 shows some bank and bit error codes for XT-class computers.

As an example, suppose an XT system displayed 0002 201. This would indicate a memory failure in bank 0 at data bit D1. You need only replace the memory IC residing at that location. Now, let's look at some symptoms.

Symptom 1: Error codes 1055 201 **or** 2055 201 **are displayed on the monitor** Both of these error codes indicate an error in the system's DIP switch settings. XTs do not use an RTC to contain a system's setup configuration, so DIP switches are used to tell the system how much memory should be present. If memory is added or removed, the appropriate switches in switch bank 2 (bits 1 to 8) and switch bank 1 (bits 3 and 4) must be set properly. Check your switch settings and reboot the computer.

Symptom 2: A PARITY CHECK 1 **error message is displayed** This error typically suggests a power supply problem—RAM ICs are not receiving the proper voltage levels. Remove all power from the computer and repair or replace the power supply.

Table 5-1. Index of IBM PC/XT error codes

XXYY 201: Memory failure

XX	Bank	YY	Bit
00	0	00	parity bit
04	1	01	D0
08	2	02	D1
0C	3	04	D2
		08	D3
		10	D4
		20	D5
		40	D6
		80	D7

Symptom 3: An XXYY 201 **error message is displayed** This is a general RAM failure indicating the bank and bit where the fault is located. XX is the faulty bank, and YY is the faulty bit. See Table 5-1 to decipher the specific bank and bit in an XT. Replace the defective IC, or bank of ICs.

Symptom 4: A PARITY ERROR 1 **message is displayed** Multiple addresses or multiple data bits are detected as faulty. In some cases, one or more ICs may be loose or inserted incorrectly in their sockets. Remove power from the system and reseat all RAM ICs. If all RAM ICs are inserted correctly, replace one IC at a time until the defective IC is located.

Troubleshooting with AT error codes

Like the XT, IBM's PC/AT was the leader of the 80286 generation. Because there was only one model (at the time), the AT also use some specific error messages to pinpoint memory (RAM or ROM) problems on the motherboard, as well as in its standard 128K and multiple 512K memory expansion devices. The 200 series error codes represent system memory errors: code 201 is a memory error, code 201 is a low order memory address line error (A0-A15), and code 203 is a high order memory address line error (A16-A23). An AT presents memory failures as AAXXXX YYYY 20X. This 10-digit code can be broken down to indicate the specific system bank and IC number, although the particular bit failure is not indicated. The first two digits (AA) represent the defective bank, while the last four digits (YYYY) show the defective IC number. It is then a matter of finding and replacing the faulty IC. Table 5-2 shows a set of error codes for early AT-class computers.

For example, suppose an IBM PC/AT displays the error message 05XXXXXX 0001 201 (disregard the Xs). This message places the error in IC 1 of bank 1 on the AT's system memory. Following are some of the common symptoms of memory failure.

Symptom 1: The number 164 **is displayed on the monitor** This is a memory size error, indicating that the amount of memory found does not match the amount of memory listed in the AT's CMOS setup. Run the AT CMOS system setup routine. Make sure that the listed memory amount matches the actual memory amount. If memory has been added or removed from the system, you should have to adjust the

Table 5-2. Index of IBM PC/AT error codes

AAXXXX YYYY 20X: Memory failure	
AA: Bank	**YYYY: Failed IC number**
00, 01, 02, 03	System Bank 0
04, 05, 06, 07	System Bank 1
08, 09	128K Memory Expansion
10, 11, 12, 13 14, 15, 16, 17	1st 512K Memory Expansion
18, 19, 1A, 1B 1C, 1D, 1E, 1F	2nd 512K Memory Expansion
20, 21, 22, 23 24, 25, 26, 27	3rd 512K Memory Expansion
28, 29, 2A, 2B 2C, 2D, 2E, 2F	4th 512K Memory Expansion
30, 31, 32, 33 34, 35, 36, 37	5th 512K Memory Expansion

figure in the CMOS setup to reflect that change. If CMOS setup parameters do not remain in the system after power is removed, try replacing the battery or RTC.

Symptom 2: An INCORRECT MEMORY SIZE **message is displayed** This message is displayed if the CMOS system setup is incorrect, or if there is an actual memory failure that is not caught with a numerical 200-series code. Check your CMOS system setup as described in symptom 1 and correct the setup if necessary. If the error persists, there is probably a failure in some portion of RAM.

Without a numerical code, it can be difficult to find the exact problem location, so adopt a divide-and-conquer strategy. Remove all expansion memory from the system, alter the CMOS setup to reflect base memory (system board) only, and retest the system. If the problem disappears, the fault is in some portion of expansion memory. If the problem still persists, you know the trouble is likely in the base or system board memory. Take a known-good RAM IC and swap RAM ICs until you locate the defective device.

If you successfully isolate the problem to the memory expansion board(s), you can adopt the same strategy. Return one board at a time to the system, updating the CMOS setup to keep track of available memory. When the error message reappears, you have found the defective board. Use a known-good RAM IC and begin a systematic swapping process until you have found the defective IC.

Symptom 3: A ROM ERROR **message is displayed** To guarantee the integrity of system ROM, a check-sum error test is performed as part of the POST. If this error occurs, one or more ROM locations may be faulty. The only alternative is to replace the system BIOS ROM(s) and retest the system.

Symptom 4: A PARITY CHECK **error or numerical 200-series error is displayed** The system has identified a specific bit-level or address-line fault in at least one memory device. With a numerical error, you can find the bank and IC that has failed. It is then a simple matter of replacing the defective IC and retesting the system. Use Table 5-2 to locate the bank and IC in an AT system.

A PARITY CHECK error, however, is not so specific as to the fault location. You should again use a divide-and-conquer strategy, as outlined in symptom 2, to isolate the general failure area. Then you can find the defective IC through trial and error.

Troubleshooting with POST/boot error messages

Since the introduction of 80286-class computers, there has been a tremendous amount of diversity in the design and layout of memory systems. Although the basic concepts of memory operation remain unchanged, every one of the hundreds of computer models manufactured today uses unique memory arrangements. Specific numeric (bank and bit) error codes have long since been rendered impractical in newer systems, where megabytes can be stored in just a few ICs. Today's 80386-class and 80486-class computers use generic POST and bootstrap error codes. The address of a fault is always presented, but there is no attempt made to correlate the fault's address to a physical IC. Fortunately, today's memory systems are so small and modular that trial-and-error isolation can often be performed rapidly. Let's look at some typical errors.

Symptom 1: An XXXX OPTIONAL ROM BAD CHECK-SUM = YYYY **error message is displayed on your monitor**   One part of the POST sequence checks for the presence of any other ROMs in the system. When another ROM is located, a check-sum test is performed to check its integrity. This error message indicates that the external or peripheral device ROM has checked bad, or its address conflicts with another device in the system. In either case, initialization cannot continue.

If you have just installed a new peripheral device when this error occurs, try changing the device's address to resolve the conflict. If the problem remains, remove the peripheral board. If this error has occurred spontaneously, remove one peripheral board at a time and retest the system until you isolate the faulty board, then replace it (or just replace its ROM, if possible).

Symptom 2: Any one of the following general RAM error messages is displayed

    Memory address line failure at XXXX, read YYYY, expecting ZZZZ
    Memory data line failure at XXXX, read YYYY, expecting ZZZZ
    Memory high address failure at XXXX, read YYYY, expecting ZZZZ
    Memory logic failure at XXXX, read YYYY, expecting ZZZZ
    Memory odd/even logic failure at XXXX, read YYYY, expecting ZZZZ
    Memory parity failure at XXXX, read YYYY, expecting ZZZZ
    Memory read/write failure at XXXX, read YYYY, expecting ZZZZ

Each of the errors shown above are general RAM error messages indicating a problem in base or extended/expanded RAM. The code XXXX is the failure address. The word YYYY is what was read back from the address, and ZZZZ is the word that was expected. The difference between these read and expected words precipitated the error.

In general, these errors indicate that at least one base RAM IC or SIMM has failed. A trial-and-error approach is usually the least expensive route in finding the problem. First, reseat each SIMM and retest the system to be sure that each SIMM is inserted and secured properly. Try a known-good SIMM in each occupied SIMM socket in series. If the error disappears when the known-good SIMM is in a slot, the old SIMM that had been displaced is probably faulty. You can go on to use specialized SIMM troubleshooting equipment to identify the defective IC, but such equipment is relatively expensive unless you intend to repair a large volume of SIMMs to the IC level.

If the problem remains unchanged even though every SIMM has been checked, the error is probably in the motherboard RAM. Because there are usually only a few RAM ICs on the motherboard, replace all of the RAM ICs (or replace the entire motherboard), and retest the system.

Symptom 3: A CACHE MEMORY FAILURE—DISABLING CACHE **error message is displayed** One or more of the fast cache memory ICs on your motherboard is defective. Your best course is to either replace the cache RAM IC(s) or replace the entire motherboard. You will probably need a schematic diagram or a detailed block diagram of your system in order to locate the cache memory IC(s).

Symptom 4: A DECREASING AVAILABLE MEMORY **message is displayed** This is a confirmation message that indicates a failure has been detected in extended or expanded memory, and that all memory after the failure has been disabled to allow the system to continue operating (although at a substantially reduced level). Your first step should be to reseat each SIMM and ensure that it is properly inserted and secured. Next, take a known-good SIMM and step through each occupied SIMM slot until the problem disappears. The last SIMM removed is the faulty one. Keep in mind that you may have to alter the system's CMOS setup parameters as you move memory around the machine. An incorrect setup can cause problems during system initialization.

Symptom 5: A MEMORY PARITY INTERRUPT AT ADDRESS XXXX **message is displayed** The system has detected a parity-bit error in at least one memory location. Again, your first step should be to reseat each SIMM and ensure that it is properly inserted and secured. Then step through each occupied SIMM slot with a known-good SIMM until the problem disappears, indicating that the last SIMM removed is faulty. If you cannot detect a faulty SIMM, the error is probably in RAM located on the system motherboard. Because there are usually few memory ICs on the motherboard, you can replace the RAM ICs or replace the entire motherboard.

Troubleshooting with beep codes

It is important to remember that error messages are displayed only after your computer's video system has been loaded and initialized. Any errors that occur in your memory system before the video system is active are not displayed. To get around this limitation, POST authors have employed a series of sequential tone patterns (called *beep codes*) that inform you of the particular error condition. The specific pattern of beeps indicates the problem. Table 5-3 presents an index of beep codes that relate to common memory parameters. These parameters are tested before the display is activated, and before the "official" memory-check procedure is performed.

Table 5-3. Index of classic POST beep codes

Beep sequence	Code definition
1-1-3	CMOS RTC Read/Write Failure
1-1-4	BIOS ROM Check-sum Error
1-2-2	DMA System or Setup Failure
1-2-3	DMA Page Register Failure
1-3-1	DRAM Refresh Failure
1-3-3	Low 64K RAM Failure
1-3-4	Low 64K RAM Odd/Even Failure
1-4-1	Low 64K RAM Address Line Failure
1-4-2	Low 64K RAM Parity Bit Failure
2-1-1	Low 64K RAM Bit 0 Error
2-1-2	Low 64K RAM Bit 1 Error
2-1-3	Low 64K RAM Bit 2 Error
2-1-4	Low 64K RAM Bit 3 Error
2-2-1	Low 64K RAM Bit 4 Error
2-2-2	Low 64K RAM Bit 5 Error
2-2-3	Low 64K RAM Bit 6 Error
2-2-4	Low 64K RAM Bit 7 Error
2-3-1	Low 64K RAM Bit 8 Error
2-3-2	Low 64K RAM Bit 9 Error
2-3-3	Low 64K RAM Bit 10 Error
2-3-4	Low 64K RAM Bit 11 Error
2-4-1	Low 64K RAM Bit 12 Error
2-4-2	Low 64K RAM Bit 13 Error
2-4-3	Low 64K RAM Bit 14 Error
2-4-4	Low 64K RAM Bit 15 Error
3-1-1	DMA #2 Register Error
3-1-2	DMA #1 Register Error
3-1-3	Interrupt Register #1 Error
3-1-4	Interrupt Register #2 Error

Although there is quite a bit for the system to check before the display becomes active, Table 5-3 focuses only on the four major areas of your computer that are vital for memory operation: CMOS setup, BIOS ROM integrity, DMA and interrupt configurations (to ensure proper system DRAM refresh), and the first 64K of system RAM. Keep in mind that the beep codes shown may vary a bit from system to system, so be sure to check your user's manual or service manual documentation for your particular computer. The first 64K of system memory (00000H to 0FFFFH) is critical, because that is where the computer loads its BIOS, DOS, user, and basic interrupt vectors and data. An error in this memory area will almost certainly result in catastrophic system failure as soon as a corresponding interrupt signal is generated.

6
Floppy disk drives

The ability to interchange programs and data between various computers is a fundamental requirement of almost every computer system. It was this type of file-exchange compatibility that helped rocket the IBM PC into everyday use and spur the personal computer industry in the 1980s. A standardized recording media and file structure also breathed life into the fledgling software industry by allowing software developers to create and distribute programs and data to a mass market of compatible computer users. The mechanism that allowed this phenomenal compatibility is the floppy disk drive, shown in Fig. 6-1.

NEC Technologies, Inc.

6-1　Underside view of an NEC floppy drive.

A floppy disk drive (also called a floppy drive or FDD) is one of the least expensive and most reliable forms of mass-storage ever used in computer systems. Virtually every one of the millions of personal computers sold every year incorporates at least one floppy drive. Most notebook and laptop computers also offer a single floppy drive. Not only are floppy drives useful for maintaining file compatibility between systems, but the advantage of a removable storage medium—the floppy disk itself—makes floppy drives an almost intuitive backup system. Although floppy drives have evolved through a number of phases from 8" (20.32 cm) to 5.25" (13.34 cm) to 3.5" (8.89 cm), their basic components and operating principles have changed very little. This book looks at 5.25" and 3.5" drives.

The disks

Before getting into a detailed discussion of drive construction and operation, it is important that you become familiar with magnetic recording principles and media. One of the intriguing aspects of a floppy drive is that the drive mechanism itself does not permanently retain any information. It is the medium that is placed inside the drive that actually contains useful information. In the case of floppy drives, the media consists of a small, thin plastic disk (usually 3 mil mylar) that is coated on both sides with a thin layer of sensitive magnetic material.

5.25" (13.34 cm) disks

The 5.25" diskette is shown in Fig. 6-2. The outer shell, which actually measures 13.97 cm, is a tough, flexible plastic that is ultrasonically welded together during manufacture. Within the shell are two layers of nonwoven cloth. The circular disk itself fits within the two cloth layers. Cloth reduces any friction that might be generated as the disk rotates, and helps to remove any debris from the medium's surfaces.

The large hole in the disk center is the *spindle hub,* where the drive spindle clamps the disk in place. Because the disk is relatively free to move within its shell, it can usually float to assume the best clamping position. As the hub is prone to damage from clamping wear, many disks have protective hub rings to reinforce the disk

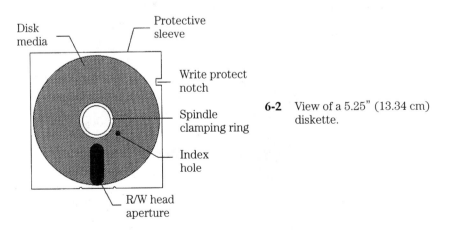

6-2   View of a 5.25" (13.34 cm) diskette.

Disk media — Protective sleeve

Write protect notch

Spindle clamping ring

Index hole

R/W head aperture

medium. A rectangular notch cut from the right side of the jacket is the write-protect notch. When this notch is exposed, the disk can be written to. If the notch is covered, writing is prohibited. Any simple adhesive label can be used to cover the write-protect notch.

The small hole near the center hub is the *index hole,* which aligns with a small hole cut into the circular diskette itself. Old, hard-sectored floppy drives used the index hole to note precise radial disk position. Today, however, the index hole serves little practical purpose, because disks are *soft-sectored.* The large, oblong hole at the bottom of a disk is the *head aperture*—the place where a drive's read/write heads come into contact with the disk's medium. It is vitally important that you do not touch the head aperture. Dust, dirt, finger prints, sweat and bodily oils, or any other foreign matter that reaches the medium can damage the disk medium—often permanently. This is the compelling reason why all 5.25" disks should be kept in their paper disk sleeves when not in use.

3.5" (8.89 cm) disks

By itself, a thin, flexible disk of medium is extremely vulnerable to damage from rough handling, dust, spills, and scratches. As a result, it is important to protect the medium from damage at all times. Protection is accomplished by mounting the medium in a hard plastic shell, as shown in Fig. 6-3. The design was originally introduced by the Sony Corporation. Perhaps the most striking aspect of a 3.5" disk is the hard shell itself which is scratch resistant and very difficult to bend. A spring-loaded metal shroud called the *head access cover* protects the exposed medium when the disk is removed from a drive. When a disk is inserted properly, a loading mechanism in the drive pulls the metal cover aside so that magnetic heads can contact the disk.

There are other attributes of a 3.5" disk that you should be aware of. To ensure that the disk is inserted properly, one corner of the disk shell is cut out. The disk medium is also attached to a solid metal drive hub that is accessible only from the disk's underside. If the disk is inserted into a drive upside down, the disk simply will not be accepted. When inserted properly, the drive's spindle interlocks with the metal drive hub. The hub shape ensures that the medium does not slip against the spindle motor. A write-protect hole in one corner of the disk is covered with a plastic

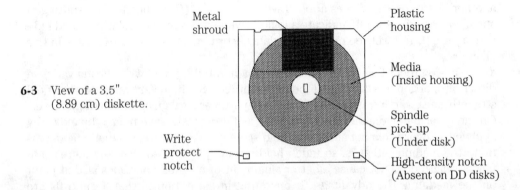

6-3   View of a 3.5"
(8.89 cm) diskette.

Metal shroud

Plastic housing

Media (Inside housing)

Spindle pick-up (Under disk)

Write protect notch

High-density notch (Absent on DD disks)

slider. When the slider is moved to cover the hole, disk write operations are permitted. When the slider is moved to expose its hole, disk write operations are inhibited—the disk can only be read. Finally, the drive must be able to differentiate between double-density and high-density disks. An additional hole is punched in the disk body to indicate a high-density disk. If the hole is missing, the disk is double-density.

Magnetic storage concepts

Magnetic storage media have been attractive to computer designers for many years —long before the personal computer had established itself in homes and offices. This popularity is primarily due to the fact that magnetic media is nonvolatile. Once information is stored, no electrical energy is needed to maintain the information. While electrical energy is used to read and write magnetic data, magnetic fields do not change on their own, so data remains intact until other forces act upon it. In most systems, such force is provided by other magnetic fields that are generated by electrical means. It is this smooth, straightforward transition from electricity to magnetism and back that has made magnetic storage such a natural choice. This part of the chapter describes the basic concepts of the magnetic media used in floppy drives.

The medium

As you have already seen, the medium is the physical material which actually holds recorded information. For floppy drives, the medium is a small mylar disk coated on both sides with a precisely formulated magnetic material called the *oxide layer*. Disk manufacturers use their own particular formulas for magnetic coatings, but most coatings are based on a naturally magnetic element (such as iron, nickel, or cobalt) that has been alloyed with nonmagnetic materials or rare earths.

The fascinating aspect of these magnetic layers is that each and every particle acts as a microscopic magnet. Each magnetic particle can be aligned in one orientation or another under the influence of an external magnetic field. If you have ever magnetized a screwdriver's steel shaft by running a permanent magnet along its length, you have already seen this magnetizing process in action. For a floppy disk, microscopic points along the disk's surfaces are magnetized in one alignment or another by the precise forces applied with read/write (R/$\overline{W}$) heads. The shifting of alignment polarities would indicate a logic 1, while no change in polarity would indicate a logic 0. You will see more about data recording and organization later in this chapter.

In analog recording, the magnetic field generated by read/write heads varies in direct proportion to the signal being recorded. Such linear variations in field strength cause varying amounts of magnetic particles to align as the medium moves. On the other hand, digital recordings such as floppy disks save binary 1s and 0s by applying an overwhelming amount of field strength. Very strong magnetic fields saturate the medium—that is, so much field strength is applied that any increase in field strength does not cause a better alignment of magnetic particles at that point on the medium. The advantage to operating in saturation is that 1s and 0s are remarkably resistant to the degrading effects of noise that can sometimes appear in analog magnetic recordings.

Although the orientation of magnetic particles on a disk's medium can be reversed by using an external magnetic field, particles tend to resist the reversal of polarity. *Coercivity* is the strength with which magnetic particles resist change. Higher-coercivity material has a greater resistance to change, so a stronger external field is needed to cause changes. High coercivity is generally considered to be desirable up to a point, because signals stand out much better against background noise and signals resist natural degradation because of age, temperature, and random magnetic influences. As you might expect, a highly coercive medium requires a more powerful field to record new information.

Another advantage of increased coercivity is greater information density for medium. The greater strength of each medium particle allows more bits to be packed into less area. The move from 5.25" to 3.5" floppy disks was made possible due largely by development of a more coercive magnetic layer. This coercivity principle also holds true for hard drives, which you will see in the next chapter. In order to pack more information onto ever-smaller platters, the medium must be more coercive.

Coercivity is a common magnetic measurement, with units in *oersteds* (pronounced *or-steds*). The coercivity of a typical floppy disk can range anywhere from 300 to 750 oersteds. Hard drive and magneto-optical (MO) drive media usually offer coercivities up to 6000 oersteds or higher.

The central premise of magnetic storage is that it is static—once recorded, information is retained without any electrical energy. Such stored information is presumed to last forever, but in actual practice, magnetic information begins to degrade as soon as it is recorded. A good magnetic medium reliably remembers (or retains) the alignment of its particles over a long period of time. The ability of a medium to retain its magnetic information is known as *retentivity*. Even the best-formulated floppy disks degrade eventually, although it could take many years before an actual data error materializes.

Ultimately, the ideal answer to media degradation is to refresh (or write over) the data and sector ID information. Data is rewritten normally each time a file is saved, but sector IDs are written only once, when the disk is formatted. If a sector ID should fail, you will see the dreaded Sector Not Found disk error, and any data stored in the sector cannot be accessed. This failure also occurs in hard drives. Little can be done to ensure the integrity of floppy disks other than maintaining one or more backups on freshly formatted disks. However, commercial software is available for restoring disks (especially hard drives).

Magnetic recording principles

Having seen the basic magnetic storage concepts, you can begin to apply those concepts to floppy disks as they are used in actual practice. The next few sections show you some of the principles behind magnetic recording, and the ways in which data is organized on a disk.

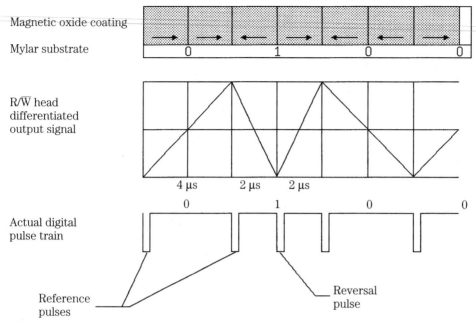

Magnetic oxide coating

Mylar substrate

R/W head
differentiated
output signal

4 µs   2 µs   2 µs

Actual digital
pulse train

Reference
pulses

Reversal
pulse

6-4　Flux transitions in floppy disks using MFM.

The first step in understanding digital recording is to see how binary data is stored on a disk. Binary 1s and 0s are not represented by discrete polarities or magnetic field orientations as you might have thought. Instead, binary digits are represented by the presence or absence of *flux transitions* as illustrated in Fig. 6-4. By detecting the change from one polarity to another instead of simply detecting a discrete polarity itself, maximum sensitivity can be achieved with very simple circuitry.

In its simplest form, a logic 1 is indicated by the presence of a flux reversal within a fixed time frame, while a logic 0 is indicated by the absence of a flux reversal. Most floppy drive systems insert artificial flux reversals between consecutive 0s to prevent reversals from occurring at great intervals. You can see some sample magnetic states recorded on the medium in Fig. 6-4. Notice that the direction of reversal does not matter at all—it is the reversal event that defines a 1 or 0. For example, the first 0 uses left-to-right orientation, while the second 0 uses a right-to-left orientation, but both can represent 0s.

The second trace in Fig. 6-4 represents an amplified output signal from a typical read/write head. Notice that the analog signal peaks wherever there is a flux transition—long slopes indicate a 0, and short slopes indicate a 1. When such peaks are encountered, peak detection circuits in the floppy drive cause marking pulses in the ultimate data signal. Each bit is usually encoded in about 4 microseconds.

Often, the most confusing aspect to flux transitions is the artificial reversals. Why reverse the polarities for consecutive 0s? Artificial reversals are added to guarantee synchronization in the floppy disk circuitry. Remember that data read or written to a floppy disk is serial, and without any clock signal, such serial data is asynchronous of the drive's circuitry. Regular flux reversals (even if added artificially) create reference pulses that help to synchronize the drive and data without use of clocks or other timing signals. This approach is loosely referred to as the *modified frequency modulation* (MFM) recording technique.

The ability of floppy disks to store information depends upon being able to write new magnetic field polarities on top of old or existing orientations. A drive must also be able to sense the existing polarities on a disk during read operations. The mechanism responsible for translating electrical signals into magnetic signals (and vice versa) is the read/write head. In principle, a head is little more than a coil of very fine wire wrapped around a soft, highly permeable core material, as illustrated in Fig. 6-5.

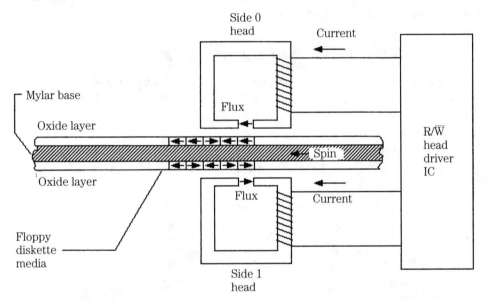

6-5   Floppy drive recording principles.

When the head is energized with current flow from a driver IC, a path of magnetic flux is established in the head core. The direction (or orientation) of flux depends on the direction of energizing current. To reverse a head's magnetic orientation, the direction of energizing current must be reversed. The small head size and low current levels needed to energize a head allow very high-frequency flux reversals. As magnetic flux is generated in a head, the resulting tightly focused magnetic field aligns the floppy disk's particles at that point. In general practice, the current signal magnetizes an almost microscopic area on the medium. R/$\overline{W}$ heads actually contact the medium while a disk is inserted into a drive.

During a read operation, the heads are left unenergized while the disk spins. Just as varying current produces magnetism in a head, the reverse is also true— varying magnetic influences cause currents to be developed in the head. As the spinning medium moves across a R/$\overline{W}$ head, a current is produced in the head coil. The direction of induced current depends on the polarity of each flux orientation.

Induced current is proportional to the flux density (how closely each flux transition is placed) and the velocity of the medium across each head. In other words, signal strength depends on the rate of change of flux versus time.

Data and disk organization

The next concern in floppy disk technology is where the data is actually located, and how that data is organized. You cannot place data just anywhere on the disk—the drive would have no idea where to look for the data later on, or if the data was valid. In order for a disk to be of use, information must be sorted and organized into known, standard locations. Standard organization ensures that a disk written by one drive is readable by another drive in a different machine. Table 6-1 compares the major parameters of several floppy drive types.

Table 6-1. Comparison of floppy drive specifications

Parameter	3.5" Drives		5.25" Drives	
	HD	DD	HD	DD
Drive spindle speed (RPM)	300/360	300	360	300
Megabytes/drive	1.4	.720	1.2	.360
Encoding format	MFM	MFM	MFM/FM	MFM/FM
Tracks/inch (tpi)	135	135	96	96
Bits/inch (bpi)	17,434	8,717	9,870	5,922
Tracks/side	80	80	80	40
Sectors/track	18	9	15	9
Bytes/sector	512	512	512	512
Data transfer Rate (Kbits/sec)	500	500	500 (MFM) 250 (FM)	250 (MFM) 125 (FM)

Newest – – – – – – – – – – – – – – – Oldest

It is important to note that a floppy disk is a two-dimensional entity possessing both height and width (depth is irrelevant here). This two-dimensional characteristic allows disk information to be recorded in concentric circles, which creates a random access type of medium. Random-access means that it is possible to move around the disk almost instantly to obtain a desired piece of information. This is a much faster and more convenient approach than sequential recording, as is used with magnetic tape.

Floppy disk organization is not complicated, but there are several important concepts that you must be familiar with. Figure 6-6 illustrates a typical 3.5" floppy disk. The disk itself is rotated in one direction (usually clockwise) under read/write heads which are perpendicular to the disk's plane. The path of the disk beneath a head describes a circle. As a head steps in and out along a disk's radius, each step describes a circle with a different circumference—somewhat like lanes on a highway.

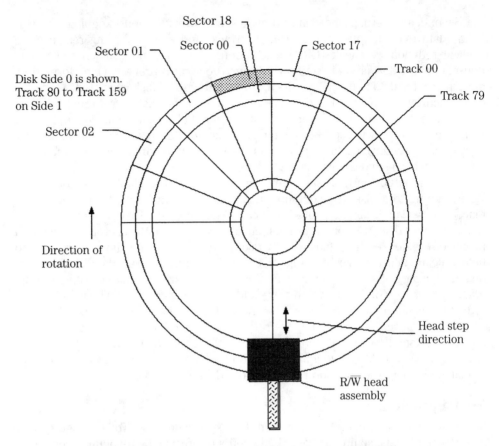

Sector 18

Sector 01 — Sector 00 — — Sector 17

Disk Side 0 is shown.
Track 80 to Track 159
on Side 1

Track 00

Track 79

Sector 02

Direction of
rotation

Head step
direction

R/W̄ head
assembly

6-6   Data organization on a 3.5" high-density floppy disk.

Each of these concentric "lanes" is known as a *track*. A typical 3.5" disk offers 160 tracks—80 tracks on each side of the medium. Tracks have a finite width that is defined largely by the drive size, head size, and medium. When a R/W̄ head jumps from track to track, it must jump precisely the correct distance to position itself in the middle of the new track. If positioning is not correct, the head can encounter data signals from two adjacent tracks. Faulty positioning almost invariably results in disk errors. Also notice that the circumference of each track drops as the head moves toward the disk's center. With less space and a constant rate of spin, data is most dense on the innermost tracks (79 or 159, depending on the disk side) and least dense on the outermost tracks (0 or 80).

Every track is broken down into smaller units called *sectors*. There are 18 sectors on every track of a 3.5" disk. Sectors serve two purposes. First, a sector stores 512 bytes of data. With 18 sectors per track and 160 tracks per disk, a disk holds 2880 sectors. At 512 bytes per sector, a formatted disk can handle about 1,474,560 bytes of data. In actual practice, this amount is often slightly less, allowing for boot sector and file allocation information. Sectors are often referred to as *clusters*, although technically, a cluster can range from 512 bytes to 8096 bytes.

Second, and perhaps more important, a sector provides housekeeping (or over-head) data that identifies the sector, the track, and error checking results from cyclical redundancy check (CRC) calculations. The location of each sector and housekeeping information is set down during the *format* process. Once formatted, only the sector data and CRC results are updated when a disk is written. Sector ID and synchronization data is never rewritten unless the disk is reformatted. This extra information means that each sector actually holds more than 512 bytes, but you have access only to the 512 data bytes in a sector during normal disk read/write operations. If sector ID data is accidentally overwritten or corrupted, the data in the afflicted sector becomes unreadable.

It is very important that the computer keep track of available space on a disk. When writing to a disk, the computer must check the disk first to determine the places where data is already stored so it can write to sectors that are unused. When reading from a disk, the computer must check to determine the sectors that contain pieces of the desired file—files usually take many sectors, and the sectors used to hold a file are not necessarily contiguous. In order to track the used and free sectors on a disk, a map of each sector is maintained on the disk. This map is called the *file allocation table* (or FAT). As files are added and erased, the FAT is updated to reflect the contents of each sector. The FAT is typically held on track 00.

As you can see, a working FAT is critical to the proper operation of a disk. If the FAT is accidentally overwritten or corrupted, the entire disk can become useless. Without a viable FAT, the computer has no other way to determine what files are available or where they are spread throughout the disk.

Media problems

Magnetic media have come a long way in the last decade or so. Today's high-quality magnetic materials, combined with the benefits of precise, high-volume production equipment, produce disks that are exceptionally reliable over normal long-term use in a floppy disk drive. However, floppy disks are removable items, so the care they receive in physical handling and the storage environment where they are kept greatly impacts their life span.

The most troubling and insidious problem plaguing floppy disk media is the accidental influence of magnetic fields. Any magnetized item in close proximity to a floppy disk poses a potential threat. Permanent magnets such as refrigerator magnets or magnetic paper clips are prime sources of stray fields. Electromagnetic sources like telephone ringers, monitor or TV degaussing coils, and all types of motors can corrupt data if the medium is close enough. The best policy is to keep all floppy disks in a dedicated container placed well away from stray magnetic fields.

Disks and other magnetic media are also subject to a wide variety of physical damage. Substrates and media are manufactured to very tight tolerances, so anything that alters the precise surface features of a floppy disk can cause problems. The introduction of hair, dirt, or dust through the disk's head access aperture, wide temperature variations, fingerprints on the medium, or any substantial impact or flexing of the medium can cause temporary loss of contact between medium and head. When loss of contact occurs, data is lost and a number of disk errors can occur. Head wear and the accumulation of worn oxides also effects head contact. Once again, storing disks in a dedicated container located well out of harm's way is often the best means of protection.

Drive construction

Now that you have learned about the floppy disk and its medium, it's time to study the drive mechanism in detail. A floppy disk drive is a rather remarkable piece of mechanical engineering. It must accept disks of varying quality from a variety of manufacturers, and align and spin the disk at a very precise rate (300 or 360 RPM) accurate to within 1 or 2% A drive must also be able to position a set of loaded (clamped) read/write heads precisely to any track on the disk within a few mils (thousandths of an inch), and reach the desired destination track in under a few milliseconds. Above all, the drive must function reliably over a long period of time with a minimum of maintenance. A solid understanding of floppy drive components will make your troubleshooting much easier. Figure 6-7 shows an exploded diagram for a Teac 3.5" floppy disk drive.

At the core of a floppy drive is the *frame assembly* (15). It is the primary structure for mounting the drive's mechanisms and electronics. Frames are typically made from die cast aluminum to provide a strong, rigid foundation for the drive. The *front bezel* (18) attaches to the frame to provide a clean, cosmetic appearance, and offers a fixed slot for disk insertion and removal. For 3.5" drives, bezels often include a small colored lens, a disk ejection button hole, and a flap to cover the disk slot when the drive is empty. The *spindle motor assembly* (17) uses an outer-rotor dc motor fabricated onto a small PC board. The motor's shaft is inserted into the large hole in the frame. A disk's metal drive hub automatically interlocks to the spindle. For 5.25" disks, the center hole is clamped between two halves of a spindle assembly. The halves clamp the disk when the drive lever is locked down. The *disk activity LED* (20) illuminates through the bezel's colored lens whenever spindle motor activity is in progress.

Just behind the spindle motor is the drive's *electronics package* (16). The electronics PC board contains the circuitry needed to operate the drive's motors, read/write heads, and sensors. A standardized interface is used to connect the drive to a floppy drive controller. The *read/write head assembly* (7; also sometimes called a head carriage assembly), holds a set of two read/write heads. Head 0 is the lower head (on the underside of the disk), and head 1 is on top. In order to move the head carriage assembly in and out along a disk, a *head stepping motor* (12) is used to ensure head movements are even between tracks or parts of a disk. A threaded rod at the motor end is what actually moves the heads. A *mechanical damper* (5) helps to smooth the disk's travel into or out of the 3.5" drive.

When a disk is inserted through the bezel, the disk is restrained by a *diskette holder assembly* (2). To eject the disk, you press the *ejector button* (19) which pushes a *slider mechanism* (3). When the ejector button is fully depressed, the disk disengages from the spindle and pops out of the drive. For 5.25" drives, the disk is released whenever the drive door is opened. Your particular drive might contain other miscellaneous components. Finally, the entire upper portion of a drive can be covered by a *metal shield* (1).

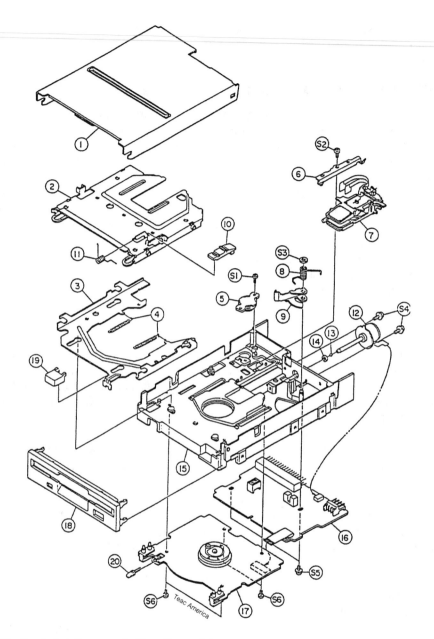

6-7 Exploded diagram of a Teac floppy drive.

Read/write heads

Read/write heads are at the heart of all magnetic disk systems. When a disk is inserted between a set of heads, the head assembly clamps down to bring the heads and media into contact. The disk medium is coated with a very light lubricant to

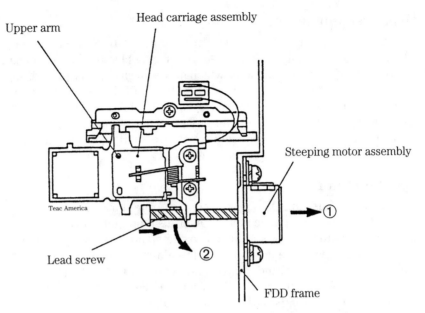

6-8   Close-up view of a read/write head assembly.

reduce friction. Figure 6-8 shows a close-up view of a head assembly. Notice how the assembly is supported on both sides to maintain stability. The right side of the assembly is supported by a sliding *guide shaft*, while the left side is firmly attached to a bracket that runs along the *lead screw* of the stepping motor. Because of the electrical coil wiring in the heads, each head has its own small flexible plastic cable (FPC) that is attached to a connector on the drive's electronics PC board.

In actual practice, a read/write head is more than simply a single coil of wire around a tiny core. Most heads are actually composed of three cores: two read/write cores and an erase core. You can visualize this configuration in the layout and schematic of Fig. 6-9. The erase head is powered whenever the drive is writing in order to clear any existing flux transitions before the read/write cores lay down new information. If a read operation is taking place, the erase core is left unpowered.

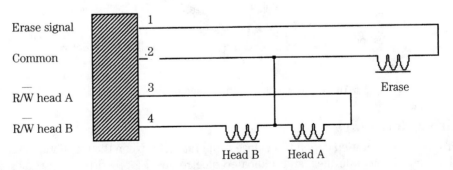

6-9   Schematic of a typical floppy drive read/write head.

Head stepping motor

The read/write heads are positioned from track to track using a stepping motor attached to a precision lead screw. As you saw in chapter 2, a stepping motor is a unique form of ac induction motor which moves in small, very precise angular steps. Each step is signalled by circuitry on the drive's PC board. As the stepping motor turns, the lead screw turns. This pushes or pulls the head carriage a precise linear distance across the disk radius. The exact amount of linear motion depends on the number of steps needed to complete a motor revolution, and the number of threads on the lead screw (known as *screw pitch*).

Spindle motor

A floppy drive must spin its disk at a constant rate during read or write operations. This is the task of the spindle motor. Older desktop floppy drives used a bulky constant speed motor that was attached to the spindle assembly with a rubber belt. Today's small, low-profile drives use an integrated brushless dc motor, in which the rotor serves as a flywheel and spindle, and the stator windings are actually fabricated onto the motor PC board (Fig. 6-10). When spindle rotation is required, an IC on the motor PC board cycles the board's stator windings on and off at a rate which accelerates the spindle to a desired speed (300 or 360 RPM) and maintains that constant speed. Spindle rotation is regulated with feedback obtained from a sensor at the spindle.

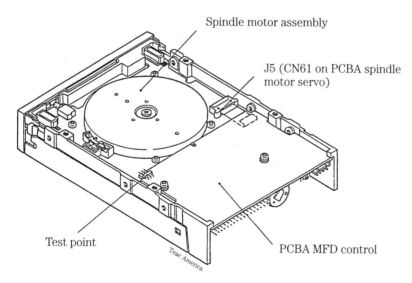

6-10   View of a floppy drive spindle motor assembly.

Drive electronics

Proper drive operation depends on close cooperation between the magnetic medium, electromechanical devices, and dedicated electronics. Floppy drive electronics are responsible for two major tasks: controlling the drive's physical operations, and managing the flow of data in or out of the drive. These tasks are not nearly as simple as they sound, but the sleek, low-profile drives in today's computer systems are a far cry from the clunky, full-height drives found in early systems. Older drives needed a large number of ICs spanning several boards that had to be fitted to the chassis. The drive in your computer, however, is probably implemented with only a few highly-integrated ICs that are neatly surface-mounted on two small, opposing PC boards. This part of the chapter discusses the drive's operating circuits. A complete block diagram for a Teac 3.5" (8.89 cm) floppy drive is illustrated in Fig. 6-11. The diagram is shown with a floppy disk inserted.

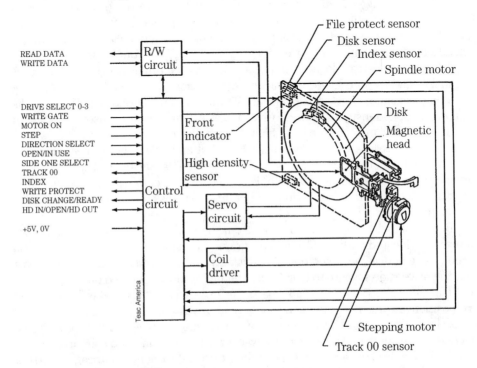

6-11   Electronic layout of a floppy drive.

Sensors

As you look over Fig. 6-11, notice that there are four very important sensors required to govern drive operations: the *file-protect* or *write-protect sensor,* the *disk sensor,* the *index sensor,* and the *track 00 sensor.* A 3.5" drive also incorporates a fifth sensor to check for a high-density medium. Sensors are used to check certain physical conditions so that drive electronics do not cause system errors or drive damage. Take a moment to familiarize yourself with these sensors before you start troubleshooting. As a rule, sensors are either mechanical switches that react to the physical presence of a disk, or optoisolators that detect the presence of light. Keep in mind that different drive manufacturers might use sensor types interchangeably depending on the task at hand.

Write-protect sensors are used to detect the position of a disk's file-protect tab. For 3.5" disks, the write-protect hole must be covered to allow both read and write operations. If the hole is open, the disk can only be read. Mechanical contact switches are commonly used as write-protect sensors, because it is a simple matter for the write-protect notch to actuate a small switch when the disk is first inserted. If the hole is open, the switch is not actuated. For 5.25" disks, write protect is handled in the opposite way. The write-protect notch cut into the jacket side must be uncovered to allow both reading and writing. Covering the notch prohibits writing. A 5.25" drive typically uses an optoisolator to check the notch condition.

Before the drive can operate at all, a disk must be inserted properly and interlocked with the spindle. The disk sensor detects the presence or absence of a disk. Like the write-protect sensor, disk sensors are often mechanical switches that are activated by disk contact. If drive access is attempted without a disk in place, the sensor causes the drive's logic to induce a DOS "Disk Not Ready" error code. It is not unusual to find an optoisolator acting as a disk sensor.

The electronics of a 3.5" drive must be able to differentiate whether the disk contains double-density or high-density media. A high-density sensor looks for the hole that is found near the top of all high-density disk bodies. A mechanical switch is typically used to detect the high-density hole, but an LED/detector pair can also be used. When the hole is absent (as is the case in a double-density disk), the switch is activated upon disk insertion. If the hole is present (indicating a high-density disk), the switch is not actuated. All switch conditions are translated into logic signals used by the drive electronics.

Before disk data can be read or written, the system must read the disk's boot information located in the FAT. While programs and data can be broken up and scattered all over a disk, however, the FAT must always be stored at a known location so that the drive knows where to look for it. The FAT is always located on track 00—the first track of disk side 0. The track 00 sensor provides a logic signal when the heads are positioned over track 00. Each time a read or write is ordered, the head assembly is stepped to track 00. Although a drive "remembers" how many steps should be needed to position the heads precisely over track 00, an optoisolator or switch senses the head carriage assembly position. At track 00, the head carriage interrupts the optoisolator or actuate the switch. If the drive supposedly steps to track 00 and there is no sensor signal to confirm the position (or the signal occurs before the drive has finished stepping), the drive assumes that a head positioning error has occurred. Head step counts and sensor outputs virtually always agree unless the sensor has failed or the drive has been physically damaged.

Spindle speed is a critically important drive parameter. Once the disk has reached its running speed (300 or 360 RPM), the drive must maintain that velocity for the duration of the disk access process. Unfortunately, simply telling the spindle motor to move is no guarantee that the motor is turning—a sensor is required to measure the motor's speed. This is the job of the index sensor. Signals from an index sensor are fed back to the drive electronics which adjusts spindle speed in order to maintain a constant rotation. Most drives use optoisolators as index sensors, which detect the motion of small slots cut in a template or the spindle rotor itself. When a disk is spinning, the output from an index sensor is a fast logic pulse sent along to the drive electronics. Keep in mind that some index sensors are magnetic. A magnetic sensor typically operates by detecting the proximity of small slots in a template or the spindle rotor, but the pulse output is essentially identical to that of the optoisolator.

Circuits

The drive electronics package contains four primary circuits that you should be familiar with: the *servo circuit*, the *coil driver circuit*, the *read/write circuit*, and the *control circuit*. Drive electronics also handle the physical interface connecting the drive to the motherboard. Operation of these circuits is critical to the drive.

The coil driver circuit is responsible for operating the head carriage stepping motor. A driver circuit accepts logic signals from the control circuit and converts those logic pulses into the voltage and current levels needed to work a stepping motor. The coil driver is typically a single, surface-mount IC, although some older drive designs might use discrete transistors.

The servo circuit performs two functions in a floppy disk drive. First, a servo drives the spindle motor. The circuit (usually located on the spindle motor PC board) accepts logic signals from the control circuit and generates the precise sequence of outputs needed to work the spindle motor's windings. The servo circuit also accepts pulse signals from the index sensor, then uses those pulses to regulate spindle motor speed. Servo circuits are usually implemented as a single IC, and a small series of discrete components. Figure 6-12 illustrates an assembly for a servo motor board.

The control circuit is the heart of the entire floppy drive. Control circuits are responsible for translating logic signals from the drive's physical interface into logic signals that operate the read/write, servo, and coil driver circuits. A control circuit also accepts the logic signals returned from each of the five drive sensors, and

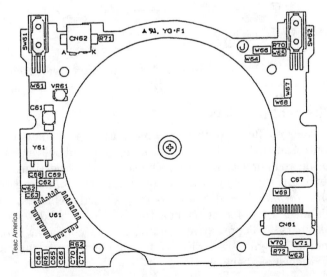

6-12 A spindle motor PC board assemble.

reports their conditions to the physical interface. Control circuits are usually implemented as a single surface-mount IC in an 80- to 100-pin QFP.

The read/write circuit interacts directly with the drive's read/write heads. During a read operation, the read/write circuit accepts and amplifies analog magnetic signals from the heads, then differentiates the analog signals to create a waveform such as in Fig. 6-4. After some external analog filtering with discrete components, the filtered analog signal is returned to the read/write circuit, where the signal is converted into a logic waveform representing the read data. Write operations are more straightforward. Data is channeled directly from the physical interface into a write driver, which translates logic signals into high-energy pulses used to cause flux transitions on the medium. The high-energy pulses are sent directly to the read/write heads. Some drives provide a separate read/write circuit, but many drives now implement these circuits as a part of the control circuit ASIC. The main logic board for a floppy drive is shown in Fig. 6-13.

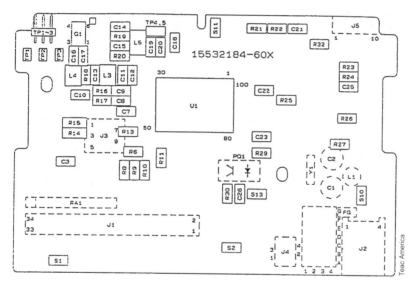

6-13　A floppy drive main logic PC board.

Physical interface

Obviously, a floppy drive is only one part of your computer. The drive must receive control and data signals from the computer, and deliver status and data signals back to the computer as required. The series of connections between a floppy disk PC board and the floppy disk controller IC on the motherboard is known as the *physical interface*. The advantage to using a standard interface is that various drives and ICs made by different manufacturers can be "mixed and matched" by computer designers. A floppy drive working in one computer should operate properly in another computer regardless of the manufacturer, as long as the same physical interface scheme is being used.

For most PC drives, a physical interface includes two cables: a power cable and a signal cable. Both cable pinouts are illustrated in Fig. 6-14. The classic power connector is a 4-pin mate-and-lock connector, although many low-profile drives used in laptops and notebooks use much smaller connector designs. Floppy drives require two voltage levels: +5.0 Vdc for logic, and +12 Vdc for motors. The return (ground) for each supply is also provided at the connector. The signal connector is typically a 34-pin insulation displacement connector (IDC) cable. Notice that all odd-numbered pins are ground lines, while the even-numbered pins carry active signals. Logic signals are all TTL-level signals.

In a system with more than one drive, the particular destination drive must be selected before any read or write is attempted. A drive is selected using the

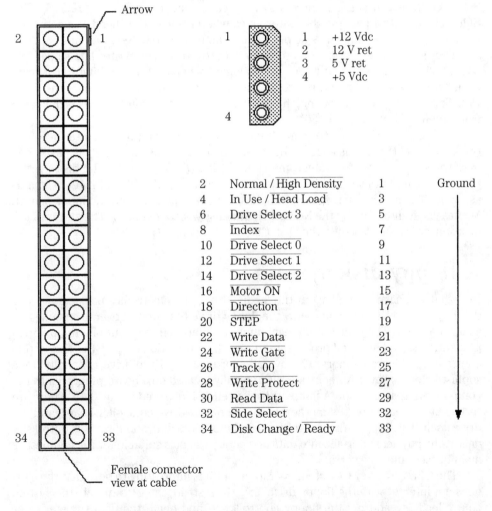

6-14 Pinout diagram for a classical floppy interface.

appropriate Drive Select pinouts (Drive Select 0 to 3) on pins 10, 12, 14, and 6 respectively. For notebook or subnotebook systems where only one floppy drive is used, only Drive Select 0 is used—the remaining Select inputs can be disconnected. The spindle motor servo circuit is controlled through the Motor On signal (pin 16). When pin 16 is logic 0, the spindle motor should *spin up*, or come to an operating speed. The medium must be spinning at the proper rate before reading or writing can take place.

To move the read/write heads, the host computer must specify the number of steps a head carriage assembly must move, and the direction in which steps must occur. A Direction Select signal (pin 18) tells the coil driver circuit whether the heads should be moved inward (toward the spindle) or outward (away from the spindle). The Step signal (pin 20) provides the pulse sequence that actually steps the head motor in the desired direction. The combination of Step and Direction Select controls can position the read/write heads over the disk very precisely. The Side Select control pin (pin 32) determines whether head 0 or head 1 is active for reading or writing—only one side of the disk can be manipulated at a time.

There are two signals needed to write data to a disk. The Write Gate signal (pin 24) is logic 0 when writing is to occur, and logic 1 when writing is inhibited (or reading). After the Write Gate is asserted, data can be written to the disk over the Write Data line (pin 22). When reading, the data that is extracted from the disk is delivered from the Read Data line (pin 30).

Each of the drive's sensor conditions are sent over the physical interface. The track 00 signal (pin 26) is logic 0 whenever the head carriage assembly is positioned over track 00. The Write Protect line (pin 28) is logic 0 whenever the disk's write-protect notch is in place. Writing is inhibited whenever the Write Protect signal is asserted. The index signal (pin 8) supplies a chain of pulses from the index sensor. Media type is indicated by the Normal/High-density sensor (pin 2). The status of the disk sensor is indicated over the Disk Change Ready line (pin 34).

A floppy disk system

Now that you have learned about the media, drive, and electronics package in some detail, you need to understand how the floppy drive fits into the overall scheme of a small computer. The transfer of meaningful information into or out of a floppy drive is an intricate and involved process, requiring the interaction of the CPU, the system controller, and core memory. The overall coordination of the drive is handled by a sophisticated floppy drive controller IC typically located on a board plugged into the computer's expansion slot. A floppy drive system is illustrated in Fig. 6-15. There are three major areas here; the motherboard, the floppy drive controller board, and the drive itself. The floppy drive controller translates serial data and discrete control signals at the physical interface into data and control signals suitable for the computer's main busses, and vice versa.

The CPU is the key to system operation, but it is interesting to note that the CPU does not interact with the floppy drive directly. Instead, the CPU directs the system controller IC to address the floppy controller IC and begin the data transfer to or from the drive. Any instructions or subroutines needed to operate the floppy drive

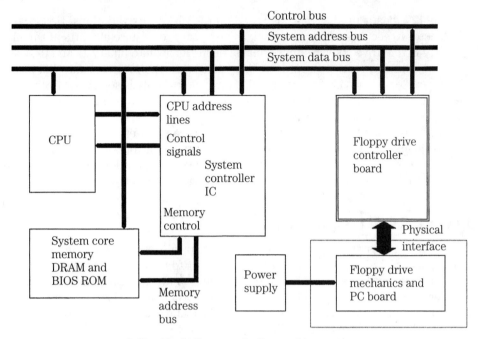

6-15 Block diagram of a floppy drive system.

are taken by the CPU from the BIOS ROM in core memory. The floppy controller instructs the drive to step to track 00 and read the FAT. This initial step learns the location of all assigned and free clusters. If the disk was changed before access was requested, the new FAT data would have to be determined anyway. The drive's read/write heads then step to the appropriate location to begin reading or writing.

Data being written to a floppy drive is taken from core memory (DRAM) one byte at a time by the floppy controller using direct memory access (DMA) techniques. The data is translated into serial form, then sent one bit at a time over the Write Data line of the physical interface. Control signals are sent along the interface simultaneously to handle the drive's motors, sensors, and so on. If data is being copied from another drive, that drive must be read first into a section of core memory, then that portion of memory is written to the desired drive. After data arrives at the floppy drive control circuit, bits are converted into drive signals which are written to the disk as magnetic flux transitions.

When data must be read from a floppy drive, the process is very similar. The CPU orders the system controller to address the floppy drive controller IC, then sends data instructions that cause the floppy drive to load a program or data file. Any data or subroutines needed to operate the floppy drive are contained in BIOS ROM. The floppy controller board instructs the drive to step to track 00 and read the FAT to determine the disk sector and track where the desired file begins. If the desired file is not found in the FAT, an error code is sent back to the CPU, which responds with a DOS error code. Once the sector and track file location is found, the heads are stepped to that location.

The R/W heads produce signals based on the disk's flux variations. Heads step from sector to sector and track to track as necessary to acquire all parts of the file. Circuitry in the drive converts those analog head signals into binary 1s and 0s. Data is sent in serial form across the physical interface to the floppy drive controller board where serial data is translated into parallel form, actual data is separated from error checking information, and the resulting parallel data is moved into core memory through the system controller across the computer's main busses.

In actual practice, the process of signalling, data transfer, and control is much more complex than just described, but the intention here is to give you an idea of the major processes involved. The concepts of floppy system operation will be invaluable to you during the testing and troubleshooting sections that follow.

Drive testing and alignment

Floppy disk drives (Fig. 6-16) are electromechanical devices. Their motors, lead screws, sliders, levers, and linkages are all subject to eventual wear and tear. As a result, a drive can develop problems that are due to mechanical defects instead of electronic problems. Fortunately, few mechanical problems are fatal to a drive. With the proper tools, you can test a troublesome drive and often correct problems simply through careful cleaning and alignment.

6-16 A 5.25" (13.34 cm) floppy drive.

NEC Technologies, Inc.

Tools and equipment

Drive alignment is not a new concept. Technicians have tested and aligned floppy drives for years using oscilloscopes and test disks containing precise, specially recorded data patterns. You might already be familiar with the classic "cat's eye" and "index burst" alignment patterns seen on oscilloscopes. This type of manual alignment requires that you find the right test point on your particular drive's PC board, locate the proper adjustment in the drive assembly, and interpret complex (and sometimes confusing) oscilloscope displays. In many cases, manual alignment required a substantial investment in an oscilloscope, test disk, and stand-alone drive exerciser equipment to run a drive outside of the computer.

Although manual drive-alignment techniques are still used today, they are largely being replaced by automatic alignment techniques. Software developers have created interactive control programs to operate with their specially recorded data disks. These software toolkits provide all the features necessary to operate a suspect drive through a wide variety of tests while displaying the results numerically or graphically right on a computer monitor (Fig. 6-17). As you make adjustments, you see real-time results displayed on the monitor. Software-based testing eliminates the need for an oscilloscope and stand-alone test equipment. You also do not need to know the specific signal test points for every possible drive. There are two popular toolkits on the market: AlignIt, by Landmark Research International Corp., and DriveProbe, by Accurite Technology Incorporated. This part of the chapter introduces you to these toolkits.

AUTOMATIC Drive Test   'Esc'- For Previous Menu

Test	Track	Head 0 Data	Head 1 Data	Test Limits	Results	
Speed	NA	300 RPM / 199.7 mS		300 ± 6 RPM	Pass	NA
Eccentricity	44	100 uI	NA	0 ± 300 uI	Pass	NA
Radial	0	96% 50 uI	100% 0 uI	60 – 100 %	Pass	Pass
Radial	40	93% -100 uI	90% -150 uI	60 – 100 %	Pass	Pass
Radial	79	96% 50 uI	90% -150 uI	60 – 100 %	Pass	Pass
Azimuth	76	6 Min	4 Min	0 ± 30 Min	Pass	Pass
Index	0	414 uS	407 uS	400 ± 600 uS	Pass	Pass
Index	79	397 uS	380 uS	400 ± 600 uS	Pass	Pass
Hysteresis	40	100 uI	NA	0 ± 250 uI	Pass	NA

uI = Micro-inches   uS = Microsecond   mS = Millisecond
Min = Minutes   NA = Not Applicable   NT = Not Tested

Note: Radial is expressed as LOBE RATIO and OFFSET from track center line.
Auto Test Completed 'Esc' For Previous Menu

6-17   Automatic floppy drive test suite.

Accurite Technologies Inc., San Jose, CA

Drive cleaning

Floppy drive read/write heads are not terribly complex devices, but they do require precise positioning. Heads must contact the disk medium in order to read and right information reliably. As the disk spins, particles from the disk's magnetic coating wear off and form a deposit on the heads. Accumulations of everyday contaminants such as dust and cigarette smoke also contribute to deposits on the heads. Head deposits present several serious problems. First, deposits act as a wedge, forcing heads away from the disk surface. This results in lost data, read/write errors, and generally unreliable and intermittent operation. Deposits tend to be more abrasive than the head itself, so dirty heads can generally reduce a disk's working life. Finally, dirty heads can cause erroneous readings during testing and alignment. Because alignment disks are specially recorded in a very precise fashion, faulty readings yield erroneous information that can actually cause you to misalign the drive. As a routine procedure, clean a drive thoroughly before you test or align it.

Read/write heads can be cleaned manually or automatically. The manual method is just as the name implies. Using a high-quality head cleaner on a soft, lint-free, anti-static swab, scrub both head surfaces by hand. Wet the swab but do not soak it. You might need to repeat the cleaning with fresh swabs to ensure that all residual deposits are removed. Be certain that all computer power is off before manual cleaning, and allow a few minutes for the cleaner to dry completely before restoring power. If you do not have head-cleaning chemicals on hand, you can use fresh ethyl or isopropyl alcohol. The advantage to manual cleaning is thoroughness—heads can be cleaned very well with no chance of damage due to friction.

Most software toolkits provide a cleaning disk and software option that allows you to clean the disk automatically. With computer power on and the software toolkit loaded and running, insert the cleaning disk and choose the cleaning option from your software menu. Software then spins the drive for some period of time—10 to 30 seconds should be adequate, but do not exceed 60 seconds of continuous cleaning. Choose high-quality cleaning disks that are impregnated with a lubricant. Avoid "bargain," off-the-shelf cleaning disks that force you to wet the disk. Wetted cleaning disks are often harsh, and prolonged use can actually damage the heads from excessive friction. Once the drive is clean, it can be tested and aligned. Eight tests are used to gauge the performance of a floppy drive: clamping, spindle speed, track 00, radial alignment, azimuth alignment, head step, hysteresis, and head width. Not all tests have adjustments that can correct the corresponding fault.

Clamping

As you have seen, a floppy disk is formatted into individual tracks laid down in concentric circles along the medium. Because each track is ideally a perfect circle, it is critical that the disk rotate evenly in a drive. If the disk is not on center for any reason, it does not spin evenly. If a disk is not clamped evenly, the eccentricity introduced into the spin can be enough to allow heads to read or write data to adjoining tracks. A clamping test should be the first test performed after the drive is cleaned, because high eccentricity can adversely affect disk tests. Clamping problems are more pronounced on 5.25" drives, in which the soft mylar hub ring is vulnerable to damage from the clamping mechanism.

Start your software toolkit from the computer's hard drive, then insert the alignment disk containing test patterns into the questionable drive. Select a clamping or eccentricity test and allow the test to run for awhile. You will probably see a display similar to the one shown in Fig. 6-18. Typical software toolkits can measure eccentricity in terms of microinches from true center. If clamping is off by more than a few hundred microinches, the spindle mechanism should be replaced. You can also simply replace the floppy drive. Try reinserting and retesting the disk several times to confirm your results. Repeated failures confirm a faulty spindle system.

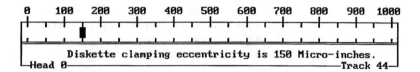

```
   0    100   200   300   400   500   600   700   800   900   1000
```

Diskette clamping eccentricity is 150 Micro-inches.

Head 0   Track 44

Drive 1 Selected as [3 1/2" 1.4Mb 300 RPM]   Location: Track 44 Head 0

6-18   Screen display of a floppy drive eccentricity test. Accurite Technologies Inc., San Jose, CA

Spindle speed

The disk medium must be rotated at a fixed rate in order for data to be read or written properly. A drive that is too fast or too slow might be able to read files that it has written at that wrong speed without error, but the disk might not be readable in other drives operating at a normal speed. Files recorded at a normal speed also might not be readable in drives that are too fast or too slow. Such transfer problems between drives is a classic sign of speed trouble (usually signalled as general disk read/write errors). Drive speeds should be accurate to within ±15%, so a drive running at 300 RPM should be accurate to ±4.5 RPM (295.5 to 304.5 RPM), and a drive running at 360 RPM should be accurate to within ±5.4 RPM (354.6 to 365.4 RPM).

After cleaning the read/write heads and testing disk eccentricity, select the spindle speed test from your software menu. The display will probably appear much like the one in Fig. 6-19. Today's floppy drives rarely drift out of alignment because rotational speed is regulated by feedback from the spindle's index sensor. The servo circuit constantly adjusts motor torque to achieve optimal spindle speed. If a self-compensating drive is out of tolerance, excess motor wear, mechanical obstructions, or index sensor failure is indicated. Check and replace the index sensor, or the entire spindle motor assembly as shown in Fig. 6-20. You can also replace the entire floppy drive.

Track 00 test

The first track on any floppy disk is the outermost track of side 0, or track 00. This track is critical because it contains file allocation information vital for finding disk files. The particular files saved on a disk can be broken up and spread out all over the disk, but the FAT data must always be in a known location. If the drive cannot fin

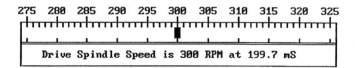

```
MOTOR SPEED Test _____ 'Esc'- For Previous Menu
```

```
275  280  285  290  295  300  305  310  315  320  325
```

Drive Spindle Speed is 300 RPM at 199.7 mS

Drive 1 Selected as [3 1/2" 1.4Mb 300 RPM]   Location: Track 0   Head 0

6-19   Screen display of a floppy drive speed test. Accurite Technologies Inc., San Jose, CA

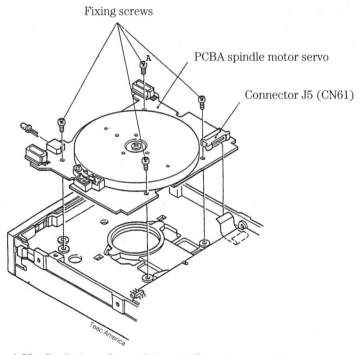

6-20   Replacing a floppy drive spindle motor assembly.

track 00 reliably, the system might not be able to boot from the floppy drive or to use diskettes. Floppy drives use a sensor such as an optoisolator to physically determine when the R/W̄ heads are over the outermost track.

Select the track 00 test from the software menu and allow the test to run. A track 00 test measures the difference between the actual location of track 00 versus the point at which the track 00 sensor indicates that track 00 is reached. The difference should be less than ±1.5 mils (thousandths of an inch). A larger error might cause the drive to encounter problems reading or writing to the disk. The easiest and quickest fix is to alter the track 00 sensor position. This adjustment usually involves loosening the sensor and moving it until the monitor display indicates an acceptable reading. Remember that you only need to move the sensor a small fraction, so a patient, steady hand is required. The track 00 sensor is almost always located along the head carriage lead screw. Mark the original position of the sensor with indelible ink so that you can return it to its original position if you get in trouble. Figure 6-21 illustrates one solution to adjusting the track 00 sensor.

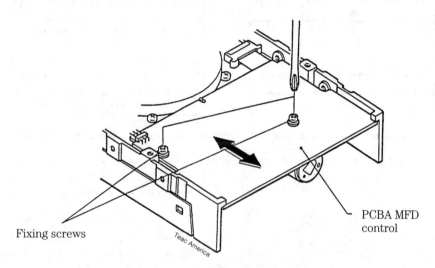

Fixing screws

PCBA MFD control

6-21   Adjusting the track 00 sensor.

Radial alignment

The alignment of a drive's read/write heads with the disk is critical to reliable drive operation, because alignment directly affects contact between heads and medium. If head contact is not precise, data read or written to the disk might be vulnerable. The radial alignment test measures the head's actual position versus the precise center of the outer, middle, and inner tracks (as established by ANSI standards). Ideally, read/write heads should be centered perfectly when positioned over any track, but any differences are measured in microinches. A radial alignment error more than several hundred microinches suggests a head alignment error.

Select the radial alignment test from your software toolkit and allow the test to run. A typical radial alignment test display is illustrated in Fig. 6-22. If you must perform an adjustment, you can start by loosening the slotted screws that secure the stepping motor shown in Fig. 6-23, and gently rotate the motor to alter the lead screw position. As you make adjustments with the test in progress, watch the display for the middle track. When the error is minimized on the inner track, secure the stepping motor carefully to keep the assembly from shifting position. Use extreme caution when adjusting radial head position—you only need to move the head a

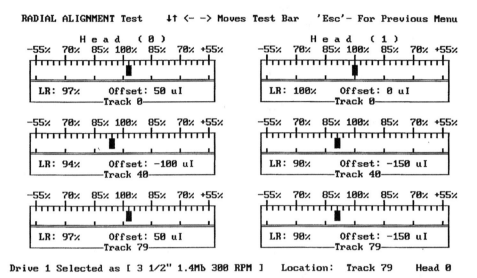

6-22 Screen display of a radial alignment test. Accurite Technologies Inc., San Jose, CA

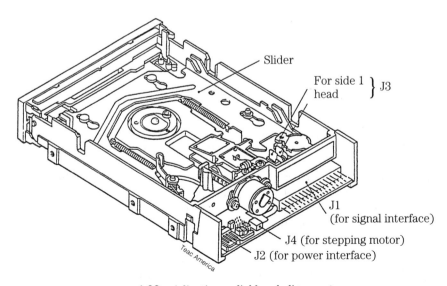

6-23 Adjusting radial head alignment.

little, so a very steady hand is needed. Recheck the track 00 sensor to make sure the sensor position is acceptable. If you can't sufficiently adjust the radial head alignment, the drive should be replaced.

Azimuth alignment

Not only must the heads be centered perfectly along a disk's radius, but the heads must also be perfectly perpendicular to the disk plane. If the head azimuth is off by more than a few minutes (1/60°), data integrity can be compromised and disk interchangeability between drives—especially high-density drives—can become unreliable. When the heads are perfectly perpendicular to the disk (at 90°), the azimuth should be 0'.

Select the azimuth test from your software toolkit and run it. Figure 6-24 shows an azimuth alignment test display. An azimuth alignment test measures the rotation (or twist) of read/write heads in terms of ±minutes. A clockwise twist is expressed as a positive (+) number, while a counterclockwise twist is expressed as a negative (−) number. Heads should be perpendicular to within about ±10'. Note that most floppy drives do not allow easy azimuth adjustments. Unless you want to experiment with the adjustment, it is often preferable to replace a severely misaligned drive.

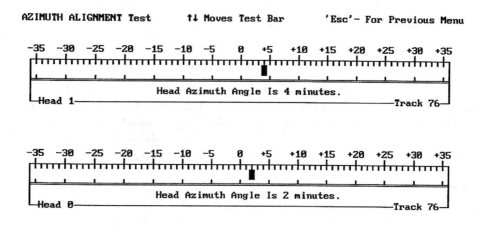

6-24   Screen display of an azimuth alignment test. Accurite Technologies Inc., San Jose, CA

Head step

The head step (or index step) test measures the amount of time between a step pulse from the coil driver circuits and a set of timing mark data recorded on the test disk. In manual oscilloscope adjustments, this would be seen as the "index burst." Average index time is typically 200 μs for 5.25" drives, and 400 μs for 3.5" drives. In automatic testing with your software toolkit, you will see time measurements for both heads on the inner and outer tracks as shown in Fig. 6-25. The actual range of acceptable time depends on your particular drive, but variations of ±100 μs or more are not unusual.

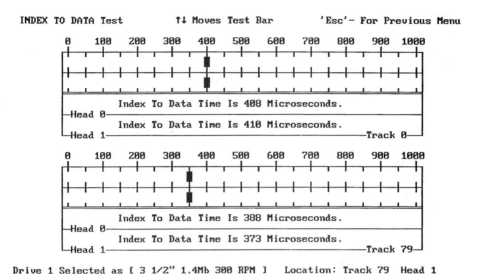

6-25   Screen display for an index-to-data test. Accurite Technologies Inc., San Jose, CA

If the head step timing is too far off, you can adjust it by moving the index sensor as shown in Fig. 6-26. As with all other drive adjustments, you need only adjust the sensor a very small amount, so be extremely careful when moving it. Again, a steady hand is very important. Make sure that you secure the sensor when you finish the timing adjustment.

Hysteresis

It is natural for wear and debris in the mechanical head positioning system to result in some "play"—that is, the head does not wind up in the exact same position when moving from the outside in as when moving from the inside out. Excessive play, however, makes it difficult for the drive to find the correct track reliably. Testing is done by starting the heads at a known track, stepping the heads out to track 00, then stepping back to the starting track. Head position is then measured and recorded. The heads are then stepped in to the innermost track, then back to the starting track. Head position is measured and recorded again. Under ideal conditions, the head carriage should wind up in precisely the same place (zero hysteresis), but natural play almost guarantees some minor difference. You can see a typical hysteresis test measurement display in Fig. 6-27. If excessive hysteresis is encountered, the drive should be replaced, because it is difficult to determine exactly where the excess play is caused in the drive.

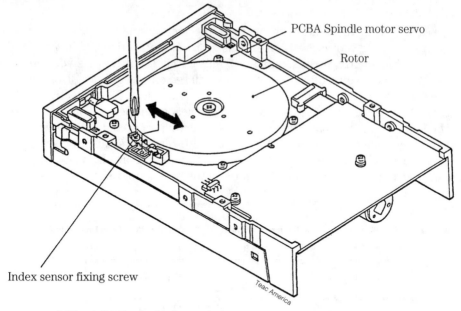

6-26 Adjusting index burst timing.

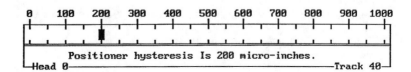

```
POSITIONER HYSTERESIS Test                    'Esc'- For Previous Menu




     0    100   200   300   400   500   600   700   800   900  1000
     |     |     |     |     |     |     |     |     |     |     |
    |||||||||||█||||||||||||||||||||||||||||||||||||||||||||||||
           Positioner hysteresis Is 200 micro-inches.
    └Head 0───────────────────────────────────────────Track 40┘
```

Drive 1 Selected as [3 1/2" 1.4Mb 300 RPM]   Location: Track 1   Head 0

6-27 Screen display of positioner hysteresis test. Accurite technologies Inc., San Jose, CA

Head width

Another test of a drive's read/write heads is the measurement of their effective width. Effective head widths are 12 or 13 mils for 5.25" double-density drives, 5 or 6 mils for 5.25" high-density drives, and 4 or 5 mils for all 3.5" drives. As you run the head width test with your software toolkit, you will see effective width displayed on the monitor as shown in Fig. 6-28. As R/W heads wear down, their effective width increases. If the effective width is too small, the heads can be contaminated with oxide buildup. When too-small head widths are detected, try cleaning the drive again to remove any remaining contaminates. If the width reading remains too small (or measures too large), the heads or head carriage might be damaged. You can replace the R/W head assembly as in Fig. 6-29, but often the best course is simply to replace the entire drive.

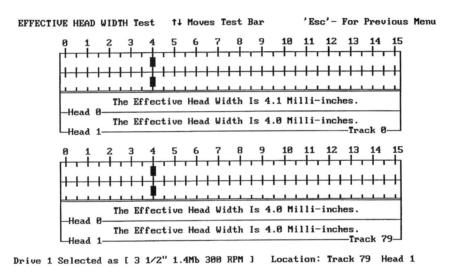

6-28 Screen display of head width test. Accurite Technologies Inc., San Jose, CA

Troubleshooting floppy disk systems

Beyond the process of testing and alignment, you must often deal with more serious or catastrophic drive failures. This section of the chapter is concerned with drive problems that cannot be corrected with cleaning or mechanical adjustments. To perform some of the following tests, you should have a known-good diskette that has been properly formatted. The disk can contain files, but be certain that any such files are backed up properly on a hard drive or another floppy disk—if you can't afford to lose the files on the disk, don't use it. For these procedures, refer to the floppy drive diagrams in Figs. 6-11 and 6-15. If you intend to overhaul a drive periodically, you need a battery of spare parts. Table 6-2 shows a list of regular spare parts for a Teac floppy drive, an approximate replacement interval, and the average time needed to replace each part.

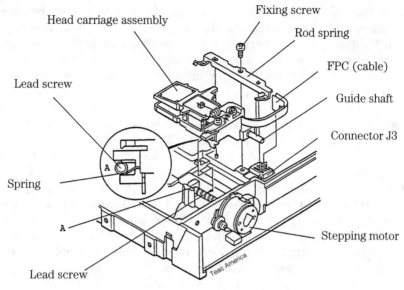

6-29 Replacing a read/write assembly.

Table 6-2. Recommended floppy drive spare parts

Part	Approximate interval	Time (minutes)
Spindle motor	20,000 motor-on hours or 3×10^6 seeks	45
Stepping motor assembly.	3×10^6 seeks	30
Drive electronics board	As required	30
Plastic front bezel	As required	2
Plastic eject button	As required	3
Eject damper	50,000 ejects	5

Symptom 1: The floppy drive is completely dead. The disk does not even initialize when inserted   Begin troubleshooting by inspecting the diskette itself. When a 3.5" disk is inserted into a drive, a mechanism should pull the disk's metal shroud away and briefly rotate the spindle motor to ensure positive engagement. Make sure that the disk is properly inserted into the floppy drive assembly. If the diskette does not enter and seat correctly in the drive, disk access is impossible. Try several different diskettes to ensure that the test diskette is not defective. It might be necessary to partially disassemble the computer to access the drive and allow you to see the overall assembly. Free or adjust any jammed assemblies or linkages to correct disk insertion. If you cannot get diskettes to insert properly, change the floppy drive.

If the diskette inserts properly but fails to initialize, carefully inspect the drive's physical interface cabling. Loose connectors or faulty cable wiring can easily disable a floppy drive. Use your multimeter to measure dc voltages at the power connector. Place your meter's ground lead on pin 2 and measure +12 Vdc at pin 1. Ground your meter on pin 3 and measure +5 Vdc at pin 4. If either of both of these voltages is low or missing, troubleshoot your computer power supply.

Before disk activity can begin, the drive must sense a disk in the drive. Locate the disk sensor and use your multimeter to measure voltage across the sensor. When a disk is out of the drive, you should read a logic 1 voltage across the sensor output. When a disk is in place, you should read a logic 0 voltage across the sensor (this convention might be reversed in some drive designs). If the sensor does not register the presence of a disk, replace the sensor. If the sensor does register the presence of a disk, use your logic probe to check the Disk Change/Ready signal (pin 34) of the physical interface. If the interface signal does not agree with the sensor signal, replace the control circuit IC on the drive PC board. You can also replace the entire drive control PC board, or replace the entire drive outright.

At this point, the trouble is probably in the floppy drive PC board, or the floppy drive controller board. Try replacing the floppy drive PC board assembly. This is not the least expensive avenue in terms of materials, but it is fast and simple. If a new floppy drive PC board corrects the problem, reassemble the computer and return it to service. Retain the old floppy drive board for parts. If a new drive PC board does not correct the problem (or is not available), replace the entire drive. Again, you can retain the old floppy drive for parts. If a new floppy drive assembly fails to correct the problem, replace the floppy controller board. Obviously, you have to disassemble the computer to get at the motherboard and expansion boards.

Symptom 2: The floppy drive rotates a disk, but does not seek the desired track This type of symptom generally suggests that the head stepping motor is inhibited or defective, but all other floppy drive functions are working properly. Begin by disassembling the computer and removing the floppy drive. Carefully inspect the head positioning assembly to be certain that there are no broken parts or obstructions that could jam the read/write heads. You might want to examine the mechanical system with a disk inserted to be certain that the trouble is not a disk alignment problem that is interfering with head movement. Gently remove any obstructions that you find. Be careful not to accidentally misalign any linkages or mechanical components in the process of clearing an obstruction.

Remove any diskette from the drive and reconnect the drive's signal and power cables. Apply power to the computer and measure drive voltages with your multimeter. Ground your multimeter on pin 2 of the power connector and measure +12 Vdc at pin 1. Move the meter ground to pin 3 and measure +5 Vdc on pin 4. If either voltage is low or absent, troubleshoot your computer power supply.

Once you are confident that the drive's mechanics are intact and appropriate power is available, you must determine whether the trouble is in your floppy drive PC board or floppy drive controller IC on the motherboard. Use your logic probe to measure the Step signal in the physical interface (pin 20). When drive access is requested, you should find a pulse signal as the floppy controller attempts to position the read/write heads. If Step pulses are missing, the floppy drive controller board is probably defective and should be replaced.

If Step pulses are present at the interface, check the pulses into the coil driver circuit. An absence of pulses into the coil driver circuit indicates a faulty control circuit IC. If pulses reach the coil driver, measure pulses to the stepping motor. If no pulses leave the coil driver, replace the coil driver IC. When pulses are correct to the stepping motor but no motion is taking place, replace the defective stepping motor. If you do not have the tools or inclination to replace surface-mount ICs, you can replace the drive PC board, or replace the entire drive.

Symptom 3: The floppy drive heads seek properly, but the spindle does not turn   This symptom suggests that the spindle motor is inhibited or defective, but all other functions are working properly. Remove all power from the computer. Disassemble the system enough to remove the floppy drive. Carefully inspect the spindle motor, drive belt (if used), and spindle assembly. Make certain that there are no broken parts or obstructions that could jam the spindle. If there is a belt between the motor and spindle, make sure the belt is reasonably tight—it should not slip. Also examine the floppy drive with a diskette inserted to be certain that the disk's insertion or alignment is not causing the problem. You can double-check your observations using several different diskettes. Gently remove any obstructions that you find. Be careful not to cause any accidental damage in the process of clearing an obstruction. **Note:** Do not add any lubricating agents to the assembly. Gently vacuum or wipe away any significant accumulations of dust or dirt.

Remove any diskette from the drive and reconnect the floppy drive's signal and power cables. Restore power to the computer and measure drive voltages with your multimeter. Ground the multimeter on pin 2 and measure +12 Vdc on pin 1. Move the meter ground to pin 3 and measure +5 Vdc on pin 4. If either voltage is low or absent, troubleshoot the computer's power supply.

When you are confident that the floppy drive is mechanically sound and appropriate power is available, you must determine whether the trouble is in the floppy drive PC board or the floppy drive controller board. Use your logic probe to measure the Motor On signal in the physical interface (pin 16). When drive access is requested, the Motor On signal should become true (in most cases an active low). If the Motor On signal is missing, the floppy drive controller board is probably defective and should be replaced.

If the Motor On signal is present at the interface, check the signal driving the servo circuit. A missing Motor On signal at the servo circuit suggests a faulty control circuit IC. If the signal reaches the servo circuit, the servo IC is probably defective. You can replace the servo IC, but the best option is usually to replace the spindle motor PC board assembly as a unit. If you cannot do that, you can replace the floppy drive.

Symptom 4: The floppy drive does not read from or write to the diskette. All other operations appear normal   This type of problem can manifest itself in several ways, but your computer's operating system usually informs you when a disk read or write error has occurred. Begin by trying a known-good, properly formatted diskette in the drive. A faulty diskette can generate perplexing read/write problems. If a known-good diskette does not resolve the problem, try cleaning the read/write heads as described in the previous section. **Note:** Do not run the drive with a head cleaning disk inserted for more than 30 seconds at a time, or you risk damaging the heads with excessive friction.

When a fresh diskette and clean read/write heads do not correct the problem, you must determine whether the trouble exists in the floppy drive assembly or the floppy controller IC. If you cannot read data from the floppy drive, use your logic probe to measure the Read Data signal (pin 30). When the disk is idle, the Read Data line should read as a constant logic 1 or logic 0. During a read cycle, you should measure a pulse signal as data moves from the drive to the floppy controller board. If no pulse signal appears on the Read Data line during a read cycle, use the oscilloscope to measure analog signals from the read/write heads. If there are no signals from the read/write heads, replace the head or head carriage assembly as in Fig. 6-30. When signals are available from the read/write heads, the control circuit IC is probably defective and should be replaced. If you are unable to replace the IC, you can replace the drive's control PC board, or you can replace the entire drive. If a pulse signal does exist during a read cycle, the floppy disk controller board is probably defective and should be replaced.

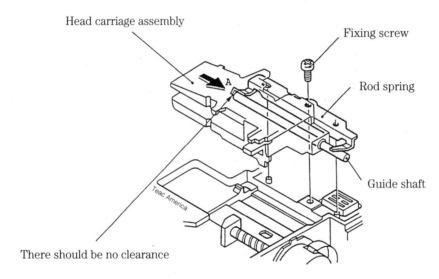

6-30   View of a read/write head assembly.

When you cannot write data to the floppy drive, use your logic probe to measure the Write Gate and Write Data lines (pins 24 and 22 respectively). During a write cycle, the Write Gate should be logic 0 and you should read a pulse signal as data flows from the floppy controller IC to the drive. If the Write Gate remains logic 1 or there is no pulse on the Write Data line, replace the defective floppy controller board. When the two Write signals appear as expected, check the analog signal to the read/write heads with your oscilloscope. If you do not find analog write signals, replace the defective control circuit IC. If analog signals are present to the heads, try replacing the heads or the entire head carriage assembly, or replace the entire drive.

Symptom 5: The drive is able to write to a write-protected disk   Before concluding that there is a drive problem, remove and examine the disk itself to ensure that it is actually write-protected. If the disk is not write-protected, write-protect it appropriately and try the disk again. If the disk is already protected, use your multimeter to check the drive's write-protect sensor. For an unprotected disk, the sensor output should be a logic 1, while a protected disk should generate a logic 0 (some drives might reverse this convention). If there is no change in logic level across the sensor for a protected or unprotected disk, try a new write-protect sensor.

If the sensor itself appears to function properly, check the Write Protect signal at the physical interface (pin 28). A write-protected disk should cause a logic 0 on the Write Protect line. If the signal remains logic 1 regardless of whether the disk is write-protected or not, the control circuit IC in the drive is probably defective. If you are unable to replace the IC, change the drive PC board or replace the entire floppy drive outright.

Symptom 6: The drive can only recognize either a high- or double-density medium, but not both   This problem usually appears in 3.5" drives during the disk-format process when the drive must check the medium type. In most cases, the normal/high-density sensor is jammed or defective. Remove the disk and use your multimeter to measure across the sensor. You should be able to actuate the sensor by hand (either by pressing a switch or interrupting a light path) and watch the output display change accordingly on your multimeter. If the sensor does not respond, it is probably defective and should be replaced.

If the sensor itself responds as expected, check the normal/high-density signal at the physical interface (pin 2). A double-density disk should cause a logic 1 output, while a high-density disk should cause a logic 0 signal. If the signal at the physical interface does not respond to changes in the density sensor, the control circuit IC on the drive PC board is probably defective. If you are unable to replace the control circuit IC, you can replace the drive PC board, or you can replace the entire floppy drive.

7
Hard disk drives

A number of drawbacks limit the usefulness and reliability of floppy disks. Even the finest floppy system is slow to save and recall data, consumes a substantial amount of power relative to other areas of your computer, and is prone to media failure and incompatibility problems between various disks. Floppy drives are also limited in their storage capacity. Massive operating systems and multimegabyte application programs simply need more than a single 1.2Mb or 1.44Mb disk for storage. Switching between multiple disks is a cumbersome and unreliable solution. The demands for a massive, permanent storage device gave rise to the hard disk drive (called a hard drive or HDD) in the early 1980s (Fig. 7-1). Ultimately, the ability to store large quantities of data has only helped to fuel further computer development. Today, hard drives are standard equipment in desktop computers, and available in virtually every notebook and subnotebook computer now in production. This chapter presents the technology and principles of hard disk drives, and provides you with some solutions for drive testing and troubleshooting.

Drive concepts

The first step in understanding hard drives is to learn the basic concepts involved. Many of the terms covered for floppy drives in chapter 6 also apply to hard drives, but the additional performance requirements and operating demands placed on hard drives have resulted in an array of important new ideas.

In principle, a hard disk drive (Fig. 7-2) is very similar to a floppy drive. A magnetic recording media is applied to a substrate material which is then spun at a high rate of speed. Magnetic read/write heads in close proximity to the media can step rapidly across the spinning media to detect or create flux transitions as required. When you look closely, however, you can see that there are some major physical differences between floppy and hard drives.

7-1   A Maxtor 7000 series hard drive.

7-2   A Quantum ProDrive SCSI hard drive.

Platters and media

Where floppy disks use magnetic material applied over a thin, flexible substrate of mylar or some other plastic, hard drives use rugged, solid substrates called *platters*. You can clearly view the platters of a hard drive in Fig. 7-3. A platter is typically made of aluminum because aluminum is a light material, it is easy to machine to desired tolerances, and holds its shape under the high centrifugal forces that occur at high rotation rates. Because a major advantage of a hard drive is speed, platters are rotated at about 3600 RPM—ten times the rate of floppy drives. Platters are also made from other materials such as glass and ceramic. Both materials are appealing because of their low thermal coefficient, inherent flatness, and the ability to with-stand high rotating forces. A hard drive generally uses two or more platters.

7-3 A Maxtor 1.24Gb hard drive.

Maxtor Corp.

Hard drives must be capable of tremendous recording densities—well over 10,000 bits per inch (BPI). To achieve such substantial recording densities, platter media is far superior to the oxide media used for floppy disks. First, the media must possess a high coercivity so that each flux transition is well defined and easily discernible from every other flux transition. Coercivity of hard-drive media typically exceeds 1400 oersteds. Second, the media must be extremely flat across the entire platter surface to within just a few microinches. Hard-drive read/write heads do not actually contact their platters, but ride within a few microinches over the platter surfaces. A surface defect of only a few microinches can collide with a head and destroy it. Such a *head crash* is often a catastrophic defect that requires hard drive replacement. Floppy drive heads do contact the media, so minor surface defects are not a major concern. You will learn more about head flight and surface defects later in this chapter.

A hard-drive medium is a thin-film which has long since replaced magnetic oxides. Thin-film medium is a microscopic layer of pure metal (or a metal compound) which is bonded to the substrate surface through an interim layer. The medium is then coated with a protective layer to help survive head crashing. Figure 7-4 illustrates the cross-section of a typical hard-drive platter. Thin-film medium also tends to be very flat, so read/write heads can be run very close to the platter surfaces.

Air flow and head flight

Read/write heads in a hard disk drive must travel extremely close to the surface of each platter, but can never actually contact the media while the drive is running. The heads could be mechanically fixed, but fixed-altitude flight does not allow for shock or natural vibration that is always present in a drive assembly. Instead, read/write heads are made to float within microinches of a platter surface by suspending the heads on a layer of moving air. Figures 7-5 and 7-6 illustrate the typical air flow in a hard drive. Disk rotation creates a slight cushion that elevates the heads. Also notice

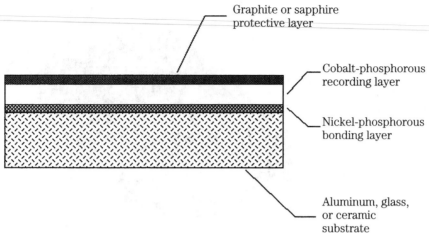

7-4   Cross-sectional view of a typical hard drive platter.

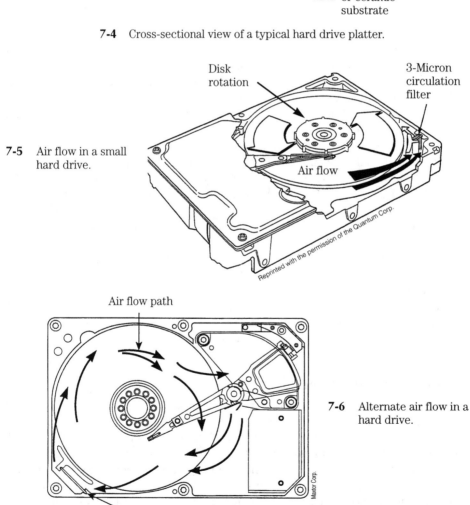

7-5   Air flow in a small hard drive.

7-6   Alternate air flow in a hard drive.

that some air is channeled through a fine filter that helps to remove any particles from the drive's enclosure.

It is important to note that all hard drives seal their platter assemblies into an air-tight chamber. The reason for such a seal is to prevent contamination from dust, dirt, spills, or strands of hair. Contamination that lands on a platter's surface can easily result in a *head crash*. A head crash can damage the head, the media, or both— any physical damage can result in an unusable drive.

Consider the comparison shown in Fig. 7-7. During normal operation, a hard drive's read/write head flies above the medium at a distance of only about 10 microns (microinches). Technical professionals relate that specification to a jumbo jet flying 30 feet above the ground at 600 miles per hour. It follows, then, that any variation in surface flatness due to platter defects or contaminates can have catastrophic effects on head height. Even an average particle of smoke is ten times wider than the flying height.

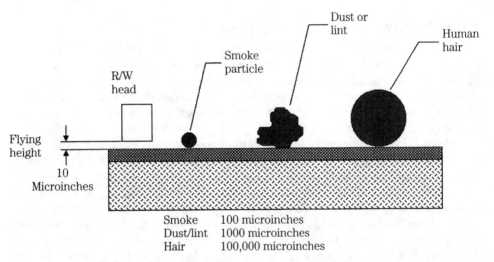

7-7   Comparison of typical contaminants with flying height.

With such proportions, you can understand why it is critically important that the platter compartment remain sealed at all times. The platter compartment can only be opened in a *cleanroom* environment. A cleanroom is a small, enclosed room where the air is filtered to remove any contaminants larger than 3 microns. Hard-drive assemblers wear gloves and cleanroom suits that cover all but their faces—even masks cover their mouth and nose to prevent breath vapor from contaminating the platters. If you specialize in hard-drive repair and want your own cleanroom area, you can purchase a CleanSphere such as the one shown in Fig. 7-8. This small environmental chamber from National Labnet filters contaminants 3 microns or larger. You can place the drive and its parts inside the sphere, filter the air until it is clean enough to open the drive, then work on the drive through glove holes in the sphere.

7-8 A CleanSphere work
environment.
National Labnet Co.

Areal density

It is desirable to pack as much information as possible in the media of hard-drive platters. The *areal density* of a medium describes this maximum amount of capacity in terms of megabytes per square inch. Today's hard drives (Fig. 7-9) used in small computers use media supporting 100 to 200 Mb/sq. in. As you might imagine, physically smaller platters must hold media with a higher areal density to offer storage capacities similar to larger drives.

There are several major factors that affect areal density. First, the actual size of magnetic particles in the media places an upper barrier on areal density—smaller particles allow higher areal densities. Larger coercivity of the media and smaller read/write heads with tighter magnetization fields allow higher areal densities. Finally, head height—the altitude of a read/write head over the platter surface—controls density. The closer a read/write head passes to its media, the higher areal densities can be. As heads fly further away, magnetic fields spread out, resulting in lower densities. Surface smoothness is then a major limiting factor in areal density, because smoother surfaces allow read/write heads to fly closer to the media.

Reprinted with the permission of Quantum Corp.

7-9 A Quantum
Hardcard EZ
integrated drive
and control.

Latency

As fast as a hard drive is, it does not work instantaneously. There is a finite period of delay between the moment that a read or write command is initiated over the drive's physical interface, and the moment that desired information is available (or placed). This delay is known as *latency*.

More specifically, latency refers to the time it takes for needed bytes to pass under a read/write head. If the head has not quite reached the desired location yet, latency can be quite short. If the head has just missed the desired location, the head must wait almost a full rotation before the needed bits are available again, so latency can be rather long. In general, a disk drive is specified with *average latency* which (statistically) is time for the spindle to make half a rotation. For a disk rotating at 3600 RPM (or 60 rotations per second), a full rotation is completed in 16.7 ms:

$$\frac{1\text{ s}}{60\text{ rotations/s}} = 0.0167\text{ s/rotation, or }16.7\text{ ms/rotation}$$

Average latency is then 8.3 ms:

$$\frac{16.7\text{ ms}}{2} = 8.3\text{ ms}$$

Disks spinning at 5400 RPM offer an average latency of 5.5 ms, and so on. As a rule, the faster a disk spins, the lower latency will be. Ultimately, disk speed is limited by centrifugal forces acting on the platters.

Tracks, sectors, and cylinders

As with floppy drives, you cannot simply place data anywhere on a hard-drive platter—the drive would have no idea where to look for data, or if the data is even valid. The information on each platter must be sorted and organized into a series of known, standard locations. Each platter side can be considered as a two-dimensional field possessing height and width. With this type of geometry, data is recorded in sets of concentric circles running from the disk spindle to the platter edge. A drive can move its read/write heads over the spinning media to locate needed data or programs in a matter of milliseconds. Every concentric circle on a platter is known as a track. A platter generally contains from 312 to 2048 tracks. Figure 7-10 shows data organization on a simple platter assembly. Note that only one side of the three platters is shown.

While each surface of a platter is a two-dimensional area, the number of platter surfaces involved in a hard drive (four, six, eight, or more) bring a third dimension into play. Because each track is located directly over the same tracks on subsequent platters, each track in a platter assembly can be visualized as a cylinder that passes through every platter. The number of cylinders is equal to the number of tracks on one side of a platter. Consider the multiple platters for the drive in Fig. 7-11.

Once a read/write head finishes reading one track, the head must be stepped to another (usually adjacent) track. This stepping process, no matter how rapid, does require some finite amount of time. When the head tries to step directly from the end of one track to the beginning of another, the head arrives too late to catch the new

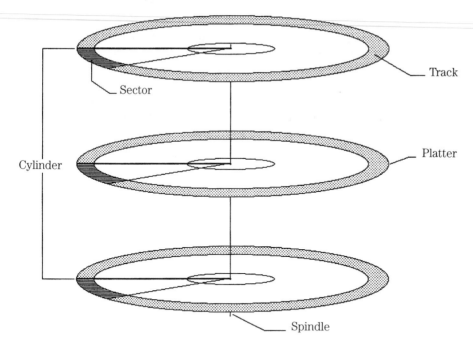

7-10 Data organization on a typical hard drive.

7-11 A quantum ProDrive LPS hard drive.

track's index pulse(s), so the drive has to wait almost an entire rotation to synchronize with the track index pulse. By offsetting the start points of each track as in Fig. 7-12, head travel time can be compensated for. This *cylinder skewing* technique is intended to improve hard-drive performance by reducing the disk time lost during normal head steps. A head should be able to identify and read the desired information from a track within one disk rotation.

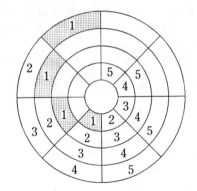

7-12 An example of sector/cylinder skew.

Tracks are broken down even further into small segments called sectors. As with DOS floppy disks, a sector holds 512 bytes of data, along with error-checking and housekeeping data that identifies the sector, track, and results calculated by cyclical redundancy checking (CRC). The location and ID information for each sector is developed when the drive is formatted. After formatting, only sector data and CRC bytes are updated during writing. If sector ID information is accidentally overwritten or corrupted, the data recorded in the afflicted sector becomes unreadable.

Figure 7-13 shows the layout for a typical sector on a Maxtor SCSI drive. As you can see, there is much more than just 512 bytes of data. The start of every sector is marked with a pulse. The pulse signalling the first sector of a track is called the *index pulse*. There are two portions to every sector: an address area and data area. The *address area* is used to identify the sector. This is critically important because the drive must be able to identify precisely which cylinder, head, and sector is about to be read or written. This location information is recorded in the "address field," and is followed by two bytes of cyclical redundancy check (CRC) data. When a drive identifies a location, it generates a CRC code which it compares to the CRC code recorded on the disk. If the two CRC codes match, the address is assumed to be

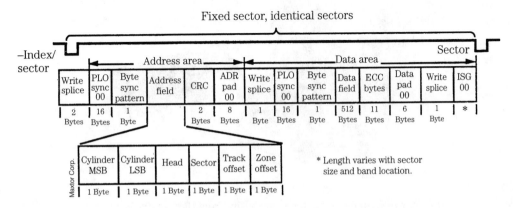

7-13 Sector layout of a typical hard drive.

valid, and disk operation can continue. Otherwise, an error has occurred and the entire sector is considered invalid. This failure usually precipitates a catastrophic DOS error message.

After a number of bytes are encountered for drive timing and synchronization, up to 512 bytes can be read or written to the "data field." The data is processed to derive eleven bytes of ECC error-checking code using Reed-Solomon encoding. If data is being read, the derived ECC is compared to the recorded ECC. When the codes match, data is assumed to be valid and drive operation continues. Otherwise, a data read error is assumed. During writing, the old ECC data is replaced with the new ECC data derived for the current data.

It is interesting to note that only the data and ECC fields of a sector are written after formatting. All other sector data remains untouched until the drive is reformatted. If a retentivity problem eventually allows one or more bits to become corrupt in the address area, the sector fails.

Sector sparing

Not all sectors on a hard drive are usable. When a drive is formatted, bad sectors must be removed from normal use. The *sparing* process works to ensure that each track has access to the appropriate number of working sectors. When sparing is performed *in-line* (as a drive is being formatted), faulty sectors cause all subsequent sectors to be shifted up one sector. In-line sparing is not widely used.

Field defect sparing, performed after the format process is complete, assigns or remaps faulty sectors to other working sectors located in spare disk tracks that are reserved for that purpose. For example, the Hewlett-Packard Kitty Hawk drive (Fig. 7-14) uses field defect sparing. It reserves a full 16 tracks for spare sectors. Faulty sectors are typically marked for reallocation when the disk is formatted.

7-14 A 1.3" form factor 20/40Mb hard drive from Hewlett-Packard Co.

The only place where faulty sectors are absolutely not permitted is on track 00. Track 00 is used to hold a hard drive's partition and FAT information. If a drive cannot read or write to track 00, the entire drive is rendered unusable. If a sector in track 00 fails during operation, reformatting the drive to lock out the bad sector does not necessarily recover the drive's operation. Track 00 failures usually necessitates reformatting the drive from scratch or replacing it entirely.

Landing zone

The read/write heads of a hard drive fly within microinches of their respective platter surfaces—held aloft with air currents produced by the spinning platters. When the drive is turned off, however, the platters slow to a halt. During this *spindown period,* air flow falls rapidly, and heads can literally crash into their platter surfaces. Whenever a head touches a platter surface, data can be irretrievably destroyed. Even during normal operation, a sudden shock or bump can cause one or more heads to skid across their surfaces. Although a drive can usually be reformatted after a head crash, all current data and programs must be reloaded from scratch.

In order to avoid head crash during normal spindown, a cylinder is reserved (either the innermost or outermost cylinder) as a *landing zone*. No data is stored on the landing zone, so any surface problems caused by head landings are harmless. Most drives used in small computers automatically move the head assembly over the landing zone before spindown, then gently lock the heads into place until power is restored. Locking helps to ensure that random shocks and vibrations do not shake the heads onto adjacent data-carrying tracks and cause damage while power is off.

Interleave

The *interleave* of a hard drive refers to the order in which sectors are numbered on a platter. Interleave was a critical factor in older desktop computer systems where the core logic (i.e., CPU and memory) was relatively slow compared to drive performance. It was necessary to create artificial delays in the drive to allow core logic to catch up. Delays were accomplished by physically separating the sectors (numbering contiguous sectors out of order). This ordering forced the drive to read a sector, then skip one or more sectors to reach the next subsequent sector. The drive would have to make several rotations before all sectors on a track could be read.

The ratio of a sector's length versus the distance between two subsequent sectors is known as the *interleave factor*. For example, if a drive reads a sector and skips a sector to reach the next sequential sector, its interleave factor would be 1:3, and so on. The greater the interleave, the more rotations that are needed to read all the sectors on a track, and the slower the drive is. To achieve highest disk performance, interleave should be eliminated.

Because core logic today is so much faster than even the fastest hard drive, the issue of interleave is largely irrelevant. Drives no longer interleave their sectors, so all sectors are in sequential order around the track, and the interleave factor is 1:1— all data on a track can be read in one disk rotation (minus latency). An interleave factor of 1:1 yields optimal drive performance.

Write precompensation

A hard drive spins its platters at a constant rate. This is known as *constant angular velocity* (CAV). While constant rotation requires only a very simple motor circuit, extra demands are placed on the medium. Tracks closer to the spindle are physically shorter than tracks toward the platter's outer edge. Shorter tracks result in shorter sectors. For inner sectors to hold the same amount of data as outer sectors, data must be packed more densely on the inner sectors—each magnetic flux reversal is actually smaller. Unfortunately, smaller flux reversals produce weaker magnetic fields in the read/write heads during reading.

If the inner sectors are written with a stronger magnetic field, flux transitions stored in the media are stronger. When the inner sectors are then read, a clearer, more well-defined signal results. The use of increased writing current to compensate for diminished disk response is known as *write precompensation*. The track where write precompensation is expected to begin is specified in the drive's parameter table in CMOS system setup. Write precompensation filled an important role in early drives that used older, oxide-based media. Today's thin-film media and very small drive geometries result in low signal differences across the platter area, so write precompensation (although still specified) is rarely meaningful anymore.

Drive parameters

A host computer must know the key parameters of its installed hard drive before the drive can be used. There are six parameters that a system must know: the number of cylinders, heads, and sectors, as well as the track where write precompensation begins; what track the landing zone is on; and the drive's formatted capacity. These parameters are stored in the computer's CMOS setup memory. If a new drive is installed, the CMOS setup can easily be updated to show the changes. Table 7-1 illustrates an example of drive parameters.

It is possible to draw some interesting information about a drive by looking at its parameters. Consider the Fujitsu drive from Table 7-1. You can immediately see that it is a 54Mb drive with 754 cylinders (tracks per platter surface). Because only four heads are used, you know there are two platters (two heads per platter). There are 35 sectors per track. Write precompensation begins at track 375 (roughly the middle track) and continues through track 754. When the drive is shut down, the heads must park over track 754 for landing (nearest to the spindle).

Table 7-1. An example of drive parameters

Parameter	CDC 9420 x –51	Fujitsu M2241AS	Maxtor XT8760E
Cylinders	989	754	1632
Heads	5	4	15
Sectors per track	35	35	52
Write precompensation	0	375	none
Landing zone	989	754	1631
Capacity (M)	89	54	652

The CDC drive provides 89Mb in 989 cylinders. Each track is broken into 35 sectors. Notice that there are 5 heads, so three platters are available, but one side of one platter is left unused by data. Write precompensation begins right at track 00, so enhanced current is used all over the drive. The landing zone for the CDC drive is also on the innermost track (989). As you can see, a parameter table can provide a great deal of valuable information.

Data transfer rate

Information must be transferred back and forth between the computer's core logic and the drive mechanism. The *data transfer rate* specifies just how fast bits can be sent between a host system and drive. Data transfer rate is generally specified either in megahertz (MHz) or megabytes per second (Mb/s). Remember that the Mb/s rate should be 1/8 of the MHz rate. The rate of data transfer is a specification that depends on a variety of system conditions: the class and speed of the CPU, core logic overhead (or bus utilization), the physical interface architecture in use, and the design of the hard drive itself.

Today, the major limiting factor of data transfer rate is the physical interface, because core logic and hard drives can operate exceptionally fast. Drives using the IDE interface can transfer data up to 4Mb/s over an 8-bit data bus, while the newer SCSI-2 interface runs up to 10Mb/s.

Encoding

Binary information must be translated into flux transitions (or *encoded*) for storage on magnetic media. Not only must data be stored, but it is desirable to manipulate data in order to fit more information into limited media space. As you saw in chapter 6, floppy drives make use of FM and MFM encoding schemes to encode data. Both FM and MFM encoding cause a 1:1 relationship between the bit being recorded and the flux transition recorded on the disk (1 bit = 1 flux transition). Such a relationship is straightforward, but is certainly not the most efficient way to encode data. Many hard drives today make use of the Run Length Limited (RLL) encoding scheme.

RLL encoding represents each byte of data as a unique series of 16 flux transitions. There are 65,536 possible 16-bit codes (2^{16}), but engineers have chosen 256 of those 16-bit combinations to represent each possible byte. Each combination is chosen so that it records easily on the available media. The objective is to choose codes that space digital 1s farther apart—this makes it easier for control circuitry to read and write. Each 16-bit code is actually placed on the media in a much denser fashion than floppy drives. As a result, there are twice as many bits to represent a byte, but the bits are placed many times closer together, which saves space.

Consider the *2,7 RLL* scheme. Bytes are converted into 16-bit words where each logic 1 is separated by 2 to 7 logic 0s (thus the term 2,7 RLL). Table 7-2 illustrates some sample conversions. Note that logic 1s never have less than two 0s between them. As a result, there are 2/3 fewer flux transitions per bit (on average). There are twice as many bits, but only 1/3 the number of flux changes. Encoding with 2,7 RLL offers over 50% more storage capacity than MFM encoding, as well as a 50% increase in the data transfer rate (twice the number of bits being read in the same period of

**Table 7-2. An example of
binary-to-2, 7 RLL conversion**

Binary data	2,7 RLL interpretation
11	1000
10	0100
011	001000
010	100100
0011	0000 1000
0010	0010 0100
000	000100

time). Keep in mind that packing so much data requires media with a high coercivity (usually 600 oersteds or more).

An advanced version of RLL encoding is 3,9 RLL. In this version, bytes are still translated into 16 bit patterns, but each binary 1 is separated by 3 to 9 logic 0s. The 3,9 RLL scheme can pack 50% more data on a drive than 2,7 RLL (100% more than MFM encoding), and an even higher data transfer rate. Note that the read/write circuitry required to operate a 3,9 RLL drive must be faster and offer a wider bandwidth than other encoding schemes.

Disk caching

Ideally, a mass-storage device should respond instantaneously—data should be available the moment it is requested. Unfortunately, the instant access and transfer of data is virtually impossible with today's magnetic (and optical) storage technologies. The inescapable laws of physics govern the limitations of mechanical systems such as spindles and head stepping, and mechanical delays will always be present in drive systems to some extent.

The problem now facing computer designers is that mechanical drive systems—as fast and precise as they are—are still far slower than the computer circuitry handling the information. In the world of personal computers, a millisecond is a very long time. For DOS-based systems, you often must wait for disk access to be completed before DOS allows another operation to begin. Such delays can be irritating when the drive is accessing the huge programs and data files that are typical of current software packages. Designers have developed a technique called *drive caching* to increase the apparent speed of drive systems.

Caching essentially allocates a small amount of solid-state memory to act as an interim storage area (or *buffer*). A cache is typically loaded with information that is anticipated to be required by the system. When a disk read is initiated, the cache is checked for desired information. If the desired information is actually in the cache (a cache hit), that information is transferred from the cache buffer to the core logic at electronic rates—no disk access occurs, and very fast data transfer is achieved. If the desired information is not in the cache (a cache miss), the data is taken from the hard disk at normal drive speeds with no improvement in performance. A variety of complex software algorithms are used to predict what disk information to load and save in a cache. Figure 7-15 illustrates the caching algorithm used by Quantum Corp. for some of their ProDrive hard drives.

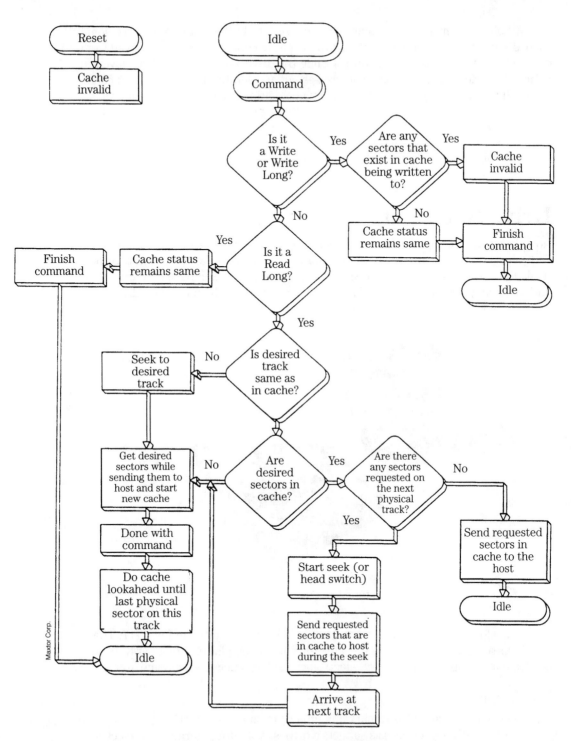

7-15 A cache control algorithm.

Although the majority of caches are intended to buffer read operations, some caches also buffer write operations. A write cache accepts the data to be saved from core logic, then returns system control while the drive works separately to save the information. Keep in mind that a cache does not accelerate the drive itself. A cache merely helps to move your system along by not waiting for as many drive delays.

In terms of general implementation, a cache can be located on the hard drive itself, with the hard drive controller IC, or in the main memory in core logic. For most computers using system-level hard-drive interfaces (IDE or SCSI), any cache is usually located on the drive itself. You will see more about drive caches later in this chapter.

Drive construction

Now that you have a background in major hard-drive concepts and operations (Fig. 7-16), it is time to take a drive apart and show you how all the key pieces fit together. While it is somewhat rare that you should ever need to disassemble a hard drive, the understanding of each part and its placement will help you to appreciate drive testing and the various hard-drive failure modes.

7-16   A Quantum ProDrive ELS hard drive.

An exploded diagram for a Quantum hard drive is illustrated in Fig. 7-17. There are six areas that this book concentrates on: the frame, platters, read/write heads, head actuators, spindle motor, and electronics package. Let's look at each area.

The frame

The mechanical frame (1) is remarkably important to the successful operation of a hard drive. The frame (or chassis) affects a drive's structural, thermal, and electrical integrity. A frame must be rigid, and provide a steady platform for mounting the

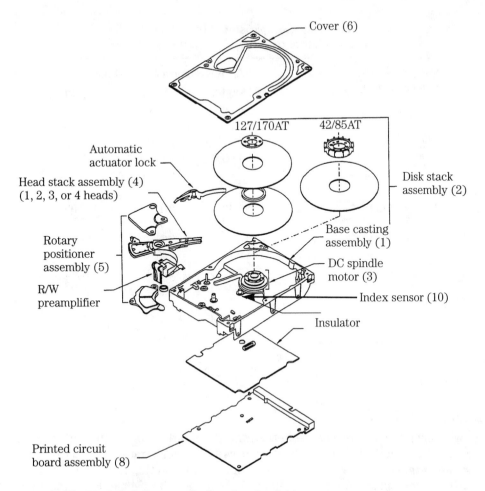

Cover (6)

127/170AT 42/85AT

Automatic
actuator lock

Head stack assembly (4)
(1, 2, 3, or 4 heads)

Disk stack
assembly (2)

Rotary
positioner
assembly (5)

Base casting
assembly (1)

DC spindle
motor (3)

R/W
preamplifier

Index sensor (10)

Insulator

Printed circuit
board assembly (8)

7-17   Exploded diagram of a Quantum hard drive. <small>Reprinted with the permission of Quantum Corp.</small>

working components. Larger drives typically use a chassis of cast aluminum, but the small drive in your notebook or pen-computer might use a plastic frame. The particular frame material really depends on the *form factor* (dimensions) of your drive. Table 7-3 compares the form factors of several drive generations.

Platters

As you read early in this chapter, the platters (2) are relatively heavy-duty disks of aluminum, glass, or ceramic. Platters are coated on both sides with a layer of magnetic material (the actual medium) and coated with a protective layer. Finished and polished platters are then stacked and coupled to the spindle motor (3); some drives might use only one platter. Before the platter stack is fixed to the chassis, the read/write head assembly (4) is fitted in between each disk. There is usually one head per platter side, so a drive with two platters should have three or four heads. During drive operation, the platter stack spins at 3600 RPM or more.

Table 7-3. Comparison of form factor nomenclature to actual drive dimensions

Form factor nomenclature		Approximate dimensions		
		Height	Width	Depth
5.25" full-height *	mm	82.60	145.54	202.69
	in	3.25	5.73	7.98
5.25" half-height *	mm	41.28	145.54	202.68
	in	1.63	5.73	7.98
3.5" half-height **	mm	41.28	101.60	146.05
	in	1.63	4.00	5.75
3.5" low-profile **	mm	25.40	101.60	146.05
	in	1.00	4.00	5.75
2.5" low-profile	mm	19.05	70.10	101.85
	in	0.75	2.76	4.01
1.8" low-profile	mm	15.00	51.00	77.00
	in	0.59	2.00	3.03
1.3" low-profile	mm	10.50	36.50	50.8
	in	0.41	1.44	2.00

* Used in desktop systems only

** Used in desktops and some older laptops

Read/write heads

As with floppy drives, read/write heads form the interface between a drive's electronic circuitry and magnetic media. During writing, a head translates electronic signals into magnetic flux transitions that saturate points on the medium where those transitions take place. A read operation works roughly in reverse. Flux transitions along the disk induce electrical signals in the head which are amplified, filtered, and translated into corresponding logic signals. It is up to the drive's electronics to determine whether a head is reading or writing.

Early hard drive read/write heads generally resembled floppy drive heads—soft iron cores with a core of 8 to 34 turns of fine copper wire. Such heads were physically large and relatively heavy, which limited the number of tracks available on a platter surface, and presented more inertia to be overcome by the head positioning system.

Virtually all current hard drive designs have abandoned the classic wound-coil heads in favor of thin-film read/write heads. Thin-film heads are fabricated in much the same way as ICs or platter media using photochemical processes. The result is a very flat, sensitive, small, and durable read/write head, but even thin-film heads use an air gap and 8 to 34 turns of copper wire. Small size and light weight allow for smaller track widths (more than 1000 tracks per platter side) and faster head travel time. The inherent flatness of thin-film heads helps to reduce flying height to only 5 microns or so.

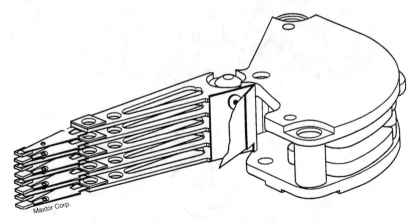

Maxtor Corp.

7-18   A conventional head/actuator assembly.

In assemblies, the heads themselves are attached to long metal arms that are moved by the head actuator motor(s) as shown in Fig. 7-18. Read/write preamp ICs are typically mounted on a small PC board that is attached to the head/actuator assembly. The entire subassembly is sealed in the platter compartment, and is generally inaccessible unless opened in a cleanroom environment. The compartment is sealed with a metal lid/gasket configuration (6).

Head actuators

Unlike floppy motors that step their read/write heads in and out, hard drives swing their heads along a slight arc to achieve radial travel from edge to spindle. Many hard drives use *voice coil motors* (also called *rotary coil motors* or *servos*) to actuate head movement. Voice coil motors (5) work using the same principle as analog meter movements: a permanent magnet is enclosed within two opposing coils (Fig. 7-19). As current flows through the coils, a magnetic field is produced which opposes the permanent magnet. Head arms are attached to the rotating magnet, so the force of opposition causes a deflection that is directly proportional to the amount of driving current. Greater current signals result in greater opposition and greater deflection. Cylinders are selected by incrementing the servo signal and maintaining the signal at the desired level. Voice coil motors are very small and light assemblies that are well suited to fast access times and small hard drive assemblies.

The greatest challenge to head movement is to keep the heads centered on the desired track. Otherwise, aerodynamic disturbances, thermal effects in the platters, and variations in voice coil driver signals can cause head positioning error. Head position must be constantly checked and adjusted in real time to ensure that desired tracks are followed exactly. The process of track following is called *servoing* the heads. Information is required to compare the head's expected position to their actual position—any resulting difference can then be corrected by adjusting the voice coil signal. Servo information is located on the platters using a variety of techniques.

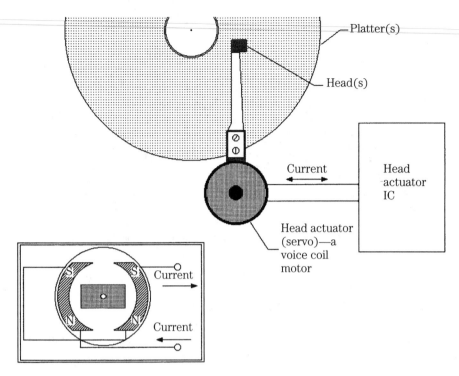

7-19 Simplified operation of a rotary coil motor.

Dedicated servo information is recorded on a reserved platter side. For example, a two-platter drive using dedicated servo tracking might use three sides for data, but use a fourth surface exclusively for track locating information. Because all heads are positioned along the same track (a cylinder), a single surface can provide data that is needed to correct all heads simultaneously. *Embedded servo information,* however, is encoded as short bursts of data placed between every sector. All surfaces can then both hold data and provide tracking information. The servo system uses the phase shift of pulses between adjacent tracks to determine whether heads are centered on the desired track, or drifting to one side or another. For the purposes of this book, you need not be concerned with the particular tracking techniques—only be aware that tracking information must be provided to keep the heads in proper alignment.

Spindle motor

One of the major factors that contributes to hard drive performance is the speed at which the media passes under the read/write heads. Media is passed under the read/write heads by spinning the platters at a high rate of speed (at least 3600 RPM). The *spindle motor* is responsible for spinning the platters. A spindle motor is typically a brushless, low-profile dc motor that is similar in principle to the spindle motors used in floppy disk drives.

An *index sensor* (10) provides a feedback pulse signal that detects the spindle as it rotates. The drive's control electronics (8) use the index signal to regulate spindle speed as precisely as possible. Today's drives typically use magnetic sensors that detect iron tabs on the spindle shaft, or optoisolators that monitor holes or tabs rotating along the spindle. The spindle motor and index sensor are also sealed in the platter compartment.

Older hard drives used a rubber or cork pad to slow the spindle to a stop after drive power is removed, but newer drives use a technique called *dynamic braking*. When power is applied to a spindle motor, a magnetic field is developed in the motor coils. When power is removed, the magnetic energy stored in the coils is released as a reverse voltage pulse. Dynamic braking channels the energy of this reverse voltage to stop the drive faster and more reliably than physical braking.

Drive electronics

Hard drives are controlled by a suite of remarkably sophisticated circuitry. The drive electronics board (8) mounted below the chassis contains all of the circuitry necessary to communicate control and data signals with the particular physical interface, maneuver the read/write heads, read or write as required, and spin the platters. Each of these functions must be accomplished to high levels of precision. In spite of the demands and complexity involved in drive electronics, the entire circuit can be fabricated on a single PC board similar to the one shown in Fig. 7-20.

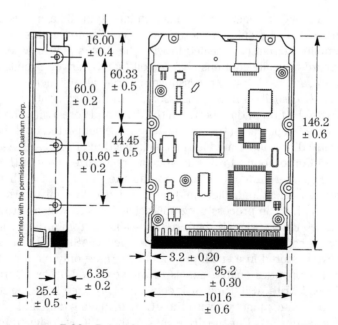

7-20　Drive electronics mounted in a base casting.

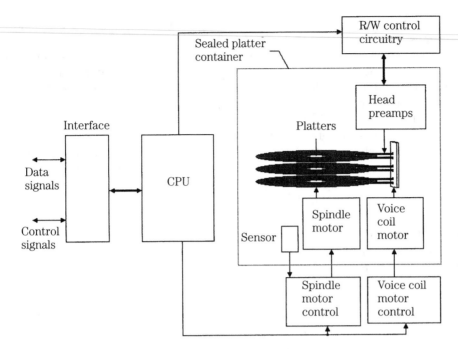

7-21   Block diagram of a generic hard drive.

Figure 7-21 illustrates a generic block diagram for a typical hard drive electronics system. Notice that the spindle motor, voice coil motor, index sensor, and read/write preamplifier circuitry is sealed in with the drive's platter assembly. The electronics PC board typically contains a voice coil (servo) driver circuit, a spindle motor driver circuit, and read/write processing circuitry—all of which is overseen by a drive controller IC (usually a microprocessor). An interface controller circuit is added to coordinate the flow of data between the drive and core logic. The interface controller that is used depends on the physical interface supported by the drive.

A practical hard disk is illustrated in the block diagram of Fig. 7-22. As you look over the Quantum Corporation's ProDrive, you can recognize many of the key elements shown in Fig. 7-21. You should understand the purpose of each part. The heart of this drive is a microcontroller (µC). A µC is basically a customized version of a microprocessor that can process program instructions as well as provide a selection of specialized control signals that are not available from ordinary microprocessors. A µC can be considered an application-specific IC (ASIC). The program that operates this drive is stored in a small programmable read-only memory (PROM). The microcontroller provides enable signals to the voice-coil driver IC, read/write preamplifier IC, read/write ASIC, and disk controller/interface ASIC. A controller/ interface ASIC works in conjunction with the µC by managing data and control signals on the physical interface. For the drive shown, the ASIC is designed to support a SCSI interface, but variations of this model can use interface ASICs that support IDE interfaces (physical interfaces are covered in the next section).

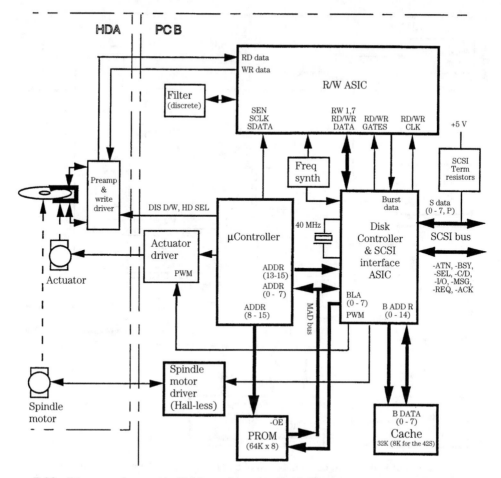

7-22   Diagram of a practical high-performance hard drive. Reprinted with the permission of Quantum Corp.

The primary activity of the controller/interface ASIC is to coordinate the flow of data into or out of the drive. Figure 7-23 shows a detailed view of the disk controller and SCSI interface ASIC. The controller determines read or write operations, handles clock synchronization, and organizes data flow to the read/write ASIC. The controller also manages the local cache memory. Commands received over the physical interface are passed on to the μC for processing and response. The frequency synthesizer helps to synchronize the controller and read/write ASIC. Finally, the disk controller ASIC is responsible for selecting the head position and controlling the spindle and motor driver.

The read/write ASIC shown in Fig. 7-24 is another major IC on the drive's PC board. A read/write ASIC accepts data from the controller IC and translates data into serial signals that are sent to the write driver for writing. The read/write ASIC also receives signals amplified by the read preamp, and translates serial signals into parallel digital information available to the controller ASIC. A discrete filter affects the

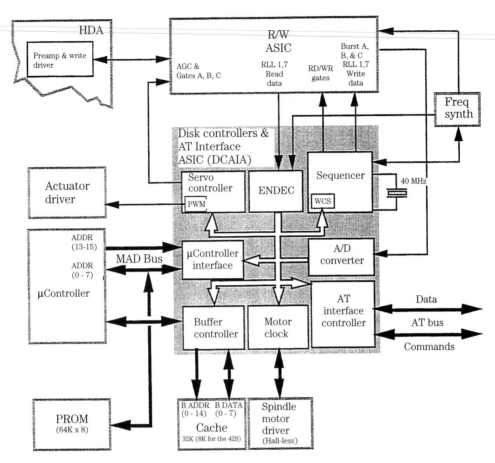

7-23 Detailed block diagram of a hard disk drive controller/interface IC.
Reprinted with the permission of Quantum Corp.

way in which analog signals are handled. Read/write heads are connected directly to
the read preamplifier/write driver IC, which is little more than a bidirectional amplifier IC.

The actuator driver accepts a logic enable signal from the μC and a proportional
logic signal from the controller ASIC. The actuator driver then produces an analog
output current that positions the read/write heads by driving a voice coil motor. The
spindle motor driver is turned on and off by a logic enable signal from the controller
ASIC. Once the spindle motor driver is enabled, it self-regulates its speed using feedback from an index sensor.

All components within the dotted area marked "HDA" are located within the
sealed platter compartment while other components in the area marked "PCB" are
located on the drive PC board. Most of the drive's intelligence is contained in the μC,
controller ASIC, and read/write ASIC.

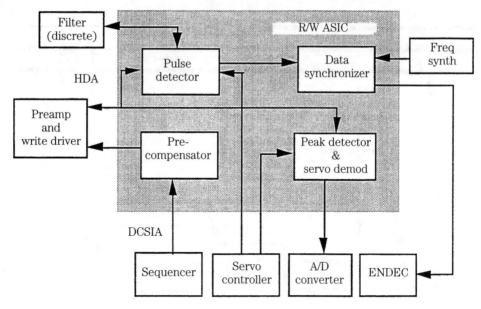

7-24   Detail of a read/write ASIC.

A system view

So far, you have only learned about the hard drives themselves. However, there is much more involved in hard-drive operation. The *physical interface* only connects a drive to your host computer system, but the drive must obtain access to your computer's main busses in order to actually serve a practical purpose. Bus access is provided by the *host controller*. In the early days of desktop hard drives, a controller board was needed. The drive would connect to the host controller board which, in turn, would plug into an expansion slot in the host computer's motherboard (or backplane). Older cards were usually packed with ICs, or combined on the same card with floppy drive controller circuitry. Today, a hard drive host controller is usually implemented as a single ASIC located on a miniature expansion board attached to the motherboard. Some computers offer motherboards designed specifically for a particular interface, and implement the controller circuit and connector directly on the motherboard. You then need only plug the drive cable directly into the motherboard. This approach leaves an expansion slot free. The hard-drive controller ASIC translates commands and data on the computer busses into commands and data sent over the physical interface, and vice versa. Figure 7-25 shows a basic illustration of the parts comprising a complete hard-drive system.

As with most other aspects of your computer, hard-drive access for reading or writing originates in the system CPU during execution of a program in core memory (DOS, Windows, or some other application). It is interesting to note that the CPU does not interact with the hard drive directly. Instead, the CPU instructs the system controller to address the hard-drive controller and begin data transfer into or out of the drive. Any program subroutines needed to operate the hard drive are taken by

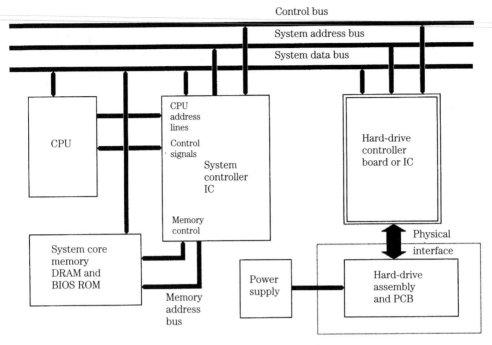

7-25   Block diagram of a complete hard-drive system.

the CPU from BIOS ROM in core memory. Transfer takes place to and from memory using direct memory access (DMA) techniques.

In actual practice, the process of drive signalling, data transfer, and control is a rather complex and involved procedure that is beyond the scope of this book. For the purposes of this chapter, it is important that you understand how the hard drive interacts with the rest of your computer.

Drive interfaces

Hard drives were not included in the earliest PC designs. Instead, hard drives developed as an add-on device that could either be included in new computers or added as an after-market item. As a result, there was no natural bus-level interface that allowed a stand-alone drive to work with a CPU's control, address, and data busses. Hard drives needed a host controller card which could plug into the computer's busses. Then there was the problem of connecting the drive to its controller card. This connection between a drive and its controller card (or controller IC in a small computer) is the physical interface. Although there are limitless variations of connectors and signals, four physical interface standards and their variations have developed since the early 1980s: ST506, ESDI, IDE, and SCSI. Table 7-4 presents a comparison of interface characteristics for your reference.

Table 7-4. Comparison of hard-drive interface characteristics

Parameter	ESDI	IDE	SCSI-1	SCSI-2	SCSI-3
Data bus width (bits)	1	8/16	8	8/24	8/32
Interface cable conductors	34/20	40	50	50/68	50/68
Maximum cable length (meters)	3.0	0.5	6.0	6.0	?
Data transfer rate (Mbps)	10.0	?	32.0	80/320	?
Data transfer rate (MHz)	10.0	?	4.0	10.0	?

? – a highly variable or not well-established parameter

ST506

The *ST506* interface dates back to 1980, and is largely regarded to be the ancestor of all modern hard-drive interfaces. The serial interface works at 5 Mbits per second using the same MFM encoding as floppy drives. Later versions of ST506 use RLL encoding instead of MFM at 17 sectors per track (512 bytes per sector). ST506 drives performed head stepping with stepping motors. ST506 drives are "dumb" (device-level) devices. Like floppy drives, ST506 drives must be told explicitly what to do and when to do it. This necessitates a complex and demanding controller board residing on a plug-in expansion board. The host computer addresses the controller board through the main computer busses and sends instructions to the controller's on-board registers.

The physical interface for an ST506 drive consists of three cables: a 4-pin power cable, a 34-pin control cable, and a 20-pin data cable. The control cable is responsible for carrying explicit operating signals to the drive such as Drive Select, Cylinder Select, Head Select, and so on. The data cable supports differential read and write lines. Figure 7-26 shows the cable pinouts for an ST506 interface. Both digital cables are flat or twisted-pair ribbon cable.

The 34-pin control cable uses 17 differential signals. Differential connections are well-suited for resisting the influence of noise and for carrying signals over long distances. You should notice that almost all signals are active-high. There are three Head Select inputs (pins 14, 18, and 4 respectively) that select one of up to eight read/write heads for reading or writing. The Write Gate input (pin 6) is logic 1 during write operations and logic 0 during read operations. A Seek Complete output (pin 8) tells the controller when the heads have been moved the desired step distance. Track 000 (pin 10) is an output informing the controller when the heads move from track 001 to 000.

A Write Fault output (pin 12) tells the controller if an error has occurred during the write operation. There are a number of write faults, including:

- Write Current in a head without the Write Gate signal true
- No Write Current in the head with Write Gate true and the drive selected
- Write Gate true when heads are off the desired track, or dc power to the drive is outside acceptable limits

The Sector/Address Mark Found signal (pin 16) sends an output pulse to the controller when the head is positioned correctly. An Index output (pin 20) provides

	1	+12 Vdc
	2	12 V ret
	3	5 V ret
	4	+5 Vdc

	Sig. Pin	GWD Pin
Reserved	2	1
Head Select 2	4	3
Write Gate	6	5
Seek Complete	8	7
Track 000	10	9
Write Fault	12	11
Head Select 0	14	13
Sector/Address Mark	16	15
Head Select 1	18	17
Index	20	19
Ready	22	21
Step	24	23
Drive Select 1	26	25
Drive Select 2	28	27
Drive Select 3	30	29
Drive Select 4	32	31
Direction In	34	33

	Sig. Pin	GWD Pin
Drive Selected	1	2
reserved	3	4
reserved	5	6
reserved	7	8
reserved	9 & 10	11
+ Write Data	13	12
– Write Data	14	15
+ Read Data	17	16
– Read Data	18	19 & 20

7-26   Pinout diagram for an ST506 hard-drive interface.

a brief pulse whenever a track's index data mark has just passed under the read/write heads. An index pulse appears every 16.6 ms for a disk spinning at 3600 RPM (once per revolution).

The Ready output (pin 22) tells the controller when drive speed and dc power are acceptable, and the track 000 signal is true—the drive is considered ready for operation. A pulse on the Step input (pin 24) causes the head stepping motor to move one track position. The direction in which the heads actually step depends on the Direction In input condition (pin 34). Finally, there are four Drive Select inputs (pins 26, 28, 30, and 32) used to identify which drive must be accessed.

Although the data cable carries 20 conductors, there are really only three meaningful signals. Four Reserved lines (pins 3, 5, 9, and 10) are not used at all. The Drive Selected output (pin 1) acknowledges to the controller when its drive address matches the drive address specified on the control cable's Drive Select lines. Differential Write Data lines (pins 13 and 14) transmit serial data to the drive from the controller. Differential Read Data signals (pins 17 and 18) send serial data read from the disk to the controller.

ESDI

The *Enhanced Small Device Interface* (ESDI) came into being early in 1983 in an effort to replace the already obsolete ST506 and its variant, the ST412. ESDI drives make extensive use of RLL encoding, with 34 sectors per track and a direct 1:1 interleave factor. The ESDI scheme employs data separator/encoder circuitry on the drive itself, where ST506 drives placed the circuitry on the controller card. With data separator/encoder circuitry already on the drive, an ESDI drive need only send straight binary over its data lines. This approach gives ESDI the potential for serial data rates up to 24 Mbits per second. Another improvement to ESDI is the use of *buffered seeks,* which allow the drive (not the controller) to manage head step movement. The ESDI drive need only receive a single step command from its controller which could refer to single or multiple track steps.

The pinouts for ESDI cables are illustrated in Fig. 7-27. As you look over the pinout labels, you will notice that virtually all of the signals are active-low logic (denoted by the bar over their names). Physically, the cable layout is very similar to the ST506 approach. The 34-pin control cable uses differential signalling and many of the same signals used for ST506. ESDI is also a "dumb" interface, wherein most of the drive's intelligence is located on the controller card. The drive must be told explicitly what to do and when to do it.

There are four Head Select lines (pins 2, 4, 14, and 18) that select one of up to 16 read/write heads on the drive for reading or writing. The Write Gate signal (pin 6) enables the selected head for writing. A Config/Status Data line (pin 8) responds to the controller's request for information by sending 16 or more serial condition bits back to the controller. A Transfer Request input (pin 24) indicates that the host system wants to begin a data transfer, while the Transfer Acknowledge output (pin 10) sends a handshaking signal to the controller when a data transfer is permitted to begin. The Attention output (pin 1 2) is sent by the drive when the controller must read drive status—usually due to a fault.

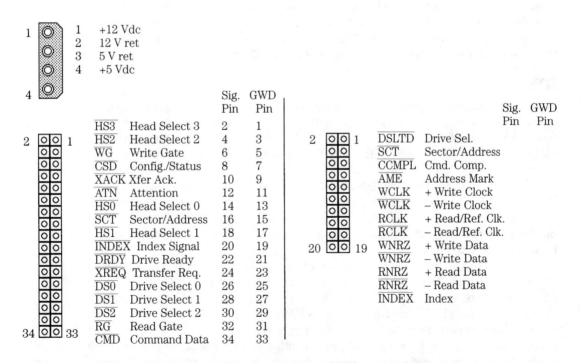

7-27 Pinout diagram for an ESDI hard-drive interface.

The Sector/Address Mark Found line (pin 16) outputs a pulse to the controller whenever a sector's address data passes under a head. An Index signal (pin 20) produces a pulse every 16.6 ms corresponding to a track's index mark data. The Drive Ready line (pin 22) outputs a signal to the controller when the drive is at operating speed and is ready to accept commands. A Read Gate signal (pin 32) enables the selected read/write head for a read operation. Commands and data can be sent from controller to drive using the 16-bit serial line called Command Data (pin 34). Finally, three Drive Select lines (pins 26, 28, and 30 respectively) form a binary value corresponding to the drive number which the computer wants to access.

The 20-pin data cable uses a mix of differential and single-ended signals. A Drive Selected output (pin 1) tells the controller that the selected drive is responding to commands. The Sector/Address Mark Found (pin 2) is essentially the same signal used in the 34-pin cable, but is available at all times. When the ESDI drive has finished its last function, it outputs a Command Complete signal (pin 3) to tell the host that a new command can be accepted. An Address Mark Enable signal (AME, pin 4) causes the drive to search for the next address mark. The AME can also be used to enable writing address marks and sync data fields to the disk during the format process. The +Write Clock and –Write Clock (pins 7 and 8) are used for synchronizing write data. The +Read/Reference Clock and –Read/Reference Clock (pins 10 and 11) are used for synchronizing read data, and for determining the drive's appropriate data transfer rate.

Write data is carried to the drive over the +Write Data and –Write Data lines (pins 13 and 14), and read data is carried to the controller by the +Read Data and –Read Data lines (pins 17 and 18). Finally, an Index signal (pin 20) generates a pulse signal each time the platters rotate. This index signal serves the same purpose as the index signal in the 34-pin cable, but it is available at all times.

IDE

The *Intelligent Drive Electronics* or *Integrated Drive Electronics* (IDE) interface is one of the most popular and widely used system-level interfaces for hard drives today. All the circuitry required to operate an IDE drive is located on the hard-drive PC board. An IDE interface connects a hard drive to the controller board (or motherboard) over a 40-pin connector, as shown in Fig. 7-28. Software routines needed to communicate with an IDE drive are already embedded in the BIOS ROM of any IBM PC/AT (or compatible) system. Because the controller for an IDE interface can usually be implemented as a single ASIC, an IDE controller can often be provided right on the motherboard itself. By plugging an IDE drive directly into a motherboard, an expansion slot can be saved.

A complete IDE interface is composed of two cables: a 4-pin power cable and a 40-pin signal cable. Both cable pinouts are illustrated in Fig. 7-29. The classical power connector is a 4-pin mate-and-lock connector. To maintain conventions with floppy drive systems, IDE hard drives use +5 Vdc and +12 Vdc. The return (ground) for each supply is also provided on the power connector.

The signal cable is typically a 40-pin insulation displacement connector (IDC) cable. Both the even- and odd-numbered wires are signal-carrying lines. Also note that some of the signal labels have dark bars over their names. The bar indicates that

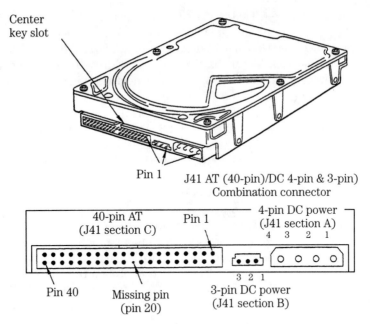

7-28 IDE connector configuration. <small>Reprinted with the permission of Quantum Corp.</small>

1	+12 Vdc
2	12 V ret
3	5 V ret
4	+5 Vdc

2	Ground	1	$\overline{\text{Reset}}$
4	DD8	3	DD7
^	DD9	5	DD6
8	DD10	7	DD5
10	DD11	9	DD4
12	DD12	11	DD3
14	DD13	13	DD2
16	DD14	15	DD1
18	DD15	17	DD0
20	key pin	19	Ground
22	Ground	21	DMARQ
24	Ground	23	$\overline{\text{DIOW}}$
26	Ground	25	$\overline{\text{DIOR}}$
28	reserved	27	$\overline{\text{IORDY}}$
30	Ground	29	$\overline{\text{DMACK}}$
32	$\overline{\text{IOCS16}}$	31	INTQ
34	PD1AG	33	DA1
36	$\overline{\text{DA2}}$	35	$\overline{\text{DA0}}$
38	CS3FX	37	$\overline{\text{CS1FX}}$
40	Ground	39	DASP

7-29 Pinout diagram for an IDE hard-drive interface.

the particular signal is active low. That is, the signal is true in the logic 0 state instead of being true in the logic 1 state. All signal lines on the IDE interface are fully TTL-compatible, where a logic 0 is 0.0 to +0.8 Vdc, and a logic 1 is +2.0 to +3.0 Vdc.

Data points and registers in the hard drive are addressed using the Drive Address Bus lines DA0 to DA2 (pins 35, 33, and 36 respectively) in conjunction with the Chip Select Drive inputs CS1FX and CS3FX (pins 37 and 38). When a true signal is sent along the Drive I/O Read (DIOR, pin 25) line, the drive executes a read cycle, while a true on the Drive I/O Write (DIOW, pin 23) line initiates a write cycle. The IDE interface provides TTL-level input and output signals. There are 16 bidirectional data lines (DD0 to DD15, pins 3 to 18) used to carry data bits into or our of the drive. Once a data transfer is completed, a DMA Acknowledge (DMACK, pin 29) signal is provided to the drive from the hard-disk controller IC. Finally, a true signal on the drive's Reset line (pin 1) restores the drive to its original condition at power on. A Reset is sent when the computer is first powered on or rebooted.

The IDE physical interface also provides a number of outputs back to the motherboard. A Direct Memory Access Request (DMARQ, pin 21) is used to initiate the transfer of data to or from the drive. The direction of data transfer depends on the condition of the DIOR and DIOW inputs. A DMACK signal is generated in response when the DMARQ line is asserted or made true. IORDY (pin 27) is an I/O Ready signal that keeps a system's attention if the drive is not quite ready to respond to a data transfer request. A drive Interrupt Request (INTQ or INTRQ, pin 31) is asserted by a drive when there is a drive interrupt pending (i.e., the drive is about to transfer information to or from the motherboard). The Drive Active line (DASP, pin 39) becomes logic 0 when there is any hard-drive activity occurring. A Passed Diagnostic (PDIAG, pin 34) line provides the results of any diagnostic command or reset action. When PDIAG is logic 0, the system knows that the drive is ready to use. Finally, the 16-bit I/O control line (IOCS16, pin 32) tells the motherboard that the drive is ready to send or receive data. Notice that there are several return (ground) lines (pins 2, 19, 22, 24, 26, 30, and 40), one unused pin (28), and a key pin (20), which is removed from the male connector. Figure 7-30 illustrates the timing for an IDE system.

SCSI

The *Small Computer Systems Interface* (SCSI; pronounced *scuzzy*) is more than just a hard-drive interface. SCSI is a stand-alone bus architecture capable of transmitting 8-bit data words at speeds up to 4 Mbps. In actual operation, SCSI is very much like a regular computer bus where a formal *protocol* or sequence of events is needed to communicate between devices. As a result, the computer is not concerned with the particular aspects or conditions of the drive—the hard drive contains its own comprehensive on-board intelligence to complete each task. A host system sends high-level commands to the SCSI bus and waits for the results. The original specification for SCSI was published in 1986. Two other enhanced versions, SCSI-2 and SCSI-3, are now available. Like the IDE interface, a SCSI drive needs only to be connected to the motherboard using a standard cable. Given the open architecture of SCSI, many other devices have adopted the SCSI interface such as tape drives, CD-ROM drives, and floptical drives. Even printers make use of the SCSI interface.

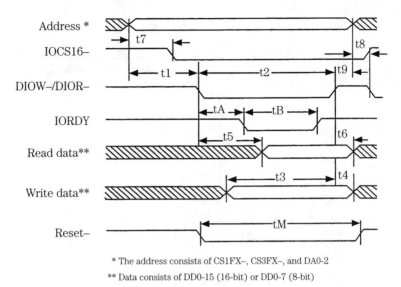

* The address consists of CS1FX–, CS3FX–, and DA0-2

** Data consists of DD0-15 (16-bit) or DD0-7 (8-bit)

7-30 IDE bus signal timing. Reprinted with the permission of Quantum Corp.

Figure 7-31 illustrates a typical SCSI connector for the signal and power cables. The power connector is often the 4-pin mate-and-lock connector. To maintain conventions with standard power supplies and floppy systems, SCSI hard drives use +5.0 Vdc and +12 Vdc. The return (ground) for each supply is also provided on the connector.

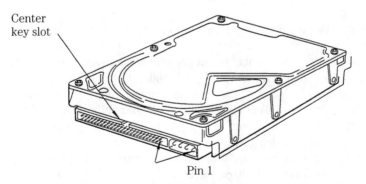

7-31 SCSI connector configuration. Reprinted with the permission of Quantum Corp.

1		1	+12 Vdc
		2	12 V ret
		3	5 V ret
		4	+5 Vdc
	4		

2		1				
			2	DB0	1	
			4	DB1	3	Ground
			6	DB2	5	
			8	DB3	7	
			10	DB4	9	
			12	DB5	11	
			14	DB6	13	
			16	DB7	15	
			18	DBP	17	
			20	Ground	19	
			22	Ground	21	
			24	Ground	23	
			26	TRMPWR	25	
			28	Ground	27	
			30	Ground	29	
			32	$\overline{\text{ATN}}$	31	
			34	Ground	33	
			36	$\overline{\text{BSY}}$	35	
			38	$\overline{\text{ACK}}$	37	
			40	$\overline{\text{RST}}$	39	
			42	$\overline{\text{MSG}}$	41	
			44	$\overline{\text{SEL}}$	43	
			46	$\overline{\text{C/D}}$	45	
			48	$\overline{\text{REQ}}$	47	
50		49	50	I/O	49	

7-32   Pinout diagram for a SCSI hard-drive interface.

The signal cable is usually a 50-pin insulation displacement connector (IDC) cable, and the signal pinouts are shown in Fig. 7-32. Notice that all of the odd-numbered lines are ground lines. This type of cable scheme helps to reduce electrical noise in the cable and ensure data integrity throughout the range of data transfer speeds. SCSI signals are carried over the even-numbered lines. Some of the signal labels have dark bars over them, indicating that the signal is active low. An active low signal is true in the logic 0 state instead of being true in the logic 1 state. Signals in the SCSI interface re fully TTL-compatible.

The communications protocol that takes place between a SCSI hard drive and motherboard is much different than that for an IDE system. When a SCSI system needs to access its hard drive, it brings its Select signal (SEL, pin 44) to a logic 0 state. The drive can also control the SEL line to initiate data transfer itself—but that is almost never done in hard drives. The Attention line (ATN, pin 32) then becomes logic 0, and the drive responds by pulling the Request line (REQ, pin 48) to a logic 0. When the drive must send back a particular control response to the system, an 8-bit message can be placed on the bidirectional data bus (DB0 to DB7, pins 2, 4, 6, 8, 10, 12, 14, and 16, respectively), and the Message signal (MSG, pin 42) is pulled to logic 0. A Data Bit Parity signal (DBP, pin 18) is used in conjunction with the data bits to provide data error-checking.

The Control/Data line (C/D, pin 46) is controlled by the hard drive. A logic 1 on the line indicates that the drive has placed a control byte on its data lines, while a logic 0 says that data is being placed on the bus. The direction of data transfer is determined by the Input/Output (I/O, pin 50) line. A logic 1 inputs data from the hard drive, while a logic 0 outputs data to the hard drive. After a data transfer has taken place, the motherboard forces the Acknowledge (ACK, pin 38) line to a logic 0 state to indicate that data has been transmitted or received. Whenever the SCSI bus is in use, the Busy (BSY, pin 36) signal becomes logic 0. When power is first applied to the SCSI drive or the computer system is rebooted, a Reset pulse (RST, pin 40) forces the drive's circuitry to initialize.

In order for a SCSI bus to operate properly, bus lines must be terminated with *pullup resistors*. Pullup resistors help ensure that each logic line behaves as expected. The power needed for each pullup resistor is provided by the Terminator Power (TRMPWR) line. Figure 7-33 shows the timing that takes place on a SCSI bus.

As a final note, remember that some small computers might not utilize the standard interface connector scheme for their particular interface, although the same major signals are required. If your computer uses a nonstandard interface connector arrangement, you need a schematic diagram to identify the appropriate pins.

Drive testing and troubleshooting

Hard disk drives (Fig. 7-34) present some challenges for computer technicians and everyday users alike. The problem with hard drives is that they are inaccessible devices. Unless you have a cleanroom environment in which to open the sealed drive platters, it is pointless to try replacing failed drive mechanics. Even if you could open a drive safely, the advances in hard-drive technology have been so fast and furious that no spare parts market has ever developed. Drive manufacturers themselves rarely bother to repair faulty drives, or invest in specialized drive testing equipment such as in Fig. 7-35. Clearly, the course for hard-drive repair is to replace faulty drives with new (usually better) devices.

Fortunately, not all hard-drive problems are necessarily fatal. True, you might lose some programs and data (which is why you should back up your hard drive frequently), but many drive problems are recoverable without resorting to drive replacement. Instead of focusing on repairing a hard drive's electronics or mechanics, today's repair tactics focus on repairing a drive's *data*. By reconstructing or relocating faulty drive information, it is possible to recover from a wide variety of drive problems.

As in any repair effort, however, you need tools to carry out the repair. In this case, you need software tools that can read and rewrite information and control drive operations. A hard drive has several important areas that can develop problems: a DOS boot area, a media descriptor, a File Allocation Table (FAT), a directory structure, and a storage area. The DOS boot area contains information vital for allowing the computer to access its file system. The media descriptor is a single byte in the FAT that identifies the type of device in use. The FAT itself contains information on sector (or cluster) allocation throughout the drive (keep in mind that sectors and clusters are not necessarily the same thing). Drives already support a

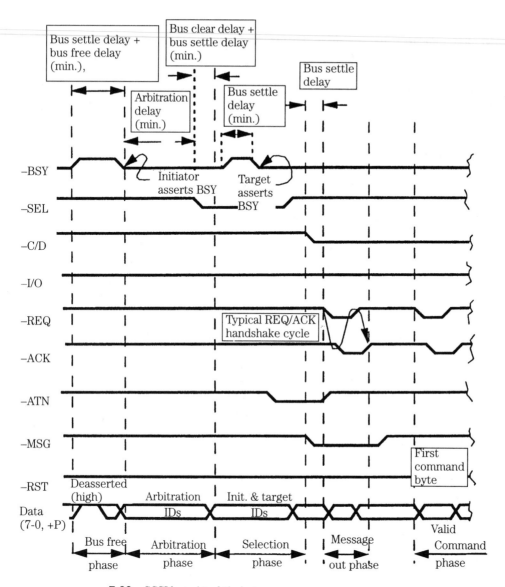

7-33 SCSI bus signal timing. Reprinted with the permission of Quantum Corp.

duplicate FAT in the event that the original FAT fails. The directory structure keeps track of each filename, file size, and how the FAT has allocated space for each file. The majority of the drive is the general storage area which actually contains the files loaded and created during normal drive operation. Software tools must be capable of interacting with and manipulating each of these areas to some degree.

7-33 Continued

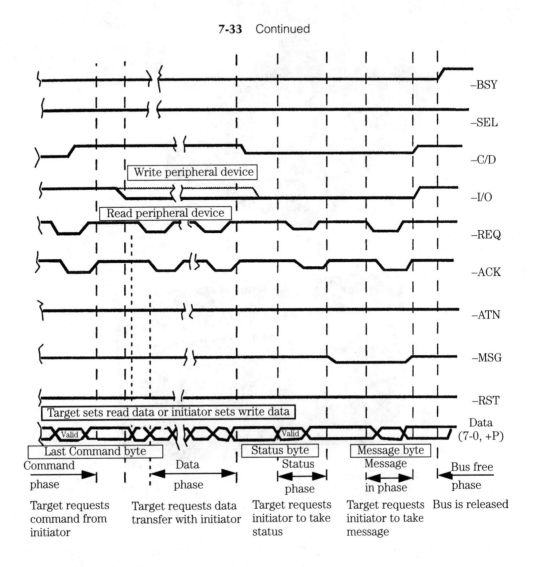

Write peripheral device

Read peripheral device

Target sets read data or initiator sets write data

| –BSY |
| –SEL |
| –C/D |
| –I/O |
| –REQ |
| –ACK |
| –ATN |
| –MSG |
| –RST |
| Data (7-0, +P) |

Last Command byte   Status byte   Message byte

| Command phase | Data phase | Status phase | Message in phase | Bus free phase |

Target requests command from initiator | Target requests data transfer with initiator | Target requests initiator to take status | Target requests initiator to take message | Bus is released

The tools on hand

Before you dig into symptoms and solutions, you should take a moment to gather your software tools. You could purchase third-party tools, but operating systems such as MS-DOS provide a number of handy diagnostic utilities that can at least get you started. Third-party software is covered later in this chapter.

You will need a floppy disk that is formatted and configured with system files so you can boot the computer to DOS from the floppy drive. Refer to your DOS manual for creating a bootable (system) floppy disk. In addition to DOS system files, your bootable disk should also contain six utilities: CHKDSK.EXE, FDISK.EXE, FOR MAT.COM, RECOVER.EXE, SYS.COM, and UNFORMAT.COM (note that all six files are available in DOS 5.0 and higher). You can also add other utilities to the floppy,

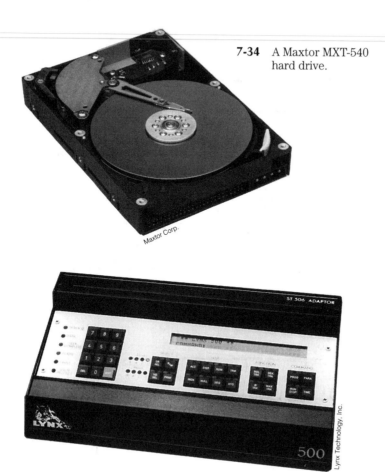

7-34   A Maxtor MXT-540 hard drive.

Maxtor Corp.

Lynx Technology, Inc.

7-35   A Lynx hard-drive tester.

but these six are the most important for our purposes. **Note:** It is highly recommended that you prepare several of these bootable disks in advance before you encounter drive problems. You might not be able to access the necessary files to create a bootable disk after a problem arises, but you can make the disk on another compatible machine if necessary.

The CHKDSK.EXE program checks the directory and FAT, and reports current disk and memory status on your monitor. Any logical errors are reported and bad sectors are marked, but CHKDSK.EXE does not locate physical disk errors. FDISK.EXE performs a low-level configuration of your hard drive's logical partition(s) prior to formatting. **Note:** Do not attempt to use low-level formatting on IDE or SCSI, because low-level formatting can ruin servo information encoded on drive platters. The FORMAT.COM file formats the drive to accept DOS files within the drive partition area specified by FDISK.EXE. Use extreme caution when using FOR MAT utilities. Formatting a disk can destroy the original data contained on it. The drive should be repartitioned (if appropriate) and reformatted only if data is unrecoverable and the drive cannot be made operable by any other means. Once the drive is reformatted, use SYS.COM to copy system files to the hard drive so it becomes bootable. The RECOVER.EXE program can be used to recover readable text or data files from a defective drive. No .EXE or .COM files can be recovered. The UNFORMAT.COM program can be used to restore a drive that had been corrupted or inadvertently formatted. As with all DOS utilities, refer to your DOS reference manual for specific information on using each function.

Off-the-shelf tools

Although programs like CHKDSK.EXE can provide basic failure information and correct a few very simple problems, most DOS utilities are not powerful or user-friendly enough to tackle serious drive corruption or data damage. Consider investing in a professional drive management package such as PC Tools Deluxe by Central Point Software or SpinRite by Gibson Research Corporation. You can purchase packages like PC Tools at almost any computer store. PC Tools Deluxe offers a series of utilities that can fix extensive data damage, rebuild corrupted file allocation and directory tables, recover lost clusters, organize disk contents to eliminate file fragmentation, and perform comprehensive backup operations. If your drive does fail, a professional software toolkit can often recover files and restore inoperable drives without ever disassembling the computer.

Troubleshooting

Now that you know what tools are available, you can take a look at some problems and software solutions. The key concept here is that a hard-drive problem does not necessarily mean a hard-drive failure. The failure of a sector or track does not automatically indicate physical head or platter damage—that is why software tools have been so successful. Even if one or more sectors are physically damaged, there are tens of thousands of sectors on a hard drive. A few bad sectors do not render a drive faulty. About the only time a drive is truly irreparable is when physical medium damage occurs on track 00, but software tools can help you to identify the scope of the problem. Always refer to the user's manual for your software tools for more information.

Symptom 1: The computer does not boot to DOS from the hard drive Every system disk, whether a floppy or hard disk, must contain DOS files in order to initialize and execute the disk operating system. If a hard drive fails to boot, one or more DOS files are probably corrupt, the partition table or boot sector (not related to the DOS boot) might be corrupt, or there might be an actual failure in the drive.

Begin your repair by booting the computer from a floppy drive using a bootable disk, and check your system CMOS setup. Just about all computers save their configuration parameters in a small section of battery-powered CMOS RAM in the Real-Time Clock (RTC). Part of the setup information includes descriptions of each installed drive type. If the small lithium battery supporting your configuration memory should fail, the setup information can be lost. As a result, your system "forgets" how it should be set up and not recognize the installed hard drive. If you find that your system's configuration has been lost, replace the CMOS RAM backup battery, reenter and save the necessary setup information. Then try rebooting the computer from its hard disk. You will probably have to disassemble at least part of your computer to install the new battery.

Here is a trick to help you with setup information: check your system's setup parameters before a problem arises, and copy the setup information into your DOS manual or user's manual. That way, you need only refer to your written notes when it is time to reload or modify a missing or corrupt setup parameter.

Install a floppy disk containing your software toolkit utilities and run the utility designed to locate and correct hard-disk problems (for *PC Tools Deluxe*, this would be the DISKFIX.EXE utility). After the fix utility has run, you might want to reload system files if necessary. Insert the DOS boot disk containing the SYS.COM file and copy system files to the hard drive according to the DOS instructions. If you do not have professional software tools on hand, you can attempt to reformat the drive and start from scratch.

If software tools cannot correct the problem, remove all power from your small computer and disassemble the system to expose the hard-drive assembly. Check the installation of signal and power cables. This check is especially important if you have just finished a repair which required you to disconnect your drive cables. Make certain that each cable is installed properly and oriented correctly. Check for any loose or broken wiring. Correct any wiring problems that you might encounter.

Remove the power cable from the hard drive, reapply power to the computer, and measure dc voltages at the power connector. Place your meter's ground lead on pin 2 and measure +12 Vdc on pin 1. Ground your meter at pin 3 and measure +5 Vdc on pin 4. If either voltage is low or absent, troubleshoot your computer power supply.

At this point, your hard-drive assembly is probably defective. However, you can test the drive by substitution. Because hard drives use standard physical interfaces, you can install the questionable drive into another computer using the same physical interface and power levels. If you can find a compatible system (you can call it the *test system*), you will have to change the test system's setup parameters before it can recognize the suspect drive. Once the testing is complete, remember to restore and recheck the test system's original drive and setup parameters. If you must change a test system's setup parameters, make it a point to keep careful notes of the original configuration for later reference.

If the suspect drive is functioning properly (and holds the files needed to boot a computer), it should be able to boot the test system, and you should have normal access to the drive. Keep in mind that the suspect drive must be the only boot device in the test system. When you prove that the suspect drive does work, try replacing the hard-drive signal cable, then try replacing the hard-drive controller board.

If you encounter the same hard-drive failure in the test system, you should replace the hard drive entirely. You then need to reformat the new drive in your system and reload all of the applications software and data files contained on the original drive. As long as the replacement drive is identical to the faulty drive, you do not have to alter any setup parameters.

Without a test system to verify operation of the hard drive, your best course is simply to replace the hard drive first. This is not always the least expensive answer, but it is much faster and easier to obtain a replacement drive than struggling to find and replace components.

Symptom 2: One or more subdirectories appear lost or damaged Both the root directory of a drive and its FAT contain references to subdirectories. If data in either the root directory or FAT is corrupt, one or more subdirectories might be inaccessible by the drive. All other subdirectories, however, are probably working just fine. The computer is probably able to load and save files normally in all other working directories.

The repair objective here is to locate and reconstruct the faulty information. If you can access your software tools on the hard drive, you should run any repair utilities available such as DISKFIX.EXE. If you cannot access your resident software tools, reboot your system with a bootable floppy disk, insert a disk containing the appropriate utilities, and run each appropriate utility. If utilities are unable to restore the defective area(s), you might have to reformat the drive to recover any inaccessible areas.

Symptom 3: There are errors during drive reads or writes As you have learned earlier in this book, magnetic information does not last forever. The ID information written into each disk sector is only written during the format process. Even though data can be rewritten to a sector regularly, its ID information is not. If ID data should fail, the drive might be unable to find an allocated sector for reading or writing, and a disk error results. This type of failure can occur sporadically over time—especially if the drive has been used for very long periods of time. Usually only one or two files are affected.

Your repair objective is to check the bad sectors and transfer as much data as possible to working sectors. Use your fix utility (such as DISKFIX.EXE) to examine the drive. Sectors that are physically faulty are marked as bad and never used again. Any sector data that is readable is recovered and placed in known-good sectors. If the error occurred in an .EXE or .COM file, the file is generally corrupt and must be replaced by copying the file from a source or backup disk. If utilities are unable to correct the problem, you might have to run CHKDSK.EXE and reformat the drive to recover the use of inaccessible areas.

Symptom 4: The hard drive was formatted accidentally Every now and then, you might attempt to format a floppy disk and forget to include the particular drive specification. If you initiate a DOS format of the hard drive, the data is lost forever—the DOS format is a destructive procedure that clears all existing data. However, if you use a non-DOS format command, a disk reconstruction program in your software toolkit can usually restore the drive contents as long as you rebuild immediately after formatting. If you cannot reconstruct the drive, you have no alternative but to reload the disk manually or from a backup.

Symptom 5: A file has been deleted accidentally This particular symptom is more of an inconvenience than an actual problem. Mistyping or forgetting to add a drive specification can accidentally erase files from places you did not intend to erase. DOS 5.0 offers an UNDELETE.EXE program that can restore the deleted file. Undeleting can be very helpful when you accidentally delete a file that took a long time to create, and there is no backup for it. Of course, if you cannot undelete a file, you must either reload it from a backup, or recreate it manually.

Symptom 6: The hard drive's root directory is damaged   A faulty root directory can cripple the entire disk, rendering all subdirectories inaccessible. A bad FAT or directory tree can sometimes be corrected by booting the computer from a bootable floppy disk, then running a fix utility from your software toolkit. In many cases, fix utilities (such as DISKFIX.EXE) can reconstruct damaged FATs or directories. If your fix utilities are unable to correct or patch the problem, you have little choice but to reformat the drive and reload it from a recent backup, or reload it from scratch.

Symptom 7: Hard-drive performance appears to be slowing down over time   Hard drives require a relatively long time to search a drive (on the order of milliseconds). Ideally, all information necessary for a file is stored in contiguous sectors and tracks, and the drive can access the maximum amount of information in the shortest possible time. Unfortunately, as files are updated and saved, they become scattered in noncontiguous sectors and tracks throughout the drive. *File fragmentation* demands much more seek and access time from a drive. The solution is to *unfragment* the drive using a software utility.

Boot your computer from a bootable floppy disk, then run an unfragment utility in your software toolkit (such as COMPRESS.EXE, found in *PC Tools Deluxe*). As a general rule, there should be no terminate-and-stay-resident (TSR) programs running when a drive is unfragmented. Also, files are rearranged and moved from one place to another on the drive during the unfragment process, so any files that have been deleted might be totally unrecoverable after unfragmenting the drive.

8
Memory cards

Magnetic media do not last forever. Over time and use, magnetic particles eventually lose their orientation. Stray magnetic fields can also upset the alignment of magnetic flux patterns. Just one bad bit can render a program or data file unusable. Wide, frequent fluctuations in environmental conditions can also contribute to media breakdown. Magnetic media require relatively large, intricate, and delicate mechanisms to transport the media and heads. Such drawbacks make floppy and hard drives susceptible to failures from mechanical wear and tear, as well as impact shock and physical abuse. Finally, magnetic drives require motors and electronic driver circuitry; both require substantial amounts of power to operate. Even with the power reduction features found in many of today's computers (especially notebook and pen-computers), mechanical drives constitute a large part of a system's power requirement.

Solid-state memory cards take advantage of advanced memory ICs and packaging techniques to provide mass-storage in the form of credit-card-size modules (Fig. 8-1). Integrated circuits (especially memory ICs) are reaching a level of sophistication where they can now handle the large volume of information once handled only by magnetic media. Although memory cards are still far more expensive per megabyte than magnetic media, cards are generally considered to be an efficient and reliable alternative to magnetic media. After all, memory cards have no moving parts. They also require no drive mechanism, so there is nothing to wear out, except perhaps for the card's connectors.

Memory cards use very little power compared to magnetic drives, and all data is accessible within nanoseconds. Cards are not influenced by external magnetic fields, and they are more rugged than floppy disks. This chapter introduces you to conventional memory card technology, as well as mass-storage cards that can store up to 20Mb per card or more. Both classes of memory card are quickly gaining acceptance in all types of computers and "intelligent" instruments.

8-1 A 20Mb Mitsubishi Flash EEPROM card.

Memory concepts

Before getting into a detailed discussion of particular memory cards, you should understand some of the important concepts involved in memory card technology. If you are already familiar with memory devices in general, you might want to skip this section, reviewing it later for reference.

Storage cells

Computers require programs and data in order to perform any meaningful function. Such information must be kept where it is either immediately available to the micro-processor, or accessible in a short period of time. To the computer, all "information" is stored as a series of binary digits (1s and 0s), where a 1 represents the presence of a signal, and a 0 represents the absence of a signal. In computer systems, the volt-age levels representing each bit must be stored in an electronic circuit—a memory device. Each bit is kept in its own individual circuit where it can be copied (read) to a waiting device. Some memory circuits also allow a bit to be copied to the memory circuit (written). Any circuit that holds a bit as a voltage level is known as a *storage cell*. By combining storage cells into arrays, circuits can be created to hold millions of bits. Today, large storage cell arrays are fabricated as integrated circuits (memory ICs). Memory cards use sophisticated memory ICs to store the most information possible in the smallest amount of space.

There are many types of circuits that are capable of retaining bit information. Which ones are actually used depends on the characteristics desired of a particular memory device, and the number of storage cells that must be placed on an IC die. There are typically six types of storage cells used in memory cards: SRAM, DRAM, ROM, PROM, EEPROM, and Flash EEPROM. Each type of cell offers unique features to memory cards.

Cell organization

Storage cells must be organized into a coherent array (or matrix) as illustrated in Fig. 8-2. A memory array is essentially a two-dimensional arrangement laid out as N rows and M columns. The exact numbers for N and M depends on the particular memory array. Storage cells within the array are selected by address decoding circuitry in the IC. There can be any number of addresses, so long as the number is a power of 2. For example, a memory array can offer 1024 addresses (2^{10}), 2048 addresses (2^{11}), or sizes up to 16,777,216 addresses (2^{24}). Even larger memory arrays are being designed.

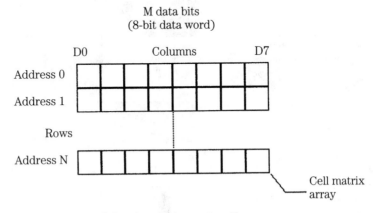

8-2   A typical storage cell array.

Controlling the array

Of course, it takes much more then storage cells to make a working memory IC. Circuitry is needed to decode and select the proper memory cells, and channel data into or out of the array as required. Figure 8-3 shows the three sets of signals required to handle a memory array: address signals, data signals, and control signals. For the purposes of this book, the internal circuitry of ICs is unimportant, but you should understand the role each circuit plays.

Address signals are used to select the rows and columns where desired bits are stored. The number of cells that can be addressed depends on the number of address lines—more address lines allow more cells to be selected. For the IC in Fig. 8-3, there are two *control signals*: a Chip Select ($\overline{CS}$), and a Read/Write ($R/\overline{W}$) signal. Chip Select is an enable signal that controls the flow of data to the IC. When $\overline{CS}$ is logic 1, the IC is disabled, and data will neither enter or leave the IC (regardless of what address is selected). The data lines of a disabled memory IC are neither logic 1 or logic 0, but a "high-impedance" state, which effectively disconnects the IC from all other ICs that might share its bus lines. When $\overline{CS}$ is logic 0, the IC is enabled, and data will leave (or enter) the IC normally at the locations specified by address lines.

All memory devices can be read, and many devices (but not all) can be written to (ROMs and PROMs cannot be written to once programmed). A Read/Write signal

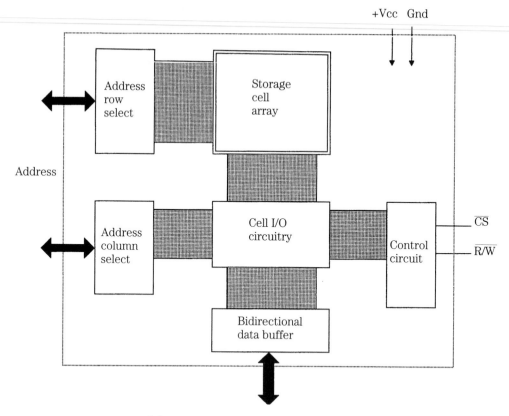

8-3   Block diagram of a simple RAM IC.

is supplied to tell the array which direction data is traveling in. When R/$\overline{\text{W}}$ is logic 1, the IC is in the read mode, and data at the specified address will appear on the IC's *data lines*. If R/$\overline{\text{W}}$ is logic 0, the IC is in the write mode (assuming the IC can be written to), and data on the IC's data lines will be stored in the cells specified by the address lines.

Access time

Even with electronic circuitry, the data held in storage cells is not instantaneously available to external systems. There is a certain finite delay between the time when a valid address is selected, and the data at that address becomes valid at the memory IC's data lines. This time delay is known as *access time*. You will recall from chapters 6 and 7 that typical access time for magnetic media is in the millisecond range. Access time for semiconductor memory devices, however, is on the order of nanoseconds—six orders of magnitude faster than magnetic media. Solid-state memory data might not be instantly available, but it is as close as technology can get for the moment.

Random access memory

The ability to manipulate memory contents quickly and efficiently is a critical aspect of any computer system. A computer must be able to access only desired pieces of data from memory without having to continually weed through large blocks of information (such as reading a tape from start to finish). It is also desirable to access and change individual memory bits (if necessary) without rewriting large portions of data. The ability to address data and read or write at the individual bit level is known as *random access* operation. Floppy disk and hard disk drives support random access as well, even though their bits are stored as magnetic flux transitions instead of electrical signals. There are two classic types of random access memory (or RAM): static RAM and dynamic RAM.

Static RAM (or SRAM) stores bits in cells that act like switches—electricity is turned on (logic 1) or off (logic 0). In actual practice, each SRAM storage cell is a flip-flop circuit that is set or reset when written. The flip-flop stores the condition of that bit until it is altered by a subsequent write operation (or lost when power is removed). The advantage to static RAM is data stability. Once a bit is stored, it will be held indefinitely without any further interaction with the system. The disadvantages to SRAM are limited array size and relatively large power requirements. After all, each flip-flop is a small circuit consisting of transistors, diodes, and passive components. Flip-flop circuits dissipate power continuously regardless of whether the memory array is being accessed or not. Power dissipation results in heat, so there is a finite limit to just how many flip-flops can be fabricated onto a single memory IC die. Today's SRAMs are limited to roughly 262,144 cells (256 Kbits), although the cell arrangement can take a variety of configurations (e.g., 32 Kbits x 8, or 64 Kbits x 4).

Dynamic RAM (or DRAM) stores bits in the form of electrical charges on incredibly small, solid-state capacitors. A single MOS transistor is added to each capacitor to act as a switch and control element. The presence or absence of a charge defines whether the bit is logic 1 or logic 0. By making each capacitor very small, charges can be added or withdrawn in only a few nanoseconds. The advantages to a DRAM are low power consumption and high storage density. Because each bit can be stored with no more than a capacitor and transistor, it is possible to hold far more bits in a DRAM than an SRAM IC. Today's DRAMs can hold 16,777,216 bits (16 Mbits, or 64 times the upper capacity of SRAM technology). There are 64 Mbit DRAMs on the drawing board now. Bit conditions are stored as static charges, so current only flows when the capacitor is being charged or discharged. Power requirements are kept to an absolute minimum, so DRAMs are ideal for small computers such as laptops or notebooks.

Unfortunately, DRAMs are not nearly as simple to operate as SRAMs. No capacitor is perfect (especially microscopic capacitors), so charge will eventually drain away through the capacitor's insulating material and control circuitry. With such small capacitors, a charge will not last more than a few milliseconds. After several milliseconds, charge levels are irretrievably lost and data becomes corrupted. To preserve the charge levels in a memory array, each storage cell must be periodically refreshed. It is the need for regular, active maintenance that earned these memory devices the term "dynamic."

Refresh

In order to refresh a DRAM IC, each row of storage cells must be read and rewritten to the array. Note that it is not necessary to select a full address—only an array row needs to be selected (the particular columns can be ignored). Once selected, the row of storage bits is written into a sense/refresh amplifier, which recharges the appropriate storage capacitors and rewrites each bit (1 or 0) to the array. Thus, the entire memory array can be refreshed by simply reading each row in sequence every few milliseconds. Two new control signals are also needed: the Row Address Refresh ($\overline{\text{RAS}}$) and the Column Address Refresh ($\overline{\text{CAS}}$).

Figure 8-4 illustrates this concept with a DRAM block diagram. DRAMs do not accept all address lines simultaneously. Instead, addresses are segregated into low (row) and high (column) segments that are multiplexed to the appropriate select circuit. For example, the lower (row) bits are placed on the address lines first, and the $\overline{\text{RAS}}$ is pulsed low. The row portion of the address causes the selected row of bits to be "amplified" by the sense/refresh amplifiers—logic 0s remain logic 0s, and logic 1s are recharged to their full value. That row is then successfully refreshed. The upper (column) bits are then placed on the address line and the $\overline{\text{CAS}}$ line is pulsed low. The column portion of the address selects the particular bits of the row to be placed on the data lines (for a read operation). If a write operation is called for, the R/$\overline{\text{W}}$ line must be logic 0 and valid data must be available on the data bus before $\overline{\text{CAS}}$ is asserted. The new data bits are then placed in their corresponding places in the storage array, and the old bits are replaced. During the next refresh cycle, the new bits are refreshed.

Of course, if the memory is not being accessed for reading or writing, it still must be refreshed to ensure data integrity. Fortunately, refresh can be accomplished simply by reading each row in sequence—refresh circuitry does not have to specify any column address for refresh to take place. This *row-only refresh* technique helps to speed the refresh process. Although refreshing DRAM every few milliseconds might seem like a constant chore, a small computer can execute quite a few instructions before being interrupted by a refresh. Milliseconds are a long time to a computer. This chapter does not discuss refresh any further because DRAM cards utilize the refresh signals and circuitry built into your small computer. Refer to chapter 5 for more about memory ICs.

Attribute memory

One of the greatest challenges facing memory cards is cross-compatibility—the ability to use various card types from different manufacturers in the same card slot. There are quite a few card sizes and types currently in production, and many more card models will be available by the time you read this book. How does the computer know when you have replaced your 2Mb SRAM card with a 20Mb Flash card or 512K OTPROM card? You should understand that a computer capable of accepting mem-

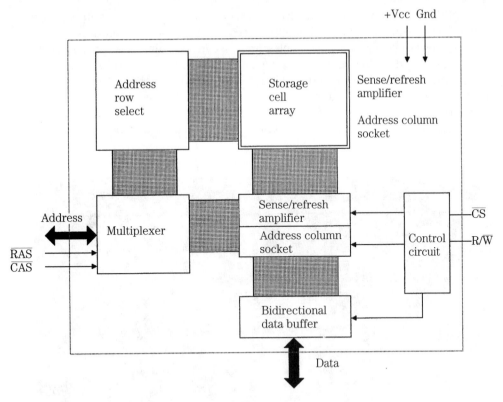

8-4   Block diagram of a simple DRAM IC.

ory cards must be able to detect and adjust to the diverse attributes of each card it might encounter, even though each card might use the same physical interface.

The best analogy to this is the hard drive, which is available in a staggering array of capacities, heads, cylinders, sectors, and so on. All those drives, however, can use the same physical interface. A computer interacts properly with a hard drive because you enter the drive's key parameters in the computer's CMOS setup routine. The same basic problem exists for memory cards. However, memory cards are intended to be transient items—inserted and removed at will. Imagine the inconvenience of having to reenter a card's key parameters each time a new card is inserted. Even a single typing error can be disastrous for some cards and their contents.

The patron organization of memory card standards, the Personal Computer Memory Card Industry Association (PCMCIA) has supported a standard for memory card services that defines the software interface for accessing cards (currently called PCMCIA 2.0). The interface can either be a device driver loaded when the computer boots, or designed directly into BIOS ROM or the operating system. In order for this driver system to work, each card must be able to identify itself to the computer. The complete characteristic and ID data for a memory card is held in the *attribute memory area* of each individual card.

Attribute memory contains a surprising amount of information—it must, considering the huge number of potential differences in card layout and features. Attribute memory tells the computer how much storage a card contains, the particular device type (memory, disk, I/O, and so on), the card's data format, speed capabilities, and many other variables. It is important to note here that the PCMCIA standard 2.0 supports devices other than strictly memory cards, such as modem/fax modules, actual hard drives using the PCMCIA interface such as the Maxtor drive in Fig. 8-5, network modules, and more. For the purposes of this book, you need only be concerned with memory cards.

8-5   A Maxtor hard drive using a PCMCIA card interface.

Attribute memory typically contains setup information that falls into one of four categories of PCMCIA's Card Identification System (CIS)—otherwise known as the card's *metaformat*. These four categories, or layers, are:

- the basic compatibility layer, indicating how the card's storage is organized
- the data recording format layer, specifying how blocks of card information are to be stored
- the data organization layer, defining the card's operating system format (e.g., DOS, Microsoft's FlashFile system, PCMCIA's XIP, etc.)
- any specific standards needed to support an operating system.

At the time of this writing, attribute memory runs up to 8K, but that figure will likely increase with the demand for additional attributes.

Attribute memory is kept in a separate memory area apart from the card's ordinary memory (called *common memory* by the PCMCIA). The CIS data contained in attribute memory is a collection of related data blocks that are interlinked rather like a chain. Each link in the chain (a *data block*) is called a *tuple*, and can be up to 128 bytes long. The first byte of a tuple encodes the function of that tuple and its parameters. The second byte links to the next tuple (if any) and specifies the precise number of bytes in that tuple. Because you know how long the present tuple is, you know exactly where the next tuple begins. Table 8-1 lists a series of tuples used in the PCMCIA 2.0 standard. Individual card manufacturers are also free to add their own unique tuples to support proprietary features. It is not necessary for you to know the precise operation of each tuple, but it can help you to be familiar with their nomenclature and general purpose.

Table 8-1. Common tuple codes for PCMCIA-compatible memory cards

Code (hex)	Tuple	Description
00	CISTPL_NULL	A null (ignored) tuple
01	CISTPL_DEVICE	Device information tuple showing available common memory
02–07	reserved	Reserved device tuple
08–0F	reserved	Reserved tuple
10	CISTPL_CHECKSUM	Check-sum control tuple
11	CISTPL_LONGLINK_A	Attribute memory control tuple
12	CISTPL_LONGLINK_C	Common memory control tuple
13	CISTPL_LINKTARGET	Link target control tuple
14	CISTPL_NO_LINK	No-link control tuple
15	CISTPL_VERS_1	Version/product information tuple
16	CISTPL_ALT_STR	Alternate language string tuple
17	CISTPL_DEVICE_A	Attribute memory device information
18	CISTPL_JEDEC_C	JEDEC program information for common memory
19	CISTPL_JEDED_A	JEDEC program information for attribute memory
1A	CISTPL_CFIG	Configurable-card tuple
1B	CISTPL_ENTRY	Configuration-entry tuple
1C	CISTPL_DEVICE_0C	Other operating information for common memory
1D	CISTPL_DEVICE_0A	Other operating information for attribute memory
1E	CISTPL_DEVICEGEO	Memory geometry of card
1F	CISTPL_DEVICEGEO_A	Geometry of attribute memory
40	CISTPL_VERS_2	Level-2 version tuple
41	CISTPL_FORMAT	Format tuple
42	CISTPL_GEOMETRY	Card memory geometry
43	CISTPL_BYTE_ORDER	Byte ordering tuple
44	CISTPL_DATE	Date card was last formatted
45	CISTPL_BATTERY	Date battery was last replaced
46	CISTPL_ORG	Operating system; DOS, XIP, etc.
FF	CISTPL_END	End of tuples

Note: CISTPL stands for **C**ard **I**nformation **S**ystem **T**uple

Card construction

Before you learn about the various types of memory cards that are available, you should have a good understanding of card construction and the major subassemblies that can be found on every card (Fig. 8-6). The earliest PCMCIA cards measured only 3.4" (8.65 cm) long, 2.1" (5.4 cm) wide, and 0.1" (0.33 cm) thick. These dimensions are typical of Type I cards, and their basic dimensions remain the same today. However, it is extremely difficult to fit some electronic devices into such a small thickness, so the PCMCIA 2.0 standard allows for thicker cards. The Type II card measures the same length and width as Type I cards, but Type II cards are 0.2" (0.5 cm) thick. The Type III card also measures the same length and width as Type I, but is 0.4" (1.05 cm) thick. The Type III form factor allows the card to be used for PCMCIA-compatible hard-drive units. A 0.7" (1.80 cm) Type IV card has been proposed, but is not yet part of the PCMCIA standards. Figure 8-7 shows a comparison of memory card dimensions.

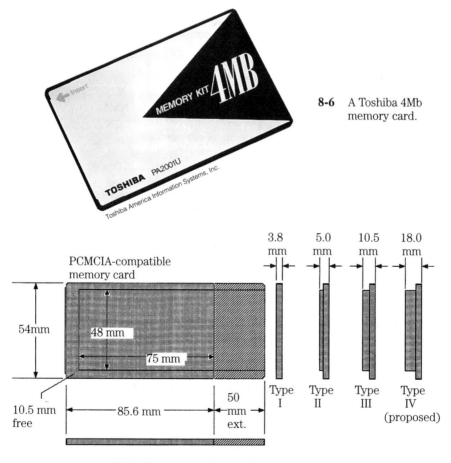

8-6   A Toshiba 4Mb memory card.

8-7   Form factor for typical memory cards.

It is interesting to note that the larger memory cards still provide 2.1" rails for insertion into standard connectors. All additional electronics in the card is stored in the *bubble,* which is actually about 1.8" (4.8 cm) wide and 2.9" (7.5 cm) long. As you might expect, the actual physical aperture for a card must be large enough to accept a card's extended height, even though the rails and connector are identical for every card. PCMCIA 2.0 also allows card length to be extended by 1.9" (5.0 cm) to hold even more circuitry. The PCMCIA has recommended standards for battery orientations and write-protect switch placement (if used). The only part of the memory card that has not yet been standardized is the rear edge (opposite to the card face, which actually plugs into a connector) where modem, fax, and LAN cards (generally called I/O cards) offer connectors for external cabling. Plans are currently underway to standardize rear edge connectors. Keep in mind that a non-PCMCIA card might adhere to some PCMCIA standards, or none at all.

Inside the card

The inside of a memory card is not complicated, but it is very compact—there is a metal shell encasing a PC board. There are also a few minor components such as spacers, a write-protect switch (optional), and one or more batteries (optional). Figure 8-8 shows you a cutaway view of a Mitsubishi memory card. It is really the PC board itself that is the masterpiece of modern circuitry. Notice that the main PC board uses Thin, Small-Outline Package (TSOP) ICs, which are surface-mounted to both sides of the board. The PC board is clamped within its shell using a series of nonconductive spacers. Given the number of ICs and the card's capabilities, it is sometimes difficult to believe that the PC board actually fits into a shell only 0.2" thick (Type II). Many cards use the Type II dimensions.

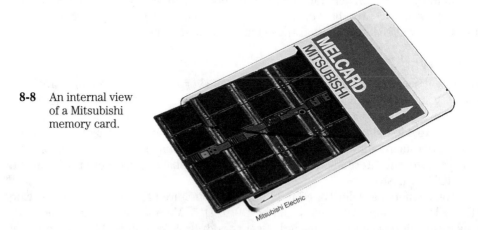

8-8 An internal view of a Mitsubishi memory card.

Another important consideration in memory card design is the control and suppression of electrostatic discharge (ESD). Susceptibility to ESD is perhaps the single aspect of memory cards where magnetic media is superior. Static electricity must be prevented from reaching the card's PC board, where IC damage can occur. Once a card is inserted into a system (Fig. 8-9), a discharge tab at the physical interface connector carries away any accumulation of charges to system ground. Until the card is inserted, it protects its circuitry from damage using the Faraday cage principle, the same used by antistatic bags to protect their contents. The shell of most memory cards is constructed either of metal (such as stainless steel) or some type of metalized plastic. Both shell halves are bonded together by a small spring that you can see in Fig. 8-9. Any charge introduced to the card is quickly dispersed over the entire shell surface instead of being allowed to enter the card.

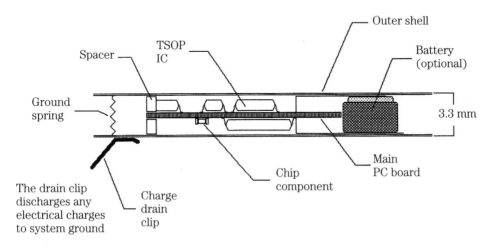

8-9 Cross-section of a typical memory card.

Memory cards can generally be broken down into four key areas: memory, support logic, power control/backup, and connector. Figure 8-10 illustrates each of these areas. The next sections looks at these four parts in detail.

Memory

Memory ICs are the most important elements of every solid-state memory card. The capacity and data bus width (8, 16, or 32 bits) is determined by the choice and configuration of memory ICs. For example, eight 256K x 8 bit SRAM ICs can be configured to provide 2M x 8 bits or 1M x 16 bits, and so on. Various sizes of memory ICs can provide many different possible card configurations. The type of memory ICs that are used will determine the type of memory card that is constructed (i.e., SRAM, OTPROM, or flash).

The memory card illustrated in Fig. 8-10 is configured for a data bus 8-bits wide (D0 to D7). A 16-bit data bus would be D0 to D15. Memory array size determines how many address lines are needed. Twenty address lines (A0 to A19) can directly address 2^{20} or 1,048,576 unique locations. Keep in mind that memory cards use a standard interface for the same purpose as floppy or hard drives, so there might be more address lines available to a card than it can use. For example, a 256K x 8-bit memory card requires only 18 address lines (A0 to A17) to address the card's 2^{18} or

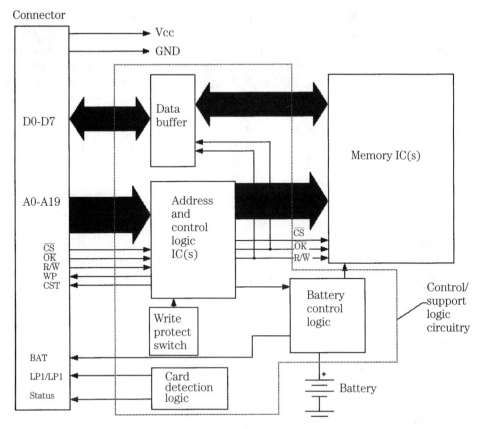

Connector

D0-D7

A0-A19

$\overline{\text{CS}}$
$\overline{\text{OK}}$
$\text{R}/\overline{\text{W}}$
WP
CST

BAT

LP1/LP1

Status

Vcc

GND

Data buffer

Memory IC(s)

Address and control logic IC(s)

$\overline{\text{CS}}$
$\overline{\text{OK}}$
$\text{R}/\overline{\text{W}}$

Write protect switch

Battery control logic

Control/ support logic circuitry

Card detection logic

Battery

8-10   Example block diagram of a memory card.

262,144 bytes. As long as the interface provides enough address lines to operate the inserted card, any additional lines from the interface can simply be ignored, or used as Chip Select signals in the memory array.

Support logic

Memory alone is not enough to make a memory card. Multiple memory ICs must be addressed and selected on demand by the card interface . Support logic is needed to ensure that the memory card ICs are properly connected to your computer's physical card interface. Data travelling to and from the memory card is handled within the card by a bidirectional data buffer. A buffer does not alter data, but merely amplifies the existing data to guarantee signal integrity.

A write cycle causes data on the card controller's data bus to be read into the memory card and stored at the memory location specified on the card's address pins. A read cycle allows data at the location specified in the memory card's address pins to be output to the card's interface data bus.

Address decoding and control logic are important aspects of a memory card's supporting logic. When there are multiple memory ICs on a card, each memory IC shares data and address lines. Decoding logic determines exactly which of the common ICs need to be activated. Control logic in the card interprets the variety of control signals occurring over the physical interface. The desired memory IC is activated with a Chip Select ($\overline{CS}$) signal. A logic 0 selects an IC while a logic 1 allows the IC to remain idle. The Read/Write ($R/\overline{W}$) signal defines whether data is entering (write) or leaving (read) the card. A logic 0 indicates a write operation and a logic 1 will cause a read. During a read operation, the Output Enable ($\overline{OE}$) signal allows the addressed data in the selected memory IC to be available at the bidirectional data buffer, which directs data out of the card.

Memory cards also generate some control signal outputs that are interpreted by the memory card controller IC. A Write Protect (WP) signal is available on most volatile memory cards. Write Protect signals are generated by a small switch on the card itself and serves much the same purpose as the write-protect notch on floppy diskettes. A logic 1 on the write-protect line prevents new data from being written to the card. The card's overall condition is fed back to the memory card controller using a card status (CST) line.

There are two card detect pins ($\overline{CD1}$ and $\overline{CD2}$) that are used by the host to identify a properly inserted card. If one or both card detect signals are absent, the host system will generate an error and refuse to interact with the card. Logic is also needed to control card power. A voltage sensing/comparison circuit within the card detects when external power is available. When external power is applied (the card is plugged into a running system), the card stops drawing backup power from its internal battery. If your computer is turned off or the card is removed from its slot, the voltage detector monitors external power loss and automatically reconnects the card's battery.

Power source

Solid-state memory cards have one primary source of power: the host computer system. Ideally, a memory card should not require any power when it is removed from a system, but SRAM cards (and some flash card designs) use one or more lithium coin cells to maintain memory contents when system power is not available. Under normal circumstances, SRAM batteries should be able to support a card's contents for several years. Figure 8-11 illustrates battery placement in a simple SRAM card.

Connector

You might think that connectors are rather trivial items. In memory cards, however, connectors are a critical concern (Fig. 8-12). A typical 60- or 68-pin memory card must be able to withstand regular insertions and removals over a period of many years. If even one pin in the computer or receptacle in the card should become loose or intermittent, the entire card could be rendered useless. Most commercial-grade memory cards are rated for 10,000 insertion/removal cycles. Some industrial-grade cards designed for harsh environments can withstand only 5000 insertion/removal cycles. Be suspicious of connectors and sockets whenever you are troubleshooting memory card systems. Figure 8-13 shows an up-close view of an AMP memory card connector interface.

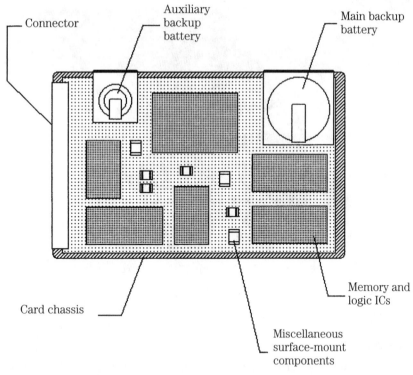

Connector

Auxiliary
backup
battery

Main backup
battery

Card chassis

Memory and
logic ICs

Miscellaneous
surface-mount
components

8-11 Internal view of a typical SRAM card.

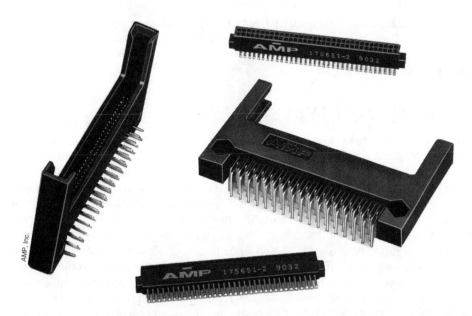

AMP, Inc.

8-12 A selection of AMP memory card connectors.

8-13 Memory card insertion.

Variations

Of course, the memory card elements presented above might not be needed for every type of memory card. For instance, nonvolatile cards such as OTPROM cards do not require an internal backup battery. DRAM cards cannot support a battery at all. Support logic will also vary widely from card to card depending on data bus width and memory IC arrangement. A DRAM card does not need a write-protect switch. Finally, the connectors used with memory cards reflect the particular interface for which the card was designed.

Memory card types

Memory cards (Fig. 8-14) are generally categorized by the type of memory that each card incorporates. They are either temporary (volatile) or permanent (nonvolatile). A volatile card typically uses some type of RAM to hold its information. Unless a battery backup is used, a volatile card loses its data when withdrawn from the host system, or when system power is turned off. Volatile memory cards can usually be rewritten easily and quickly whenever the need arises. Nonvolatile memory cards employ some class of ROM ICs to hold data. Battery backup is not required because ROM devices retain data even in the absence of power. However, nonvolatile memory cards can only be written once, or at best are extremely cumbersome to erase and rewrite. If you want to be very specific, you can classify memory cards according to their particular memory ICs. This chapter covers six types of memory cards: SRAM, DRAM, ROM, OTPROM, EEPROM, and Flash. Table 8-2 summarizes the characteristics of each card type.

8-14 Memory cards and an
Adtron card drive.

Adtron Corp.

Table 8-2. Comparison of memory card parameters

	SRAM	OTPROM	Mask ROM	EEPROM	DRAM	Flash
Access time (ns)	80–200	250	200–250	250	60–150	250
Battery	Yes	No	No	No	No	No
Capacity	8Mb	4Mb	32Mb	.25Mb	16Mb	40Mb
R/W life	Infinite	1	None	10K	Infinite	100K
Multiplexed addressing	No	No	No	No	Yes	No
Refresh	No	No	No	No	Yes	No
Standby power (mW)	.08	.13	2	3.5	320	3.2
Active power (W)	.5	.25	.2	.3	2	.15

1. Some Flash EEPROM cards containing Flash and SRAM use one or more batteries to backup the SRAM portion of the card.

2. Original Flash EEPROM cards offered a scant few R/W cycles, but some manufacturers are developing long-life cards with 100,000+ cycle capacity.

SRAM cards

Static RAM (SRAM) cards are generally considered to be general-purpose work-horse cards. Based on SRAM ICs, an SRAM card is capable of straightforward reading or writing up to 8Mb. With fair access times (80 to 200 ns) and moderate power requirements (0.5 W), the SRAM card is ideal as a floppy disk replacement. Static RAM enjoys an exceptionally long read/write cycle life, so SRAM cards are typically very reliable. You usually find SRAM cards used in data collection systems and notebook and subnotebook computers to back up or transfer files between compatible machines. Because static RAM is volatile memory, battery power is used to maintain card contents when removed or inserted into an unpowered system. Lithium coin cells are installed in the card to provide power.

Figure 8-15 shows a block diagram for a typical SRAM card. At the core, you will see a memory array of 1M x 8 bit SRAM. This is the card's common memory. There is also a 64-Kbit (8K x 8 bit) attribute memory area. Address lines A0 to A19 enter the card and are buffered by the address bus buffer. A small address decoding circuit generates the Chip Enable ($\overline{CE}$) signals that activate particular memory devices within the array. The 16-bit data bus (D0 to D15) has a bidirectional data buffer, where data is split into two sets of 8 bits (one set is paralleled to the 8-bit attribute memory). Control signals enter the card where they are intercepted by a control logic circuit. Output Enable ($\overline{OE}$) and Read/Write (R/$\overline{W}$, also known as Write Enable) signals are developed and distributed to the memory and data buffer. The $\overline{REG}$ line is used by the host system to access the attribute memory. The Write Protect (WP) condition, set by the write-protect switch, is output to the host system. Notice that both Card Detect signals ($\overline{CD1}$ and $\overline{CD2}$) are simply tied to ground. If either of those pins fail to make contact, the host system will know that the card is not inserted properly.

Power to the card is controlled by a voltage protection circuit. When +Vcc is applied to the card, batteries are not used. If the card is removed from its host

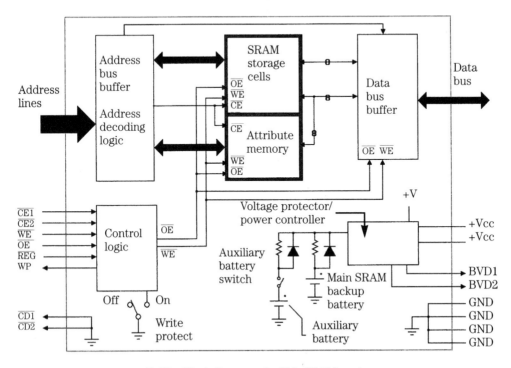

8-15   Block diagram of a 1Mb SRAM card.

system, +Vcc disappears and the main SRAM backup battery supplies power to the system. Two battery voltage detect signals (BVD1 and BVD2) keep the host system informed of the status for one or two batteries. For the SRAM card of Fig. 8-15, a second battery is included as an auxiliary backup. When the main battery must be changed, a small switch is closed to invoke the auxiliary cell, which continues to maintain card contents while the main battery is replaced. After the main battery is replaced, the backup switch can be opened to disengage the auxiliary cell. Without an auxiliary battery scheme, the card would lose its data the moment its main battery was removed for replacement.

DRAM cards

Dynamic RAM cards are much easier and more convenient to install than other forms of expansion memory such as DIPs or SIMMs. A DRAM card need only be inserted into a waiting slot in your computer's housing, whereas you must disassemble the computer to install ICs or SIMMs. Current DRAM cards typically hold up to 16Mb—twice the capacity of current SRAM cards. Extremely short access times (60 to 150 ns) make DRAM devices ideal for both expansion and core memory. Like SRAM devices, DRAM ICs enjoy a long working life under continuous read/write cycles. However, DRAM cards require a measurable amount of power to support the continuous refresh of huge memory volumes. Because it would be impractical to incorporate refresh circuitry (or sufficient battery power to operate the refresh circuitry) on a DRAM card, the card is not suited for data transfer or backup—it would lose all contents the moment it was removed or power was shut down. As a result, DRAM cards are used almost exclusively as expansion memory modules for laser printers (Fig. 8-16) and small computers.

Texas Instruments, Inc.

8-16 An OTPROM card used to hold font styles for a laser printer.

The block diagram for an 8Mb DRAM card is shown in Fig. 8-17. As you look over the diagram, you will notice that the bulk of the card consists of 1 Mbit DRAM devices, along with a small amount of address buffer and refresh control circuitry. It is interesting to note that many DRAM cards work through an 88-pin physical interface that supports up to 36 bits of data. If you look at the arrangement of DRAM banks, you will see that there are 4 banks providing 8 bits each (32 bits), plus 4 banks providing only 1 bit each (4 bits) for a total of 36 bits of data.

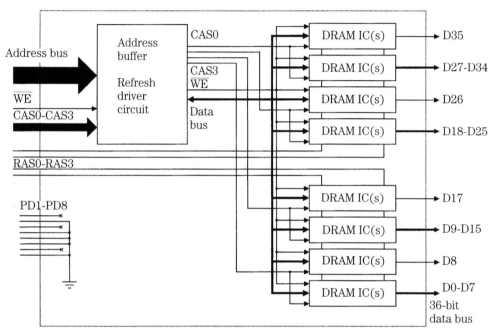

8-17   Block diagram of an 8Mb DRAM card.

Although there are only ten address lines to the card (A0 to A9), remember that DRAM uses multiplexed addressing. This results in twenty functional address lines that can directly access 2^{20} or 1,048,576 locations. The lower (row) address bits are placed on the bus first, then latched into the desired DRAM bank with a row address strobe ($\overline{RAS}$) signal. The upper (column) address bits are placed on the bus next, then latched into the desired DRAM bank with a column address strobe ($\overline{CAS}$) signal. Bidirectional data can then move into or out of the DRAM ICs directly depending on the write enable or read/write (WE or R/$\overline{W}$) signal condition. There are eight additional signal lines (PD1 to PD8) used to form a *presence detect table,* which tells the host system about card configuration, memory banks, access time, refresh rate, and so on. Presence lines form somewhat of a hard wired attribute reference for DRAM cards.

EEPROM cards

Electrically Erasable Programmable Read Only Memory (EEPROM) cards offer some unique characteristics. EEPROMs are classified as nonvolatile, rewritable memory because they will not lose their contents when power is removed, yet they can be erased and rewritten. No battery is needed to back up EEPROM contents when power is removed. While this might sound like a tremendous advantage, there are some physical drawbacks associated with EEPROM use. First, EEPROMs are slow-access devices (250 ns or more) with a rather limited write cycle life of only 10,000 cycles or so. In other words, the average EEPROM storage cell can be erased and rewritten about 10,000 times before failing (it can be read indefinitely). Also, EEPROMS are not writable at the bit level like RAM ICs. An EEPROM must erase and rewrite entire blocks of information (even if only one bit within that block is changed). As a result, the write process can be exceedingly slow. EEPROM cells are somewhat large, so most EEPROM cards are limited to about 196K of storage—certainly not large enough to distribute entire software packages. In many instances, EEPROM cards are used to hold short data lists or programs that are still in the development stage.

Figure 8-18 shows a block diagram for a 196K EEPROM card. Compared to the other card designs you have seen so far, the EEPROM card is rather simple, but it still contains the major elements found in other memory cards. EEPROM ICs make up the bulk of the memory card. The array in Fig. 8-18 uses 24 individual 8K EEPROMs to provide its 196K capacity. With so many ICs in a single package, the

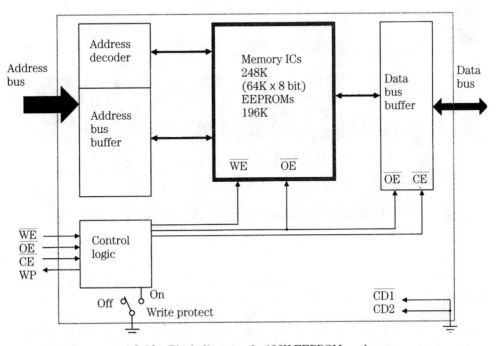

8-18   Block diagram of a 196K EEPROM card.

card might be an extended length Type II card. Eight data bits (D0 to D7) enter the card through the bidirectional data bus buffer, and 18 address lines (A0 to A17) are handled by an address bus buffer. Some higher-order address signals are used to create the 24 Chip Select ($\overline{CS}$) signals that enable each EEPROM in the array. The Output Enable ($\overline{OE}$), Write Enable ($\overline{WE}$), and Card Enable ($\overline{CE}$) signals are processed by the control logic and distributed throughout the card. A write-protect switch generates a Write Protect (WP) signal that is sent back to the host system.

OTPROM cards

A One-Time Programmable ROM (OTPROM) card is an excellent tool for software development and limited-run program distribution. Once a program is developed and debugged on an SRAM or EEPROM card, the program can be loaded (or burned) onto an OTPROM card. OTPROM card programmers such as the one shown in Fig. 8-19 can be used to create single copies or hundreds of copies depending on the need. After an OTPROM card is burned, it can never be erased or rewritten. Fortunately, the OTPROM is nonvolatile, so it will retain its information permanently without the need for battery backup.

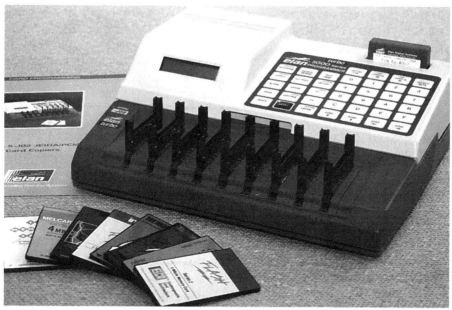

The Elan 5-J08 PCMCIA card copier manufactured and distributed by Elan Digital Systems, Ltd., Fareham, Hampshire, UK, and distributed by Elan Systems, Inc.. Morgan Hill, CA 95037, USA.

8-19   A memory card copier.

A 4Mb OTPROM card is illustrated in the block diagram of Fig. 8-20. Memory is configured as a 2M × 16 bit (4Mb) array. Address lines A0 to A21 are buffered and decoded, then provided to the OTPROM IC array. Data is handled through a bidirectional data buffer, but after the device is programmed, data can only be read from the card. In order to program an OTPROM device, one or more high-voltage pulse

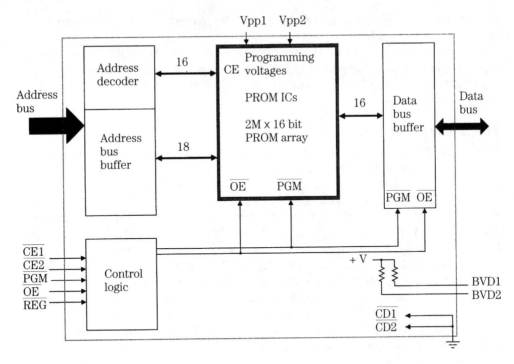

8-20 Block diagram of a 4Mb OTPROM card.

signals must be provided from the programming system. These programming voltages (Vpp1 and Vpp2) supply the energy needed to burn the appropriate bits in the memory array. Two Card Enable signals ($\overline{CE1}$ and $\overline{CE2}$), an Output Enable ($\overline{OE}$), and a Write Enable ($\overline{WE}$, listed in Fig. 8-20 as PGM) signal work to control the card. When the PGM line is logic 1, the card will be read. If the PGM line is logic 0, the card *tries* to write, but writing will only occur in conjunction with programming voltages. The $\overline{REG}$ signal is asserted by the host when accessing the card's attribute memory area. Two card detect signals ($\overline{CD1}$ and $\overline{CD2}$) are used by the host to indicate when the card is properly inserted. Battery voltage signals (BVD1 and BVD2) are available, but serve no purpose in OTPROM cards. Both battery signals are merely tied to the card's +Vcc line.

Mask ROM cards

A mask ROM memory card (or ROM card) is the purest of all the nonvolatile memory cards. Mask ROM devices are programmed during their manufacturing process, so by the time a new card is assembled, it already contains all the information it will ever hold. The program or data contents are specified by the organization purchasing the cards for distribution. Mask ROM is also the simplest, densest (up to 32Mb), and least expensive type of memory. These factors make ROM cards an ideal medium for large-scale software package distribution. Large, well-established packages such as Lotus 1-2-3 can be mass-produced on ROM cards. Once a ROM card is manufactured, however, its contents can never be altered. No battery is needed to back up the card's contents.

The internal design of a ROM card is very similar to the OTPROM card shown in Fig. 8-20, but writing signals and functions are removed. Address buffering, chip select generation, data buffering out of the card, and control logic are otherwise identical to OTPROM cards.

Flash EEPROM cards

A flash EEPROM card offers significant improvements over ordinary EEPROM cards. The greatest advantage is memory capacity—flash EEPROM cards are used to store massive amounts of data (up to 20Mb), yet offer roughly the same speed (200 to 250 ns) and power requirements as ordinary EEPROM cards. Figure 8-21 illustrates a solid-state "mass-storage" device from SunDisk Corporation in California. Flash EEPROM also suffers from some of the limitations found in EEPROMs. Cycle life is an important factor. Older flash cards were only rated for about 10,000 write cycles, but new flash devices have improved to 100,000 write cycles and more. As with ordinary EEPROMs, flash memory must also be written in blocks—not at the bit level. Block operation slows the card's performance, but the convenience of 20 to 40Mb in a credit-card-size device often makes up for slower operation. Finally, flash cards are nonvolatile, so no battery backup is needed to sustain the flash EEPROM components. At the time of this writing, flash EEPROM cards continue to improve in speed and cycle life.

8-21   A SunDisk mass-storage memory card.

Figure 8-22 illustrates the block diagram for a 2Mb flash EEPROM card. An array of flash EEPROM ICs are configured to provide 1M x 16 bits (16 Mbit) or 2Mb of storage. Data (D0 to D15) is handled through a bidirectional 16-bit data buffer, while 21

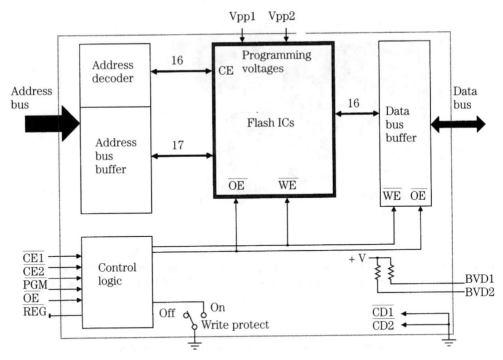

8-22 Block diagram of a 2Mb Flash card.

address lines (A0 to A20) are introduced through an address bus buffer. Address lines are decoded to generate 16 chip select ($\overline{CS}$) signals. Two write voltage signals (Vpp1 and Vpp2) are used when data is written to the card. Memory and data bus operation are managed by control logic.

An Output Enable ($\overline{OE}$), Write Enable ($\overline{WE}$), two Card Enable ($\overline{CE1}$ and $\overline{CE2}$), and a $\overline{REG}$ input control the card's operations. A write-protect switch is interpreted by card control logic that provides a Write Protect (WP) signal to the host system. Two Card Detect lines ($\overline{CD1}$ and $\overline{CD2}$) are grounded to tell the host when the card is properly installed. Battery voltage signals (BVD1 and BVD2) are powered directly from the host's supply voltage (+Vcc), because the flash card uses no batteries. The only time a flash card uses batteries is to back up a small amount of SRAM incorporated into the card.

Card interfaces

As with floppy and hard drives, there must be an organized arrangement of signals that connect a memory card (Fig. 8-23) to host system. A standardized physical interface ensures that memory cards made by various unrelated manufacturers will operate properly in any compatible socket. The problem with memory cards today, however, is that they are still a relatively immature technology—each major card manufacturer has created their own proprietary interface and connector scheme. Fortunately, the PCMCIA (largely supported by card manufacturers) has adopted

8-23 Two memory cards from Texas Instruments.

two primary standards; the 68-pin interface and the 88-pin interface. Most card manufacturers now offer PCMCIA-compatible memory cards in addition to their own proprietary schemes. This section introduces you to the PCMCIA interfaces, as well as other interfaces used by card manufacturers. Table 8-3 presents the definitions used for each interface label.

Table 8-3. Index of memory card interface signals

Vbb	Battery voltage detect	
Vcc	+ Supply voltage	
Vss	Ground (return)	
Vpp1 or Vpp2	Programming voltage lines	[input]
CE1, CE2, or CE	Card enable	[input]
OE	Data output enable	[input]
WE	Write enable (same as R/W)	[input]
R/W	Read/Write (same as WE)	[input]
WE/PGM	Write or Program	[input]
RDY/BSY	Ready/Busy condition	[output]
WP	Write protect	[output]
CD1, CD2, or CD	Card detect lines	[output]
RFU	Reserved for future use	[unused]
NC or NU	Not connected or not used	[unused]
REG	Access attribute memory	[input]
BVD1 or BVD2	Battery voltage detects	[output]
A0-A?	Address lines	[input]
D0-D?	Data lines	[I/O]
CAS	Column address strobe	[input]
RAS	Row address strobe	[input]
DQ0-DQ?	Data lines (same as D0-D?)	[I/O]
PD1-PD?	Presence detect signals	[output]

Table 8-3. Continued

DET	Detect card (same as CD)	[output]
CS1 or CS2	Card select	[input]
ROM/RAM	IC card type	[output]
MR	Memory read only (same as WP)	[output]
CST	Card present (same as CD)	[output]
PGM2	Auxiliary programming input	
S1 or S2	Write to lower or upper bits	[input]
B0, B1, or B2	Card type (same as PD1-PD?)	[output]

PCMCIA 68-pin interface

The PCMCIA 68-pin interface (Fig. 8-24) is endorsed by many card manufacturers as a good, general-purpose card interface. The use of 68 pins allows enough signals to support operation by all cards except DRAM cards. The 68-pin interface offers 16 data lines (D0 to D15) and 26 address lines (A0 to A25) with I/O control signals for Card Enable, Output Enable, Read/Write (program) operation, Ready/Busy, Write Protect, Card Detect, Refresh (limited DRAM), attribute memory access, and battery voltage detection. There are also two programming voltage inputs to write flash

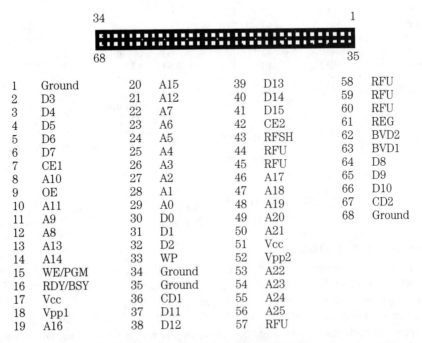

1	Ground	20	A15	39	D13	58	RFU
2	D3	21	A12	40	D14	59	RFU
3	D4	22	A7	41	D15	60	RFU
4	D5	23	A6	42	CE2	61	REG
5	D6	24	A5	43	RFSH	62	BVD2
6	D7	25	A4	44	RFU	63	BVD1
7	CE1	26	A3	45	RFU	64	D8
8	A10	27	A2	46	A17	65	D9
9	OE	28	A1	47	A18	66	D10
10	A11	29	A0	48	A19	67	CD2
11	A9	30	D0	49	A20	68	Ground
12	A8	31	D1	50	A21		
13	A13	32	D2	51	Vcc		
14	A14	33	WP	52	Vpp2		
15	WE/PGM	34	Ground	53	A22		
16	RDY/BSY	35	Ground	54	A23		
17	Vcc	36	CD1	55	A24		
18	Vpp1	37	D11	56	A25		
19	A16	38	D12	57	RFU		

8-24 Pinout diagram for a 68 pin PCMCIA card.

and ordinary EEPROM cards. All data, address, and control signals operate at standard TTL levels. In low-voltage systems, the +Vcc might be +3.3 or +3.0 Vdc.

PCMCIA 88-pin interface

While the 68-pin interface is well-suited for many types of memory cards, it is not as good for DRAM cards. The 36 data lines (D0 to D35) alone are incompatible with the 68-pin standard. An 88-pin interface was devised specifically to handle DRAM applications. Figure 8-25 shows the pinout for an 88-pin interface. The 14 address lines (A0 to A13) are multiplexed to effectively provide 28 lines or 2^{28} (268,435,456, or 256M) direct addresses. Multiplexing and refresh are accomplished with four $\overline{RAS}$ and four $\overline{CAS}$ signals. Eight presence detection signals (PD1 to PD8) are hardwired within the card to tell the host what type of memory configuration is available. The only other control signal is the write enable ($\overline{WE}$) line. Notice that the 88-pin standard lacks many of the ancillary control signals found in the 68-pin interface.

1	Ground	19	A8	37	Vcc	55	nc	73	Ground
2	DQ0	20	A10	38	DQ11	56	Ground	74	PD5
3	DQ1	21	A12	39	DQ12	57	A1	75	PD7
4	DQ2	22	RAS0	40	DQ13	58	A3	76	PD8
5	DQ3	23	CAS0	41	DQ14	59	A5	77	nc
6	DQ4	24	CAS1	42	DQ15	60	A7	78	nc
7	DQ5	25	Vcc	43	DQ16	61	A9	79	DQ35
8	DQ6	26	RAS2	44	Ground	62	A11	80	DQ27
9	Vcc	27	Vcc	45	Ground	63	Ground	81	DQ28
10	DQ7	28	PD2	46	DQ18	64	A13	82	DQ29
11	Vcc	29	PD4	47	DQ19	65	RAS1	83	DQ30
12	DQ8	30	PD6	48	DQ20	66	CAS2	84	DQ31
13	A0	31	nc	49	DQ21	67	Ground	85	DQ32
14	A2	32	nc	50	DQ22	68	CAS3	86	DQ33
15	Vcc	33	DQ17	51	DQ23	69	RAS3	87	DQ34
16	A4	34	DQ9	52	DQ24	70	WE	88	Ground
17	Vcc	35	Vcc	53	DQ25	71	PD1		
18	A6	36	DQ10	54	DQ26	72	PD3		

8-25 Pinout diagram for an 88-pin PCMCIA card.

Panasonic 34-pin interface

The 34-pin interface shown in Fig. 8-26 has been used by Panasonic to support specialized SRAM, OTPROM, Mask ROM, and EEPROM cards. Although the card's 20 address lines (A0 to A19) will directly access a respectable 1,048,576 (1M) locations, the data bus is limited to only 8 bits (D0 to D7), which renders the 34-pin card unusable in almost all high-performance computer applications. Control signals include the familiar Write Enable ($\overline{WE}$), Output Enable ($\overline{OE}$), and Card Enable ($\overline{CE}$). The

17   1

```
ooooooooooooooooo
ooooooooooooooooo
```

34   18

1	Vcc	18	A10
2	A14	19	A1
3	A12	20	CE
4	WE	21	A17
5	A7	22	A15
6	A13	23	A16
7	A18	24	A0
8	A19	25	D7
9	A6	26	D0
10	A8	27	D6
11	A5	28	D1
12	A9	29	D5
13	A4	30	D2
14	A11	31	D4
15	A3	32	D3
16	OE	33	DET
17	A2	34	GND

8-26   Pinout of a Panasonic 34-pin memory card.

only unusual control here is the DET signal, which detects card insertion—the same card-detect output function as $\overline{CD1}$ and $\overline{CD2}$ in the 68-pin interface, but DET uses active-high logic.

Maxell 36-pin interface

Figure 8-27 shows a 36-pin card interface used by customized Maxell cards. One major difference is the connector itself. The 36-pin interface uses a PC board card-edge connector with finely printed and plated fingers instead of an actual pin connector. The 36-pin interface provides 18 address lines (A0 to A17), so the card can address only 262,144 (256K) locations. Each location can only hold 8 bits (D0 to D7), so the cards are generally not used in 16-bit systems. Two Card Select inputs ($\overline{CS1}$ and CS2) are used to activate the card. Notice that $\overline{CS1}$ is an active-low signal, and CS2 is an active-high signal. The Card Detect line ($\overline{CD}$) tells the host system when the card is inserted properly. A Read/Write ($R/\overline{W}$) line controls data flow through the card, and the ROM/$\overline{RAM}$ signal tells the host system what type of memory is built into the card.

Maxell 38-pin interface

The pinout for a Maxell 38-pin interface is illustrated in Fig. 8-28. The 38-pin interface is also a card-edge connector configuration with 18 address lines (A0 to A17) and 8 data lines (D0 to D7), so this design too is generally inappropriate for high-performance applications. Two Card Select signals ($\overline{CS1}$ and CS2), an Output Enable

36   1

Pin	Signal	Pin	Signal
1	A17	19	D3
2	A16	20	D4
3	A14	21	D5
4	A15	22	D6
5	nc	23	D7
6	A12	24	CS2
7	A7	25	A10
8	A6	26	OE
9	A5	27	A11
10	A4	28	A9
11	A3	29	A8
12	A2	30	A13
13	A1	31	nc
14	A0	32	R/W
15	D0	33	Vcc
16	D1	34	CS1
17	D2	35	ROM/RAM
18	GND	36	CD

8-27   Pinout of a Maxell 36-pin memory card.

38   1

Pin	Signal	Pin	Signal
1	GND	20	Vcc
2	A17	21	A16
3	nc	22	A15
4	D3	23	A12
5	D4	24	A7
6	D5	25	A6
7	D6	26	A5
8	D7	27	A4
9	CS1	28	A3
10	A10	29	A2
11	OE	30	A1
12	A11	31	A0
13	A9	32	D0
14	A8	33	D1
15	A13	34	D2
16	A14	35	MR
17	R/W	36	nc
18	CS2	37	Vbb
19	CD	38	GND

8-28   Pinout of a Maxell 38-pin memory card.

($\overline{OE}$), a Card Detect ($\overline{CD}$), and a Read/Write (R/$\overline{W}$) signal are included in the 38-pin design, but two new signals are the Memory Read Only (MR), which acts as a write-protect for memory contents, and the Battery Voltage Level signal (Vbb). Both Maxell interfaces support SRAM, OTPROM, and Mask ROM cards. Note that EEPROM and DRAM cards are not supported because there are no programming voltage or refresh lines in the interface.

Epson 40-pin interface

Figure 8-29 shows the Epson 40-pin card interface. Like the Maxell interfaces, the Epson 40-pin design uses a PC board card-edge connector configuration. The interface provides 23 address lines (A0 to A22) to operate 8,388,608 (8 M) locations, but the 8-bit data bus (D0 to D7) restricts the card's use to low-end processing systems or data collection devices. The Write Enable ($\overline{WE}$), Output Enable ($\overline{OE}$), and ROM/$\overline{RAM}$ signal lines are already familiar, but the Card Enable ($\overline{CE}$), Write Protect ($\overline{WP}$), and Card Present ($\overline{CST}$) signals are all inverse logic from other card interface designs—most other designs use CE, WP, and CD. This is a decent interface for simple, low-end applications if you favor a card-edge connector.

40			1

1	Vcc	21	CE
2	Vbb	22	OE
3	A0	23	D0
4	A1	24	D1
5	A2	25	D2
6	A3	26	D3
7	A4	27	D4
8	A5	28	D5
9	A6	29	D6
10	A7	30	D7
11	A8	31	A17
12	A9	32	A18
13	A10	33	A19
14	A11	34	A20
15	A12	35	A21
16	A13	36	A22
17	A14	37	WP
18	A15	38	CST
19	A16	39	ROM/RAM
20	WE	40	GND

8-29 Pinout of an Epson 40-pin memory card.

Epson 50-pin interface

The Epson 50-pin card interface shown in Fig. 8-30 is also a card-edge connector interface. However, the 50-pin design offers some advantages over the 40-pin version. The 21-line address bus controls 2,097,152 (2 M) locations, but each location can

1	GND	26	CE2
2	A1	27	WP
3	A2	28	OE
4	A3	29	CST
5	A4	30	Vbb
6	A5	31	Vcc
7	A6	32	Vpp
8	A7	33	D0
9	A8	34	D1
10	A9	35	D2
11	A10	36	D3
12	A11	37	D4
13	A12	38	D5
14	A13	39	D6
15	A14	40	D7
16	A15	41	D8
17	A16	42	D9
18	A17	43	D10
19	A18	44	D11
20	A19	45	D11
21	A20	46	D12
22	nc	47	D13
23	WE	48	D14
24	ROM/RAM	49	D15
25	CE1	50	GND

8-30   Pinout of an Epson 50-pin memory card.

hold 16 bits (D0 to D15). A larger data bus makes the interface suitable for more demanding computer applications. The 50-pin interface also supports EEPROM or flash memory devices with its programming voltage pin (Vpp1). The Write Enable ($\overline{\text{WE}}$), ROM/$\overline{\text{RAM}}$ signal, Card Enable inputs ($\overline{\text{CE1}}$ and $\overline{\text{CE2}}$), Write Protect (WP), Output Enable ($\overline{\text{OE}}$), Card Present ($\overline{\text{CST}}$), and Battery Voltage Detect (Vbb) signals are all similar to the previous interfaces.

Epson/Texas Instruments 60-pin interface

One of the first major attempts to create a "standard" DRAM card is highlighted in the interface of Fig. 8-31. The 60-pin DRAM interface has been used by both Epson Corporation of America and Texas Instruments (TI still uses the interface). The interface offers an extended data bus of 18 bits (D0 to D17) and 11 address lines A0 to A10). Remember that DRAM addresses are multiplexed and latched with $\overline{\text{RAS}}$ and $\overline{\text{CAS}}$ signals, so 11 address signals effectively yield 22 address bits capable of accessing 2^{22} or 4,194,304 unique locations. Two row address select ($\overline{\text{RAS0}}$ and $\overline{\text{RAS1}}$) and two column address select ($\overline{\text{CAS0}}$ and $\overline{\text{CAS1}}$) signals serve to multiplex the address lines and refresh memory. A Write Enable ($\overline{\text{WE}}$) determines whether data is read or written to the card. Five Presence Detect signals (PD1 to PD5) are usually hardwired within the card to provide its memory attributes to the host system.

59   1

60   2

1	GND	27	D1	53	A10
2	PD3	28	D11	54	nc
3	PD1	29	D3	55	CAS1
4	PD2	30	Vcc	56	Vcc
5	WE	31	D4	57	PD5
6	Vcc	32	D12	58	PD4
7	nc	33	GND	59	GND
8	nc	34	D13	60	nc
9	GND	35	D5		
10	A0	36	D14		
11	nc	37	D6		
12	nc	38	Vcc		
13	A1	39	D7		
14	Vcc	40	D15		
15	A2	41	GND		
16	A3	42	D16		
17	GND	43	CAS0		
18	A4	44	A5		
19	D8	45	A6		
20	D17	46	Vcc		
21	D0	47	A7		
22	Vcc	48	A8		
23	D1	49	GND		
24	D9	50	A9		
25	GND	51	RAS0		
26	D10	52	RAS1		

8-31 Pinout of an Epson/TI 60-pin memory card.

Mitsubishi 50-pin interface

Figure 8-32 illustrates a 50-pin card-edge memory card interface used by Mitsubishi for SRAM, OTPROM, Mask ROM, and EEPROM cards. The 16-bit data bus (D0 to D15) is better suited for 16-bit CPU systems, and 23 address lines (A0 to A22) can access 8,388,608 individual locations for significant storage capacity. An active-high Card Detect (CD) signal tells the host system when a card is properly installed. A single programming voltage (Vpp1) line is available for EEPROM cards. The Card Enable ($\overline{CE}$), Output Enable ($\overline{OE}$), and Write Enable ($\overline{WE}$) signals control the majority of a card's operations. An auxiliary Program signal ($\overline{PGM2}$) enables writing to EEPROM devices. Finally, a Write Protect (WP) signal is generated by the card's write-protect switch condition to enable or inhibit the host system from writing to the card.

Mitsubishi 60-pin interface

The Mitsubishi 60-pin interface of Fig. 8-33 is intended for SRAM, OTPROM, Mask ROM, and EEPROM/Flash EEPROM cards instead of DRAM cards as with the

50   1

1	GND	26	D5
2	CD	27	D6
3	Vpp1	28	D7
4	A22	29	D8
5	A21	30	D9
6	A20	31	D10
7	A19	32	D11
8	A18	33	D12
9	A17	34	D13
10	A16	35	D14
11	A15	36	D15
12	A12	37	CE
13	A7	38	A10
14	A6	39	OK
15	A5	40	A11
16	A4	41	A9
17	A3	42	A8
18	A2	43	A13
19	A1	44	A14
20	A0	45	WK
21	D0	46	PGM2
22	D1	47	WP
23	D2	48	nc
24	D3	49	Vcc
25	D4	50	GND

8-32   Pinout of a Mitsubishi 50-pin memory card.

Epson/TI 60-pin interface. With a 16-bit data bus (D0 to D15) and a 23-bit address bus (A0 to A22), the interface can address 8,388,608 locations. Such memory capacity and data bus width is ideal for computer applications. A battery voltage line (Vbb) outputs battery level information to the host, while two individual programming voltages (Vpp1 and Vpp2) support a variety of EEPROM and Flash EEPROM cards. Two active-high Card Detect outputs ($\overline{CD1}$ and $\overline{CD2}$) tell the host system when the card is inserted properly. A Card Enable ($\overline{CE}$), Output Enable ($\overline{OE}$), and Write Enable ($\overline{WE}$) signal manage the card's operations. A Write Protect ($\overline{WP}$) line indicates the condition of the card's write-protect switch. There are also three hard-wired lines (B0, B1, and B2) used to indicate the card type, and two bytewise controls ($\overline{S1}$ and $\overline{S2}$).

A card drive system

Now that you have learned about memory cards and their physical interfaces, you can see how memory cards are integrated into your computer (Fig. 8-34). In the case of DRAM cards, high-speed access for reading and writing generally requires that the card have direct access to the computer's main busses—in effect, the host system treats DRAM cards as if they were an extension of the core memory. For most other

```
59                                                        1
┌─────────────────────────────────────────────────────┐
│ ▢□□□□□□□□□□□□□□□□□□□□□□□□□□□□□ │
│ □□□□□□□□□□□□□□□□□□□□□□□□□□□□□□ │
└─────────────────────────────────────────────────────┘
60                                                        2
```

1	nc	25	D1	49	A9
2	Vbb	26	D9	50	nc
3	Vpp1	27	D2	51	A8
4	Vpp2	28	D10	52	B0
5	A12	29	GND	53	A13
6	CD1	30	GND	54	B1
7	A7	31	D3	55	A14
8	A15	32	GND	56	B2
9	A6	33	D4	57	WE
10	A16	34	D11	58	CD2
11	A5	35	D5	59	Vcc
12	A17	36	D12	60	Vcc
13	A4	37	D6		
14	A18	38	D3		
15	A3	39	D7		
16	A19	40	D14		
17	A2	41	CE		
18	A20	42	D15		
19	A1	43	A10		
20	A21	44	S1		
21	A0	45	OE		
22	A22	46	S2		
23	D0	47	A11		
24	D8	48	WP		

8-33   Pinout of a Mitsubishi 60-pin memory card.

memory cards, however, a controller board is needed to connect the card's physical interface to the computer's main busses. Desktop systems use a host controller board that plugs into the computer's motherboard. Computers use highly integrated card controller ICs that are located directly on the system motherboard. The card controller is often an ASIC designed specifically for the physical interface being used. Figure 8-35 shows a block diagram for a typical card drive system.

Each card slot represents a physical interface such as the PCMCIA 68-pin interface discussed earlier in this chapter. In addition to signal lines, a power supply is needed to provide +Vcc, ground, and any required programming voltages (Vpp) to the card(s). The card controller board/IC connects to the host system's address, data, and control busses, so the card controller translates higher level commands from the host into control and card address signals. From a system perspective, memory cards are each treated as a logical drive (e.g., A:, B:, D:, and so on).

It is interesting to note that the term "card drive" is rather misleading. Unlike floppy drives and hard drives using intricate and involved mechanical assemblies and electromagnetic head devices, a "card drive" (Fig. 8-36) contains no mechanical components at all except perhaps for the card's connector and a small card ejection

8-34   An external card drive for notebook computers.

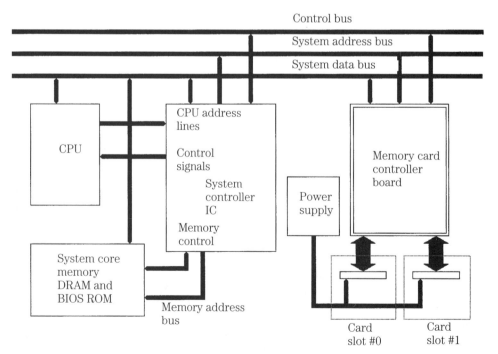

8-35   Block diagram of a complete card system.

8-36   Adtron memory card drives.

lever. All the circuitry required for a card drive system is either in the memory card itself, or is located on the host system's motherboard in the form of a card controller IC or board. In many designs, the card rail is actually mounted right on the host motherboard adjacent to the card controller. The net result is a small, simple, and shock-resistant mass-storage system.

During card access, the CPU addresses the system controller and causes the system controller to address the card controller for reading (or writing, if possible). Any instructions or program routines needed by the CPU can be taken from BIOS ROM (if the card system has been designed as an integral part of the computer), or device drivers loaded on system startup. Microsoft provides several device drivers for use with memory card systems. CARDDRV.EXE allows the core logic to access memory cards as FAT-formatted, DOS-compatible media. CARDBIOS.EXE is a BIOS interface used by CARDDRV.EXE, and MEMCARD.EXE is a device driver utility to configure and maintain memory cards. In very new computers such as pen computers or palmtop computers, the card controller is actually integrated into the system controller ASIC.

As Table 8-4 shows, a PCMCIA-compatible memory card can be kept in any one of three states: standby, read, or write. Card modes are based on combinations of physical interface signals generated by the card controller in response to commands sent by the system's core logic. Each card mode offers some unique characteristics.

The standby mode is active whenever the card is idle. The card controller IC makes both Card Enable signals ($\overline{CE1}$ and $\overline{CE2}$) logic 1. In that state, all data bits from the card (D0 to D15) become effectively disconnected by a high-impedance (HiZ) condition at the card's data bus buffer regardless of any other control signals.

In the read mode, data can be read as the lower 8 bits (lower byte), the upper 8 bits (upper byte), the entire 16 bits simultaneously (word), and the odd (upper) byte only. Bytewise operations allow the 16-bit PCMCIA interface to be backward-compatible with 8-bit data bus systems. In order to read from a card, the Output Enable ($\overline{OE}$) must be logic 0 and the write enable ($\overline{WE}$) line must be logic 1. To read an upper or lower byte, Card Enable 2 ($\overline{CE2}$) must be logic 1, and Card Enable 1 ($\overline{CE1}$) must be logic 0. In this condition, the upper 8 data lines are at high-impedance. When address line A0 is at logic 0, the lower 8 data lines output the

Table 8-4. PCMCIA 68-pin card operation

Function	CE2	$\overline{CE1}$	A0	$\overline{OE}$	$\overline{WE}$	D8-D15	D0-D7
Standby	H	H	x	x	x	HiZ	HiZ
Read (low byte)	H	L	L	L	H	HiZ	Low B
(high byte)	H	L	H	L	H	HiZ	Up B
(word 16 bit)	L	L	x	L	H	Up B	Low B
(odd byte only)	L	H	x	L	H	Up B	HiZ
Write (low byte)	H	L	L	H	L	x	Low B
(high byte)	H	L	H	H	L	x	Up B
(word 16 bit)	L	L	x	H	L	Up B	Low B
(odd byte only)	L	H	x	H	L	Up B	x

lower byte of the desired word. If A0 is logic 1, the lower 8 data lines output the upper byte of the desired word. To read the entire byte, both Card Enable signals ($\overline{CE1}$ and $\overline{CE2}$) must be logic 0. Address A0 then becomes irrelevant, and the entire addressed word appears across D0 to D15. To address odd bytes only, Card Enable 2 ($\overline{CE2}$) must be logic 0, and Card Enable 1 ($\overline{CE1}$) must be logic 1. Address A0 is also not relevant, but only the upper 8 bits of each addressed word appear at D8 to D15 (the lower 8 bits are in the high-impedance state).

The same selections are available in the write mode: lower byte, upper byte, entire word, and odd byte only. This assumes that the inserted card contains media that can be written to (i.e., SRAM or EEPROM). Writing requires that the Output Enable ($\overline{OE}$) be logic 1, and the Write Enable ($\overline{WE}$) signal be logic 0. To write an upper or lower byte, Card Enable 2 ($\overline{CE2}$) must be logic 1, and Card Enable 1 ($\overline{CE1}$) must be logic 0. When address line A0 is logic 0, the data on the lower 8 bits of the data bus (D0 to D7) will be written into the lower byte of an addressed word. If A0 is made logic 1, data on the lower 8 bits of the data bus will be written to the upper byte of an addressed word. To write an entire 16-bit data word to a card, both Card Enable signals ($\overline{CE1}$ and $\overline{CE2}$) must be logic 0. Then, the entire 16 bits of data on D0 to D15 are written to the addressed location without regard for A0. To write odd bytes only, Card Enable 2 ($\overline{CE2}$) must be logic 0, and Card Enable 1 ($\overline{CE1}$) must be logic 1. The 8 bits appearing on data bits D8 to D15 are then written to the upper byte of the selected word.

Troubleshooting memory card systems

Despite their small size, memory cards are remarkably complex devices. Flash EEPROM cards are even more sophisticated. As a result, memory cards are some of the densest and most intricate electronic assemblies that you will encounter. Such demanding circuitry is very unforgiving even in the hands of experienced trouble-shooters, unless you have the precise tools and equipment to deal with them, so this book will consider memory cards as component parts. Card drives (Fig. 8-37) are very straightforward.

8-37 An internal memory card drive.

Symptom 1: The SRAM or flash card loses its memory when powered down or removed from the system Because flash cards make use of advanced EEPROMs, you might wonder why batteries would be incorporated. Some flash cards use a small amount of SRAM to speed the transfer of data to or from the card. Batteries are needed to back up the SRAM only. If your memory card does not appear to hold its memory, you should start your investigation by removing the memory card and testing its batteries. Make sure the card's batteries are inserted properly. Use your multimeter to check the battery voltage(s). Replace any memory card batteries that appear marginal or low. You should expect a 2- to 5-year backup life from your memory card batteries, depending on the amount of card memory—more memory results in shorter battery life. All battery contacts should be clean and bright, and contacts should make firm connections with the battery terminals.

Try a known-good memory card in your system. You can verify a new or known-good memory card on another computer with a compatible card slot. If another card works properly, your original memory card is probably defective and should be replaced. It is not recommended that you open or attempt to troubleshoot a memory card without comprehensive experience in surface-mount device repair and high-quality surface-mount desoldering equipment.

Symptom 2: You are unable to access the card for reading. You might not be able to write to the card either Begin troubleshooting by checking memory card compatibility (programmed OTPROM cards and mask ROM cards cannot be written to). If a memory card is not compatible with the interface used by your small computer, the interface cannot access the card. For example , a PCMCIA-compatible 68-pin card will probably not work in a non-PCMCIA 68-pin card slot, and vice versa. Try a known-good compatible card in the suspect card slot. Also check your CON FIG.SYS or AUTOEXEC.BAT files to be sure that any required device drivers have been installed during system initialization.

If you have difficulty writing to an SRAM or flash card, inspect the card's write-protect switch. A switch left in the protected position prevents new information from being written to the card. Move the switch to the unprotected position and try the memory card again.

If you cannot write to EEPROM or Flash EEPROM cards, check your programming voltages (Vpp1 and Vpp2). Without high-voltage pulses, new data cannot be written to such cards. Measure Vpp1 and Vpp2 with your oscilloscope with the card removed from your system (it might be necessary to ground the card detect lines ($\overline{\text{CD1}}$ and $\overline{\text{CD2}}$) to fool the host system into believing that a card is actually installed. You will probably have to disassemble the computer's housing to gain easy access to the motherboard's card connector. If one or both programming pulses are missing during a write operation, check the power supply output(s). When high-voltage supplies are missing, troubleshoot your computer's power supply. If programming voltages are present, there might be a defect in the card controller IC or board, or any discrete switching circuitry designed to produce the programming pulses. Try replacing the card controller.

The memory card might be inserted incorrectly. Two Card Detect signals are needed from a PCMCIA-compatible card to ensure proper insertion. If the card is not inserted properly, the host system will inhibit all card activities. Remove the card and reinsert it completely. Make sure the card is straight, even, and fully inserted. Try the memory card again.

If trouble remains, remove the card and inspect the connector on the card and the one inside the computer. Check for any contacts that are loose, bent, or broken. It might be necessary to disassemble the computer in order to inspect its connector, but a clear view with a small flashlight will tell you all you need to know. Connections in the computer that are damaged or extremely worn should be replaced with a new connector assembly. When a memory card connector is worn or damaged, the memory card should be replaced

If your results are still inconclusive, try a known-good memory card in the system. Keep in mind that the new card must be fully compatible with the original one. Make sure that there are no valuable or irreplaceable files on the known-good card before you try it in a suspect system. If a known-good card works properly, then the old memory card is probably damaged and should be replaced.

If a known-good card also does not work, the original card is probably working properly. Your final step is to disassemble the computer and replace the memory card controller or drive. A defective controller can prevent all data and control signals from reaching the card.

9

Tape drives

One of the unfortunate truths of all forms of mass-storage is that, sooner or later, the medium will fail. As the medium goes, so goes the valuable data recorded there. Even with the remarkable levels of reliability offered by today's storage systems, the loss of even a single bit can have catastrophic consequences for your computer system. The best, most proven method of protecting yourself against storage failures is to produce one or more duplicates of the storage system's contents—you know this as the backup procedure.

Floppy disks are a favorite backup medium. Cheap, light, and fast, a floppy disk is an excellent choice for copying individual files such as word processor documents or CAD drawings, but floppy disks are limited in their storage capacity. Extensive backup operations can require a handful of floppies. Backing up an entire hard drive can require boxes of floppy disks and a cumbersome, time-consuming swap and copy procedure. For businesses with large, rapidly changing databases, accounting, inventory, and payroll files, tape drive systems (Fig. 9-1) are capable of storing hundreds of megabytes on a single tape cartridge. This chapter explains the construction and operation of typical tape drives, and offers some maintenance and troubleshooting procedures that can help you resolve tape drive problems.

Media

Magnetic tape is the oldest form of magnetic mass-storage. Tape systems served as the primary mass-storage medium for older mainframes (obsoleting the aging punched-card and punched-paper-tape environment of the day). Tape systems proved to be inexpensive and reliable—so much so that even the original IBM PC was outfitted with a drive port for cassette tape storage. With the development of floppy and hard drives, tape systems became obsolete as a primary storage method, but retain a valuable role as backup systems.

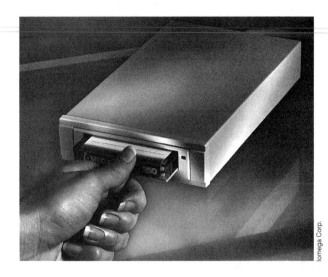

9-1 An Iomega TAPE250 tape drive.

Although the size, shape, and standards used for tape packaging and recording has advanced, the tape itself is virtually unchanged in principle from the very first incarnation. Figure 9-2 illustrates a tape cartridge used in an Iomega tape backup system. A tape is a long, slender piece of polyester substrate that is much more flexible than the mylar substrate used in floppy disks. Polyester also sustains a bit of stretch to help the tape negotiate the high tensions and sharp turns encountered in today's tape cartridge assemblies. As with all other magnetic storage media, the substrate is coated with a layer of magnetic material that is magnetized to retain digital information. Many different coatings have been tried through the years, and many tapes still employ coatings of conventional magnetic oxides similar to older floppy disk coatings. More exotic coatings such as metal films and pure metal particles suspended in a binder material are also used.

Drive roller
Write protect

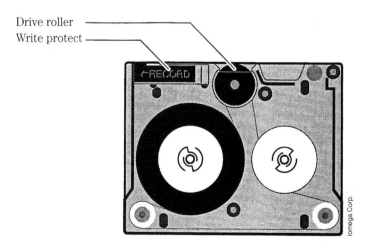

9-2 A typical minicartridge.

The recording principles for magnetic media are presented in chapters 6 and 7, so you can refer there for additional background, but you must understand here that tapes are *sequential* media, not random access media. A tape drive stores its data sequentially along the length of its medium. Unlike a floppy disk or a hard disk, which stores bits along a two-dimensional plane that read/write heads can access in milliseconds, tapes must be searched bit by bit from beginning to end in order to locate a desired file. A tape search can take minutes—far too long for use as primary storage. There are four major approaches to tape packaging: reels, cassettes, quarter-inch cartridges, and helical-scan cartridges. Due to the age and expense of reel-to-reel tape storage systems, they will not be covered in this book.

Cassette tapes

The audio cassette as we know it today was originally developed and patented by the Phillips Corporation as a way of overcoming the disadvantages of open reel audio tape. Phillips created a self-contained tape module that was small, compact, relatively rugged and reliable, and offered a reasonably high-fidelity that appealed to the consumer market. As personal computers entered the marketplace, the conventional audio cassette and cassette tape player were viewed as a simple, inexpensive storage system. Even the original IBM PC provided a cassette interface port. However, the slow speed and access techniques required for cassette tapes soon led to the introduction and widespread adoption of inexpensive 5.25" (13.34 cm) floppy disk drives. Cassette tape drives disappeared from personal computer systems virtually overnight.

However, Teac Corporation has reintroduced the compact cassette as a refined, data-only digital cassette (called a D/CAS). Teac's new high-speed cassette transport mechanism (Fig. 9-3) uses the D/CAS to provide tape backup storage with performance levels equal to the better cartridge systems. Teac D/CAS tapes are intentionally incompatible with conventional audio cassettes. While dimensions between audio and digital cassettes are very similar, digital cassettes have a single large notch

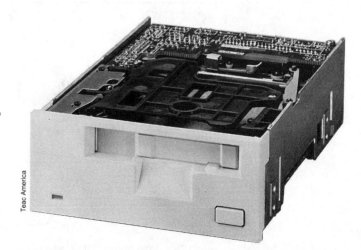

9-3 A Teac MT-2ST/F tape drive.

Teac America

on the cassette housing that allows a D/CAS to fit in the drive, but prohibits audio cassettes from being used. The notch also prohibits the D/CAS from being inserted into the drive upside-down. An auto-reverse mechanism allows both sides of the tape to be used. A typical Teac D/CAS system stores 160Mb on a tape; newer models can store up to 600Mb. Teac plans to increase that limit even further in the next few years. You will see more of Teac's D/CAS drive system in this chapter.

Quarter-inch cartridge

The concept of the quarter-inch tape cartridge (QIC) is identical to the compact cassette tape: a plastic shell contains two spools that hold a length of tape. Enclosing the tape supply in a prefabricated shell eliminates the need for handling open reel tape, or threading the tape through the labyrinth of a mechanical handling system. The original QIC was introduced by 3M in the early 1970s as a recording medium for telecommunication system programming and high-volume data acquisition.

While QIC and cassette tapes are similar in appearance, the means used to drive them are radically different. Cassette tapes are driven using a capstan drive system, wherein the tape is pulled by a take-up reel as it winds across a read/write head. A QIC (Fig. 9-4) uses a small belt that loops around and contacts both the supply and take-up spools, as well as a rubber drive wheel. The capstan in a QIC system contacts the drive wheel (but not the tape), so only the belt's contact friction is used to drive the tape. Drive forces are spread evenly over a long length of tape, so the tape can be moved faster and sustain more direction reversals than a cassette. Tape reliability and working life are greatly improved. Because the components needed to handle the tape are already contained in the QIC shell, the drive mechanism is simple, as only a motor and read/write head are required.

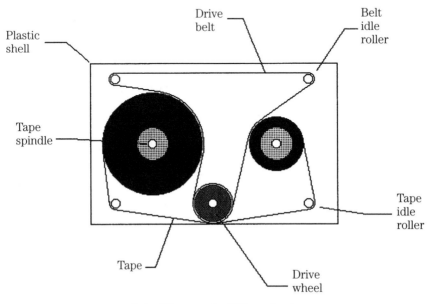

9-4 Diagram of a QIC mechanism.

With the introduction of personal computers and the subsequent discard of audio cassettes as mass-storage devices, the QIC emerged as the premier tape medium, but early QIC systems were riddled with incompatibilities—each manufacturer had their own ideas about how QIC systems should work. A number of tape drive companies met in the early 1980s to decide on a set of standards for the new QIC devices. In 1987, this group of industrial manufacturers formed an organization called the QIC Committee. The QIC Committee is responsible for developing standards for all aspects of tape drive construction and application.

A classic QIC can be identified by its general dimensions. The cartridge is 6" (15.24 cm) wide, 4" (10.16 cm) long, and 5/8" (1.59 cm) deep—roughly the size of a VHS video cassette. While dimensions have not changed significantly through the years, there have been several versions of "standard" quarter-inch cartridges. The 3M Company produced the DC300A-model cartridge. Original DC300As used 300' (91.44 m) of tape at a recording density of 1600 bits per inch. Subsequent drive upgrades allowed the DC300A to hold about 1Mb (formatted). Further drive enhancements allowed the DC300A cartridge design to hold up to 15Mb. Keep in mind that such advances have been due to changes in the drive—not the tape itself.

The amount of tape was doubled from 300' (91.44 m) to 600' (182.88 m) in the DC600 cartridge, and the designation was changed to DC6000. The last three digits in the DC6000 family represent the capacity of the cartridge. For example, a DC6040 would hold 40Mb, a DC6120 would hold 120Mb, and so on. DC6000-series cartridges today can hold 1Gb or more depending on the particular tape drive the tape is being used in. Whenever you see a tape or tape drive associated with a DC6000 designation, you must use a standard 6" x 4" QIC with 600' (182.88 m) of tape.

A series of standards for QICs has been developed by the QIC Committee as illustrated in Table 9-1. The first standard (QIC-20) offered a 9-track, 5Mb drive for the DC300A QIC. From that point, all subsequent QIC tape drives were designed using DC6000 cartridges. The QIC-24 provided a 9-track, 60Mb drive, QIC-120 drives could handle up to 125Mb, and QIC-150 drives stored up to 250Mb on 18 tracks. From then on, the number shown with "QIC" represented the standard's storage capacity on a DC6000 cartridge using 30 tracks: QIC-1000 (1Gb), QIC-1350 (1.35Gb), and QIC-2100 (2.1Gb).

Table 9-1. Comparison of quarter inch cartridges

Standard	Description	Capacity
QIC-02	9-track, DC300 cartridge	15Mb
QIC-24	9-track, DC6000 cartridge	60Mb
QIC-120	9-track, DC6000 cartridge	125Mb
QIC-150	18-track, DC6000 cartridge	250Mb
QIC-525	18-track, DC6000 cartridge	525Mb
QIC-1000	30-track, DC6000 cartridge	1Gb
QIC-1350	30-track, DC6000 cartridge	1.35Gb
QIC-2100	30-track, DC6000 cartridge	2.10Gb

DC300	300' spool
DC600	600' spool
DC6000	600' spool

The major drawback to standard QICs is their overall large size—they do not fit in today's small drive bays, so most QIC systems are external desktop devices. To address the need for smaller QIC systems, the QIC Committee created the mini-cartridge, a 3.25" x 2.5" x ⅝" (8.26 cm x 6.35 cm x 1.59 cm) assembly holding about 205' (62.48 m) of quarter-inch tape. Minicartridges use a DC2000 designation, where the last three digits in the number reflect the cartridge's capacity. For example, a DC2080 minicartridge is designated to hold 80Mb, and so on. Any time you see a tape or tape drive associated with a DC2000 designation, you must use a minicartridge.

Standards have also been developed for minicartridges by the QIC Committee as shown in Table 9-2. QIC-40 was a simple, inexpensive tape backup standard that used an ordinary floppy drive interface controller to store up to 40Mb. Another interesting aspect of the QIC-40 specification is that the standard also covers data formatting. Sectors and tracks are allocated for files in much the same way that floppy or hard drive space is allocated. Any bad sectors are also listed to prohibit data storage in defective media areas. As with floppy disks, QIC-40 tapes must be formatted prior to their use. The enduring advantage to QIC-40 formatting is that the tape can be randomly accessed like a floppy disk (although much slower), without having to search the entire tape to find a file. Files can also be appended, as the QIC-40 drive can find free space on the formatted tape.

Table 9-2. Comparison of QIC minicartridges

Standard	Description		Capacity
QIC-40	20-track,	DC2000 cartridge	40 Mb
QIC-100	12/24-track,	DC2000 cartridge	40 Mb
QIC-80	32-track,	DC2000 cartridge	80–120 Mb
QIC-128		DC2110 cartridge	86 Mb
		DC2165 cartridge	128 Mb
QIC-500M		QIC-143 cassette	500 Mb

DC2000   205' spool

Today, QIC-40 tape systems are inexpensive and easy to use, but QIC-80 has become a very popular minicartridge tape standard. QIC-80 extends the QIC-40 approach by placing 32 tracks across the tape and increasing the data density, which effectively raises storage capacity to 80Mb (formatted). Although QIC-80 systems can read but not write older QIC-40 systems, QIC-80 drives are compatible with conventional floppy drive controllers.

The QIC-100 standard is actually older than the QIC-80 standard, and can only support capacities of 40Mb. The advantage of QIC-100 was its performance because it used specialized interface hardware for high data transfer rates. QIC-100 stores data on 12 or 24 tracks recorded in a serpentine (back and forth) fashion. For practical purposes, you might never encounter tape drives using a QIC-100 system or its 86Mb successor, the QIC-128 standard.

New standards for QIC minicartridges are constantly being developed. The QIC-500M standard is intended to eventually replace QIC-80 systems. A QIC-500M drive should be able to pack 500Mb on a minicartridge without using any data compression at all. The QIC-500M standard is also intended to be compatible with QIC-40 and QIC-80 systems, and connect to your computer using a conventional floppy drive interface.

Helical scan tapes

The rate at which data is transferred in tape systems has long been an issue. Transfer rates of 250 or 500 Kbits per second (floppy drive rates) can seem extraordinarily slow when there are hundreds of megabytes (even gigabytes) to move onto a tape. Because the conventional tape systems you have seen so far move tape across stationary heads, data transfer rates are ultimately limited by the tape speed—and a tape can be moved only so fast. Data transfer is also affected by the drive electronics, but even new encoding techniques are of limited utility. Tape drive designers realized that the head and tape can be moved simultaneously to increase the relative speed between the two, while allowing the tape transport mechanism itself to continue operating at a normal speed.

It was discovered that a set of R/W heads mounted on a cylindrical drum could be spun across a length of moving tape wrapped about 90° around the drum's circumference, as illustrated in Fig. 9-5. The drum itself would be offset (or cantered) at a slight angle relative to the tape's path of travel. During normal operation, the spinning drum describes a *helical* path (thus the term *helical scan*) across the tape as in Fig. 9-6. Such a helical pattern allows more information to be written to the tape faster than conventional stationary head systems. There are currently two major helical recording systems: digital audio tape (DAT) and 8 mm tape. DAT heads are canted about 6°, while 8 mm tape heads use a 5° tilt. DAT heads spin at 2000

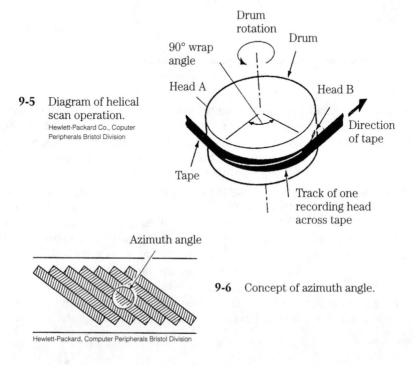

9-5   Diagram of helical scan operation.
Hewlett-Packard Co., Coputer Peripherals Bristol Division

9-6   Concept of azimuth angle.

Hewlett-Packard, Computer Peripherals Bristol Division

RPM, and lay down 1869 tracks (traces) in every linear inch (2.54 cm) of tape. Each trace is only 4 mm wide.

Data can be packed very tightly on DAT tapes because each trace (or scan line) is recorded at a unique *azimuth angle*. Each head in the drum is skewed slightly from the perpendicular such that the data on adjacent traces is oriented very differently. During playback, a head responds well to signals written in the same orientation, but it responds poorly to signals written in the other orientation, so blank space between each signal is not required. Another advantage to helical scan is data integrity. By adding two more heads to the rotating drum (total of four heads), data can be read immediately after writing. Any errors that are detected can be corrected by repeating the data on subsequent traces until data is valid. Physically, helical scan tape is 3.81 mm wide and wound into a plastic cartridge roughly the size of a credit card. Figure 9-7 illustrates a typical DAT cartridge. A DAT usually packs 1.3 to 2.0Gb of data in up to 90 m of 1450-oersted tape.

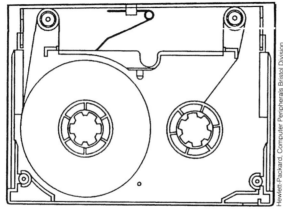

Hewlett-Packard, Computer Peripherals Bristol Division

Illustration actual size

9-7 Diagram of a DAT cartridge.

The greatest disadvantage to helical scan tape systems is the additional mechanical complexity required to wrap the tape around a spinning drum. Where cassettes, QICs, and minicartridges allow only a single point of contact with a stationary R/W head, a helical scan tape must be pulled out and away from its shell and wrapped around the rotating drum, as illustrated in Fig. 9-8. Note the series of rollers and guides that are needed to properly position and tension the tape. The amount of wrap depends on the particular system. Figure 9-9 shows four standard wrap angles ranging from 270° for a VHS-C system to 90° for a DAT system.

An 8 mm tape is twice as wide as the DAT medium, and is housed in a 3.75" (9.53 cm) x 2.5" (6.35 cm) x 0.5" (1.27 cm) cassette that appears rather like a VHS cassette. Using file compression techniques, 8 mm systems can store up to 10Gb on a single cassette. The exorbitantly high cost of 8 mm tape backup systems are well beyond the means of most hobbyists and enthusiasts, and even some small companies. This book will not deal with 8 mm systems any further.

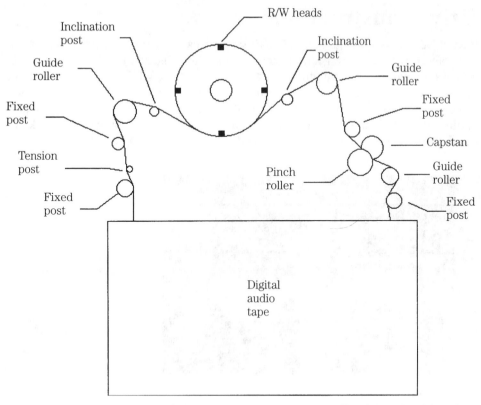

9-8   A tape path used in helical tape systems.

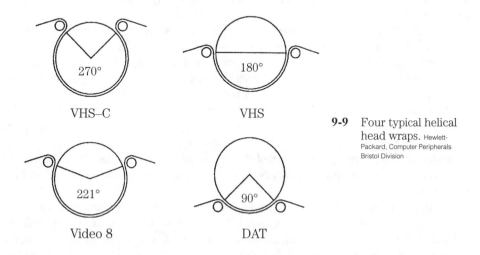

9-9   Four typical helical head wraps. Hewlett-Packard, Computer Peripherals Bristol Division

Drive construction

Having gained an understanding of basic tape types and concepts, you can now see how tape drives are physically designed and built (Fig. 9-10). This construction information can be very helpful during troubleshooting. While the construction of most fixed-head tape drives is not terribly complex, it is rather involved and delicate. Helical scan tape drives, however, can offer significant technical challenges because of the added heads and tape handling mechanisms. For the purposes of this book, we will discuss the mechanical and electrical design of fixed-head tape drives.

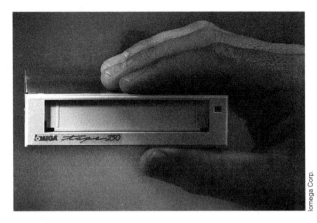

9-10 An Iomega internal TAPE 250 tape drive.

Iomega Corp.

Mechanical construction

The mechanical assembly for a Teac D/CAS tape drive mechanism is illustrated in the exploded diagram of Fig. 9-11. At the core of the assembly is the *drive chassis* (1), also called the *transport subassembly*. This chassis forms the foundation for all other drive components including two PC boards. The chassis is built with four assemblies already in place: two *loading base assemblies*, a *lever base assembly*, and a *loading arm assembly*. These mechanical assemblies are responsible for loading and ejecting the tape. When you encounter difficulties with tape loading or unloading, you should suspect a problem in one or more of these mechanical areas. The chassis mechanics are also responsible for allowing tapes to be inserted on one side only (Side A). If the tape is inserted with side B up, the mechanics do not allow the tape to seat in the drive. A *front bezel/door assembly* (28) and an *eject button* (29) give the drive its cosmetic appearance once the completed drive is mounted in its drive bay.

A D/CAS tape is transported through the drive using two reel motors: a *forward reel motor* (9) and a *reverse reel motor* (10). These are both dc motors that are driven by control circuitry on the *drive control PC board* (26). Ideally, these reel motors should turn at a constant rate of speed, but tape speed tends to vary as tape is unwound from one spool and wound onto another. To keep tape velocity constant, the tape contacts an *encoder roller* (15) which drives an *encoder assembly* (12). Data generated by the encoder is used to regulate reel motor speed—much the same

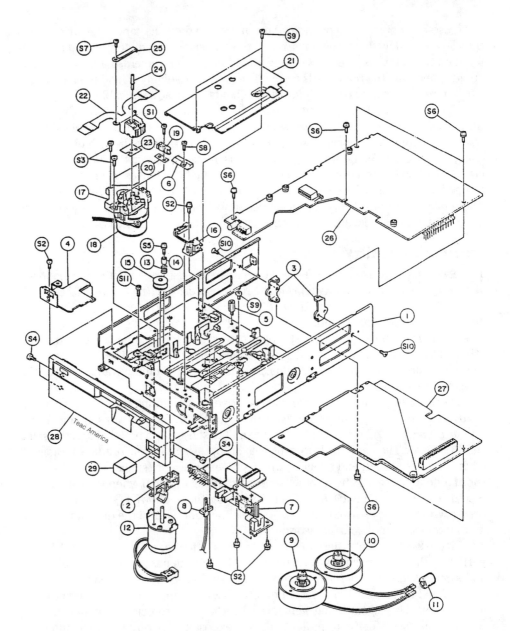

9-11 Exploded diagram of a Teac D/CAS tape drive.

way that an index sensor is used to regulate spindle speed in a floppy or hard drive. Tension on the encoder roller is maintained and adjusted by tweaking the *encoder spring* (13) and *pin spring* (14) with a screw.

D/CAS tape is separated into individual tracks along the tape's width. The *read/write head assembly* (22) is actually composed of five separate magnetic heads: two read heads, two write heads, and an erase head. During a write operation, the erase head erases any previous data that existed on the tape. The write heads then lay down new flux transitions, and the read heads immediately reread the written data to ensure its integrity. During a read operation, the erase and write heads are idle, and only the read heads respond. The head assembly is held in place with a *head mounting screw* (24). A *clamp* (25) holds the head's flat cable.

The head assembly is mounted to a *head seek assembly* (17) through an *electrical isolation sheet* (23). A head seek unit raises or lowers the head to the desired track as the tape moves past. A *stepping motor* (18) drives the head seek assembly using a lead screw. As the stepping motor turns in one direction, the force of rotation is translated to linear motion by the lead screw—the head moves in a fashion similar to head stepping in a floppy drive. There are also several *tape guides* (6 and 19). The remainder of mechanical parts are generally brackets and screws. Always make it a point to note the location of all screws and brackets during disassembly.

Electronic circuitry

The electronics involved in the Teac D/CAS drive are also called out in the exploded view in Fig. 9-11. There are two printed circuit boards: the *drive control PC board* (26) and the *drive interface PC board* (27). The drive control board contains all the circuitry necessary for operating the drive's physical devices such as the read/write heads, the reel motors, and the stepping motor, and for reading the encoder and other drive sensor elements. A drive interface board contains the high-level processing circuitry needed to communicate with a host computer, and operate the drive control board.

There are three discrete sensors in the drive (not counting the encoder): a *cassette load sensor* (7), a *file protect sensor* (7), an *LED hole sensor* (8), and a *sensor guide pair* (16). Notice that cassette and file sensors are both held on the same sub-PC board. The cassette load sensor is an optoisolator that produces a logic 0 when a tape is absent, and a logic 1 when a tape is present (similar to the disk sensor of a floppy drive). A file protect sensor produces a logic 0 when the tape is protected (writing is inhibited), and a logic 1 when writing is allowed (similar to a floppy drive's write-protect sensor). All sensors are important parts of the drive and its ability to interact with the outside world.

Figure 9-12 presents these major electronic sections as a block diagram. The left portion of the diagram shows you how a D/CAS tape will interact with the R/$\overline{\text{W}}$ head and system sensors. When the cassette is inserted properly, it will engage into the forward and reverse reel motors. A properly inserted tape also asserts the cassette load sensor. The signal being generated by the file protect sensor depends on whether the cassette's write-protect notch is exposed or covered. The beginning of tape (BOT) and end of tape (EOT) contain a short series of holes. An LED source is placed on one side of the tape, and a sensor is placed on the other side. When EOT and BOT holes are encountered, a pulse signal is returned to drive control circuitry. During reading or writing, a read/write head assembly is engaged to contact the tape. The encoder wheel also contacts the tape. Resulting encoder signals are used by drive control circuits to regulate tape speed by adjusting reel speed. The head is mounted to its track-seeking stepping motor, which is also operated by drive control circuits.

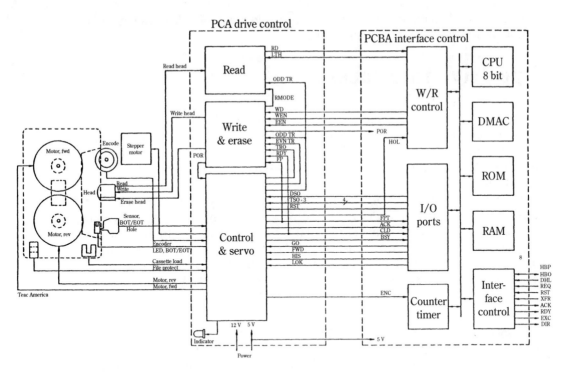

9-12   Electrical block diagram of a Teac D/CAS tape drive system.

The tape drive control PC board handles the drive's physical operations and processes all sensor readings. Analog head signals are processed through a read circuit where they are converted into logic signals and sent along to the read/write head control circuit on the drive's interface control PC board. Write signals leave the R/W control circuit in logic form and are sent to the write/erase circuit on the drive control PC board. Logic write signals are converted to analog signals and sent to the R/W head. During writing, the write/erase circuit also actuates the erase head to clear any previous data before new data is written. The drive control board is managed by the control/servo circuit, which communicates with I/O ports on the drive interface board. The control/servo circuit also lights an LED on the drive's front panel when any drive activity takes place.

The tape drive interface control PC board is a microprocessor-driven system that handles high-level drive operations. A CPU is responsible for processing system instructions provided by an on-board ROM, as well as any variables or data information held in RAM. The CPU handles the physical interface through the interface control circuit, and directs the drive's control board utilizing I/O circuits. Data flowing into or out of the drive is processed through a write/read control circuit. System synchronization is maintained by reading the counter/timer circuit being driven by the control/servo circuit. The particular layout and control structure of your particular tape drive might vary quite a bit from the Teac system illustrated here, but all major operating areas should be present. You might also encounter several functions integrated into a single high-density ASIC, so you should regard Fig. 9-12 as more of a conceptual guideline than an absolute rule.

Tape drive interfaces

Regardless of a drive's sophistication or recording technology, a tape drive is merely another computer peripheral—it is useless by itself. The drive must connect to a computer (referred to as the host) in order to serve a useful function. Because the drive is operated by the host system, there must be some means of carrying data and control signals into and out of the drive. Signal exchange is accomplished over the physical interface. There are a myriad of possible signal interface schemes, but manufacturers prefer to utilize a number of standard interfaces. A standard interface allows a tape drive built by any manufacturer to run properly on a given computer. There are, however, a small number of manufacturers that choose to implement a custom interface scheme. A host controller board interfaces the drive's signals to the computer's main busses. Tape drive interfaces usually fall into three categories: SCSI, floppy drive, and proprietary.

SCSI

The Small Computer Systems Interface (SCSI) is a system-level device interface that can service a wide range of peripheral devices (e.g., printers, CD-ROMs, hard drives, tape drives, and so on). A SCSI host controller board is required in your computer in order to interface a 50-pin SCSI signal cable to your system's main busses. A single host controller board can support up to 8 SCSI devices simultaneously. The advantages of SCSI is flexibility and performance. Data can be transferred very quickly, and multiple devices can share the same bus system. See chapter 7 for a detailed discussion of the SCSI standard.

Floppy interface

Because of the relatively slow data transfer rates found in tape systems (typically 500 Kbits/second), most tape drives are ideally suited to use ordinary floppy drive controllers. Floppy drive controllers use a 34-pin interface cable to the drive. Floppy drive controllers are handy because they are very inexpensive, readily available, and compatible with older generations of computers. Refer to chapter 6 for a discussion of the standard floppy drive interface.

Proprietary interface

SCSI and floppy drive interfaces have their share of drawbacks in tape drive systems. The tremendous speed and performance potential of the SCSI technique is often wasted on tape systems—SCSI is simply too fast. No tape drive made can possibly hope to utilize a SCSI bus to its full potential. A floppy drive interface occupies the other end of the performance spectrum at a slow 250 to 500 Kbits/second. While this data rate is just about right for older tape systems, new tape systems are being limited by these floppy drive rates. In order to achieve the highest possible performance for a tape system, tape drive manufacturers are providing *accelerated host controllers* which handle the optimum data transfer rate. Accelerated controllers are often available as options, so the tape drive will operate with a native floppy drive controller (at floppy drive rates), or can operate much faster with an accelerated controller board.

Proprietary interfaces are usually "plug-and-play" systems—the manufacturer provides any cables and connectors necessary to set up and use their system. In some cases, the manufacturer also supplies the backup software that controls the drive. You will have to refer to a schematic or detailed block diagram for your proprietary tape system to learn the name and function of each signal pin. The proprietary controller board translates the interface cable signals into signals needed by the computer's main busses.

Drive operations

Now that you have learned about tape standards, drive construction, and interfaces, you should understand how the tape drive operates in conjunction with the computer and software. This section gives you an overview of general backup operations for QIC/minicartridge and DAT systems.

QIC/minicartridge

The backup process begins when you insert a formatted tape into the drive (note that some proprietary systems can format a blank tape on-the-fly). The tape cartridge itself contains all the mechanisms for driving and maneuvering the tape. The formatted tape typically contains up to 32 parallel *tracks* as illustrated in Fig. 9-13. Every track is divided into smaller parts called *blocks,* each with 512 or 1024 bytes. A set of 32 blocks is known as a *segment.* The first eight blocks in a segment are usually reserved for error correction (EC) data. The directory of backed up information is placed on tape track 0, or on another separate track reserved for directory data.

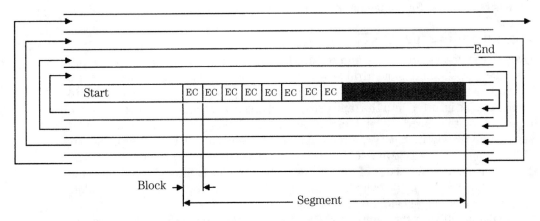

9-13   Illustration of QIC tape layout and recording patterns.

The backup software (such as *PC Tools Deluxe, Norton Backup, Central Point Backup,* or a proprietary backup package) then initiates the drive's backup procedure. Software reads the hard drive's file allocation table (FAT), locates each file to be backed up, and allocates a buffer in RAM (usually about 32K). Data is loaded from each desired file into the RAM buffer, including header information identifying the file and its directory. RAM data is dumped to the tape controller. If error correction is built into the controller, the controller will calculate the necessary error correction codes, otherwise, the software will calculate the error correction codes. Error correction codes are included with RAM data before being sent along to the drive. The RAM buffer is then cleared, and backup software can begin filling the buffer again. The tape controller board starts the tape moving, and transfers the data to the drive. Data is broken down into blocks for storage, and a cyclic redundancy check (CRC) code is added to the end or each block to help with error correction.

As the tape writes data, a redundant read head checks the tape to verify that the data has been recorded correctly. If all data is verified as correct, the tape drive will accept new data from its controller board in the computer. Otherwise, the data will be rewritten on a subsequent piece of tape. As tape reaches the end, sensors in the drive detect a series of holes and the head assembly shifts to another track to continue recording. After all data is transferred, some additional housekeeping information is written to the tape, and the backup is complete. The tape should be removed from the drive, write-protected, and stored in a safe place.

When restoring a hard drive from tape, the tape drive reads the tape's directory to locate the desired file(s), then advances the drive to the start of the first file. Data is read into a small buffer, and the tape drive controller card calculates a CRC code for the loaded data. The controller card compares its calculated CRC code against the CRC code recorded for each block. If the codes match, data is assumed to be valid. Data can then be transferred to a system RAM buffer where backup/restore software distributes the data to the hard drive. If the CRC codes do not match for some reason, an error is flagged, and error correction processing is attempted based on the error correction (EC) codes stored at the start of the segment. Backup software is responsible for managing the overall restoration process.

Digital audio tape (DAT)

Overall, the process of backup and restoration on DAT systems is similar to the process used for QIC and minicartridge systems. The most striking differences occur in the way data is read and written to the tape. Backup begins when a blank, unprotected DAT is inserted into the tape drive. Mechanisms in the drive draw a length of tape out of the cartridge and create an artificial 90° wrap around a circular-segmented read/write head. The recording head itself is a squat cylinder consisting of four magnetic heads: two read heads and two write heads. Both sets of heads are 180° apart on opposing sides of the cylinder. The cylinder is tilted 5° or 6° and spun at about 2000 RPM. As the cylinder spins, each head traces out a diagonal line along the tape that is roughly eight times the tape's width.

Backup software then initializes the drive's backup procedure. Software proceeds to read the hard drive's FAT, locates each file to be backed up, and allocates a large system RAM buffer (usually 512K to 1Mb). Data from each desired file is loaded into the RAM buffer while the tape controller card causes the drive to begin searching for a blank tape area. When the tape is ready, the RAM buffer is dumped to the tape controller card where error correction and housekeeping information is added. Prepared data is then sent along to the drive circuitry.

The write heads place the data in parallel diagonal (helical) tracks along the tape. Read heads are used to read back the corresponding data just laid down by the write head (i.e., read head A checks write head A). If the data matches, operation continues normally. If data does not match, the entire trace is rewritten on the next head rotation. Both write heads are aligned at different angles, so the orientation of each trace on the tape alternates. The use of alternating orientations allows the read heads to easily discern adjoining traces and eliminates the need to add blank spaces between each helical trace. When all desired files have been backed up, the drive rewinds the tape to a directory area, and a directory of backed up files is recorded.

Restoring a hard drive from a DAT is virtually identical to restoring from a QIC tape. Software allocates a system RAM buffer and causes the drive to read its directory. The drive then advances the tape to the desired file location, and uses its read heads only to copy file data to the controller card. Circuitry in the controller card initiates error checking to verify or correct data, then passes the prepared data to the system RAM buffer. Software reads the RAM buffer and copies the data to the hard drive as required.

Tape drive cleaning and troubleshooting

Tape drive systems (especially DAT systems) are among the most complex and expensive mass-storage devices. The motors, sensors, and mechanisms in a typical tape drive are all prone to eventual failure. Even the natural wear that occurs in mechanical systems has an impact on drive performance and data error rates. This section provides some general cleaning guidelines and a series of basic troubleshooting procedures.

Drive cleaning

As with floppy disk drives, tape drives bring magnetic media directly into contact with magnetic read/write heads. Over time and use, magnetic oxides from the tape rub off onto the head surface. Oxides (combined with dust particles and smoke contamination) accumulate and act as a wedge that forces the tape away from the head surface. Even if you never need to disassemble your tape drive, you should make it a point to perform routine cleaning. This improves the working life of your recording media and can significantly reduce the occurrence of data errors.

The objective of cleaning is to remove any buildup of foreign material that has accumulated on the read/write heads. The most common cleaning method uses a prepackaged cleaning cartridge. The cartridge contains a length of slightly abrasive cleaning material. When cleaning tape is run through the drive, any foreign matter on the head is rubbed away. The cleaning tape can often be used for several cleanings before being discarded. Some cleaning tapes are run dry, while others have to be dampened with an alcohol-based cleaning solution. The advantage to a cleaning cartridge is simplicity—the procedure is quick and you never have to disassemble the drive. Because QIC tape moves much more slowly across a head than floppy media does, you need not worry about damaging the read/write head due to friction. DAT heads do move across the tape quickly, however, so you must be cautious about cleaning times. You will have better results over the long term using dry cleaning cartridges that are impregnated with a lubricating agent to reduce friction.

You can also clean R/$\overline{W}$ heads manually, which is convenient during a repair when the drive is already opened. Start by vacuuming away any debris in the drive. Use a small, hand-held vacuum to reach tight spots. Heads can be cleaned with a fresh, lint-free swab dipped lightly in a head-cleaning solution. If no head cleaning solution is available, use fresh ethyl or isopropyl alcohol. Rub the head gently but firmly to remove any debris. You can use several swabs to ensure a thorough cleaning. Allow the head to dry completely before running a tape.

Remember that these are only general guidelines. Refer to the user's manual or reference manual for your particular drive to find the cleaning recommendations, procedures, and cautions listed by the manufacturer. Every drive has slightly different cleaning and preventive maintenance procedures. Some drives also require periodic lubrication.

Drive troubleshooting

Now you will see a selection of basic symptoms and solutions for tape drive mechanisms (Fig. 9-14). Bear in mind that tape drives (especially DAT drives) contain a substantial amount of mechanical and electromechanical components. Given the nature of mechanical parts, many problems will be mechanically oriented. If you are involved with tape drive repair in any volume, you might consider stocking an assortment of replacement parts as shown in Table 9-3. Many of the illustrations used in the following procedures and throughout this chapter are for the D/CAS tape system manufactured by Teac.

Teac America

9-14 A Teac D/CAS tape drive.

Table 9-3. Recommended replacement parts for Teac D/CAS

Part	Recommended period	Repair time (minutes)
Head assembly	50,000 passes	30
Reel motors (forward and reverse)	40,000 passes	25
Encoder assembly and roller	as required	40
Stepping motor	as required	30
Sensors	as required	15
Drive or interface PC boards	as required	15
Tape	approximately 5000 passes	N/A

Symptom 1: The tape drive does not work at all   Begin your repair by checking for obvious setup and configuration errors. First, make sure that power is available to the drive (a power indicator will usually be lit on the drive). An internal tape drive is usually powered from the host computer, so place your voltmeter's ground lead at power pin 2 and measure +12 Vdc at pin 1. Place the voltmeter ground at power pin 3 and measure +5 Vdc at pin 4. External drives are almost always powered from a separate ac adaptor or power supply, but a few proprietary drives can be powered through their interface cables. Check the output of any external ac adaptor or power supply. If the ac adaptor output is low or nonexistent, replace the ac adaptor.

Check that the interface cable between drive and tape controller card is connected properly. Also check that your backup software is running and properly configured to your particular drive. If you are troubleshooting a new, unproven installation, inspect the tape controller board address, interrupt, and DMA settings —configuration conflicts can lock up a software package or render a drive inoperative. Check the tape itself to be sure it is inserted properly and completely.

If power, interface cables, and software setup check properly, your trouble is likely in your drive or host controller. Ideally, your next step would be to isolate further by substitution. Try a known-good tape drive and/or controller card in your system. For most of us, however, tape drives are few and far between, so simply plugging in a compatible system from a friend or colleague is not nearly as likely as it would be with floppy or even hard drives.

If your tape drive is being controlled by an ordinary floppy drive controller board, turn system power off and try disconnecting the tape drive and plugging in a floppy drive. When power is restored, you might have to disable any TSRs that manage the tape drive, and change the CMOS system setup so that the floppy drive will be recognized. If the test floppy drive works properly, you can be confident that the controller board works properly. The problem is then likely to be found in the tape drive, or there is still a problem in your tape system setup. If you cannot get the test floppy drive to work, the floppy controller board might be defective, so try a new controller board. If a new controller board supports the test floppy drive, return the floppy drive to its original port, reinstall the tape drive, restore the system setup for the tape drive, and try the tape drive again.

If your tape drive uses a proprietary, accelerated, or SCSI controller board, use your logic probe to check the data and handshaking lines along the interface cable. Refer to your user's manual or service manual for interface pin numbers and descriptions. If handshake and data signals appear active when a backup is initiated, but no drive activity takes place, the interface circuitry in the drive is probably defective. If handshake signals from the drive are idle or incorrect, the drive is also probably faulty. Try replacing the drive interface PC board, or replace the drive entirely. If one or more handshake lines from the controller board appear idle or incorrect, the drive's controller board is probably defective and should be replaced. If the tape drive uses a SCSI bus and there is more than one SCSI device on the bus, check that the other devices (e.g., the hard drive, CD-ROM, printer, and so on) are working properly. If all SCSI devices appear inoperative, the SCSI controller board is probably defective and should be replaced. If other SCSI devices appear to work normally, the SCSI controller board is probably alright, and the problem is most likely in your SCSI tape drive.

Symptom 2: The tape does not read or write, but the tape and head seem to move properly   You will probably find read/write errors indicated by your backup software. Start your repair by inspecting the tape cartridge itself. The cartridge should be inserted completely and properly into the drive, and sit firmly over the reel as shown in Fig. 9-15. If the current tape is inserted properly, try loading from

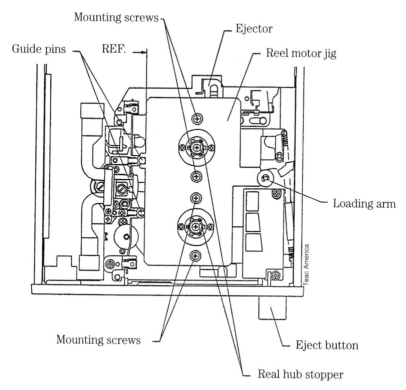

9-15   The reel area of a tape drive.

another tape. Old tapes might have degraded to a point where data can no longer be read or written reliably. If an alternate tape works properly, discard and replace the old tape.

If other tapes are also unreadable, the problem is likely in your tape drive. Open the drive's upper housing (or remove the drive from its drive bay) and measure the head signals with your oscilloscope. If you are attempting to write, check the write and read signals. If you are only reading, check just the read signals. Note that you will need a very sensitive setting on your oscilloscope to view R/$\overline{\text{W}}$ signals. If you find write signals but no verifying read signals, the read/write head assembly is defective. Replace the read/write head assembly as illustrated in Fig. 9-16. If read and write signals are missing, the head or head control circuit is probably defective. Try replacing the drive's control PC board. If a new PC board fails to correct the problem, replace the R/$\overline{\text{W}}$ head or replace the drive outright. If both read and write signals are present, there is trouble elsewhere in the drive's control circuitry. Try replacing the drive's control PC board or the drive's interface PC board.

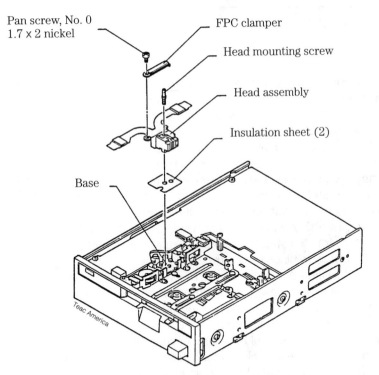

9-16   Replacing the tape drive read/write head.

Symptom 3: The R/$\overline{\text{W}}$ head does not step from track to track   The remainder of the drive appears to work properly. This problem can also result in tape read or write errors. The head assembly must step across very small tracks laid out along the width of the tape. Most tapes are formatted with 12 to 24 tracks. When the tape reaches its end, the head is positioned to another track, tape direction reverses, and

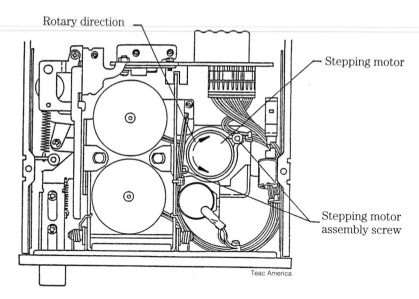

Rotary direction

Stepping motor

Stepping motor
assembly screw

Teac America

9-17   Head stepping motor illustration.

reading or writing continues. There are two physical elements responsible for positioning a R/W head: the head stepping motor and a mechanism called the head seek
assembly. A defect or jam in either one of these components can prevent the head
from moving. You can see the stepping motor in the underside view of Fig. 9-17.

Check the LED/sensor pair that detect the EOT/BOT holes. If the LED transmitter or phototransistor receiver is defective, the drive will not know when to
switch tracks. Remove the tape and place your multimeter across the receiving sensor. As you alternately pass and interrupt the light path from transmitter to receiver,
you should see the logic output from the detector sensor switch from logic 1 to logic
0 (or vice versa). If the sensor does not work, replace the LED and phototransistor,
and try the sensor pair again. If the sensor pair still malfunctions, replace the drive's
control PC board, or replace the entire drive.

Use your oscilloscope to measure the driver signals operating the stepping
motor. When stepping occurs, you should see a series of high-voltage pulses on each
motor line (except for ground). Let the tape approach its end and check for stepping
signals. If no stepping signals are present, there is a problem in the drive's control PC
board. Try replacing the control PC board, or replace the drive outright. If signals are
present, uncouple the head seek assembly from the stepping motor and try again. If
the stepping motor steps with the head assembly uncoupled, replace the head seek
assembly. If the freed motor still refuses to step, replace the defective stepping
motor.

Note: When working with the head movement assembly, be extremely careful to
mark the original position of all mechanical components, and to reinstall new components to those exact locations. Care is necessary to ensure that the R/W head
assembly is returned to its original location. A poorly located head assembly can read
and write to the wrong tracks and cause even greater problems.

Symptom 4: The tape does not move, or its speed does not remain constant

When a tape is set into motion for reading or writing, it is vitally important that tape speed remain constant. Tape speed is a function of the reel motors and the encoder, which produces speed feedback signals. Begin by removing the tape and check for any accumulation of dust and debris that might be interfering with drive operation. Carefully clear away any obstruction that you find.

If the tape does not move at all, check the dc motor signal across the reel motor(s) with your multimeter. When activated, there should be about +12 Vdc across the forward or reverse motor, depending on the tape's initial direction. If no excitation voltage is present, there is probably a fault in the drive's control PC board. Try replacing the drive control PC board, or replace the entire drive. If drive voltage is present but the tape does not turn, replace both reel motors as in Fig. 9-18.

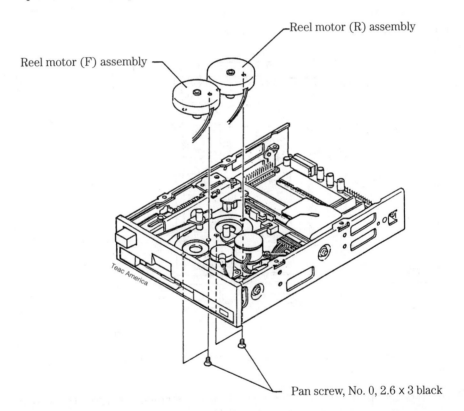

9-18   Replacing the tape reel motors.

If the reel motors turn as expected but their speed is not constant, the problem might be in the encoder. Tape is normally kept in contact with a rubber encoder roller. As tape moves, the encoder roller turns and spins the encoder. Pulse signals from the encoder are used by the drive control PC board to regulate reel motor speed. Check the encoder roller. Tighten the encoder roller if it is loose or worn; a heavily worn encoder roller should be replaced. Make sure one roller turn results in one encoder turn—the roller must not slip on the encoder shaft. Place your logic probe on the encoder output and check for pulses as the tape moves. If there are no pulses, replace the defective encoder. If pulses are present, replace the drive's control PC board, or replace the entire drive.

Symptom 5: There are problems in loading or ejecting the tape   Most of the mechanisms for loading or unloading a tape are incorporated directly into the drive chassis itself, as shown in Fig. 9-11. Physical abuse and the accumulation of dust and debris can eventually cause problems in your tape handling mechanisms. Before you disassemble your drive, however, check your tape very carefully. Old tapes can jam or wear out, and some tapes (such as Teac's digital cassette shown in Figs. 9-19 and 9-20) can only be inserted into the drive in one orientation. Try a fresh tape and make sure that the tape is inserted properly into the drive.

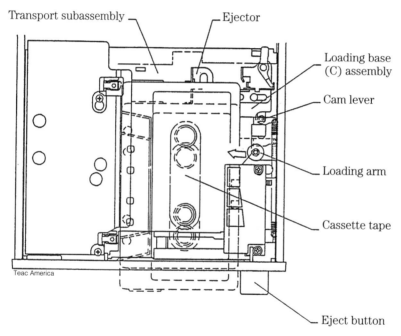

Transport subassembly — ┐   ┌— Ejector

Loading base
(C) assembly

Cam lever

Loading arm

Cassette tape

Teac America

Eject button

9-19   Top view of the Teac tape drive loading mechanism.

If the tape continues to load or unload with resistance, expose the drive's mechanical assemblies and inspect all levers and linkages for any signs of obstruction or damage. Gently clear away any obstructions that you find. You can use a fresh, dry cotton swab to wipe away any accumulations of debris. Do not add any lubricant to the load/unload mechanism unless there was lubricant there to begin with—and then use only the same type of lubricant. Replace any components that show signs of unusual wear.

Use extreme caution when working with tape assemblies. Mechanical systems are very precisely designed, so make careful notes and assembly diagrams during

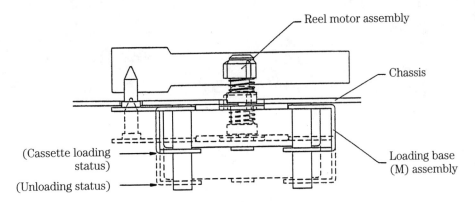

9-20   Side view of the Teac tape drive loading mechanism. Teac America

disassembly. An improperly reassembled mechanical system can damage the tape, or hold the tape in an improper position, resulting in read/write or motor speed errors.

Symptom 6: The drive writes to write-protected tapes   When a tape is write-protected, the drive should not be able to write to that protected tape. Your first step should be to remove and inspect the tape itself. Check to make sure that the write-protect lever is in the "protect" position. If the protect lever is not in the right place, the tape can be written. If the tape protect lever is set properly, expose the drive mechanism and place your voltmeter across the sensor's output. Alternately interrupt and free the optoisolator beam by hand and watch the sensor's output on your multimeter. If the output switches logic levels as you actuate the sensor manually, the trouble is probably in the drive's control PC board. Replace the drive control PC board, or replace the entire drive. If the output does not shift logic levels as expected, the sensor might be defective. Replace the write-protect sensor and repeat your test. If the sensor remains inoperative, replace the drive control PC board, or replace the entire drive.

Symptom 7: The drive does not recognize the beginning or end of the tape A tape drive must know when the end or beginning of a tape has been reached. The majority of tapes use a series of small holes at each end of the tape. An optoisolator provides a pulse signal to the drive control PC board when holes pass by. Begin by removing the tape and checking for the presence of end holes. The wrong type of tape (i.e., a tape without holes) can cause problems for the drive. If the wrong type of tape is being used, retry the system using the correct type of tape.

Focus next on the BOT/EOT sensor, which is an optoisolator located across the tape path (an LED on one side and a detector on the other). Remove the tape, expose the system, and place your multimeter across the detector's output. Alternately interrupt and free the light path by hand and watch the detector's output on your multimeter. If the output switches logic levels as expected, the trouble is probably in the drive's control PC board. Replace the drive control PC board, or replace the entire drive. If the output does not shift as expected, replace the LED source and detector elements together and retest the sensor pair. If the sensor remains inoperative, replace the drive control PC board or replace the entire drive.

10
Optical drives

The push for ever-greater and more reliable information storage has been a relent-less one. Every few years, technological breakthroughs and enhancements yield stunning improvements in the way computer users store and access information. Classic magnetic storage (floppy, hard, and tape drives) is now being challenged by a family of storage systems using light instead of (or in addition to) magnetic fields to read and write information to storage media. These optical drives, such as the one shown in Fig. 10-1, offer three major advantages that are yet unmatched by magnetic technology.

First, optical storage is capable of huge data densities. Because light beams can be focused to a much smaller spot than magnetic fields, optical drives can achieve at

10-1 A Tandy CD-ROM drive.

least 10 times the data density of current magnetic drives. Continuous advances in optical technology and media materials promise to push data density 100 times beyond what it is today. Optical storage media is also one of the most long-lasting media, with expected lifetimes that are measured in terms of centuries instead of years. Because the media are primarily plastic, they are inexpensive to produce. Finally, optical media are removable. These rugged, high-density disks can be removed and handled in the open air; most media surfaces can even tolerate a bit of scratching. While today's optical storage systems cannot replace hard drives, they are a common and beneficial accessory. For our purposes here, you will learn about two optical technologies now in general use: CD-ROM and floptical.

CD-ROM systems

With the introduction of the audio compact disk (CD), designers demonstrated that huge amounts of digital information can be stored simply and very inexpensively on a common, nonmagnetic medium—the silvery plastic disks that you have become familiar with. Audio CDs carry data as mechanical pits on the disk surface. The pits are pressed into the CD media using high-volume pressing equipment much like that used to make plastic LPs. The pressed CDs are then coated with protective plastic. Data is read by spinning the disk and reading the changes in reflectivity between pit and nonpit areas. To measure reflection, a light source is required. A semiconductor laser diode is used to provide the tightly focused light energy that is required. Refer to chapter 2 for more about laser diodes.

CD-ROM media work exactly the same way. In fact, many CD-ROM players also play audio CDs if the host computer is running the appropriate software to interpret the audio information. However, an audio CD player cannot read CD-ROMs—data from CD-ROMs would simply be presented as audible noise. Today, CD-ROM players are common and affordable peripherals for your computer. CD-ROM disks are only a little more expensive than many disk-based software packages.

Mastering

CD-ROMs start life as a huge collection of data stored in a large, 1Gb or 2Gb hard drive. When enough information is available to make a CD-ROM product, the data must be transferred from the original, computer-based storage to a prototype CD-ROM called a *master*. A master CD is a glass disk with a light-sensitive photoresist coating. The master is placed into a *CD burner* that reads information from the master source files (in the computer), formats the data for the proper CD-ROM standard, then uses the converted information to fire a high-power laser, which cuts spots on the master's photoresist coating.

Mastering lays out pits in a spiral track along the master CD identically to the final CD product. Once the master is exposed by the laser, the master disk is *developed*—areas of photoresist exposed by the laser are washed away, leaving the desired pits. Theoretically, this developed master should be usable. Once the master is produced, duplicates must be manufactured. A negative of the master (pits raised) is produced using an electroplating or photopolymer processes. It is these negatives that are used to "stamp" the actual production duplicates of the CD-ROM. Duplication is usually done by injection-molding hot polycarbonate plastic into a chamber containing the stamper. Polycarbonate material is light and tough, so CDs usually stand a good chance of survival in the real world.

The medium

Once the polycarbonate disks are being produced, there are finish steps that must be performed to transform a clear plastic into a viable, data-carrying medium. The clear polycarbonate disk is given a silvered (reflective) coating so that it reflects laser light. Silvering coats all parts of the disk side (pits and lands) equally. After silvering, the disk is coated with a tough, scratch-resistant lacquer that seals the disk from the elements. Finally, a label can be silk-screened onto the finished disk before it is tested and packaged. Figure 10-2 illustrates each of these layers in a cross-sectional diagram. The finished disk itself is about 4.72" (12.0 cm) in diameter with a 1.5 cm spindle hole in the center. CDs are roughly 1.2 mm thick.

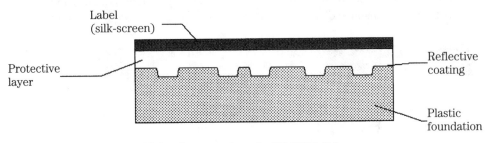

10-2   Cross-section of a CD-ROM disk.

CDs are not segregated into concentric tracks and sectors as magnetic media are. Instead, CDs are recorded as a single, continuous spiral track running from the spindle to the lead out area. Figure 10-3 shows the spiral pattern recorded on a CD. The inset illustrates the relationship between the pits and lands. Each pit is about

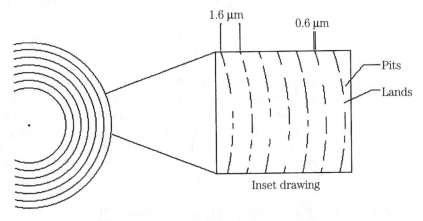

10-3   Close-up view of CD-ROM disk tracks.

0.12 μm (micrometers) deep and 0.6 μm wide. Pits and lands can range from 0.9 μm to 3.3 μm in length. There are approximately 1.6 μm between each iteration of the spiral. Given these microscopic dimensions, a CD-ROM offers about 16,000 tracks per inch (tpi)—much more than floppy disks or hard disks.

Recording the medium

Optical disks such as CDs use a highly focused laser beam and laser detector to sense the presence or absence of pits. Figure 10-4 illustrates the reading behavior. The laser/detector pair is mounted on a carriage that follows the spiral track across the CD. A laser is directed at the underside of the CD, where it penetrates more than 1 mm of clear plastic before shining on the reflective surface. When laser light strikes a land, the light is reflected toward the detector which, in turn, produces a very strong output signal. As laser light strikes a pit, the light is slightly out of focus. As a result, most of the incoming laser energy is scattered away in all directions, so very little output signal is generated by the detector. As with floppy and hard drives, it is the transition from pit to land (and back again) that corresponds to binary levels, not the presence or absence of a pit or land.

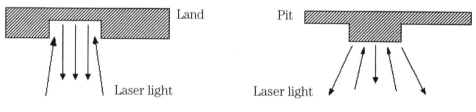

10-4   Reading pits and lands.

EFM and CD storage

A complex decoding process is necessary to convert the arcane sequence of pits and lands into meaningful binary information. The technique of *eight-to-fourteen modulation* (EFM) is used with CD-ROMs. You will recall from chapter 7 that 2,7 RLL encoding can be used to place a large number of bits into a limited number of flux transitions. The same is true for CDs using EFM. User data, error correction information, address information, and synchronization patterns are all contained in a bit stream represented by pits and lands.

Magnetic media encodes bits as flux transitions—not the discrete orientation of any magnetic area. The same concept holds true with CD-ROMs: binary 1s and 0s do not correspond to pits or lands. A binary 1 is represented wherever a transition (pit-to-land or land-to-pit) occurs. The length of a pit or land represents the number of binary 0s. Figure 10-5 illustrates this concept. EFM encoding equates each byte (8 bits) with a 14-bit sequence (called a *symbol*) where each binary 1 must be separated by at least two binary 0s. Table 10-1 shows part of the EFM conversion. Three bits are added to merge each 14-bit symbol together.

A CD-ROM *frame* is composed of 24 synchronization bits, 14 control bits, 24 of the 14-bit data symbols you saw previously, and eight complete 14-bit error correc-

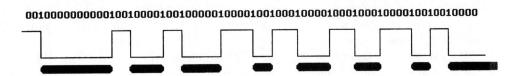

10-5   CD-ROM data encoding.

**Table 10-1. A sample of
eight-to-fourteen modulation codes**

Number	Data bit pattern	EFM equivalent
0	00000000	01001000100000
1	00000001	10000100000000
2	00000010	10010000100000
3	00000011	10001000100000
4	00000100	01000100000000
5	00000101	00000100010000
6	00000110	00010000100000
7	00000111	00100100000000
8	00001000	01001001000000
9	00001001	10000001000000
10	00001010	10010001000000

tion (EC) symbols. Each symbol is separated by an additional 3 merge bits, bringing the total number of bits in the frame to 588. Thus, 24 bytes of data is represented by 588 bits on a CD-ROM expressed as a number of pits and lands. There are 98 frames in a data *block*, so each block carries 98 x 24 or 2048 bytes (2352 with error correction, synchronization, and address bytes). The average CD-ROM can deliver 153.6K of data (75 blocks) per second to its host controller.

Remember that the CD-ROM is recorded as one continuous spiral track running around the disk, so ordinary sector and track ID information does not apply well. Instead, information is divided in terms of 0 to 59 *minutes*, and 0 to 59 *seconds* recorded at the beginning of each block. A CD-ROM (like an audio CD) can hold up to 79 *minutes* of data. However, many CD-ROMs tend to limit this to 60 minutes since the last 14 minutes of data are encoded in the outer 5 mm of disk space, which is the most difficult to manufacture and keep clean in everyday use. There are 270,000 blocks of data in 60 minutes. At 2048 data bytes per block, the disk's capacity is 552,950,000 bytes (553Mb). If all 79 minutes are used, 681,984,000 bytes (681Mb) are available in 333,000 blocks. Most CD-ROMs run between 553Mb and 630Mb in normal production.

Standards and software

There is one primary standard for CD-ROM: the ISO 9660 format, which is an update of the High Sierra data format standard of 1985. There are thousands of titles today that support the ISO 9660 format. Keep in mind that a drive designed to operate with the slightly older High Sierra format might not read an ISO 9660 disk, but a drive designed with the ISO 9660 standard should read disks written in the High Sierra format with no trouble.

Because DOS does not directly support CD-ROMs yet, you need a device driver capable of operating the specific drive (every drive uses a slightly different driver), along with a DOS CD-ROM extension driver such as Microsoft's MSCDEX (version 2.2 or later). If you work on a variety of different drives, you need to know which drivers are needed with which drive. Once your software and drive are properly installed, the computer treats the CD-ROM just as it would any DOS drive—complete with its own DOS drive letter. You can then access the CD-ROM's directory or execute any executable file(s) found on the installed disk. The only limitation is that you cannot save information to the CD-ROM.

CD-ROM drive construction

Like the magnetic drives you have seen so far in this book, CD drives are impressive pieces of engineering. The drive must be able to accept standard-size disks from a variety of sources, and each disk can contain an assortment of unknown surface imperfections. The drive must then spin the disk at a *constant linear velocity* (CLV) —that is, the disk speed varies inversely with the tracking radius. As tracking approaches the disk edge, disk speed slows, and vice versa. Keep in mind that CLV is different than the *constant angular velocity* (CAV) method used by floppy and hard drives, which moves the medium at a constant speed. The purpose of CLV is to ensure that CD-ROM data is read at a constant rate. A CD drive must be able to follow the spiral data path on a spinning CD-ROM accurate to within less than 1 μm along the disk's radius. The drive electronics must be able to detect and correct any unforeseen data errors in real time, operate reliably over a long working life, and be available for a low price that computer users have come to expect.

You can begin to appreciate how a CD drive achieves its features by reviewing the exploded diagram of Fig. 10-6. At the center of the drive is a cast aluminum or rigid stainless steel *frame assembly*. As with other drives, the frame is the single primary structure for mounting the drive's mechanical and electronic components. The *front bezel, lid,* drive-in-use LED *lens,* and *eject button* attach to the frame, providing the drive with its clean cosmetic appearance, and offering a fixed reference slot for CD insertion and removal. Keep in mind that many drives use a sliding tray, so the front bezel (and the way it is attached) is not the same for *every* drive.

The drive's electronics package is split into several PC board assemblies. The *main PCB* handles drive control and interfacing, and the *headphone PCB* provides an audio amplifier and jack for headphones. The bulk of the drive's actual physical work, however, is performed by a main CD subassembly, called a *caddy* or *engine*, which are often manufactured by only a few companies. As a result, many of the diverse CD-ROM drives on the market actually use identical engines to hold, spin, read, and eject the disk. This interchangeability is part of the genius of CD-ROM drives—a single subassembly performs 80% of the work. Sony, Phillips, and Toshiba are the primary manufacturers of CD-ROM engines, but other companies such as IBM and Ikka are also producing caddys.

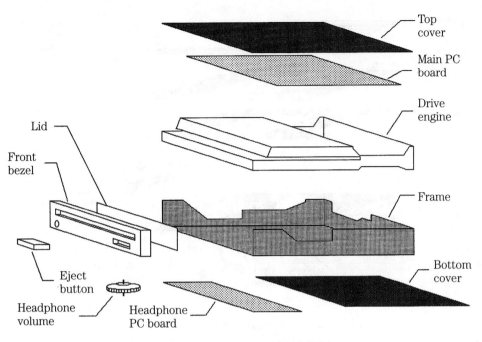

10-6 Exploded diagram of a CD-ROM drive.

The upper and lower sides of a typical drive engine are shown in Figs. 10-7 and 10-8 respectively. The upper view of the engine features a series of mechanisms that accept, clamp, and eject the disk. The foundation of this engine is the *BC-7C assembly*. It acts as a subframe to which everything else is mounted. Note that the subframe is shock-mounted with four rubber feet to cushion the engine from minor bumps and ordinary handling. Even with such mounting, a CD-ROM drive is a delicate and fragile mechanism. The *slider assembly*, the *loading chassis assembly*, and the *cover shield* provide the mechanical action needed to accept the disk and clamp it into place over the drive spindle, as well as free the disk and eject it on demand. A number of levers and *oil dampers* (not shown) serve to provide a slow, smooth mechanical action when motion takes place. A *motorized load/unload assembly* drives the load/unload mechanics.

The serious work of spinning and reading a disk is handled under the engine. A *spindle motor* is mounted on the subframe and connected to a *spindle motor PC board*. A *thrust retainer* helps keep the spindle motor turning smoothly. The most critical part of the CD engine is the *optical device* containing the 780 nm (nanometer) 0.6 mW gallium aluminum arsenide (GaAlAs) laser diode and detector, along with the optical focus and tracking components. The optical device slides along two guide rails and shines through an exposed hole in the subframe. This combination of device mounting and guide rails is called a *sled*.

The sled must be made to follow the spiral data track along the disk. While floppy disks (using clearly defined concentric tracks) can easily make use of a stepping motor to position the head assembly, a CD drive ideally requires a *linear motor*,

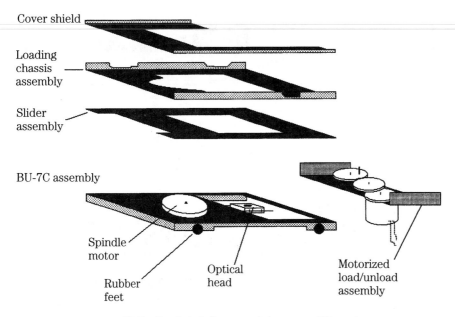

Cover shield

Loading
chassis
assembly

Slider
assembly

BU-7C assembly

Spindle
motor

Rubber
feet

Optical
head

Motorized
load/unload
assembly

10-7 Exploded diagram of the upper CD engine.

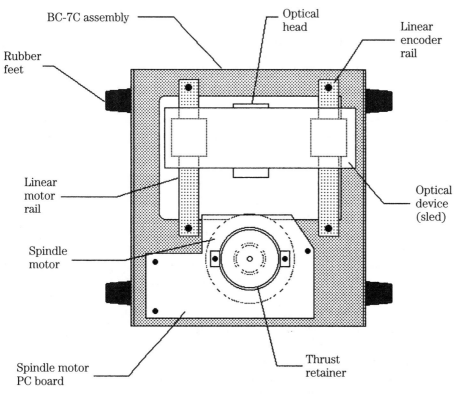

BC-7C assembly

Optical
head

Linear
encoder
rail

Rubber
feet

Linear
motor
rail

Optical
device
(sled)

Spindle
motor

Spindle motor
PC board

Thrust
retainer

10-8 Underside view of the BC-7C assembly.

which acts much like the voice coil motor used to position hard drive read/write heads. By altering the signal driving a sled motor and constantly measuring and adjusting the sled's position, a sled can be made to track very smoothly along a disk —free from the sudden, jerky motion of stepping motors. Some CD drives still use stepping motors with an extremely fine-pitch lead screw to position the sled. Figure 10-8 illustrates the sled motor and linear encoder mounted on opposite sides of the subframe's aperture. The drive's main PC board is responsible for managing these operations.

CD-ROM optics

The CD-ROM is read by reflecting a laser beam off the disk's data carrying surface and measuring the amount of returned light. In actual practice, however, this is a much more intricate and involved process than you might imagine. The optical device illustrated in Fig. 10-9 helps you appreciate how delicate and fragile such a device is. A laser diode is shown at the device's base. The typical laser diode is fabricated using gallium (called a gallium aluminum arsenide diode) and emits about 0.6 mW (600 μW) of laser power at a wavelength of 780 nm.

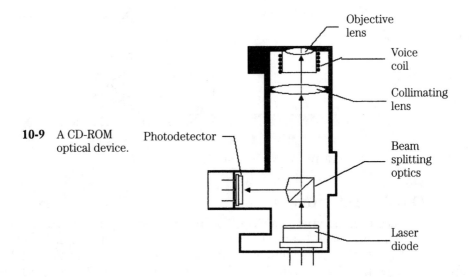

10-9 A CD-ROM optical device.

As you can see, the laser beam diverges (or spreads out) as energy leaves the diode. This is unacceptable for measuring the microscopic track data on a CD. Laser light must be directed and tightly focused to achieve acceptable reading characteristics. After the laser light passes through beam splitting optics, a *collimating lens* directs the light to an *objective lens* that focuses laser light to a precise point. The focal point is intended to be in the land area, not in the pit area. A small voice coil— very similar in principle to the electromagnetic earpiece generating sound in your telephone's handset—makes minute, almost indiscernible changes in objective lens position to maintain a precise focus. Drive electronics controls the voice coil focusing mechanism.

When focused light bounces off a land area, the focused light returns through the objective and collimating lenses where it is reflected 90 degrees into the photo-detector by the beam splitting optics. The photodetector produces a strong signal when stimulated by laser light. When focused light bounces off a pit area, the light is scattered, so very little light returns to be picked up by the photodetector. Only a small signal (or none at all) is produced under that condition. The optical device chamber (Fig. 10-10) is always kept sealed to prevent dust and debris from obstructing or interfering with light.

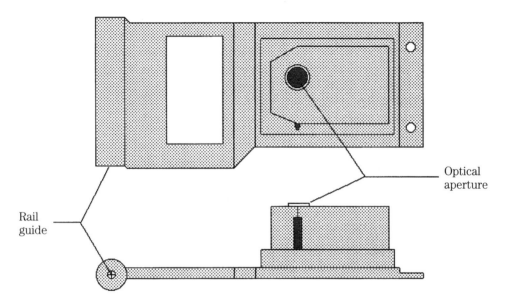

10-10   View of a CD-ROM optical device.

CD-ROM drive electronics

The electronics package used in a CD-ROM drive is illustrated in Fig. 10-11. The drive electronics are somewhat more complex than that of a floppy drive. The electronics package can be divided into two major areas: the controller section and the drive section. Much of the reason for a CD-ROM's electronic sophistication can be traced to the controller section. Much of the controller circuitry is dedicated to handling a SCSI interface. This allows the drive's intelligence to be located right in the CD drive itself. You need only connect the drive to a system-level interface board and set the drive's device number to establish a working system. Standard system-level drives relieve a lot of overhead operations from the host computer system.

The drive portion of the CD drive's electronics is dedicated to managing the drive's physical operation, as well as data decoding (EFM) and error correction. Drive circuitry converts an analog output from the laser diode into an EFM signal that is, in turn, decoded into binary data and Cross-Interleaved Reed-Solomon Code (CIRC) information. A drive controller IC and servo processor IC are responsible for

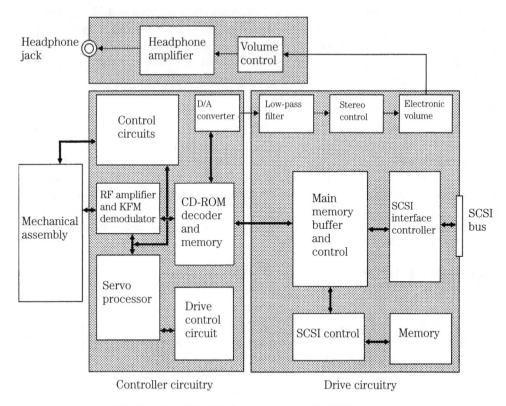

10-11 Simplified block diagram of a CD-ROM circuit.

directing laser focus, tracking, sled motor control (and feedback), spindle motor control (and feedback), and loading/unloading motor control.

With respect to CD drive electronics, you should treat the diagram of Fig. 10-11 more as a guideline than as an absolute. There are quite a few different iterations of drive electronics and interfaces; while most manufacturers use SCSI interfaces, some systems use proprietary interfaces, others use the IDE system-level interface, and a few manufacturers implement subtle, nonstandard variations on the SCSI system. Obtain manufacturer's service data wherever possible for specific information on your particular drive.

CD-ROM interfaces

Regardless of a CD drive's sophistication, it is merely another computer peripheral, and it is rather useless by itself. The drive must connect to a host computer in order to serve a useful function. Because the CD drive is operated by the host system, there must be some means of carrying data and control signals into and out of the drive. Signal exchange is accomplished over the physical interface. There are a number of possible signal interface schemes, but manufacturers prefer to utilize a

number of standard interfaces. A standard interface allows a drive built by any manufacturer to run properly on the same computer. There are, however, a small number of manufacturers that choose to implement a custom interface scheme. A host
controller board interfaces the CD drive's signals to the computer's main busses.
Interfaces usually fall into two categories: SCSI and proprietary.

SCSI

The Small Computer Systems Interface (SCSI) is a system-level device interface that
can service a wide range of peripheral devices (e.g., printers, CD-ROMs, hard drives,
tape drives, and so on). A SCSI host controller board would be required in your computer to interface a 50-pin SCSI signal cable to your system's main busses. A single
host controller board can support up to 8 SCSI devices simultaneously. The advantages of SCSI is flexibility and performance. Data can be transferred very quickly,
and multiple devices can share the same bus system. Refer to chapter 7 for an in-
depth discussion of the SCSI standard.

Proprietary interface

The SCSI drive interface is not well suited to CD drive systems. The tremendous
speed and performance potential of the SCSI technique is often wasted on CD-ROM
systems—SCSI is simply too fast. No CD-ROM drive made can possibly hope to utilize a SCSI bus to its full potential. In order to achieve reasonable performance for a
CD-ROM system, manufacturers can provide host controllers that handle the optimum data transfer rate (usually about 150 K/second). Proprietary controllers are
often available as options, so the drive can operate with a native SCSI drive controller, or can operate with a proprietary controller board.

Proprietary interfaces are usually "plug-and-play systems"—the manufacturer
provides any cables and connectors necessary to set up and use their system. In
most cases, the manufacturer also supplies the driver software that controls the
drive. You have to refer to a schematic or detailed block diagram for your proprietary
CD drive system to learn the name and function of each signal pin. The proprietary
controller board translates the interface cable signals into signals needed by the
computer's main busses.

Troubleshooting CD-ROM drives

Note: When attempting a CD-ROM repair, exercise extreme caution. Optical tracking systems are very delicate and are aligned at the factory for precise operation.
Any replacement or adjustment of optical components (even when replacing other
components such as the linear actuator) can throw the drive so far out of alignment
that it is unusable. Do not attempt to repair a CD-ROM drive that you need unless
you have a lot of confidence and experience. CD-ROMs can be very unforgiving. As
always, never attempt a repair that might void your warranty. If you do attempt a
repair, replace at the subassembly level, and disassemble the drive as little as possible—keep things together whenever you can.

Symptom 1: The drive has trouble accepting or rejecting a CD   This problem is typical of motorized CD-ROM drives, where the disk is accepted into a slot, or placed in a motorized tray. Before performing any disassembly, check the assembly through the CD slot for any obvious obstructions. If there is nothing obvious, expose the assembly and check each linkage and motor drive gear very carefully. Carefully remove or free any obstruction. Be gentle when working around the load/unload assembly. Note how it is shock mounted in four places.

Disconnect the geared dc motor assembly and try moving the load/unload mechanism by hand. If you feel any resistance or obstruction, you should track it down by eye and by feel. Replace any worn or damaged part of the mechanism, or replace the entire load/unload assembly. Also check the geared motor for any damage or obstruction. Broken or slipping gear teeth can interfere with the transfer of force from motor to mechanism. Replace any damaged gears or replace the entire geared assembly.

If the load/unload mechanism fails to work at all, the drive motor might not be functioning. If the motor does not function, measure the voltage across the dc motor. When a load or unload event occurs, you should read a positive or negative voltage across the motor. If voltage appears but the motor does not move, replace the defective motor. If no voltage appears, there is a problem in the motor's driver circuitry. Track down the defective component, or replace the drive PC board.

Symptom 2: Read heads do not seek   An optical head is used to identify pits and lands along a CD-ROM, and to track the spiral data pattern as the head moves across the disk. The optical head must move very slowly and smoothly to ensure accurate tracking. Head movement is accomplished using a linear stepping motor (or *linear actuator)* to shift the optical assembly in microscopic increments—head travel appears perfectly smooth to the unaided eye. Power down the computer, expose the CD-ROM, and begin your examination by observing the head carriage assembly. Check for any objects or foreign matter that could interfere with normal carriage movement.

If the head carriage is free to move, measure the driving voltage across the linear actuator. If there is no voltage applied to the linear actuator at run-time, the motor's driver circuitry is probably defective (usually a driver or servo controller IC). Track down the defective component (if possible) or replace the drive's main PC board. If there is voltage across the motor at runtime but the motor does not move, the linear motor is probably defective. Linear actuator replacement requires drive disassembly to the chassis level, so such a procedure should only be attempted by a highly skilled and experienced individual. Careless replacement can result in a totally useless drive. It might be simpler to replace the entire drive.

Symptom 3: Disk cannot be read   This type of problem can result in a DOS level Sector not found or Drive not ready error. Before you reach for your tools, however, check the CD itself to ensure that it is the right format, inserted properly, and physically clean. Cleanliness is very important to a CD. While the laser often overlooks any surface defects in a disk , the presence of dust or debris on a disk surface can produce serious tracking (and read) errors. Try a different disk to confirm the problem. If a new or different disk reads properly, the trouble might indeed be in (or on) the disk itself. Not only must the disk be clean, but the head optics must also be clear. Gently dust or clean the head optics as suggested by your drive's particular manufacturer.

If read problems persist, check the physical interface cable. Most CD drives use SCSI interfaces, although a few still employ proprietary interfaces. If you are using multiple SCSI devices from the same controller card and other SCSI devices are operating properly, the SCSI controller board is probably alright. If other SCSI devices are also malfunctioning, try a new SCSI host controller board.

At this point, you must determine whether the defect is in the drive's optics or electronics. Use your oscilloscope to measure the analog output from the optical head. If you see a clear analog signal from the head while a disk is turning, the defect is probably in the drive's main PC board. Track down and replace the defective component (if possible) or replace the entire drive PC board outright. If no signal is being generated by the optical read head, replace the optical read head. Head replacement requires device disassembly to the chassis level, so such a procedure should only be attempted by a highly skilled and experienced individual. Careless replacement can easily result in a totally useless drive. It is simpler to replace the drive entirely.

Symptom 4: The disk does not turn   Before beginning a repair, review your drive installation and setup carefully to ensure that the drive is properly configured for operation. If the drive's Busy LED comes on when drive access is attempted (you might also see a corresponding DOS error message), the drive spindle system is probably defective. If the computer does not recognize the CD drive (e.g., Invalid drive specification), there might be a setup or configuration problem.

If your particular drive provides you with instructions for cleaning the optical head aperture, perform that cleaning operation and try the drive again. A fouled optical head can sometimes upset spindle operation.

Use your multimeter to measure voltage across the spindle motor. When turning must occur, a voltage should be present across the motor. If voltage is present but the motor does not turn, the spindle motor is probably defective and should be replaced. If no motor voltage is developed, the spindle motor driver or controller IC(s) might be defective. You can track down and replace the defective component (if possible), but you might have better results simply replacing the drive PC board.

Symptom 5: The optical head cannot focus its laser beam   As you saw earlier in this chapter, a CD drive must focus its laser beam to microscopic precision in order to properly read the pits and lands of a disk. To compensate for minute fluctuations in disk flatness, the optical head mounts its objective lens into a small focusing mechanism that is little more than a miniature voice coil actuator—the lens does not have to move very much to maintain precise focus. If focus is out or not well maintained, the laser detector can produce erroneous signals. This can result in DOS drive error messages.

Due to the incredibly small dimensions at work in a CD drive optical system, it is very difficult to establish whether a laser beam is focused or not. Try a different disk (maybe a newer disk) and see if the problem continues. If a new or different disk performs better (or worse) than your original disk, the focus is probably defective. If there is no difference in performance between various disks, focus is probably alright, and the problem lies elsewhere. Use your oscilloscope to measure the focus signal being sent to the voice coil. If a signal is present, replace the optical head assembly. Again, head replacement requires drive disassembly to the chassis level, so such a procedure should only be attempted by a skilled or experienced individual.

If there is no focus signal available to the optical head, the problem is usually in the drive PC board. Either the focus signal driver or focus controller is faulty. You can track down and replace the defective component, if possible, or you can simply replace the drive PC board outright.

Symptom 6: There is no audio being generated by the drive   Many CD-ROM drives are capable of not only reading computer data, but reading and reproducing music and sounds under computer control. Audio CDs can often be played in CD-ROM drives through headphones or speakers. Start your investigation by testing the headphones or speakers in another sound source such as a stereo. Once you have confirmed that the speakers or headphones are working reliably, check the drive's audio volume setting, which is usually available through the front bezel. Set the volume to mid-range. Check any software required to operate the CD drive's audio output to be sure that it is installed and loaded as expected. CD-ROMs cannot play audio CDs without an audio driver. Also check the line output, which drives amplified speakers or stereo inputs. If speakers work through the line output but headphones or speakers do not work through the front bezel connector, the volume control or output audio amplifier might be defective.

Use your oscilloscope to measure the audio signal into the volume control. If a signal is present into the control but is not available out of the control, the control is defective and should be replaced. If audio is present into the audio amplifier, but no signal leaves the audio amplifier, replace the defective audio amplifier. If no signal at all is present into the audio amplifier, there is a defect on the drive PC board or headphone amplifier PC board. You can track down the defective component, or you can replace the drive PC board or headphone PC board outright. You can also simply replace the drive.

Floptical drives

Where CD-ROM drives are in competition with hard disk drives for storage capacity, the *floptical* drive (Fig. 10-12) is intended to compete with the ordinary floppy disk drive. By merging both magnetic recording media and optical tracking techniques (thus the term *floptical*), more than 20Mb of data can be stored on a specially designed 3.5" (8.89 cm) diskette. Because the recording media is still magnetic, floptical drives are backwardly compatible with both high- and double-density 3.5" disks as discussed in chapter 6. Drives, diskettes, and controller boards are available from several sources, but Iomega Corporation is one of the premier providers of floptical products. This section presents the major technologies and operations of a floptical drive.

10-12 An internal Iomega
floptical drive.

Iomega Corp.

Floptical technology

As you saw in the earlier chapters on magnetic drives, the amount of data that can
be stored on a disk is dependent on two key factors: the distance between the head
and media, and the ability to position the heads precisely. Because floppy drive
read/write heads actually come into contact with the disk media, a floppy drive
should (theoretically) be able to store more data per unit area than a hard drive. The
problem with floppy drives is that once a read/write head carriage leaves track 00,
there is no feedback to determine where the heads actually are—the drive just steps
the heads and hopes that they wind up in the proper place. Such "dumb" positioning
has limited floppy drives for years. If head positioning were continuously checked
and adjusted, much higher data densities could be achieved than the 135 tpi currently available on ordinary 3.5" cm floppy disks.

Floptical technology makes a number of improvements to the disk and the drive
(Fig. 10-13). The most pronounced changes are in the floptical disk medium. In principle, the medium is still a plastic disk coated with a fine, high-quality magnetic layer
(usually barium ferrite for floptical disks), but the floptical disk is segregated into far
more tracks than its conventional cousins, achieving 1245 tpi. The tracks are separated by a series of concentric grooves that are physically stamped (or laser etched)
onto the media. Each track is about 20 microns apart. These physical tracks are used
to aid head positioning. The elevated areas between each groove are called lands,
just like the elevated areas between pits on a CD. Lands provide a more reflective
surface than the grooves.

Tracking

Precision tracking is accomplished through the use of an Iomega electro-optical
(EO) head assembly as shown in Fig. 10-14. As with the optical devices of CD-ROM

10-13　An external Iomega floptical drive.

drives, floptical tracking and positioning are exceptionally delicate, and they are unforgiving if misaligned. This particular type of tracking assembly is referred to as *holographic,* because the laser beam directs a computer-generated pattern, or *hologram,* onto the floptical disk surface. Such a projection renders a pattern that covers several contiguous tracks simultaneously, so holographic tracking is typically more stable and responsive than simple optical-servo tracking that deals with only one track. The tracking patterns are compared in Fig. 10-15.

The solid-state laser is used to project a grating pattern (hologram) through a series of focusing lenses, through a beam splitting prism (called the *mirror*), and

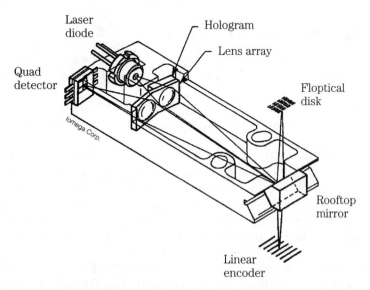

10-14　A floptical optical tracking assembly.

Optical tracking   Holographic tracking

10-15 Optical versus holographic tracking.

out of the device in two simultaneous directions. The holographic pattern is projected onto the disk, as well as a separate linear encoder. The linear encoder serves as a backup positioning mechanism. Ordinary 3.5" DD and HD floppy disks do not have tracking grooves, so the linear encoder provides *artificial* tracking information when ordinary disks are used. This is what allows ordinary floppy disks to operate reliably in floptical drives. Reflections from either the floptical disk media or the linear encoder (as appropriate) are sent back through the rooftop mirror to a multi-element photodetector (called the *quad detector*). The detector's output is used by the drive's electronics package to continually adjust head position.

Reading and writing

Head tracking and positioning is handled by an optical detection system, but floptical drives use magnetic read/write heads that operate using precisely the same principles as discussed in chapter 6. However, floptical head assemblies employ a second, ultrafine head gap to accommodate the tight track dimensions of a floptical diskette. When the drive detects a standard DD or HD floppy diskette, the standard head gaps are used. If the drive detects a floptical disk (called *Very High Density* or VHD), the ultrafine head gaps are used. Standard diskettes are encoded using MFM, while VHD diskettes are encoded using the 1,7 RLL technique.

Floptical construction

Now that you have been introduced to floptical drive concepts, you can begin to study their construction. An exploded view of an Iomega floptical drive is shown in Fig. 10-16. Its assembly is very similar to that of ordinary 3.5" floppy drives described in chapter 6. The most striking additions to a floptical drive are the optical tracking assembly and the linear read/write head assembly. Let's look at the drive piece by piece.

As with other drive systems, the *chassis* (or *frame*) is the foundation for the entire drive. Made of cast aluminum or steel, the chassis provides the rigidity and strength to support the other drive components. A molded plastic *bezel* mounts to the chassis and provides the drive's cosmetic appearance, as well as a consistent guide for inserting or removing disks. An eject button and translucent disk-in-use LED cover complete the bezel. A side rail bolts to each side of the chassis, allowing the drive to slide in and out of any half-height drive bay.

The disks are inserted, clamped, and ejected through a subassembly known as a *load/unload mechanism*, which is virtually identical to the mechanisms used in

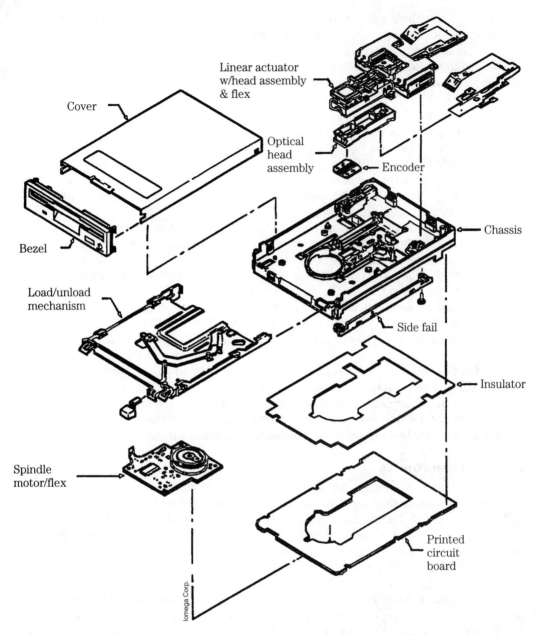

Linear actuator
w/head assembly
& flex

Cover

Optical
head
assembly

Encoder

Bezel

Chassis

Load/unload
mechanism

Side fail

Insulator

Spindle
motor/flex

Printed
circuit
board

Iomega Corp.

10-16　Exploded diagram of an Iomega floptical drive.

other 3.5" floppy drives. You should keep the load/unload mechanism together as a subassembly whenever possible—attempt disassembly only if you are experiencing problems with disk insertion or removal, as you will see in the section on floptical troubleshooting. The large hole in the chassis center accommodates the *spindle motor* and its associated driver circuit. Note that the spindle motor mounts into the chassis after the drive's main PC board is installed. The drive is controlled through the circuitry contained on a single main *printed circuit board*. You will see more about floptical drive electronics in the next part of this chapter. A nonconductive insulator is added between the main PC board and chassis to prevent any possibility of a short circuit occurring against the base chassis.

There are three main assemblies located above the chassis, other than the load/unload mechanism. The *encoder* is little more than a piece of glass engraved with an array of microfine lines. It provides tracking signals to the optical assembly whenever ordinary HD and DD floppy disks are being used. **Note:** Do not alter or adjust the encoder unless it is absolutely necessary. Throwing the encoder out of alignment can render the drive inoperative for HD and DD diskettes. Also be very careful not to foul or damage the encoder's surface—each microfine tracking line must be plainly visible to the optical assembly.

The *optical head assembly* used for tracking floptical, HD, and DD diskettes is attached to the *linear actuator/head assembly*, and positioned over the encoder. When a floptical disk is inserted, the optical head tracks across the disk using the track grooves placed on the floptical disk. When conventional HD and DD disks are inserted, the optical head tracks the encoder instead.

Disks are inserted and clamped between upper and lower magnetic read/write heads. The heads transfer information to and from the disk. Floptical heads use two head gaps—a large gap for working with conventional disks, and a smaller gap for working with very high density (VHD) floptical disks. Read/write heads are mounted on a carriage that is free to slide radially along the disk. Head movement is accomplished using a *linear actuator* (instead of a stepping motor as in ordinary floppy drives). The linear actuator provides extremely smooth incremental movement, which is vital to fine stepping. Heads and actuator are provided as a single mechanism. A metal cover helps to protect the subassemblies in the drive.

Floptical electronics

The floptical drive electronics package performs several vital functions. First, the electronics are responsible for managing the physical interface between the drive and controller board. Floptical drives typically use a SCSI interface. The electronics also operate the drive mechanisms (spindle, linear actuator, optical tracking device, and so on), and performs all the conversions and processing of data to and from the disk. Figure 10-17 illustrates the mounting arrangement for the drive electronics.

The functional block diagram for a floptical drive is shown in Fig. 10-18. A SCSI bus connects the drive to its host controller. A single, highly integrated ASIC manages the interface and provides a master drive control function. This master control IC interconnects with the spindle motor, PC board, a RAM buffer used for a cache, a CPU that performs much of the drive's on-board processing, and the read/write electronics that operate the magnetic read/write heads.

All CPUs need instructions in order to operate, and the floptical's CPU is no exception. A firmware IC supplies the program and data needed for the CPU to operate the digital servo tracking system. A diagnostic port is also available that allows the drive to be connected to a test system for in-depth, precise factory diagnostics.

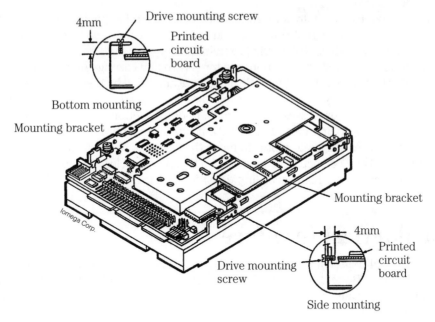

10-17 A view of floptical electronics.

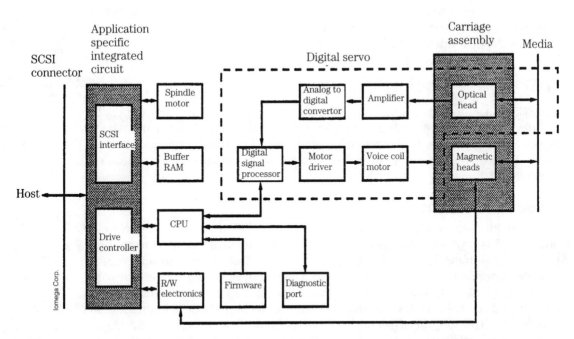

10-18 Block diagram of floptical electronics. Iomega Corp.

Factory diagnostics are vitally important when aligning and adjusting optical tracking after a repair. The actual optical tracking head and the read/write heads are mounted over the media in the carriage assembly.

The digital servo system is responsible for controlling carriage movement over a diskette. Tracking signals from the optical head are amplified by the digital servo and converted into digital signals. A digital signal processor (DSP), which is a very specialized type of CPU, processes those signals under direction of the CPU. When a track must be changed or adjusted, the DSP outputs an appropriate signal to a motor driver, which causes the linear motor to move the carriage. New tracking signals are then interpreted and corrected as needed. It is this precise, closed-loop approach to tracking that makes the high recording densities of hard drives and optical drives possible.

The floptical interface

Like other peripherals, a floptical drive is useless by itself. The drive must connect to a host computer. Because the floptical disk drive is operated by the host system, there must be a means of carrying data and control signals into and out of the drive. Signal exchange is accomplished over the physical interface. There are a number of possible signal interface schemes, but manufacturers prefer to utilize a standard interface. A standard interface allows a drive built by any manufacturer to run properly on the same computer. There are, however, a small number of manufacturers that choose to implement a custom interface scheme. A host controller board interfaces the floptical drive's signals to the computer's main busses. Interfaces usually fall into two categories: SCSI and proprietary.

SCSI

The SCSI is a system-level device interface that can service a wide range of peripheral devices. A SCSI host controller board is required in the computer to interface a 50-pin SCSI signal cable to the system's main busses. Refer to the previous section on CD-ROM drives for a brief overview of SCSI, and to chapter 7 for a detailed discussion.

Proprietary interface

The SCSI drive interface is not ideally suited to floptical drive systems. The tremendous speed and performance potential of the SCSI technique is often wasted on floppy drive systems—like CD-ROM, SCSI is simply too fast. In order to achieve reasonable performance for a floptical system, manufacturers can provide host controllers that handle the optimum data transfer rate (usually about 1.6 Mbits/second for VHD, 1.2 Mbits/second for HD, and 0.6 Mbits/second for DD). SCSI interfaces can handle more than 10 Mbits/second. Proprietary controllers are often available as options, so the drive can operate with a native SCSI drive controller, or with a proprietary controller board.

Proprietary interfaces are supplied with any cables and connectors necessary to set up and use the system. In most cases, the manufacturer also supplies the driver software that controls the drive. You must refer to a schematic or detailed block diagram for your proprietary drive system in order to determine the name and function of each signal pin. The proprietary controller board translates the interface cable signals into signals needed by the computer's main busses.

Troubleshooting floptical drives

On the surface, floptical drive troubleshooting is surprisingly similar to ordinary floppy drive troubleshooting—many of the key components perform virtually identical functions. It is important to remind you here that the optical tracking system used in floptical drives is extremely delicate and unforgiving. Factory-precise alignments are needed to achieve accurate and reliable operation. As a result, any disassembly represents a calculated risk, because replacement or adjustment of optical components can throw the drive so far out of alignment that it is unusable. Do not attempt to repair a floptical drive unless you can afford to risk ruining it. Never attempt a repair that voids your warranty. If you choose to attempt a repair, replace at the subassembly level and disassemble as little as possible.

Symptom 1: The floptical drive is completely dead. The disk does not even initialize when inserted　Begin troubleshooting by inspecting the diskette itself. When a disk is inserted into a drive, a mechanism should pull the disk's metal shroud away and briefly rotate the spindle motor to ensure positive engagement. Make sure that the disk is properly inserted into the floptical drive assembly. If the diskette does not enter and seat properly in the drive, disk access is impossible. Try several different diskettes to ensure that test diskette is not defective. It might be necessary to partially disassemble the computer to access the drive and allow you to see the overall assembly. Free or adjust any jammed assemblies or linkages to correct disk insertion. If you cannot get diskettes to insert properly, you can replace the load/unload mechanism. Remember that load/unload assembly replacement requires extensive disassembly.

If the disk inserts properly but fails to initialize, carefully inspect the drive's SCSI physical interface cabling. Loose connectors or faulty cable wiring can easily disable any drive. Use your multimeter to measure dc voltages at the power connector. Place your meter's ground lead on pin 2 and measure +12 Vdc at pin 1. Ground your meter on pin 3 and measure +5 Vdc at pin 4. If either of both of these voltages is low or missing, troubleshoot your computer power supply.

Before disk activity can begin, the drive must sense a disk in the drive. Locate the disk sensor and use your multimeter to measure voltage across the sensor. When a disk is out of the drive, you should read a logic 1 voltage across the sensor output. When a disk is in place, you should read a logic 0 voltage across the sensor (this convention might be reversed in some drive designs). If the sensor does not register the presence of a disk, replace the sensor. If the sensor does register the presence of a disk, replace the entire drive PC board, or replace the drive.

At this point, the trouble is probably in the floptical drive PC board. Try replacing the drive PC board assembly. This is not the least expensive avenue in terms of materials, but it is fast and simple. If a new floptical drive PC board corrects the problem, reassemble the computer and return it to service. If a new drive PC board does not correct the problem (or is not available), replace the entire drive. If a new drive assembly fails to correct the problem, replace the SCSI host controller board. You have to disassemble the computer to expose the motherboard and expansion boards.

Symptom 2: The floptical drive rotates a disk, but does not seek the desired track   This symptom suggests that the head positioning linear motor is inhibited or defective, but all other floptical drive functions are working properly. Begin by disassembling your computer and removing the floptical drive. Carefully inspect the head positioning assembly to be certain that there are no broken parts or obstructions that could jam the head carriage. You might want to examine the mechanical system with a disk inserted to see if the problem is disk alignment, which might be interfering with head movement. Gently remove any obstructions that you find. Be extremely careful not to misalign any optical assemblies or mechanical components in the process of clearing an obstruction.

Remove any disk from the drive and reconnect the drive's signal and power cables. Apply power to the computer and measure drive voltages with your multimeter. Ground your multimeter on pin 2 of the power connector and measure +12 Vdc at pin 1. Move the meter ground to pin 3 and measure +5 Vdc on pin 4. If either voltage is low or absent, troubleshoot your computer power supply.

Use your multimeter to measure voltage across the linear actuator during drive operation. If actuator voltage is present but the motor does not move, the linear actuator is probably defective and should be replaced. Keep in mind that linear actuator replacement requires disassembly down to the chassis level, so such a procedure should be performed only by a highly skilled or experienced individual. Careless replacement can easily result in a totally useless drive. Under some circumstances, it is advisable to replace the drive.

If no actuator voltage occurs across the linear actuator, the problem is most likely in the drive's main PC board. Either the actuator driver IC or controller IC has failed. You can track the failure to the component level, if possible, or simply replace the drive PC board. You can also replace the drive.

Symptom 3: The floptical drive heads seek properly, but the spindle does not turn   This symptom suggests that the spindle motor is inhibited or defective, but all other functions are working properly. Remove all power from the computer. Disassemble the system enough to remove the floptical drive. Carefully inspect the spindle motor and spindle assembly. Make certain that there are no broken parts or obstructions that could jam the spindle. You should also examine the drive with a disk inserted to be certain that the disk's insertion or alignment is not causing the problem. You can double-check your observations using several different diskettes. Gently remove any obstruction that you find. Be careful not to cause any accidental damage to the optical tracking head in the process of clearing an obstruction.

Remove any diskette from the drive and reconnect the floppy drive's signal and power cables. Restore power to the computer and measure drive voltages with your multimeter. Ground your multimeter on pin 2 and measure +12 Vdc on pin 1. Move the meter ground to pin 3 and measure +5 Vdc on pin 4. If either voltage is low or absent, troubleshoot your computer power supply.

Use your multimeter to measure voltage across the spindle motor during operation. If excitation voltage is present across the spindle motor but the motor does not turn, replace the defective spindle motor. You might also have to replace any sub-PC boards dedicated to the spindle motor. If no voltage is available to the spindle motor, the fault might lie in the motor's sub-PC board or the main drive PC board. If you have service documentation for your floptical drive, you can attempt to troubleshoot the problem to the component level. In most instances, you can simply replace the drive PC board. You could also replace the entire drive.

Symptom 4: The floptical drive encounters trouble reading or writing to the disk. All other operations appear normal   This type of problem can manifest itself in several ways, but your computer's operating system usually informs you when a disk read or write error has occurred. Begin by trying a known-good, properly formatted disk in the drive. A faulty diskette can generate some very perplexing read/write problems. If a known-good diskette does not resolve the problem, try cleaning the read/write heads according to manufacturer's suggestions. Do not run the drive with a head cleaning disk inserted for more than 30 seconds at a time, or you risk damaging the heads with excessive friction.

There are two major causes of read/write problems in floptical drives: trouble in the optical tracking system, and trouble in the read/write electronics. Start with the tracking system. Use your oscilloscope to measure the analog output from the laser detector during drive operation. If there is no signal (regardless of what type of disk is installed), there is no tracking information available to the drive, so reading and writing is impossible. Replace the defective optical tracking head. Remember that optical assembly replacement is very delicate, precise work that should only be attempted by an experienced individual. Careless replacement can render the drive inoperative.

Use your scope to check the read/write heads next. Measure the read signals from each head (remember that there are two gaps on each head—floptical disks use a micro-gap while regular disks use a normal-size gap). If there are no analog read signals available from the heads, the heads are probably defective and should be replaced. Replace both sets of read/write heads at the same time. Use caution to avoid misaligning the carriage or any other optical assembly.

If optical tracking signals and head signals appear intact, the problem is likely somewhere on the drive's main PC board. If you have the appropriate service documentation for your floptical drive, attempt to track down the problem to the component level if you wish. Under most circumstances, your best course is to simply replace the main drive PC board. You could also replace the drive outright.

Symptom 5: The drive is able to write to a write-protected disk   Before concluding that there is a drive problem, remove and examine the disk itself to ensure that it is actually write-protected. If the disk is not write-protected, protect it appropriately and try the disk again. If the disk is already protected, use your multimeter to check the drive's write-protect sensor. For an unprotected disk, the sensor output should be a logic 1, while a protected disk should generate a logic 0 (some drives reverse this convention). If there is no change in logic level across the sensor for a protected or unprotected disk, try a new write-protect sensor.

If the sensor appears to function properly, the fault is probably in the main drive PC board logic. You can try tracking the fault to the component level if you wish, but your best course is usually to replace the drive PC board outright.

Symptom 6: The drive does not read or write ordinary HD or DD disks properly An intricate part of floptical drive operation is optical tracking. When floptical disks are being used, the drive tracks the minute grooves pressed into the disk. When standard HD or DD floppy disks are used, however, there are no physical marks for the drive to track, so the drive uses an encoder located just below the optical tracking head to provide tracking signals. If the drive works properly with floptical disks, but not with standard disks, tracking might be interrupted.

Note: Check but do not adjust the small glass encoder located below the optical tracking head. Any accumulation of dust or debris on the encoder can interfere with tracking signals. Use a photography-grade lens brush and gently whisk away any accumulation on the encoder. You can also brush any dust or dirt from the optical tracking head aperture pointing at the encoder. Any optical interference can interrupt the light path and result in tracking or read/write problems. Remember to use extreme care when working around the drive's optics. If these actions fail to restore operation, replace the drive.

Appendix A
Materials and
system vendors

Parts, materials, test equipment, and services

B+K Precision
6470 W. Cortland St.
Chicago, IL 60635
(312) 889-1448

Elan Systems, Inc.
365 Woodview Ave., Suite 700
Morgan Hill, CA 95037
(408) 778-7267

Fessenden Technologies
116 North 3rd St.
Ozark, MO 65721
(417) 485-2501

Harddisk Technology
504-E Vandell Way
Campbell, CA 95008
(408) 374-5157

Innoventions
11000 Stancliff Rd., Suite 150
Houston, TX 77099
(713) 879-6226

Link Computer Graphics, Inc.
369 Passaic Ave., Suite 100
Fairfield, NJ 07004
(201) 808-8786

Lynx Technology, Inc.
9040 Leslie St., Unit 4
Richmond Hill, Ontario L4C-7B5
CANADA
(416) 886-7315

National Labnet
P.O. Box 841
Woodbridge, NJ 07085
(908) 549-2100

OK Industries
4 Executive Plaza
Yonkers, NY 10701
(914) 969-6800

PC Parts Express
1221 Champion Circle, Suite 105
Carrollton, TX 75006
(214) 406-8583
(800) 727-2787

Peripheral Parts Support, Inc.
219 Bear Hill Rd.
Waltham, MA 02154
(617) 890-9101

Proto PC, Inc.
2424 Territorial Rd.
St. Paul, MN 55114
(612) 644-4660

Valtron Technologies
28309 Avenue Crocker
Valencia, CA 91355
(805) 257-0333

Software tools

Accurite Technologies, Inc. (DriveProbe)
231 Charcot Ave.
San Jose, CA 95131
(408) 433-1980

Central Point Software (PC Tools)
15220 N.W. Greenbrier Pkwy. #200
Beaverton, OR 97006
(503) 690-8090
(800) 888-8199

Dysan International
218 Railroad Ave.
Milpitas, CA 95035
(408) 945-3930
(800) 422-3455

Landmark Research International, Inc. (AlignIt)
703 Grand Central St.
Clearwater, FL 34616
(800) 683-6696

Hard disk drives

ALPS USA
3553 N. First St.
San Jose, CA 95134
(408) 432-6000

AMPEX Corp.
200 N. Nash St.
El Segundo, CA 90245
(310) 640-0150

Areal Technology, Inc.
2075 Zanker Rd.
San Jose, CA 95131
(408) 436-6800

Bull HN Information Systems
250 Merrimack St.
Lawrence, MA 01843
(508) 294-6415
(800) 226-4357

Caledonian (formerly RODIME)
4301 Oak Circle Dr., #19
Boca Raton, FL 33431
(407) 750-6836

Conner Peripherals, Inc.
3081 Zanker Rd.
San Jose, CA 95134
(408) 456-4500

Core International
7171 North Federal Hwy.
Boca Raton, FL 33487
(407) 997-6044

Digital Equipment Corp.
146 Main St.
Maynard, MA 01754
(508) 493-5111

Disc Tech
925 S. Semoran, #114
Winter Park, FL 32790
(800) 553-0337

Epson America, Inc.
20770 Madrona Ave.
Torrance, CA 90503
(310) 782-0770

Fuji America
555 Taxter Rd.
Elmsford, NY 10523
(914) 789-8100

Fujitsu America
3055 Orchard Dr.
San Jose, CA 95134
(408) 432-1300

Hewlett-Packard Co.
11413 Chinden Blvd.
Boise, ID 83714
(208) 323-6000

Hitachi America
2000 Sierra Point Pkwy.
Brisbane, CA 94005
(415) 589-8300

IBM
Route 100
Somers, NY 10589
(914) 642-6400

JVC Companies of America
19900 Beach Blvd., Suite I
Huntington Beach, CA 92648
(714) 965-2610

Kalok
1289 Anvilwood Ave.
Sunnyvale, CA 94089
(408) 747-1315

Kyocera
100 Randolph Rd.
Somerset, NJ 08875
(908) 560-0060

Maxtor
211 River Oaks Pkwy.
San Jose, CA 95134
(408) 432-1700

Maxtor (formerly Miniscribe)
2190 Miller Dr.
Longmont, CO 80501
(303) 651-6000

Mega Drive Systems
489 S. Robertson Blvd.
Beverly Hills, CA 90210
(310) 247-0006

Micropolis
21211 Nordhoff St.
Chatsworth, CA 91311
(818) 709-3300

MiniStor Peripherals
2801 Orchard Pkwy.
San Jose, CA 95134
(408) 943-0165

NCL America
574 Weddell Dr., #4
Sunnyvale, CA 94089
(408) 734-1006

NEC Technologies, Inc.
1414 Massachusetts Ave.
Boxborough, MA 01719
(508) 264-8000

Okidata
532 Fellowship Rd.
Mt. Laurel, NJ 08054
(609) 235-2600

Olivetti
765 US Highway 202
Bridgewater, NJ 08876
(908) 526-8200

Quantum Corp.
500 McCarthy Blvd.
Milpitas, CA 95035
(408) 894-4000

Seagate Technology, Inc.
920 Disc Dr.
Scotts Valley, CA 95066
(408) 438-6550

Toshiba America
9740 Irvine Blvd.
Irvine, CA 92718
(714) 587-6200

Western Digital Corp.
8105 Irvine Center Dr.
Irvine, CA 92718
(714) 932-5000

CD-ROM drives

CD Technology, Inc.
766 San Aleso Ave.
Sunnyvale, CA 94086
(408) 752-8500

Chinon America, Inc.
615 Hawaii Ave.
Torrance, CA 90503
(310) 533-0274
(800) 441-0222

Hitachi Home Electronics, Inc.
401 West Artesia Blvd.
Compton, CA 90220
(310) 537-8383
(800) 369-0422

Laser Magnetic Storage Co.
4425 Arrows West Dr.
Colorado Springs, CO 80907-3489
(719) 593-7900

Liberty Systems, Inc.
160 Saratoga Ave., #38
Santa Clara, CA 95051
(408) 983-1127

NEC Technologies, Inc.
1255 Michael Dr.
Wood Dale, IL 60191-1094
(708) 860-9500
(800) 632-4636

Phillips Consumer Electronics
One Phillips Dr.
P.O. Box 14810
Knoxville, TN 37914-1810
(800) 835-3506

PLI
47421 Bayside Pkwy.
Fremont, CA 94538
(510) 657-2211
(800) 288-8754

Procom Technology, Inc.
2181 Dupont Dr.
Irvine, CA 92715
(714) 852-1000
(800) 800-8600

Sony Corp. of America
655 River Oaks Pkwy.
San Jose, CA 95134
(408) 432-0190
(800) 352-7669

Storage Devices, Inc.
6800 Orangethorpe Ave.
Buena Park, CA 90620
(714) 562-5500

Tandy Corp.
One Tandy Way
Ft. Worth, TX 76102
(817) 390-3011

TEXEL
1605 Wyatt Dr.
Santa Clara, CA 95054
(408) 980-1838
(800) 886-3935

Todd Enterprises, Inc.
224-49 67th Ave.
Bayside, NY 11364
(718) 343-1040
(800) 445-8633

Tape drives

Alloy Computer Products, Inc.
One Brigham St.
Marlboro, MA 01752
(508) 481-8500

Colorado Memory Systems, Inc.
800 S. Taft Ave.
Loveland, CO 80537
(800) 432-5858

Core International, Inc.
7171 N. Federal Hwy.
Boca Raton, FL 33487
(800) 688-9910

Everex Systems, Inc.
48431 Milmont Dr.
Fremont, CA 94538
(800) 821-0806

Iomega Corp.
1821 West Iomega Way
Roy, UT 84067
(800) 456-5522

Irwin Magnetic Systems, Inc.
2101 Commonwealth Blvd.
Ann Arbor, MI 48105
(800) 421-1879

Maynard Electronics Inc.
36 Skyline Dr.
Lake Mary, FL 32746
(800) 821-8782

Micro Solutions, Inc.
132 W. Lincoln Hwy.
DeKalb, IL 60115
(815) 756-3411

Mountain Network Solutions, Inc.
240 Hacienda Ave.
Campbell, CA 95008
(800) 458-0300

Summit Memory Systems, Inc.
100 Technology Circle
Scotts Valley, CA 95066
(800) 523-4767

Tallgrass Technologies Corp.
11100 W. 82nd St.
Lenexa, KS 66214
(800) 825-4727

Techmar, Inc.
6225 Cochran Rd.
Solon, OH 44139
(800) 422-2587

Floppy drives/floptical drives

Iomega Corp.
1821 West Iomega Way
Roy, UT 84067
(800) 456-5522

Sony Corp. of America
655 River Oaks Pkwy.
San Jose, CA 95134
(408) 432-0190
(800) 352-7669

TEAC America
7733 Telegraph Rd.
Montebello, CA 90640
(213) 726-0303

Toshiba America
9740 Irvine Blvd.
Irvine, CA 92718
(714) 587-6200

Memory cards and readers

Adtron Corp.
128 W. Boxelder #102
Chandler, AZ 85224
(602) 926-9324

Century Microelectronics
2979 Bowers Ave.
Santa Clara, CA 95051
(408) 748-7788

Databook, Inc.
10 Alder Bush
Rochester, NY 14624
(716) 889-4204

Epson America, Inc.
20770 Madrona Ave.
Torrance, CA 90503
(310) 782-0770
(310) 787-6300

Fujitsu Microelectronics, Inc.
3545 North First St.
San Jose, CA 95134
(408) 922-9000

Maxell Corp. of America
22-08 Route 208
Fair Lawn, NJ 07410
(201) 794-5900

Micron Technology
2805 East Columbia Rd.
Boise, ID 83706
(208) 368-3900

**Mitsubishi Electronics
America, Inc.**
1050 East Arques Ave.
Sunnyvale, CA 93086
(408) 730-5900

Panasonic Industrial Co.
P.O. Box 1511
Secaucus, NJ 07096
(201) 348-5266

Psion PLC
85 Frampton St.
London NW8 8NQ
ENGLAND
4471-262-5580

Rohm Corp.
3034 Owen Dr.
Antioch, TN 37013
(615) 641-2020

Samsung
(408) 954-7000

SunDisk
3270 Jay St.
Santa Clara, CA 95054
(408) 562-0500

Smart Modular Technologies
45531 Northport Loop West, Bldg. 3B
Fremont, CA 94538
(510) 623-1231

Appendix B
Summary of troubleshooting charts

Solid-state memory devices—Troubleshooting with XT error codes (chapter 5)
1055 201 or 2055 201 error

- Check/correct faulty DIP switch settings.

PARITY CHECK 1 error

- Check power supply output(s)
- Repair/replace power supply

xxyy 201 error

- Locate/replace faulty RAM IC(s)

PARITY ERROR 1

- Locate/replace defective RAM IC(s)

Solid-state memory devices—Troubleshooting with AT error codes (chapter 5)
164 (memory size) error

- Check/correct RAM size in CMOS system setup
- Check/replace CMOS backup battery

INCORRECT MEMORY SIZE error

- Check/correct RAM size in CMOS system setup
- Check/replace CMOS backup battery
- Locate/replace defective RAM IC(s)

ROM ERROR message

- Replace system BIOS ROM(s)

PARITY CHECK or 200-series error

- Locate/replace defective RAM IC(s)

Solid-state memory devices—Troubleshooting with POST/boot error codes (chapter 5)

xxxx OPTIONAL ROM BAD CHECK SUM = yyyy error

- Isolate/replace defective peripheral device/adaptor board

General RAM error

- Isolate/replace defective RAM IC(s) or SIMM(s)

CACHE MEMORY FAILURE error

- Isolate/replace defective cache memory IC(s) or SIMM(s)

DECREASING AVAILABLE MEMORY error

- Isolate/replace defective RAM device(s)

MEMORY PARITY INTERRUPT AT ADDRESS xxxx error

- Check/reseat each system SIMM
- Isolate/replace defective RAM IC(s) or SIMM(s)

Floppy disk drives—Troubleshooting floppy disk systems (chapter 6)

Drive is dead. Disk does not initialize when inserted.

- Check diskette and disk insertion
- Check all connectors and wiring
- Check drive power
- Replace floppy drive
- Replace the floppy controller IC

Drive does not seek. All other operations appear OK.

- Inspect the mechanical assembly
- Check drive power

- Check physical interface for floppy controller/drive failure
- Check/replace head stepping motor
- Replace the floppy drive

Drive does not spin. All other operations appear OK.

- Inspect the mechanical assembly
- Check drive power
- Check physical interface for floppy controller/drive failure
- Replace the floppy drive

Disk not being read/written. All other operations appear OK.

- Check/replace the diskette
- Gently clean the read/write heads
- Check physical interface for floppy controller/drive failure
- Replace R/W head assembly
- Replace the floppy drive

Drive writes to write-protected disks.

- Check the disk
- Check/replace the write-protect sensor
- Check physical interface signals
- Replace drive control circuit IC
- Replace drive PC board
- Replace entire floppy drive

Drive only recognizes double- or high-density disks.

- Check/replace disk sensor
- Check physical interface signals
- Replace drive control circuit IC
- Replace drive PC board
- Replace entire floppy drive

Hard disk drives (chapter 7)
Computer does not boot to DOS from the hard drive.

- Boot system from floppy drive
- Check system CMOS setup
- Check/replace CMOS backup battery
- Run fix utilities or reformat
- Reload system files if necessary
- Check/replace drive cables
- Check drive power
- Replace the drive

One or more subdirectories lost or damaged.

- Boot system from floppy drive
- Run fix utilities
- Reformat and reload drive

Hard drive read/write errors.

- Boot system from floppy disk
- Run fix utilities and check disk
- Replace any corrupted files
- Reformat and reload drive
- Replace the drive

Hard drive accidentally formatted.

- Rebuild the formatted drive with disk utilities
- Reformat and reload drive

File accidentally deleted.

- Undelete the file
- Recopy the file(s) manually

Drive root directory damaged.

- Boot system from floppy drive
- Run fix utilities
- Reformat and reload drive
- Replace the drive

Drive performance slows over time and use.

- Boot system from floppy drive
- Run an unfragment utility

Memory cards (chapter 8)

SRAM or flash card loses its memory when powered down or removed from the system.

- Check/replace any backup batteries
- Replace the memory card

Cannot access the card for reading or writing.

- Verify card compatibility
- Check the write-protect switch
- Check the card's insertion
- Inspect card connector(s)

- Replace the memory card
- Replace memory card controller IC

Tape drives (chapter 9)

Tape drive does not work at all.

- Check power to the drive
- Check interface wiring and connector(s)
- Check backup software configuration
- Check host controller board setup and configuration
- Check tape insertion
- Check interface signals
- Isolate drive/controller by substitution

Tape drive does not read or write, but it moves as expected.

- Check/replace tape
- Check/correct tape insertion
- Check/replace R/W head assembly
- Check/replace drive control PC board
- Check/replace the host controller PC board
- Replace the drive

Read/write head does not step from track to track.

- Check/replace BOT/EOT sensor pair
- Check head stepping signals
- Check/replace drive control PC board
- Check/replace R/W head seek assembly
- Replace the head stepping motor
- Replace the drive

Tape does not move at all or its speed does not remain constant.

- Check reel motor voltage(s)
- Check/replace drive control PC board
- Check/clear obstructions
- Replace both reel motors
- Check/adjust speed encoder roller
- Replace speed encoder roller
- Check/replace speed encoder
- Replace the drive

Tape does not load/eject properly.

- Check/replace the tape
- Check mechanical load/unload mechanisms
- Check/clear obstructions

- Replace any worn mechanical parts
- Replace the drive

Drive writes to write-protected tapes.

- Check tape's write-protect tab
- Check/replace write-protect sensor
- Check/replace drive control PC board
- Replace the drive

Drive does not recognize the beginning or end of tape.

- Check/replace the tape
- Check/replace EOT/BOT sensor pair
- Check/replace drive control PC board
- Replace the drive

CD-ROM (chapter 10)
Drive has trouble accepting or rejecting a CD.

- Check/clear obstruction(s)
- Replace any damaged linkage(s) or mechanism(s)
- Replace entire load/unload assembly
- Check/replace geared motor assembly
- Check/replace geared motor unit
- Check/replace drive control PC board
- Replace the drive

Read head does not seek.

- Check/clear obstruction(s)
- Check/replace linear actuator
- Check/replace drive control PC board
- Replace the drive

Disk cannot be read.

- Check/clean the CD
- Try a different CD
- Clean read head optics if possible
- Clean/replace interface cable
- Check/replace host interface controller board
- Check/replace drive control PC board
- Replace optical read assembly
- Replace the drive

Disk does not turn.

- Check/correct drive installation or configuration
- Clean read head optics if possible
- Check/replace the spindle motor assembly
- Replace the drive control PC board
- Replace the drive

Laser beam does not focus.

- Check/replace the optical head
- Replace the drive control PC board
- Replace the drive

No audio is produced by the drive.

- Check/replace speakers or headphones
- Check audio volume on drive
- Check/correct audio driver software
- Check/replace volume control
- Check/replace audio amplifier
- Replace headphone PC board
- Replace the drive

Floptical drives (chapter 10)

Drive is completely dead.

- Check disk insertion
- Try different disk(s)
- Check/replace load/unload assembly
- Check interface wiring and connectors
- Check drive power
- Check/replace disk sensor
- Check/replace drive control PC board
- Replace the drive

Disk rotates but heads do not seek.

- Check/clear obstruction(s)
- Check drive power
- Check/replace linear actuator
- Check/replace drive control PC board
- Replace the drive

Drive R/W heads seek properly but the spindle does not turn.

- Check/clear obstruction(s)
- Check drive power

- Check/replace spindle motor
- Replace spindle motor PC board
- Check/replace drive control PC board
- Replace the drive

Drive has trouble reading or writing to the disk.

- Try different disk(s)
- Clean read/write head(s)
- Check/replace optical tracking head assembly
- Check/replace the read/write head assembly
- Check/replace drive control PC board
- Replace the drive

Drive writes to write-protected disks.

- Check the disk
- Try different disk(s)
- Check/replace the write-protect sensor
- Check/replace drive control PC board

Drive handles floptical disks properly, but cannot handle ordinary DD or HD disks.

- Check/clean the encoder
- Check/clean the optical tracking head assembly
- Replace the drive

Glossary

access time   The time required to locate and begin transfer to or from a specific sector, track, or frame of media.

actuator   The mechanism which moves a set of read/write heads. Stepper motors and rotary voice coils are two common disk actuators .

ADC   Analog-to-digital converter. A device used to convert analog information (usually sound) to words of digital information.

address   A unique set of numbers that identifies a particular location in solid-state memory.

AFrame   The subdivision of time (seconds) from the beginning of an optical disk. One second of elapsed time is 75 frames.

allocation   The process of assigning particular areas of a disk to contain specific files.

allocation unit   A group of sectors on a particular disk that can be reserved to hold a specific file.

anode   The positive electrode of a two-terminal semiconductor device.

ANSI   American National Standards Institute. An organization that sets standards for languages, database management, etc.

architecture   Describes how a system is constructed and how its components are put together. An open architecture refers to a nonproprietary system design that allows other manufacturers to design products that work with the system.

ASCII   American Standard Code for Information Interchange. A set of standard codes defining characters and symbols used by computers.

asynchronous   Circuit operation in which signals can arrive at any point in time. A coordinating clock is not required.

attribute memory   PCMCIA cards provide fixed memory space to hold basic card information and configuration data.

azimuth   The angle (usually measured in angular minutes) of twist of a read/write head to the plane of the media.

bad block   An area of a disk (usually about a sector) that cannot reliably hold data because of bad format data or media damage.

bad track table   A listing of tracks that are damaged and cannot hold data.

base   One of the three leads of a bipolar transistor.

batch file   An ASCII file that combines several DOS commands into a single file.

baud   The rate at which bits are transferred between devices.

BCD   Binary coded decimal. The number system used commonly with compact disks.

BIOS   Basic input/output system. A series of programs that handle the computer's low-level functions.

bit   Binary digit. The basic unit of digital information written as a 0 or a 1.

block   A sector or group of sectors on a disk, or a fixed length of bytes in a memory card.

boot   The process of initializing a computer and loading a disk operating system.

boot device   A drive containing the files and information for a disk operating system.

boot sector   A section of a hard disk that holds information defining the physical characteristics and partitioning of the drive, as well as a short program that begins the DOS loading process.

bpi   Bits per inch. The number of bits placed in a linear inch of disk space.

buffer   A temporary storage place for data.

bus   One or more collections of digital signal lines.

byte   A set of eight bits. A byte is approximately equivalent to a character.

cache memory   Also called "cache." Part of a computer's RAM operating as a buffer between the system RAM and CPU. Recently used data or instructions are stored in cache. RAM is accessed quickly, so data called for again is available right away. This improves overall system performance.

caddy   A two-part protective case used with optical disk drives.

capacitance   The measure of a device's ability to store an electric charge. The unit of capacitance is the farad.

capacitor   An electronic device used to store energy in the form of an electric charge.

capacity   The amount of information that can be held in a particular storage device.

cassette   The protective outer housing of a tape or optical disk.

cathode   The negative electrode of a two-terminal semiconductor device.

CD Audio   An optical device capable of playing compact disks based on the Red Book (IEC 908) standard.

CD-ROM   Optical media containing digital data formatted to Yellow Book (ISO/ IEC 10149) standards.

chip carrier   A rectangular or square package with I/O connections on all four sides.

CIRC   Cross-interleaved Reed-Solomon code. An error-detection and correction process used with small frames of audio or data. The detection and correction algorithm is implemented in hardware.

cluster   The smallest unit of disk storage defined as one or more contiguous sectors.

CMOS   Complementary metal-oxide semiconductor. A type of MOS transistor commonly used in digital integrated circuits for high speed and low power operation.

collector   One of the three leads of a bipolar transistor.

configuration   The components that make up a computer's hardware setup.

contiguous   All together, or one right after another. Usually refers to files that are not fragmented or on separate sectors of a hard disk. Contiguous files can be accessed more quickly than fragmented or noncontiguous files.

continuous composite   A type of format that describes the physical, optical, and data formats of a magneto-optical disk.

control characters   ASCII characters that do not print out but are used to control communication.

CPU   Central processing unit. The primary functioning unit of a computer system. Also called a microprocessor.

CQFP   Ceramic quad flat pack.

cyclical redundancy check   An error-checking technique for data recording typically used by systems that perform hardware error checking.

cylinder   A collection of tracks located one above the other on the platters of a hard drive.

DAC   Digital-to-analog converter. A device used to convert words of digital information into equivalent analog levels.

DAT   Digital audio tape.

data separator   A drive circuit that extracts data from combined data and clock signals.

dedicated servo   A media surface separate from the surface used for data which contains only disk timing and positioning information.

de-emphasis   Decreasing the level of high-frequency audio signals relative to low-frequency audio signals prior to recording or playback. This helps to suppress hiss noise.

DIP   Dual in-line package.

DMA   Direct memory access. A fast method of moving data from a storage device directly to RAM.

DOS   Disk operating system. A program or set of programs that directs the operations of a disk-based computing system.

DOS extender   Software that uses the capabilities of advanced microprocessors running under DOS to access more then 640K of RAM.

drain   One of the three leads of a field-effect transistor.

ECC   Error correction code. A method used to recover a block of data during data playback.

eccentricity   Rotating out of round.

EDC   Error detection code. A method used to ensure data integrity such as the cyclic redundancy check (CRC-32).

EIA   Electronics Industry Association. A standards organization in the USA which develops specifications for interface equipment.

EIAJ   Electronic Industries Association of Japan. A Japanese standards organization which is the equivalent of the US Joint Electronic Device Engineering Council (JEDEC).

EISA   Extended Industry Standard Architecture.

embedded servo   Timing or location information placed on surfaces which actually contain data. Servo data allows read/write heads to achieve precise positioning.

emitter   One of the three leads of a bipolar transistor.

EMS   Extended memory system. A highly integrated IC controller used to access extra RAM.

encoding   The protocol defining how data patterns are changed prior to being written to the disk surface.

ESD   Electrostatic discharge. The sudden, accidental release of electrons accumulated in the body or inanimate objects. Static charges are destructive to MOS ICs and other semiconductors.

ESDI   Enhanced Small Device Interface. A popular physical interface for large-capacity hard drives that replaced the ST-506 interface. ESDI can transfer data up to 10Mb per second.

FAT   File allocation table. A table recorded on disk which keeps track of which clusters and sectors are available, which have been used by files, and which are defective.

file   A collection of related information which is stored together on disk.

file attributes   The DOS identification which denotes the characteristics of a file: copy-protected, read-only, or archival.

firmware   Program instructions held in a permanent memory device such as a PROM or EPROM.

flatpack   One of the oldest surface-mount packages with 14 to 50 ribbon leads on both sides of its body.

flux density   The number of magnetic flux transitions that can be written along a given length of disk surface.

flying height   The distance between a read/write head and a disk surface caused by a cushion of moving air.

format   The predefined pattern of tracks and sectors that must be written to a disk before the disk can retain information.

form factor   A reference to the general size class of a system or device such as a hard drive.

fragmentation   The state of a hard disk where files are stored in two or more small pieces across a disk rather than contiguously.

gate   One of the three leads of a field-effect transistor.

head   A device consisting of tiny wire coils which moves across the surface of floppy or hard disks. Heads are used to read or write information to disks.

head actuator   The mechanism that moves a read/write head radially across the surface of a hard or floppy disk.

head crash Damage to a read/write head due to collision with a disk surface of other foreign matter such as dust, smoke, or fingerprints.

high memory The RAM locations residing between 640K and 1Mb.

host adaptor The circuit board used to interface the host CPU to the CD-ROM, hard drive, floppy drive, tape drive, or other peripheral.

hot insertion/removal The ability to insert or remove a memory card from a system with the system power turned on.

hysteresis The ability of a read/write head to reach the same track position when approaching from either radial direction.

ICMA International Card Manufacturers Association.

index A subdivision of a CD-ROM track.

inductance The measure of a device's ability to store a magnetic charge. The unit of inductance is the henry.

inductor An electronic device used to store energy in the form of a magnetic charge.

IDE Integrated Drive Electronics. A physical interface standard commonly used in medium to large hard drives. IDE control electronics are housed in the drive itself instead of an external control board.

interface The hardware/software protocol contained in the drive and controller which manages the flow of data between the drive and host computer.

interleave The arrangement of sectors on a track. The common 1:1 arrangement places the sectors in consecutive order around a track.

ISA Industry Standard Architecture. The conventional IBM AT architecture.

ISO International Standards Organization.

JEDEC Joint Electronic Device Engineering Council. The US standards organization that handles packaging standards.

JEIDA Japanese Electronics Industry Development Association.

landing zone A location in a drive's inner cylinder where read/write heads can land during power-down. No data is recorded in the landing zone.

laser A narrow, intense beam of single-wavelength light used to read and write data to an optical disk.

latency The time required for data to rotate in front of properly positioned read/write heads. Latency usually measures a few milliseconds. Also called rotational latency.

LCC Leadless chip carrier. An IC package whose leads sit on the package edges.

lead-in area The area on a CD-ROM disk prior to track one which usually contains null data.

lead-out area The area on a CD-ROM disk beyond the last information track which usually contains null data.

lead spacing The distance (usually measured in mils) between adjacent leads on the sides of a package.

LEC Layered error correction. An error correction technique used CD-ROM systems.

LIF Low insertion force. A term used to describe sockets which require only a minimum force to insert or extract an IC.

load   The process of pressing read/write heads onto or toward the surface of a magnetic disk.

logic analyzer   An instrument used to monitor signals of an integrated circuit or system.

magneto-optical   Rewritable optical technology using a plastic disk with a magnetic layer.

MCP   Math coprocessor. A sophisticated processing IC intended to enhance the processing of a computer by performing floating-point math operations instead of the CPU.

media   The physical material which actually retains recorded information. For floppy and hard drives, the media is a coating of magnetic oxide.

MFM   Modified frequency modulation. The most widely used method of encoding binary data on a disk.

mil   One thousandth of an inch (0.001").

motherboard   In a small computer, the major PC board containing the CPU, core memory, and most of the system's controller ICs (also called the Main Logic Board).

MPU   Microprocessor unit. Another term for a CPU.

MQFP   Metal quad flat pack.

OC   Open collector. A circuit configuration where transistor outputs are left unconnected.

operating system   The interface between the hardware and software running on your PC.

overwrite   To write data on top of existing data, thereby erasing the original data.

page   A reference to a block of memory in a computer.

parallel port   A physical connection on a computer used to connect output devices. Data is transmitted as multiple bits sent together over separate wires. Typically used to connect a printer.

parity   A means of error checking using an extra bit added to each transmitted character.

partition   The portion of a hard disk devoted to a single operating system and accessed with a single logical letter.

PCMCIA   Personal Computer Memory Card Industry Association.

permeable   The ability of a material be magnetized.

pit   A microscopic depression in the surface of a compact disk.

platter   An actual disk inside a hard disk drive which carries the magnetic recording material.

PLCC   Plastic leaded chip carrier.

positioning time   The radial component of access time.

POST   Power-on self-test. A program in BIOS which handles the computer's initialization and self-test before loading DOS.

PQFP   Plastic quad flat pack.

QFP   Quad flat pack.

QSOP   Quality (quality semiconductor) small outline package.

Reed-Solomon Error Code   A linear algebraic formula used for error correction. See CIRC.

resistance   The measure of a device's opposition to the flow of current. The unit of resistance is the ohm.

resistor   A device used to limit the flow of current in an electronic circuit.

RLL   Run length limited. A technique for encoding binary data on a hard disk which can pack up to 50% more data than MFM recording.

RS-232   A standard for transmitting serial data.

SCSI   Small Computer System Interface. A physical interface standard for large to huge (up to 3Gb) hard drives.

sector   The smallest unit of storage on the surface of a floppy or hard disk.

seek   The radial movement of a head along a disk.

serial port   A physical connection on a computer used to connect output devices. Data is transmitted as individual bits sent one at a time over a single wire. Typically used to connect a modem or mouse.

settle time   The time required for a head to stop reliably after it has been stepped.

SIMM   Single in-line memory module. A quantity of extra RAM mounted onto a PC board terminated with a single, convenient connector.

SMT   Surface-mount technology.

SOIC   Small outline integrated circuit.

SOJ   Small outline "J" lead package.

SSOP   Shrink small outline package.

source   One of the three leads of a field-effect transistor.

spindle   The part of a hard or floppy drive which rotates the disks.

spindown   The process of removing power and decelerating a hard drive to a halt.

spinup   The process of applying power and accelerating a hard drive to running speed.

ST-506   The oldest physical interface standard for small hard drives (under 40Mb) with a data transfer rate of only 5 Mbits per second.

synchronous   Circuit operation where signals are coordinated through the use of a master clock.

track   The circular path traced across the surface of a spinning disk by a read/write head. A track consists of one or more clusters.

transfer rate   The speed at which a hard or floppy drive can transfer information between its media and the CPU, typically measured in Mbits per second.

TSOP   Thin small outline package.

TSR   Terminate and stay resident. A program residing in memory that can be invoked from other application programs.

TTL   Transistor transistor logic. Digital logic ICs using bipolar transistors.

tuple   A small block of memory in solid-state memory cards.

WORM   Write-once-read-many. An optical technology which allows data to be permanently written to a disk.

Bibliography

Alting-Mees, Adrian. 1991. *The Hard Drive Encyclopedia*. San Diego, CA: Anna-books.

Arrow Electronics Corporation. 1992. *1992 Arrow Systems Product Guide*. Melville, NY.

Bigelow, Stephen J. "Cleaning and Aligning Floppy Disk Drives." *The PC Troubleshooter* (March 1993).

Brenner, Robert C. 1988. *IBM PC Advanced Troubleshooting & Repair*. Indianapolis, IN: Howard W. Sams & Company.

Buell, Jim. "Floppy Drive Test Media Technology." *MSM* (April 1991): 47–49.

"Card Related Terms and Abbreviations." *Memory Card Systems & Design* 2 (January/February 1992): 38–40.

Greenfield, Joseph D. 1983. *Practical Digital Design Using ICs*. New York, NY: Wiley Books.

GRiD Systems Corporation. 1991. *GRiDPAD-HD/GRiDPAD-RC Computer Service Manual*. Fremont, CA.

GRiD Systems Corporation. 1991. *GRiDPAD-HD/GRiDPAD-RC Computer Technical Reference Manual*. Fremont, CA.

Hall, V. Douglas. 1980. *Microprocessors and Digital Systems*. New York, NY: McGraw-Hill.

Howard, Bill. "High-end Notebook PCs." *PC Magazine* (14 April 1992): 113–143.

Hughes, Allan. "Duplicator Drive Maintenance." *Software Manufacturing News* (15 November 1992): 28–31.

Innoventions, Inc. 1992. *SIMCHECK Owner's Manual*. Houston, TX.

Integral Peripherals, Inc. 1992. *Product Manual for the Stingray 1842*. Boulder, CO.

Iomega Corporation. 1992. *TAPE250 Technical Description Manual EN067300*.

Johnson, Jim. 1985. *Laser Technology*. Benton Harbor, MI: Heath Company.

Leach, Donald P., Albert P. Malvino. 1981. *Digital Principles and Applications.* 3d ed. New York, NY: Gregg/McGraw-Hill.

Margolis, Art. 1991. *Troubleshooting and Repairing Personal Computers.* 2d ed. Blue Ridge Summit, PA: Windcrest/McGraw-Hill.

Matzkin, Howard. "Palmtop PCs: Power By the Ounce." *PC Magazine* (July 1991): 197–226.

"Memory Upgrades." *PC Computing* (March 1992): 132–136.

Methuin, Dave. "Adding Memory: A Step-by-Step Guide." *PC Computing* (June 1991): 152–154.

Negrino, Tom. "Fast Forward Storage." *MACWorld* (November 1991): 177–185

Osborne, Adam. 1980. *An Introduction to Microcomputers.* 2d ed., Vol 1. F. Berkeley, CA: Osborne/McGraw-Hill.

Prosise, Jeff. "Tutor." Monthly column in *PC Magazine* (28 April 1992): 359–362.

Quantum Corporation. 1989. *ProDrive 40S/80S Product Manual.* Milpitas, CA.

Rosch, Winn L. 1992. *The Winn L. Rosch Hardware Bible* 2d ed. New York, NY: Brady Publishing.

Rosch, Winn L. "Choosing and Using Hard Disks." *PC Magazine* (31 December 1991): 313–331.

Rosch, Winn L. "Minicartridge Tape Backup." *PC Magazine* (14 April 1992): 185–224.

Sharp Corporation, Information Systems Division. 1990. *Sharp Service Manual OZ/IQ-8000 & OZ/IQ-8200.* Yamatokoriyama, Nara (Japan).

Smith, Jan. "Tape Backup." *PC Computing* (April 1992): 206–208.

Tandy Corporation. 1990. *Service Manual: Tandy 1500HD Laptop Computer.* Fort Worth, TX.

Tillinghast, Charles. January/February 1992. "IC DRAM Technology and Usage." *Memory Card Systems & Design* 2 (1): 28–31.

Toshiba America Information Systems, Inc. 1988. *T5100 Maintenance Manual.* Irvine, CA.

Toshiba America Information Systems, Inc. 1992. *T6400 Maintenance Manual.* Irvine, CA.

Index